ART THEN AND NOW

ART
THEN AND NOW

Kathryn Dean Lee
&
Katharine Tyler Burchwood

PICTURE EDITOR · MARION HOWE

New York
APPLETON-CENTURY-CROFTS, INC.

Preface

Art Then and Now is designed to be an introduction to ancient, medieval, and modern art with emphasis upon brevity, clarity, and readability of text. The material for this book has been gathered from many sources, for all that is said here has, at one time or another, been said elsewhere. What the authors have attempted is to consider the manifestations of art as they have appeared at various times and in various places and to relate them one to another, so that the reader may attain an overview of the art of the world. If the book succeeds in arousing a lasting interest in art, its aim has been fulfilled.

The illustrations in a history of art serve a double function. They help to clarify the text, and to awaken or heighten the reader's sense of pleasure in the visual arts. To further this potential enjoyment, a method of reproduction was selected which, while necessitating that all illustrations be grouped together in one section of the book, seemed to insure fidelity to the appearance of the originals. To insure that each picture could be printed in a visually satisfying size, it was decided to limit the number of illustrations rather than to crowd a greater number onto the available pages.

Obviously, the limits of any single book are too drastic to allow for more than a glimpse of art riches of the past or present. Choice of illustrations in an art history is also curtailed by the necessity to show certain works which are historically important, but are not sympathetic according to modern standards of taste. But as far as possible, selections of visual data were directed towards revealing that in every period and culture artists have expressed themselves in forms which have enduring vitality and universal appeal. Thus, the tense elegance of a sculptured Egyptian cat or the dignity and regal poise of a Mayan goddess carved out of stone, impress us as being no less "modern" than an animal painting by Delacroix or a

portrait study by Modigliani. The functional drama of architecture is timeless when visioned as a Greek temple on a rocky hill,
St. Peter's at Rome, or a column of skyscraper thrown against the
sky.

To strengthen visual effectiveness, we have tried to obtain lively,
modern photographs for reproduction. In bringing pictures together
on the plate pages, we have attempted to show how distinctly individual is each artist's mood and method of treatment even where
subject-matter is related.

Finally, in their choice of illustrations the authors wished to show
as many as possible of the great works of art the people of this country are fortunate enough to have in their museums. Any reproduction can give the viewer only a taste of the pleasure which seeing
the original might convey. It is to be hoped that students will be
encouraged to seek out the works of art reproduced in this book,
and the other visual treasures in our magnificent museums.

We are indebted, for their help, to a number of people. Gilbert
Longstreet, of Chicago, did much of the writing in the Egyptian
and Gothic chapters; Herbert A. Thelen and Russell B. Thomas of
the University of Chicago made valuable criticisms and comments
on the chapters they read; Tom Goodman and others offered excellent suggestions from the reader's point of view; John Coley and
Joanna Dean, of Alexander City, Alabama, assisted in the final
preparation of parts of the manuscript. Finally, the authors want
to express their thanks to Mrs. Marion Howe for her help in
assembling the photographs used in the book and in planning their
arrangement.

K. D. L.
K. T. B.

Contents

List of Illustrations

PLATES

Numbers refer to plates.

ix

TEXT

Numbers refer to text pages

ILLUSTRATION ACKNOWLEDGMENTS

The authors and editors gratefully acknowledge the generous assistance of the many individuals and organizations who made it possible to obtain the photographic materials for the book. We received indispensable help in acquiring photographs of art works in foreign collections from Miss Romana Javitz, Superintendent of the Picture Collection, Miss Muriel Baldwin, Acting Chief of the Art Division, and other members of The New York Public Library staff; and from Miss Alice Franklin, Mrs. Ruth Terrell, and other members of the staff of the Metropolitan Museum of Art Extension Division. Valuable coöperation was also received from Miss Evelyn Grier and the Sales Desk staff of the Metropolitan Museum of Art; Miss Dorothy Miller, Curator of Museum Collections, and Miss Pearl Moeller of the Museum of Modern Art; Miss Celia Vandermark of the Museum of Fine Arts, Boston; Miss Hilla Rebay and the staff of the Museum of Non-Objective Painting.

For the courtesy of allowing reproductions to be made for the book, we wish to thank the following:

Addison Gallery of American Art, Phillips Academy, Andover, Plate 154 (lower)
Albright Art Gallery, Buffalo, 187
American Baptist Publication Society, Judson Press (Ira M. Price, *Monuments of the Old Testament*), line subject in chapter 3
American Museum of Natural History, 1 (lower), 142 (3)
Mr. and Mrs. Walter C. Arensberg, 184

Langdon Warner, 79 (lower, from Langdon Warner, *Craft of the Japanese Sculptor*), 80 (upper), 81 (lower, from Langdon Warner, *Sculpture of the Suiko Period*)

Whitney Museum of Art, 156 (lower), 157 (lower), 197 (upper)

Worcester Art Museum, 48 (lower left), 74 (upper), 134 (upper), 148

Hamilton W. Wright, 5 (lower), 11 (lower), 46 (lower)

Yale University Art Gallery, 74 (lower right), 84, 146

William Zorach, 203 (lower)

Unless otherwise indicated, photographs were supplied by the individuals or organizations credited above. Photo services which supplied illustrations are listed adjacent to the reproduction. The authors are also indebted to the following for supplying photographs, Dr. Clarence Kennedy, Clarence Ward, Lillian Christensen, Margaret Cobb, Mrs. Cohn-Weiner, and to these institutions for providing photographs other than those of objects in their collections: Museum of Modern Art, 184, 194, 205 (upper), 206 (upper); The University of Chicago, The Oriental Institute, 9 (upper), 10 (upper), 13 (2); The Art Institute of Chicago, 164 (lower); Metropolitan Museum of Art, 170.

Additional photo sources are:

Alinari, Plate 25 (upper and lower right), 29 (right), 33 (right), 36 (upper), 42 (upper), 51 (upper), 83 (lower), 85 (upper), 86 (lower), 90 (lower), 104 (2), 106 (upper), 107 (upper)

Anderson, 37, 51 (lower left), 83 (upper), 85 (lower), 89 (lower), 90 (upper), 94 (lower), 95, 96 (upper), 97 (lower), 129 (2), 131 (upper)

Anderson and Spiers, *Architecture of Greece and Rome*, 39 (lower)

Archives Photographiques, 163 (upper), 173 (lower)

Boerschmann, *Chinesische Architektur*, 72 (upper)

Bohm, 98 (lower)

Brogi, 87 (lower), 88, 94 (upper), 99, 102 (upper), 103 (upper)

Bruckmann, 34 (2)

Capitan, Breuil and Peyrony, *La Caverne de Font de Gaume*, 2 (lower)

Cartailhac and Breuil, *La Caverne de Altamira*, 2 (upper), line subject in Chapter 1

Denkmäler der Renaissance, 102 (lower)

Encyclopedie Alpine, 58 (upper left)

Giraudon, 54 (upper), 165 (upper)

Japanese Temples and Their Treasures, 78 (lower), 79 (upper)

Mannelli, 103 (lower)

Mansell, 14 (lower), 26 (2)

Moscioni, 24 (upper)

ND, 54 (lower), 55 (upper)

Staatliche Bildstelle, 56 (upper)

Von Bissing, *Denkmäler Ägyptischer Sculptur*, 6 (right)

Walden, *Einblick in Kunst*, 191 (upper)

Weege, *Etruskische Malerei*, 38 (lower)

To the Reader

Picasso, one of the outstanding artists of the twentieth century, wonders why people feel that they should understand art; why they can not look at a painting or a piece of sculpture just as they listen to a bird sing—merely for enjoyment. Nevertheless, while listening to a bird sing, one is not disturbed by preconceived notions as to what kind of music the bird should produce, whereas with art it is different. Everyone knows what he likes. Ever since the old Greek philosophers held that "art is imitation of nature," people—of the Western World at least—have been influenced by that pronouncement. Even in our time, when men are taking in their stride almost incredible discoveries of a scientific or materialistic nature, a large majority of them are shocked when they view an exhibition of non-imitative art like some of Picasso's later work which is divorced from familiar or even recognizable subject-matter. Judging from remarks overheard in art galleries, many spectators do not look at pictures as they listen to the singing of the bird, or if they do, they seem to feel that the modern bird is singing decidedly out of tune. To the uninitiated a certain amount of understanding is conducive, if not necessary, to enjoyment.

Because it is only human to dislike what one does not understand, we have presented a brief account of the historical, social, and geographical backgrounds of the art epochs which are remote in time or place, and have indicated something of the philosophy or thought underlying the modern movements. Especially in earlier cultures, art was considered a necessity in the life of man, and artists produced it just as manufacturers supply commodities for our present-day needs. To make those ancient times seem more real and their art less strange, we have occasionally introduced important rulers or other personages. That prominent artists of later times, many of whom have also been important figures in the life of their day, may appear not merely as names but as living personalities, we have included some biographical material.

While notable works of art have always been produced by individuals who have broken through the conventions or limitations of their cultures, great art epochs are rare, seldom if ever recurring in the same country. They have appeared now here, now there, when a definite need produced a great demand for visual expression or when there were numerous geniuses capable of producing work of universal significance that transcends time or place. Among such periods we have emphasized: the *Egyptian,* because it was one of the first, and because the high quality of its art persisted the longest—over thousands of years; the *Greek,* in which art was a paramount manifestation of that most remarkable of the ancient cultures; the *Middle Ages* when Christian art reached its zenith in the dynamic architecture of the magnificent Gothic cathedrals; the *Italian Renaissance,* a high level of culture which marked the beginning of the modern world, during which time sculpture was still important, painting rose to prominence, and the artist occupied a high estate comparable to that accorded to the scientist of the present day; the *French,* because for two centuries Paris was the art capital of the Western world, and there the foundation was laid for the *International Art of the Twentieth Century,* which, though still controversial, is none the less vital, reflecting the infinite variety and complexity of present-day life.

The modern artist, working with visual symbols, is concerned with balancing strong tensions and opposing forces which parallel and echo those outward disturbances caused by the collision of conflicting cultures in a world made small by the highly accelerated speed of modern travel. It is not surprising that we find in a revolutionary century, which has produced such dissimilar characters as screaming dictators who ruled by force, and the calm figure of Gandhi who through his doctrine and practice of non-violence freed India from British dominion, a revolutionary art breaking all precedent, sometimes shouting for attention or, again, quietly communicating its visual message.

Indeed, two movements, the restless, emotional Romantic and the calm, quiet Classic, appear in varying degrees in almost every period of art with one or the other finally gaining ascendancy. With the romantic we associate Gothic architecture, the colorful arts of Persia, those of the Far East which hint at mystery and stir the imagination, the baroque of the seventeenth century with its restless movement, and the so-called romantic style of the early nineteenth century with emphasis on violent action and exotic subject-matter. On the other hand, the classical calls to mind the reasoned, measured art of Greece which, in its decadent state, is again reflected in the neo-classic art that succeeded the romantic style in the same century.

Painting and sculpture adorned the caves of prehistoric men before they built their houses on stilts; nevertheless, architecture has been called the "mother of the arts." During the earliest civilizations sculpture and painting, which were not practiced as separate arts, were employed as decorations for tombs, temples, or palaces. We have shown you how man built his monuments with the materials he found about him, first wood or sun-baked bricks, then the enduring stone that the Egyptians employed to erect "houses of eternity"; how the stone structures were erected in the style of their wooden prototypes until a suitable design could be devised for the new material. The Egyptians erected huge stone columns across which they laid heavy stone beams in the simplest type of construction known as the post and lintel; the Romans developed the round arch and raised heavy vaults which rested on thick walls; the Gothic builders broke the round arch and put segments of it together again to form the pointed arch that enabled them to reduce walls to a minimum and cover their cathedrals with fireproof vaults or roofs that rested on tall piers, reinforced by the picturesque flying buttresses seen on the exterior of these dynamic structures. Thus the Gothic builders of the Middle Ages achieved the maximum in stone construction. Not until the advent of steel and concrete in modern times did builders make any other important advance along structural lines.

Believing that sculpture and painting had magical powers, the cave men carved or modeled the animals which they hunted. The Egyptian sculptors worked in bas-relief, forms slightly raised from the background, or made free-standing figures known as sculpture in the round. With these they decorated their temples, and covered the walls of their tombs to make the occupant more comfortable in the hereafter. The Greeks, lovers of beauty, chose marble for their idealized statues of gods and athletes. The Gothic sculptors, more concerned with the spirit, covered the bodies of the figures which adorned their cathedrals with formless robes, thus directing the attention to facial expression. During the Italian Renaissance Michelangelo poured out his conflicting emotions in sculptured forms designed for tombs and churches. Gradually sculpture was divorced from architecture, for it became a needless expense when man began to travel too fast to see it from automobiles or airplanes. Contrasting materials and textures have superseded it as architectural decoration. Sculpture, like architecture, has progressed from geometric simplicity through forms loaded with multitudinous detail back to abstract forms and planes almost as simple as those of the pyramids. New materials including plastics have inspired new forms and subject-matter has been reduced to a minimum.

The painter covers a two-dimensional surface, wood, wall, or canvas, with colors that have a water base like fresco, tempera and transparent water-colors, or with oil paints. On such flat surfaces he may produce the illusion of forms in deep space by the use of perspective, foreshortening, and other devices which the artists of the Renaissance worked out, or like the Orientals and moderns he may suggest space by masses of strategically placed figures—not necessarily three dimensional—together with the interweaving of dark and light tones which bind them together to form a unified whole. As time went on, color became increasingly important, functioning both in the creation of form and the suggestion of space. The elements, line, light-dark, color, form, and texture which the artist arranges in an effective order to convey his visual message are comparable to the words, sentences, and paragraphs which a writer organizes to communicate his thoughts. In art, rhythm is a binding agent contributing to unity and balance in a design. It may appear as flowing lines or in the repetition of colors, angles, forms, or textures to make easy paths for the eye to follow. According to their individual interest or intent, artists often emphasize certain elements or distort their forms to dramatize a subject, to create a mood, or to increase the power of their composition.

Painting, following the same trends as sculpture, has in turn been conventionalized through the use of symbols or patterns; naturalistic, mirroring the objective world with photographic accuracy; realistic, a simplification of naturalism obtained by the elimination of details and retaining only the most important data derived from memory or observation; abstract, with objects, figures, or landscapes reduced to lines, geometric forms and planes; non-objective, completely freed from subject-matter, with emphasis placed upon the organization of the pictorial elements. At all times the supreme artist with a sensitive eye, intuitive mind, and highly developed skill in effective presentation has been able to communicate to us something of his own heightened response to familiar scenes of common emotional experiences, thus extending the range of our own limited vision or feelings.

Here we have given you merely a hint of those things which have been explained in the text. At the end of each chapter an outline of the contents has been included for your convenience in reviewing the material, to emphasize the most important characteristics of the art of the time, and in some cases to provide additional information. In this short overview of the art of the world planned for general information and as a foundation for your future more specialized study, we have omitted the so-called minor arts—small objects such as pottery, jewelry, textiles or furniture—important though they are, in order to give you better illustrative material and a shorter text. Although books may open the door to understanding and appreciation of works of art, one's enjoyment of them is increased by first-hand contact with original works of art. Nevertheless, since the benefit one derives from a new experience is in direct proportion to what he takes to it, we hope that the material presented in this introduction in statements which are so generalized that they may have little meaning for you now, will be quite clear when you review it after having read the book. We also hope that the contents of the text will help you enjoy some of the works of art which you will see just as you enjoy hearing a bird sing.

ART THEN AND NOW

CHAPTER I

Prehistoric Art

ARCHAEOLOGICAL discoveries of the past century and a half indicate that human creatures, more or less similar to ourselves, existed upon the earth a million years ago. During the Paleolithic or Old Stone Age (500,000-20,000 B.C.), Neanderthal man discovered the use of stone tools—the first axe, scraper, and spear point —which he seems to have utilized almost solely in his struggle to maintain precarious life in a hostile geographical environment. Four times within the Old Stone Age glaciers moved down from the north, covering Europe as far south as the forty-sixth parallel with a coating of ice; four times the ice sheet receded. It is possible that Neanderthal man was too busy trying to survive the rigors of his particular climate to devote time to the creation of art objects, or perhaps his mental development was too slight; at any rate, the archaeological remnants of the handiwork of this early man are wholly utilitarian.

PALEOLITHIC SCULPTURE AND PAINTING

A distinct cultural advance results when Cro-Magnon man steps upon the prehistoric scene toward the end of the Old Stone Age. His epoch, coincident with the last glacial period, marks the beginning of sculpture, engraving, and fresco. These early art endeavors have come to light through the discovery and exploration of cave dwellings found in greatest number in France and Spain. One group of caves, the Altamira, discovered in 1879 near Santander in Spain, contain a wealth of mural art which has subsequently been placed under the protection of the Spanish government.

The Paleolithic artist worked within a fairly limited range of materials—stone, bone, ivory from the mammoth, reindeer horn, and the clay of the cave floors. Wood also may have been used

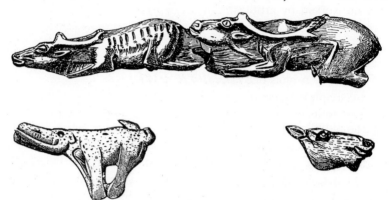

Figures carved out of ivory, reindeer horn, and stone. Above, reindeer. Lower left, a mammoth. Lower right, horse's head. Drawn after Breuil.

as a medium for art expression, but because of its perishability, no relics remain. For his palette the ancient craftsman had colors derived from common materials available either on the surface of the earth or in stream beds. These pigments, insoluble in water, were powdered from larger chunks, ground to a greater fineness in mortars, and mixed with animal grease. Although earlier cave paintings are outlined in one or, at most, two colors (black and red), later murals are polychromatic. One fresco of a bison on a ceiling in the Altamira Caves shows four distinct shades of color.

As subject-matter for his art, the Paleolithic artist chose primarily animals of the chase and human figures. Animals most frequently depicted are the horse, bison, and deer; less often the woolly rhinoceros, mammoth, wolf, chamois, and wild boar appear.

Animal representations, whether in painting, relief, or sculpture in the round, with few exceptions exhibit a high degree of realism. We surmise that the cave-dweller created his animal images in the belief that possession of these would, by magic, insure a plentiful supply of the beasts portrayed. From this it follows that the effectiveness of a carving or painting increases as its likeness to the original increases. The extent of realism attained is particularly striking when it appears in a mural painting far from the mouth of a cavern, for it becomes apparent that the artist worked from memory—the animals pictured are almost invariably alive—and that he worked by artificial light. When he depicted the human form, however, the Paleolithic artist departed from a realistic treatment in favor of conventionalism. Female figures, which predominate over the male, are most often grotesque in conception and may have been idols or symbols of a fertility cult.

The simplest aspect of a quadruped figure from the artist's point of view is its profile, and it is in this fashion that the animals which appear on the cave walls are portrayed. There is no evidence that the early painter or engraver understood the perspective which would be required, for example, in a front view. On the other hand, a definite awareness of scale is revealed by a variation in size between a mother animal and her young, or between the male and female of a species. The cave-dweller was adept in depicting his models in a variety of poses, ranging from rest to violent movement. Executed with direct simplicity, animal paintings such as the Altamira *Bison at Rest* and the Font de Gaume *Galloping Horse* (Plate 2) are representative of the vigorous mural art of the late Paleolithic period.

NEOLITHIC MAN A BUILDER

The Neolithic or Late Stone Age (20,000-5000 B.C.), which succeeded the Paleolithic, was marked by a moderation of climate as the last of the four major glaciers receded northward. Neolithic man emerged from his cave to erect buildings and establish settlements near rivers; communal life developed, based upon an agricultural rather than hunting economy. The skillful use of fire, domestication of animals, rudimentary medicine—these were some of the cultural advances achieved in the Late Stone Age. Pottery and weaving develop in this age. From the standpoint of art, however, Neolithic man's most significant contribution was the inception of architecture. Although his dwelling-places have disappeared with the passage of centuries, great stone monuments, believed to have some connection with worship or burial rites, remain to show his interest in building. The simplest of these monuments, called *menhirs*, are simple massive stones, roughly rectangular and for the most part unworked, placed on end with one portion buried in the ground. These occur singly and sometimes reach massive proportions. One menhir in France has been estimated to weigh 330 tons; not only was it raised on end—an engineering feat of some skill—but it was transported over half a mile to its present location. A series of menhirs, arranged to enclose a circular or rectangular area, is known as a *cromlech*. One of the most famous cromlechs is that at Stonehenge in England (Plate 1), dating from the late Neolithic Age. Consisting of two concentric circles of great menhirs, this structure was originally about 100 feet in diameter. An inner circle of smaller upright stones, each 22 feet high, 7½ feet broad, and 4 feet thick, is topped by stone lintels.* As in the case of menhirs, we do not know what function was served by the cromlechs, except that they were in some fashion associated with religious rites. Directly related to burial rites were the *dolmens* (stone tables), comprising two or more flat stones placed vertically to support one or more horizontal stones resting on their top edges. Some of the dolmens found in Europe bear engravings.

Examples of prehistoric art are by no means limited to Europe, although more excavation has been performed there than elsewhere. Some of the most satisfying sculpture fashioned by primitive man is found in the simple colossal rock structures on Easter Island in the Pacific. Known as the *Mysteries of Easter Island* (Plate 1), these stones are carved in human images as well as those of birds and fish. The crude forms of the statues resemble the art of contemporary savages.

Prehistory comes to a close coincident with the beginning of the Bronze Age, which started in Egypt as early as 5000 B.C. History dawns with the invention of writing. In so far as each generation profits by the knowledge and skills of previous generations, the crude but definite beginnings made in prehistoric art formed a solid foundation for the arts of later civilizations.

---

* In architecture, a horizontal timber or stone above a door or other opening, to support the structure above.

OUTLINE OF PREHISTORIC ART

TIME: Paleolithic or Old Stone Age—500,000-20,000 B.C. Neolithic or New Stone Age—20,000-5000 B.C.

BACKGROUND: Climatic changes are basic in the consideration of definitions in prehistory. Any understanding of art origins must rise from knowledge of racial beginnings combined with some study of anthropology. Masses of objective art specimens have been discovered in geological strata by researchers in the past fifty years in Europe, Asia, Africa, North and South America and the South Pacific Islands.

ARCHITECTURE: Monumental stone buildings of the Neolithic Age were characterized by vast *dolmens* (table-like formations of unhewn stone) and *menhirs* (vertical stones erected singly for religious purposes). *Cromlech,* huge stones set in circular formation in a crude but orderly arrangement, as at *Stonehenge,* England, present the first approach to architecture in western Europe.

SCULPTURE: Subject-matter: animals and man. Animals are represented realistically; human figures are conventionalized. Prehistoric relics, relief as well as sculpture in round, found in cave-dwellings.

PAINTING: Primitive hunters were the originators of painting. The greater part of early art consisted of lifelike representations of animals painted on cavern walls. Palettes of bone or stone, brushes of split reeds, colors ground from ocherous earths and combined with bone or soot and mixed with grease furnished the media of the first painters. The cave artists emphasized essential details of animal anatomy, carefully representing the hoofs, horns, heads, necks. These painters used color functionally to create form. Naturalistic color was employed to give the illusion of depth of form. Keen observation of life made the primitive painter use sure strokes, and his strong outlines enhance the beauty of his paintings, which show remarkable artistic understanding.

BIBLIOGRAPHY

BOAS, Franz, *Primitive Art* (Cambridge, Mass., Harvard University Press, 1927).

BREASTED, James H., *Ancient Times* (Boston, Ginn & Co., 1935).

KNIGHT, Charles R., *Before the Dawn of History* (New York, McGraw-Hill Book Co., Inc., 1935).

MACCURDY, George G., *Human Origins* (New York, D. Appleton-Century Co., Inc., 1924).

OSBORN, H. F., *Men of the Old Stone Age* (New York, Charles Scribner's Sons, 1924).

PARKYN, E. A., *Introduction to the Study of Prehistoric Art* (New York, Longmans, Green & Co., 1915).

PEAKE, Harold J. E., *Early Steps in Human Progress* (London, 1936).

SPEARING, Herbert Green, *The Childhood of Art*, rev. ed. (New York, Henry Holt & Co., Inc., 1930).

WELLS, H. G., *Outline of History*, rev. ed. (Garden City, N. Y., Garden City Publishing Co., 1931).

CHAPTER II

The Mystic Art of Egypt

IN A far off, forgotten age, thousands of years before Cleopatra and even before the eternal pyramids, there existed a kingdom on the banks of a great river. While the cave-man yet roamed the ice-covered steppes of the European continent, another race of men had discovered far to the south a fertile valley in the midst of a vast desert. In this oasis Nature was generous to man. She offered him a warm and sunny climate, and covered the land with rich black soil so fertile that he need only plant to reap the harvest. Within the valley, sheltered by mountain ranges on either side, the river furnished a natural and easy means of travel from one end of the land to the other.

Such were the conditions which combined to enable men in those ancient times to establish a settled mode of life and to develop a civilization in Egypt at a time when the rest of the world, or at least the Occident, was still in the Neolithic stage. Originating in the lake region of equatorial Africa, the River Nile flows northward for three thousand miles to empty into the Mediterranean Sea. For the last six hundred miles of its course it flows between the Libyan and Arabian deserts, cutting a groove through the plateau. It was this groove or valley that was settled by the early people who founded the kingdom of Egypt.

There is definite evidence that as early as seven thousand years ago a high degree of civilization existed in the valley. How many thousands of years passed before this civilization began to develop no one knows. As far as the pages of history are concerned, Egypt was born old. This agelessness is the essence of all that is Egyptian. The riddle of the Sphinx is nothing less than the riddle of Eternity.

THE LIFE-GIVING RIVER

In Egypt all life depended upon the river. Unfailingly, year in and year out, for century after century in unbroken rhythm, the Nile has overflowed its banks during the summer months and then receded, leaving the soil thoroughly irrigated and ready for a new planting of the crops. Without this annual inundation, the land would be as barren as the surrounding deserts. With each flooding the soil is enriched by silt brought down by the current from the Ethiopian highland. The width of the valley thus made habitable is seldom more than ten miles across, except in the delta where the river's several mouths branch out to empty into the sea. As Hecataeus has said, "Egypt is the gift of the Nile."

We shall frequently encounter the terms *Upper Egypt* and *Lower Egypt*. The former refers to the southern part of the country nearest the source of the river; the latter to the northern part, the delta region where it empties into the sea. In its downward course from the mountains the Nile breaks through the granite hills, forming the rapids known as the Six Cataracts. The northern-most cataract—seven miles long—formed the country's natural southern boundary. Since navigation through these rapids was possible only at flood season, and dangerous even then, the cataracts acted as barriers against invasion by the wild Nubian tribes to the south.

The protected character of the valley, the fertility of the soil, and the sunny, equable climate all combined to favor the growth of a peaceful community life, free from the hardships and interruptions of the almost continual warfare which characterizes the history of so many peoples. This does not mean, however, that life was entirely one of ease and certainty. Although the Egyptians could depend upon the river's regular inundation, constant watchfulness was required to prevent it from becoming a destructive force. Just as in our time great engineering problems are involved in controlling the floods of the Mississippi, similarly the Egyptians had to exercise much ingenuity, skill, and hard work to control the Nile. By devising an intricate irrigation system to regulate the waters and by draining the swamps, they succeeded in making an area of land comparable in size to the state of Vermont so produc-

tive that it could support a population of more than five million
people.

THE VALLEY

The landscape of the Nile valley, for the most part as flat as a
table, is extremely monotonous. Looking across the wide green
fields with their intersecting canals, one sees in the distance the
long, level lines that mark the ridges of the low cliffs terminating
the valley. The predominantly horizontal character of the view is
relieved only by vertical shadows in the cliffs made by indentations
etched there by the forces of wind and weather. These natural
cliff formations are echoed in the great Egyptian temples, particularly in *Deir-el-Bahri*, Hatshepsut's temple, which was in part hewn
from actual cliffs.

In Egypt wood had already become scarce before historical times.
Even now there remain, for the most part, only scattered palm trees,
some fruit trees introduced from other regions, and a few sycamores
and acacias. This early scarcity of wood forced builders to employ
the far more enduring stone.

Two plants, the lotus and papyrus, were of vital importance in
Egyptian life and furnished design-motifs for Egyptian art—especially notable in the capitals of the temple columns. The lotus, a
water plant somewhat like our water lily, was highly prized and
used as votive offerings or woven into necklaces much as the modern Hawaiians fashion leis from their native flowers; from the
papyrus the people obtained food, made rope, sandals, woven mats,
and—most important of all—writing material. Their hieroglyphic
system of writing—a picture language—was at a developed stage as
early as 2800 B.C. Many papyrus scrolls thus inscribed which have
been found in tombs, in dump-heaps, and elsewhere provide much
of our knowledge of the life and customs of these ancient people.

THE PHARAOH REIGNS SUPREME

In early times Egypt comprised numerous small states which
later were combined into two kingdoms, those of Upper and Lower
Egypt. After two hundred years of civil war the two kingdoms

were finally united in a single monarchy under King Menes (c. 2800 B.C.). From that time onward Egypt remained, except for brief periods, a single nation. For convenience Egyptian history thenceforth may be divided into two main epochs: the age of the tomb-builders, corresponding to the so-called Old Kingdom (c. c. 2800-2250 B.C.); and the age of the temple-builders, corresponding to the so-called Middle Kingdom (c. 2000-1780 B.C.)—after which came the Hyksos—and the New Kingdom or Empire (1546-1085 B.C.) "when Egypt ruled the East." Within each great epoch, it is customary to refer to smaller divisions of time according to the particular dynasty or line of royal succession then in power, rather than according to the Christian calendar. Thus, Menes was the first king of the first dynasty, and the whole dynastic succession dates from his reign.

In the Old Kingdom there was, under the pharaoh, a ruling class of nobles who governed the local districts and under them a bureaucracy of magistrates and tax collectors scattered throughout the country. Education and scholarship were largely under the control of the priests, who thus became more and more important and influential in the life of the people as time went on. They were supported by offerings of land or goods made to the temples they held in charge. Another caste was that of the scribes (Plate 7), somewhat comparable to our civil service employees. The common people were either slaves who toiled on the estates of the king and nobles, or else serfs who owned little more than the poor hovels in which they dwelt. As a rule, the people had to live out their lives in the class of society into which they happened to be born; nevertheless, by studying to become a scribe it was possible for a man to rise to a higher caste. In later times there arose a large and powerful middle class of merchants and tradesmen.

It was during the early days of the Old Kingdom that the three *Great Pyramids* (Plate 3)* were erected as tombs for the Pharaohs Khufu, Khafre, and Menkere, monarchs of the fourth dynasty.

---

* The three *Great Pyramids* were one of the seven wonders of the ancient world. The other six were: the *Pharos of Alexandria, Egypt* (a lighthouse), the *Hanging Gardens of Babylon,* the *Temple of Artemis* at Ephesus, the gold and ivory *statue of Zeus* at Olympia, the *Mausoleum* built by Artemisia at Halicarnassus, and the *Colossus of Rhodes.*

Their pyramids are at Gizeh, near the ancient capital of Memphis —not far from the present city of Cairo—in Lower Egypt. These gigantic monuments—in comparison with which our modern sky-scrapers are mere toothpicks—are the most famous, but by no means the only, pyramids to be found in Egypt. Some two hundred smaller ones extend along the plateau near the Nile, all the way from Gizeh to Meidum. During Greek and Roman times travelers brought back reports of these Egyptian marvels, but in medieval times Europeans knew little about Egypt except that the pyramids were there. Indeed, Egypt's great past was almost unknown to the Western world until Napoleon Bonaparte led his army there in 1798. According to custom, scientists and scholars went with the army. In 1799 a French army officer found a fragment of basalt inscribed in three languages: Greek, demotic (a sort of Egyptian shorthand) and the old hieroglyphic. This slab, known as the *Rosetta Stone* from the place where it was found, proved to be the key to the Egyptian language when its message was deciphered from the corresponding Greek version of the inscription.

As time went on the Old Kingdom disintegrated. The pharaohs became weaker and weaker, and government passed into the hands of the nobles who struggled among themselves for power. Then, after a period comparable to the so-called Dark Ages of Europe, there followed the establishment of the Middle Kingdom. By this time the capital had been moved from Memphis, near the delta, to Thebes in Upper Egypt; and Egypt was experiencing great prosperity. Trade was being carried on with the Aegean and Semitic nations to the north and east. Science, literature, and the arts were flourishing once more. Kings and nobles continued to build magnificent tombs for themselves, but instead of constructing pyramids they hollowed out caves in the cliffs, believing them to be a better safeguard against the robberies which had already dev-astated many of the earlier tombs. The *Tombs of Beni Hasan*, with their rich treasure of painted reliefs and other objects of art, belong to this period.

KINGS AND QUEENS

This prosperous era was brought to a halt by the Hyksos ("shepherd kings"), who came down through Syria and overran the whole of the Nile delta. Those who were not assimilated by the Egyptian race were eventually driven out by Ahmose, who established the eighteenth dynasty (1580-1350 B.C.). His victories mark the beginning of the New Kingdom. Now Egypt for the first time became an aggressive military power, and her boundaries were extended eastward into Asia as far as the banks of the Euphrates. Queen Hatshepsut, the wife of Thothmes III (successor of Ahmose), appears as the first great queen in history. She completely overshadowed her husband and wore masculine attire; even going so far as to strap an artificial beard to her chin and having herself addressed as "His Majesty the King." During her reign Egypt was at peace. Though she erected gold-tipped obelisks, which according to her inscriptions "reached the very heavens," her most notable monument was the rock-temple of *Deir-el-Bahri* (Plate 4), generally conceded to be the most beautiful of the Egyptian temples.

Obelisk

After the death of the Queen, Thothmes III emerged from his enforced seclusion, assumed power, and reigned for fifty years. Strange to say, he became the greatest military conqueror in Egyptian history. If Hatshepsut was the "Queen Elizabeth of Egypt," Thothmes III was its Napoleon. Like Bonaparte, he was short of stature—hardly five feet tall. He extended the empire north and east to the Euphrates and south below the third cataract in Nubia.

To commemorate his victories, Thothmes erected six great obelisks, four of which have since been taken out of Egypt. One now stands in London beside the Thames; another is in Central Park, New York City. It was brought to America in 1880, the gift of the Khedive of Egypt. It bears inscriptions by the Pharaoh Ramses

II, whose daughter, according to the Bible story, found the infant
Moses in the bulrushes. Thothmes ordered the destruction of all
of Hatshepsut's portrait statues and the obliteration of her name

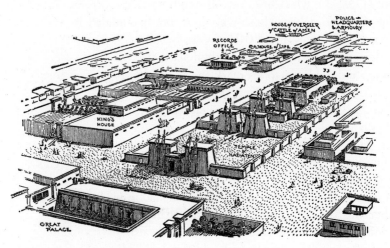

Restoration of a part of Akhetaton, ancient city founded by Ikhnaton, showing temple of Hat-Aton. (Smith)

from her tomb and temple. Fortunately his minions did not do a
thorough job of it, and one statue of her is now in the Metropolitan
Museum in New York City.

Ikhnaton (c. 14th century B.C.) is another king important in the
history of Egypt. Sometimes called the first monotheist, he tried to
make the people abandon their numerous gods in favor of one,
Aton, the sun god. He moved his capital from Thebes to Akhetaton
—the modern Tel-el-Amarna—where a sculptor's studio with many
works of art have been found. During this time there was a notable
freshness and freedom in the arts of Egypt, a brief interlude of
naturalism between two long eras of extreme conventionalism.
After his death, however, the people soon went back to their old
gods and the artists to their old forms.

Ikhnaton was succeeded by his son-in-law, Tutenkhamon, "King
Tut," who died at the early age of eighteen years and is widely
known in modern times through the discovery of his tomb, intact
with its magnificent treasures, in 1923. The mummy of the young

king was enclosed in seven coffins, one within the other, the innermost one being covered with gold. The furnishings of the chamber were unusually rich and luxurious.

If Thothmes III was the Napoleon of Egypt, Ramses II (1300-1234 B.C.) was its Louis XIV. The power of Ramses was great but his vanity was greater. Everything he did was on a large scale, and he saw to it that his every accomplishment was recorded in monumental, exaggerated fashion. His temples were the biggest, his sculptures were the most heroic, and all were inscribed with boastful records of the prowess of the Great King. For the most part, more of quantity than of quality remains to commemorate his reign, though there is one notable exception: the *rock-temple of Abu-Simbel* in Nubia, whose solemn and noble sculptures rank with the finest monuments of Egyptian art (Plate 4).

Following Ramses II, the pharaohs of the nineteenth dynasty became less powerful, and the rule of the country passed into the hands of the nobles and the priesthood. The resulting disunity laid the country open to invasion by the Assyrians and other foreign peoples, and after the year 1090 B.C. (the first year of the twenty-first dynasty), Egypt's history may be said to merge with that of its successive conquerors—the Libyans, the Assyrians again, the Persians, the Greeks (Ptolemies), and finally the Romans. After Cleopatra's time (d. 30 B.C.) once powerful Egypt was merely a Roman province.

LIFE OF THE PEOPLE

Having sketched very briefly the history of ancient Egypt, let us now consider the people themselves. Whence did they come, what did they look like, what were some of the customs of their everyday life?

To begin with, the original Egyptians were of the Caucasian race, being related more closely to the Berbers of northern Africa than to any other particular group. From an early time the strain was mingled with Oriental blood from the Asiatic invaders and immigrants and with Negro blood from Nubia and Ethiopia; but the racial character of the valley inhabitants remained predominantly Caucasian throughout.

In appearance they were slender, with red-brown skin. The women, who spent less time outdoors, were paler than the men in complexion and are thus represented in art. They accentuated their paleness by the use of a black paint (*kohl,* made from soot) applied to the eyelids and eyebrows, a practice which probably had a practical origin, namely, to protect the eyes against the glaring tropical sun. Other cosmetics were used—by men as well as women—and palettes on which they were mixed are still preserved. A famous ceremonial palette dates as far back as the time of King Menes.

For clothing men of the Old Kingdom wore a short garment of linen. Workers supplemented this with an over-garment of leather for protection. In later periods, especially with the nobility, the garment became longer and more ornate. Women dressed in a long, clinging garment which in early times was colored, but later was usually white, starched, and pleated. Examples of these finely woven linen clothes found in tombs are still to be seen in the museums, usually in an excellent state of preservation because of the dryness of the Egyptian climate. The plainness of the white garments was relieved by jewelry of gold and silver set with turquoise, lapis lazuli, amethyst, carnelian, garnet, and other semiprecious stones found in the hills of the Arabian desert. Both men and women wore wigs instead of hats when out of doors. For sanitary reasons men clipped their hair short, and women covered theirs with handkerchiefs before donning wigs. Examples of the different styles of hair-dress worn by the women are to be seen in sculpture, both in reliefs and in the round.

The average Egyptian was probably a practical and pleasure-loving person. He was perhaps the least war-minded of any of the ancient peoples. Many of the population spent their lives tilling the soil and led an uneventful existence. Others were employed in maintaining the vast irrigation system or in building the temples and monuments. The life of the nobles, on the other hand, was one of ease. They traveled up and down the Nile in private boats, accompanied by kitchen-boats which lagged just far enough behind so that the odors of cooking would not annoy the fastidious owners.

The gardens of their palaces contained artificial pools bordered by palm trees. The walls of their houses were decorated with glazed bricks in gorgeous colors, or with brightly painted low-relief carvings of scenes from outdoor life. Servants and slaves were in constant attendance. Hunting, fishing, and banqueting, the latter enlivened by musicians and dancers, offered diversion. Such illustrations serve to dispel the prevalent idea that the Egyptians were a gloomy race, too much given to introspection and thoughts of death.

Few of us would envy the "omnipotent" Pharaoh who, contrary to common belief, was subject to certain strict laws which he obeyed implicitly. These were imposed because it was thought that through some magic the well-being of the entire country was dependent upon the health of the king; he had to eat and drink sparingly, and to conduct himself so that the nation would not suffer as a result of any intemperance on his part.

RELIGION AND AFTER-LIFE

The religion of the ancients, dominated by superstition and magic, was complicated and indeterminate. Probably inconsistencies did not matter to the Egyptians, since their religion was mystical rather than intellectual. The various deities who represented forces of nature were worshipped by all Egyptians. Some of the most important were Re, the sun-god; Osiris, the god of the underworld; Isis, his wife and the symbol of motherhood; Horus, the sky-god; Nut, the sky-goddess; Shu, god of the air; Sev, god of the earth; and Seth, god of the night. One of the favorite myths of the Egyptians was that of the trinity, Osiris, Isis, and Horus, their son. According to legend, Osiris was killed by his brother, Seth, who cut his body into fourteen pieces and scattered them to the winds. This was a terrible calamity, spiritually as well as physically, for the welfare of the soul was believed to be dependent upon the earthly body. Isis, Osiris' faithful wife, collected the pieces and reassembled them; Osiris, having thus triumphed over death, became the ruler of the netherworld where he presided over the judgment of all departed souls. This myth is somewhat analogous to the idea of the Christian Resurrection—the triumph of eternal life

over death. It may also be associated with the renewal of the soil
by the river and the triumph of light when the rising sun dispels
the darkness of night.

The Egyptians believed that the soul took the form of a bird
and flew about the world at will, and that when frightened by evil
spirits it returned to the tomb for safety. In addition to the soul
there was the *ka,* a kind of protective spirit which was co-existent
with the body and remained with it after death to protect it from
mortal enemies. The necessity of the preservation of the body for
the benefit of the soul and the *ka* led to the practice of mummifica-
tion (fully developed in the eighteenth dynasty), and of furnishing
the tomb with food, furniture, oils, ointments, cosmetics, and other
adjuncts of daily life. Objects were carved or painted on the walls
of the tomb and statues of the deceased were interred, for by
magic they became real, or so the Egyptians believed. Prayers and
incantations were inscribed in the tomb to help the spirit find its
way safely through the underworld presided over by Osiris. Such
prayers and instructions were more or less codified in what we
know as the *Book of the Dead,* but which the Egyptians called the
"Book of Entrance into Light" (Plate 9).

THE PHARAOHS BUILD THEIR TOMBS

The tomb began as a round pit dug in the earth and covered
with a mound of sand. Buried with the body were the usual pots
for food and a palette for grinding paint. This crude grave, which
served the common person's need, was not deemed adequate protection for nobles or kings and the valuable objects that were buried
with them after public display in the funeral procession. Therefore
the *mastaba,* a rectangular stone bench or terrace-shaped structure
with sloping sides, was devised. A simple mastaba contained a
chapel near the entrance for the convenience of the family, who
came to bring offerings for the deceased. Underneath the stone
structure, far below the sandy surface, was the burial chamber.
The body was lowered through a shaft or taken down a set of
stairs. The opening was then filled with sand and stones to conceal the entrance. A separate shaft, the *serdab,* contained a statue

of the *ka*. The more complicated mastabas differed only in the increased number of chambers and serdabs. Near the pyramid of Khufu the numerous mastabas of the nobles were laid out in streets, like the houses of a city. Remains of them may still be seen.

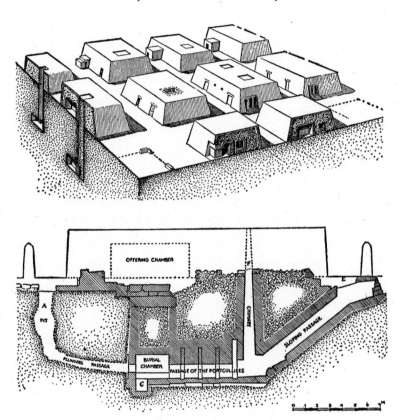

Mastaba. Exterior and cross-section. (Smith)

As the rulers grew more powerful they built their tombs higher, and during the third dynasty the simple mastaba form developed into a step-pyramid, in appearance somewhat like the set-backs of a modern skyscraper. The six-staged pyramid at Sakkara is believed to be the first structure made entirely of stone. This step-pyramid, nearly two hundred feet high, was built by the noted architect Imhotep in the third dynasty. Later in such tombs the steps were filled in with diagonal-edged blocks, thus producing the pyramid shape. These huge structures of stone masonry, with galleries leading to the burial chambers, were ingeniously vaulted in such manner as to sustain the weight of the superimposed masonry. After the body of the king was placed in the chamber provided for it, heavy stones were used to block the passage and every possible measure was taken to ensure sanctity of the tomb. Despite all of these precautions, however, robbers violated the pyramids in earliest times—tempted perhaps by the ostentatious display of valuables in the funeral processions.

The three greatest and most famous pyramids, those of *Khufu* (also called *Cheops*), *Khafre,* and *Menkere,* still remain monuments to the undying fame of their mighty builders. That of Khufu, the largest, was originally 480 feet high (part of the top is now missing, reducing its height to 450 feet), or about the height of a modern thirty-four-story skyscraper. The four sides face exactly the four points of the compass, each side being 755 feet long at its base; the whole mass of "not less than 2,500,000 cubic yards of stone" covers an area of thirteen acres. Blocks of limestone weighing two tons each were used in the construction. The transportation of such enormous blocks without the benefit of modern machinery was an amazing feat. After the stones were quarried on the opposite side of the river, they were put on rafts and shipped across at flood time to Gizeh. From the valley floor they were rope-hauled to the plateau by means of ramps. No mechanical equipment, such as block and tackle, was used. Herodotus, the Greek historian, writes that it took a hundred thousand men working twenty years to complete the task. The blocks of stone were cut so precisely that they fitted together without the slightest irregularities. When one realizes that more than two million of these huge blocks were used in the pyramid of Khufu alone, one is amazed at the potentialities of raw man-power.

In addition to the limestone and sandstone of the valley, the Egyptians used in their buildings and sculpture harder stones from Nubia and Arabia, such as red granite, obsidian, and diorite.

After the pyramid age the kings and nobles had their tombs cut directly into the rocky cliffs, like those found in the *Valley of the*

Tombs of the Kings, near Thebes. The entrances were carefully concealed to guard against robbers but even so most of these tombs were plundered in comparatively early times.

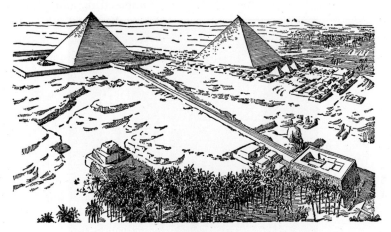

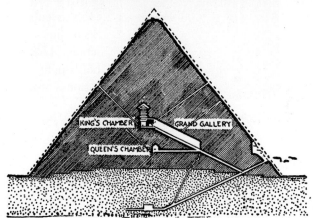

Pyramids. Above, Khufu (right) and Khafre. Below, cross-section of Khufu. (Smith)

Closely related to the tombs, especially in the Old Kingdom, were the mortuary temples. These were either connected with the tomb by a causeway or were oriented to it. The mortuary temple served as an entrance for the funeral procession, which moved up the causeway to the chapel of the pyramid where prayers and

offerings were made in behalf of the departed pharaoh. Such a
temple is that of *Khafre,* near the second largest of the great pyramids. It is simple but elegant in structure. The square supports

Valley temple, restored. Pyramid of Khafre at Gizeh.
(Smith)

and huge lintels were single pieces of highly polished red granite;
the floors were paved with alabaster. The only decorations were
rows of seated statues of the king, placed against the walls. Here,
however, we find an unusual feature. The roof over the central
portion is higher than that of the sides, leaving an opening between
the two roofs. Through this narrow space, light is admitted into
the halls. In the *Temple of Sahure,* designed for the same purpose,
columns with capitals of palm design appear. Later, when the
tombs were concealed instead of being erected out in the open, the
mortuary temples, far removed from the burial site, were still placed
on an axis with the tombs. As time went on tombs became archi-

tecturally less important while temples grew larger and more imposing.

THE COLOSSAL TEMPLES OF THE MIDDLE KINGDOM
AND EMPIRE

The typical temple of the Middle Kingdom and Empire was
built to serve the purposes of the funerary ritual. This consisted
largely of processions of people come to view the priests and kings
as they emerged from the sanctuary bearing the image of the god.
Some one has said that the Egyptian temple is a "processional road
in stone, and, like the participants in the procession, it moves with a
monotonous, measured pace." We can imagine the people moving
slowly along the avenue of sphinxes, rams, or lions symbolizing the
king, past the high obelisks, and entering the pylon gate flanked
on either side by huge statues of the pharaoh. They enter the
great colonnaded court where the common people remain while
the initiated or inner group of the cult go on to the hypostyle hall;
from here, only the high priest and the pharaoh may proceed to
the inner sanctuary where the ark containing the sacred statue
of the god and the treasure is kept. The rooms diminish in size
from front to back, and the daylight grows dimmer and dimmer as
one goes from the brilliant open outer court toward the darkness
of the sanctuary. This arrangement was no doubt intended to
inspire the common people with mystery and awe.

The entire enclosure, including the temple, the sacred lake, and
subsidiary buildings, was surrounded by a thick solid wall, the top
of which, accessible by a stairway, was wide enough to allow processions to pass around it. At Karnak the wall was thirty feet thick.
Decorations of richly colored carvings, varying from incised lines
to low reliefs, spread over these walls in continuous pattern "like
an enlarged page from a papyrus scroll."

To support the enormous weight of the stone lintels, huge
columns were placed close together. Sometimes, as in the *hypostyle hall at Karnak,* the columns were so unnecessarily thick and
close that most of the daylight was shut out (Plate 5). In order
to counteract this defect the *clerestory* was developed. In the

clerestory, the walls of the middle aisle are raised above those of the side aisles; open spaces in the middle aisle walls admit light. The capitals were usually designed with papyrus or lotus motifs (Plate 5). Fluted columns with sixteen sides, very much like the Greek Doric ones, are first met in the *Tombs of Beni-Hassan*, later in Queen Hatshepsut's temple.

Hatshepsut's cliff-temple, *Deir-el-Bahri*, built by the architect Sen-Mut, was partly carved out of a rocky hill at the foot of cliffs (Plate 4). Arranged in terraces one above the other, its colonnades are beautifully proportioned. Its walls are covered with scenes depicting the Queen's expedition to Punt. Water was brought up from the Nile to maintain the lovely gardens with their imported myrrh and incense trees. The horizontal lines of the cliff ridge and the vertical indentations in the cliffs are echoed in the long flat roofs of the temple and in the colonnades of the porches.

Lining the procession path were eight kneeling *statues of the Queen;* others in different positions stood about the court and on either side of the entrance. Each of the kneeling statues was approximately twelve feet in height. It has been suggested that the sculptor did not know how to represent a queen, since there were so few outstanding queens in all the long years of Egyptian history; therefore he represented her as a king with feminine features. However, the masculine type is believed to have been Hatshepsut's choice (Plate 8). Stylized in the Egyptian manner, the simple modeling imparts a certain elegance and charm to the statue.

In comparison to the buildings of the pyramid age, the workmanship of the great temples was in most cases inferior. This may have been due to two causes. The workmen of the earlier period were native Egyptians who might be expected to take more interest in the structures dedicated to their own religion than the slave laborers imported from abroad by the conquering pharaohs of the empire. Also, the later kings tried to complete each temple during their respective lifetimes, so that the workmanship was more hasty than in the case of the earlier builders who often depended on their successors to carry on the work which they had started. The great pyramids, as we have seen, were put together with extreme precision; no mortar was used to hold the stones together, so perfectly did they fit. But in some of the later temples, the different parts of the columns are irregularly joined and coated over with cement to conceal the imperfect workmanship. At all times, however, Egyptian architecture is impressive and monumental.

STATUES IN THE ROUND

When Egyptian sculpture is mentioned, one probably thinks first of the colossal *Sphinx* (Plate 3). Hewn directly out of a rocky hill near the pyramid of Khafre, this figure was conceived on a scale commensurate with the titanic structures which it adjoins. In its present mutilated condition it does not lend itself to detailed study as do other statues that are better preserved, but this much can be said about it: The head was possibly an idealized portrait of King Khafre himself, or it might have been intended to express the pharaoh or god-king in the abstract rather than to be a portrait of any individual human ruler. Originally it had the straight, stiff ceremonial beard found on other pharaoh-portraits of the period. The body is that of a lion lying down, symbolic of kingly power and authority.

We can study Old Kingdom sculpture better in the *statue of Ranofer*. The position of the figure was governed by rigid conventions, arrived at after many generations of experiment in the effort to express the thought of nobility, strength, and human dignity. The figure stands as straight as a ramrod, but over-stiffness is avoided by a lack of complete symmetry, and by advancing one foot slightly, as if he were about to take a step forward. The head faces directly to the front, and the arms are held straight down at the sides, close to the body. The half-nude body shows a powerful physical development, although the muscles are not brought out in anatomical detail, but rather in broad flattened masses. The figure is meant to be seen from the front and from the sides; not from angles in between. Probably this is because the sculptor had in mind the rectangular shape of the block of stone from which it was cut and wished to preserve its four-sided perpendicular character. This frontality is also characteristic of a certain stage in the evolution of a sculptural style in other countries, notably the archaic period in Greece and the early Gothic period in France. It is almost as if the sculptor were thinking of a square block of stone with high reliefs on the four sides, instead of trying to show the

human body in the round to be viewed from any angle. In the Egyptian seated figures the same frontality exists. The feet are usually placed together, pointing forward, and the hands and forearms rest on the knees and thighs. The sculptures of Ramses at the temple of Abu-Simel and of the bearded Hatshepsut exemplify this type.

Such were the statues of the kings and the nobles. But in the art of the common people we find a much greater degree of freedom, both in pose and individuality of facial expression. Not subject to the conventions of royalty, the people were free to exercise their imaginations. The *Sheikh El-Beled* is an excellent example in wood of this lifelike quality (Plate 6). Of lesser artistic importance but of considerable human interest are the small painted wooden figures that were made to be placed in the tombs, representing servants and tradesmen going about their everyday tasks. These are quite free from

Statue of Ranofer.
(Smith)

the restraint of convention, and possess a remarkable degree of animation and often humor. They were made for the tombs with the idea that they would continue to serve the master in death and the after-life (Plate 9).

RELIEFS AND PAINTINGS IN TOMB AND TEMPLE

The relief-sculpture of the Old Kingdom (and of the later periods as well) was in such low relief and so flat that it can hardly be called sculpture at all; it is more like large-scale engraving. It was usually painted, and the color-patterns are very harmonious and beautiful. This fact, together with its essentially two-dimensional character, requires us to consider it under the head of painting as well as sculpture. Such sculpture-painting covered the walls of the tombs and the temples, and often enriched the huge columns as well. One of the first things that one notices is the way in which human figures are drawn. The head is always in profile, but the eye is in front view. Again, the legs are in profile, but the shoulders in front view. This was because the artists sought to show "characterizing outlines." The character of an eye is best seen from the front, not from the side. A leg is best characterized from the profile view, and so on. Since the Egyptians were trying to represent the figure in a purely linear way, as part of the flat pattern of the whole picture, they tried to make its outlines as expressive as possible. They did not concern themselves with perspective and foreshortening, perhaps because they felt that representation of the third dimension was the task of the sculptor who worked "in the round" rather than of the artist whose medium was a flat surface.

The subject-matter of Egyptian wall reliefs covered a wide range. In them were shown people ploughing, sowing, reaping, fishing, boating, hunting, at banquet scenes, or herding cattle—in fact every facet of Egyptian life is depicted, so that we have a more complete record of their civilization than of any other ancient people. A wall painting from the *Tomb of Nakht* shows the pharaoh and his family hunting (Plate 10). These artists seemed to have an unfailing sense of design, with due consideration for spatial relationships and a continuous, flowing linear rhythm. Their color palette was a simple one: red, yellow, green, blue, with white and black. The paint was laid on in solid flat tones without modulation within an area.

During the reign of Ikhnaton (the Amarna period) the rigid conventions were relaxed. On a relief, the *Stele of Ikhnaton,* the sun-god Aton is represented by a sun disk with the head of a single cobra. Extending from it are rays terminating in hands, some of which hold the sign of life before the noses of the royal pair. The king's predecessors had demanded that they be represented as semi-divine beings, strong and wise, men in the prime of life. This idea of god-like power and wisdom was symbolized by the sphinx, with the body of a lion suggesting the strength of an

Sign of Life. Each of the three gods seated at the right holds the sign of life in his right hand. The figure at the left is a king. (Champollion)

animal, and a human head indicative of intelligence. Contrary to royal custom, Ikhnaton, who seemed to have little desire for the display of either military pomp or divine power, has permitted himself to be shown here in an intimate family scene (Plate 10). Also, the wife of the pharaoh—usually portrayed as being about one fourth the size of her royal spouse—is comparable in stature with her husband. Here the freedom and movement which characterizes the Amarna period is shown in the natural and informal poses of the figures and in the treatment of their garments.

A sculptor's studio with models well preserved has been found at the site of Ikhnaton's ancient city. In it were realistic likenesses of the king with his prominent features exaggerated almost to the point of caricature. There also were studies for the famous portrait of *Queen Nofretete* which show that the sculptor began with naturalistic models from life. The final work was made to conform to the accepted style of the period. This head, with its elaborate head-dress, well-poised upon the slender neck, the eyes and eyebrows darkened and the lips painted, conforms so closely to the present-day ideal of slender beauty that it seems surprisingly modern. From these and other models found there, one may trace the Egyptian sculptor's procedure from the initial modeling or carving to the finished product.

In the Middle Kingdom and later times many artists dispensed with the carving altogether and painted directly on the walls, which had been first coated with a layer of plaster or stucco to hold the paint. This tended to make the drawing freer and more suave, since a brush-made line is easier to apply than one carved with a stiff instrument into a hard stone surface. Many beautiful examples of this sort of work remain from the eighteenth-dynasty tombs at Thebes, capital city of the period.

Middle Kingdom sculpture in the round followed for the most part the conventions of the Old Kingdom, but it was often less monumental and majestic—perhaps the tradition was beginning to wear a bit thin. Nevertheless, there was a greater degree of individual characterization in the faces of the magnificent portraits such as those of *Queen Hatshepsut* (Plate 8), *Thothmes III*, *Ramses II* (Plate 6), and *Queen Nofretete* (Plate 6). The latter has become a symbol of queenly charm and beauty. The head of *Ikhnaton*, her husband, is portrayed with unusual attention to accurate delineation, and the gold burial mask of Tutenkhamon is another excellent example of naturalistic characterization.

A common theme in Egyptian art was the portrayal of domestic animals—cats, dogs, and donkeys. Most of these renditions are realistic and vigorous, as the Saite sculpture, *The Bronze Cat* (Plate 11). The wall paintings and reliefs of the tombs also contained numerous depictions of animals both sacred and domestic, such as the painting of *Cat Eating Fish* in the Tomb of Nakht (Plate 11).

In ceramics and jewelry the Egyptians exercised their imaginations to produce charming and distinctive patterns. They perfected the technique of glazing at a very early period, and their vases, jars, and similar utensils gleam with a rich iridescence. A metallic blue and blue-green glaze derived from copper were among their favorites.

Looking at Egyptian art as a whole, we see that it belies the common impression that the Egyptians were a gloomy, introspective race, given to contemplation of death and darkness. Alongside the solemn, awe-inspiring temples and pyramids, we find in their carvings, paintings, and other arts a constant expression of their vivid interest in the pleasures and labors of day-by-day human life. Indeed, they were so devoted to life that their whole religion was based on the desire to prolong it past the grave and into the future world. Because they thought of the after-life as a literal extension of their mortal life, they furnished and decorated their tombs to make them congenial and attractive dwelling-places in the future life.

OUTLINE OF EGYPTIAN ART

TIME: Old Kingdom—c. 2800 B.C.-2250 B.C. Middle Kingdom and Empire—2160 B.C.-c. 1100 B.C. Five hundred years of foreign domination and Saite period extended to Persian conquest in 525 B.C.

BACKGROUND: Egypt a level country between low cliffs and desert, made habitable by the Nile. Climate hot and dry, and highly preservative. Little wood, but plenty of stone such as limestone, sandstone diorite, and alabaster. Clay for making bricks. During Old Kingdom, the pharaoh supreme. Later nobles in power and priests controlled most of the wealth. Egyptians worshipped the sun-god, sky-goddess, and other gods represented as animal-headed human beings. Pharaoh, semi-divine. Emphasis upon life after death. Colossal buildings of Egypt made possible by excellent organization of almost unlimited man power.

ARCHITECTURE: Tombs most important in Old Kingdom—temples in later periods. Pits, mastabas, pyramids and tombs of kings and nobles hollowed out of cliffs. Small temples furnished entrances to covered walk leading to chapel connected with pyramid and its subsidiary smaller pyramids and mastabas. Pyramids made of precisely cut stone, laid without mortar. Solid masses with the exception of tunnels and openings for tombs of pharaoh and queen. Sphinx carved out of living rock near great pyramid. Fine engineering. Temples made of stone—workmanship inferior to that of tombs. Simple plan: Rooms and courts symmetrically placed about straight-line axis. Columns with lotiform, papyriform, flower, and bud-shaped capitals. Walls leaning slightly inward on exterior, and straight on interior. Obelisks guarded pylon gates and animals bordered the road leading to entrance. Entire temple complex surrounded by a girdle wall. Temples had clerestory lighting and ventilation. Ornamented with sculpture and painting.

SCULPTURE: Purpose both decorative and funerary. (a) Colored designs with incised outlines, (b) figures with lowered background, (c) figures in relief with background partially cut down below flat surface of the wall. All highly conventionalized, fine in design. Sculpture in the round (or free-standing); enormous figures of Pharaohs and huge animal sculpture expressive of force and power. Fine portrait sculpture in Old Kingdom, conventionalized, royal, but lifelike. Early reliefs arranged in zones. Both reliefs and sculpture in the round characterized by angularity. More freedom and naturalism during reign of Ikhnaton, after which a return to old forms, not so stiff or angular, nor so vital.

PAINTING: Adjunct of sculpture in Old Kingdom. Later, due to the use of the brush instead of incised outline, style was much freer and the line, more fluent. Extremely decorative in design.

BIBLIOGRAPHY

BREASTED, James H., *Ancient Times* (Ginn & Co., Boston, 1935).

———, *The Dawn of Conscience* (Charles Scribner's Sons, N. Y., 1935).

MASPERO, G., *Art in Egypt* (N. Y., 1930).

MEIER-GRAEFE, Julius, *Pyramid and Temple*, tr. by Roger Hinks (Macaulay Co., N. Y., 1930).

MURRAY, Margaret, *Egyptian Sculpture* (Charles Scribner's Sons, N. Y., 1930).

PETRIE, Flinders, *Egyptian Architecture* (London, 1938).

RANKE, Herman, *The Art of Ancient Egypt* (Vienna, 1936), numerous illustrations.

Ross, Sir E. D. (ed.), *The Art of Egypt Through the Ages* (Studio Publications, N. Y., 1931).

SMITH, William Stevenson, *Ancient Egypt* (Museum of Fine Arts, Boston, 1930).

STEINDORFF, George, and SEELE, Keith, *When Egypt Ruled the East* (University of Chicago Press, Chicago, 1942).

WEIGALL, Arthur, *Ancient Egyptian Works of Art* (Small Maynard & Co., Boston, 1924).

CHAPTER III

Art of the Valley of the Two Rivers

BEYOND the rich lands along the Nile, across the Isthmus of Sinai, north and east of Syria and Palestine lies the Valley of the Two Rivers. If Egypt owes its fertility to the Nile, the southern part of the Asiatic valley owes its very existence to the Tigris and Euphrates rivers. These converge to empty their silt-laden waters into the Persian Gulf; thus by a slow but continuous process extending the land far out into the water.

In ancient times these lowlands spread monotonously out to the horizon, interrupted only by fringes of palm trees along the rivers. Low bluffs rose from the rivers and stretched out into rolling prairies. Beyond the prairies were high swelling lands and the foot-hills of the snow-covered mountains which formed the northern boundary of the valley. The Euphrates furnished a water route to the highways of Syria and Palestine. These roads led to Egypt, thus establishing contact between two brilliant river-valley civilizations which paralleled and rivaled each other. It is not definitely known which is the older of the two, but present-day authorities seem to give precedence to the Asiatic civilization. There important cities such as Ur, Erech, Kish, and Lagash were already flourishing when Menes was uniting Upper and Lower Egypt into a single kingdom.

The Palestinian and Syrian corridor was the scene of many fierce battles when Egypt, abandoning her peaceful ways, made war on her Asiatic rival and when the Assyrians sacked "hundred-gated Thebes." The Hebrews have left accounts of such conflicts and their rich literature, particularly the Old Testament, contains numerous stories of those times. Two of the best known are the story of Jonah and the whale and that of the Great Flood for which Noah built his famous ark.

Like Egypt, the Tigro-Euphrates Valley was divided into lower and upper regions. The lower part, first known as Sumeria, afterwards was included in Babylonia, whereas the foot-hill land of the north was called Assyria. In modern times the valley has been called Mesopotamia and, more recently, Iraq. Both parts of the region lie within the Fertile Crescent, and form the eastern section of that inverted U-shaped strip of fabulously productive land extending westward along the northern border of the Arabian Desert and continuing southward through Syria and Palestine. Desert nomads, the Semites, and the Sumerians who were inhabitants of the grasslands were constantly warring over possession of the fertile valley. Such years of uninterrupted peace as the Egyptians, who were protected by natural barriers, enjoyed were unknown in the Asiatic valley cities whose sole defense was their thick encircling walls. Semi-barbaric peoples threatened them from all sides. Among these were the Elamites to the northeast, the Persians from the high plateaus of Iran, the fierce Hittites driven from their homes in the northwest by migrating Indo-Europeans, and also the Semitic nomads who were constantly drifting in from the deserts. All of these less fortunately situated people coveted the wealth of the rich valley. Each of the more powerful invaders occupied it for a time, bringing with them their own customs and ideas. Thus, in turn, all of them contributed to the civilization of the Land of the Two Rivers.

By 3200 B.C. the Sumerians, originally a mountain folk, had settled in widely separated, independent city-states, each of which had its own god and priest-king. As there was no strong central government, quarrels arose—chiefly over irrigation facilities—and caused war between the cities. First one city and then another established ascendancy. The loosely-knit city-states were weakened by civil strife and eventually they were conquered by their traditional enemy, the Semites, who forced their way in from the desert. After a time a Semite king, Sargon of Akkad, came into power (c. 2872 B.C.) and united the central part of the valley into one kingdom called Akkad. Sumeria was reduced to a small country bordering the Persian Gulf. Her remaining cities became increasingly Semitic in character, and finally the political power of Sumeria waned, but her culture persisted long after her cities fell. Another Semite king, Hammurabi, rose to power (c. 2000 B.C.) and made Babylon one of the greatest cities of ancient times. A raiding band of Hittites (c. 1760 B.C.) sacked and plundered it, took their booty and departed. Another Sargon (722-705 B.C.), king of the Assyrians, established the strongest military empire the world had ever known. He extended his domain from the Tigris southward to the delta of the Nile and established his capital at Sargonburg, near the ancient city of Nineveh. Assyrian power was broken when the Chaldeans revolted at the death of Ashurbanipal. Under King Nebuchadnezzar, who began his reign in 648 B.C., Babylon, the capital of the Chaldean empire, rose to heights of power and luxury hitherto unknown. Peace was enjoyed for two centuries, until the Persians under Cyrus captured the city. The fall of Babylon marked the decline of culture in the Land of the Two Rivers; great cities became mounds of mud destined to lie hidden and almost forgotten until modern archaeologists uncovered their ruins.

Prior to these discoveries the only written account we had of the valley civilizations was that found in the Old Testament of the Hebrews, a small Semitic tribe which differed from the others only in religious beliefs. Under the able leadership of King David, the Hebrews attained military strength, but during the reign of David's son, King Solomon, their power declined and they were eventually overwhelmed by the Assyrians.

Throughout the history of the valley, there were great mass migrations extending as far south as Egypt. The biblical story of Abraham, who gathered about him all of his people, his servants, his flocks and his possessions and left the city of Ur to go into the promised land was the story of a group of Israelites returning to their native Palestine.

Digging among the ruins archaeologists have found well-preserved stone statues and alabaster slabs which had fallen face down in the mud. Important tombs were located near the city of Ur. Letters and documents in cuneiform writing (wedge-shaped characters impressed upon tablets and seals of clay) have also been discovered. Through the aid of such monuments and documents scholars have been able to reconstruct the civilization of those ancient peoples.

THE SUMERIANS, RELIGION AND BURIAL CUSTOMS

The Sumerians, who were in possession of the valley at the dawn of history, invented the cuneiform system of writing, established a code of laws, learned to irrigate and control the floods, and to cultivate the land so that it yielded two and sometimes three crops a year. Since no stone was available for lintel construction, they employed sun-dried bricks and devised an arch system by means of which they could put a vaulted roof over their long narrow rooms. To protect their palaces from frequent floods they placed them on high platforms. Stories of one Great Flood have been recounted both in the Gilgamesh Epic of the Sumerians and in the Old Testament of the Hebrews.

The valley people did not devote so much of their time and thought to preparation for the future life as did the Egyptians. Instead they enjoyed the pleasures of the present. It seems that their lives were dominated by materialistic self-interest. They offered sacrifices and erected temples to propitiate the gods, to gain favor, and to insure long life. To a certain extent they were fire worshippers. Believing that the future could be foretold by the miraculous powers of astrology, they consulted priests or astrologers to ascertain the most propitious time for planting their crops, or for acting on any matter of personal concern.

The Sumerians wore sheepskin garments with the fleece on the outside, but coarsely woven cloth and linen were available for those who could afford such luxuries. The long robes of the kings and nobles were fastened on one shoulder, leaving the other bare; the women were dressed in similar garments reaching to the ankles. *Gudea* (Plate 14), thus attired in garments appropriate to his rank, was a governor of the ancient Sumerian town of Lagash. Created in fine sculptural style, this statue was hewn of green diorite over four thousand years ago. The massive head is topped by a ceremonial hat ornamented with a chiseled design. The oversize eyes are shadowed by heavy brows, a peculiar treatment which later reappeared in the sculpture that adorns the Persian palace at Persepolis. Somewhat earlier than the *Gudea* is the *Sumerian noble* (Plate 12), a conventionalized figure carved from limestone. Here the large eyes are inset with shell and lapis lazuli.

In the royal tomb excavated at Ur there were many jewels, beads, necklaces, earrings, a gold helmet which had been worn by a prince, an elaborate head-dress that once belonged to a queen, and finely-wrought gold and silver bowls—all indicative of the high quality of Sumerian art and the height of luxury to which they had attained. Through the discovery of this tomb, light has been shed upon the funeral practices of the Asiatic valley peoples which differed from those of the Egyptians, who depended upon the magic of tomb statues, paintings, and reliefs to comfort the soul of the departed. When a Sumerian priest-king was interred, his courtiers, wife, servants, soldiers, and musicians accompanied him into the beyond. It is recorded that in the funeral procession of a prince of Ur, the royal cart drawn by oxen contained the most prized possessions the deceased might desire or expect to use in the hereafter. The attendants followed the procession into the tomb and arrayed themselves about the bier. After the funerary ceremonies were completed, they all drank poison from the gold cups, some of which are still preserved. One guard remained to close the door of the tomb, and then took his own life. Seventy-four skeletons were found in the tomb. Of course, the common people did not have such elaborate ceremonies. Generally, a brick vault under the house served as a burial place for the entire family.

PALACE MORE IMPORTANT THAN TEMPLE

The palace, rather than the temple, was the most important structure in the Asiatic valley. As there was practically no wood and little stone in the southern part, the Sumerians were forced to use sun-dried bricks. The rivers provided bitumen, a soft, sticky, tar-like substance which hardened when allowed to dry in the sun. This made a waterproof covering for the bricks which were used on the outside walls at water level. Whole cities were built on large platforms high above the river level for protection from the frequent floods. Upon this raised foundation were erected battlemented walls for defense against the enemy; some of these outer walls were wide enough on top to serve as a road for chariots.

The architecture of an Assyrian sculpture-adorned palace was of the usual valley type in general plan and appearance, although much larger, more strongly fortified, and more richly ornamented. The great gates, with their flanking towers extending outward many feet beyond the walls, were approached by a wide roadway which spanned the protecting moat. This thoroughfare continued through the arched opening to a second gateway, which pierced the fortified walls of the inner city. Here were the palaces, temples and quarters that housed the king, his family, courtiers, servants, priests, accountants, the women of the court, and those who served the gods. Dominating all the architecture was the *ziggurat* (stepped-pyramid)—larger, more brilliant in color and more beautiful in shape than those of the Sumerians, for the stages were shallower in depth and more varied in height.

The gates of the main entrances to both enclosing walls and palaces were guarded by enormous *winged animals* of stone (Plate 13). These bulls with human heads and exaggerated muscles, giving the impression of mental alertness combined with physical power, are symbolical of the arrogant military character of the Assyrians. The life and energy expressed in the winged bulls are in strong contrast to the quiet, recumbent sphinxes which guarded Egyptian temples. Carved in extremely high relief, they were usually represented with five feet, so that four of them might be seen from every point of view. The vaulted roof of the gate and the walls which supported it were adorned with animal friezes of glazed brick. Ornamental bands of rosette or lotus motifs bordered the friezes, outlined the arches, and furnished colorful decorations for the overhanging battlements.

The palace was a vast, rambling, flat-roofed structure built about three courts, around which long, narrow rooms were grouped. This plan was consistently followed throughout the entire valley. In one court the king held audiences and conducted his official business;

centered around another were the servants' quarters; winding passages leading to the guarded entrance of a third provided privacy for the harem or women's section. There was only one exit to the street; all other doors and windows opened upon the inner courts. The people spent most of their evenings on the flat roofs which covered the brick vaults. The vault, arch, and dome devised by the Sumerians were used consistently throughout the valley.

Drawing after a sculpture of a human-headed bull. (Price, *The Monuments and the Old Testament*, Judson Press)

The temple, usually a part of the palace complex, included a group of buildings such as granaries, refectories, libraries, workshops, and living quarters for the priests and women who dedicated their lives to the gods. Here also was the shrine of the principal god of the city and the various gods which all of the valley people worshipped. Towering above and dominating the entire palace complex was the ziggurat, a high place for the worship of such nature deities as the sun-god and the moon-god. Its stages were recessed and the outer walls were *battered,* that is, they leaned slightly inward.

The threshold, lower walls of rooms, courts, and corridors of the palaces were ornamented with miles of carved stone and alabaster slabs above which were richly colored frescoes. Floors were inlaid with colored mosaics. Rich rugs and embroidered hangings contributed to the general effect of luxury and splendor.

The palaces were supplied with water which was conveyed from the highlands by underground pipes; for sanitation there was an adequate system of sewers. It seems that the Assyrian kings had a very comfortable place for relaxation after strenuous efforts expended upon war and hunting.

King Ashurbanipal was not only a mighty warrior but also a collector of books—cuneiform tablets—and a patron of the arts. Two thousand clay tablets from his vast library are now in the British Museum where students may compare their inscriptions with the records of the Hebrews. Nevertheless, it seems that

Ashurbanipal, like other Assyrian kings as well as the people themselves, had a reputation for cruelty far exceeding that of most ancient peoples. Their sculptured reliefs, depicting the suffering of conquered peoples or wounded and dying animals, seem to justify such a conclusion. On one of the reliefs of his palace, *Ashurbanipal and His Queen* are shown at a banquet (Plate 14). The king is looking at the decapitated head of an Elamite enemy which is dangling from the limb of a tree in his garden, a gruesome scene which presumably gave him pleasure as he drank his wine. His palace walls were covered with carvings narrating the warlike exploits of the king and his mighty armies. The sculptors were so accurate in the recording of details that we know exactly how the ancient armies used battering rams when they laid seige to a city, how they swam across rivers by means of inflated skins, and how they tortured their foes. There were also lifelike hunting scenes with the king in the act of conquering wild beasts (Plate 14). It is recorded that when Ashurbanipal fought lions, they were brought to the arena in cages and released just at the moment when the king had his bow bent and arrow poised to strike. Not all of his hunting was done under such circumstances, however, but in any case the king was victorious. The sculptor whose duty it was to accompany the party and record the valorous exploits of the king also gave sympathetic attention to the wounded beasts such as the *Dying Lioness*, whose legs were paralyzed by arrows (Plate 13). These accurately studied animals are the most impressive art forms in Assyrian sculpture.

STATUES OF THE KING

The figure of the king was always conventionalized when shown in sculptured reliefs. Standing with one foot advanced in the Egyptian manner, his expressionless face with long curled beard was turned in profile; his shoulders were shown in three-quarter view; the feet, in side view. He was clothed in a long embroidered robe reaching to his ankles. In his hand he carried a lotus flower. All the royal figures assumed the same pose; no individuality of expression was allowed. Both the long beards of the Assyrians and their exaggerated muscles signified strength and vigor. Regardless of the boastful character of their bombastic sculpture, newly exca- vated cuneiform tablets show that the Assyrians were the most efficient, painstaking, and order-loving people of antiquity. They were able administrators who, like the Romans, sought to bring order to the entire world. Nevertheless, they were ruthless in their methods of enforcing it. Their sculpture may have been intended to intimidate weaker nations so that they would surrender instead of fighting for their liberty.

BABYLON, A PROUD CITY

When Assyria fell, Babylon rose again from its ruins to become the imperial city of the Chaldean Empire. It has been called the New York or London of ancient times, just as New York, con- sidered by some to be a wicked city, is often referred to as the Babylon of modern times. The Greek traveler, Herodotus, left a first-hand account of its magnificent splendor. Through the city flowed the Euphrates, spanned by stone bridges for pedestrian use. Its ziggurat, topping the Great Pyramid of Khufu by more than a hundred feet, soared upward to reach a height never before achieved. This was the famed *Tower of Babel,* which, according to biblical records, brought down the wrath of Jehovah upon the Babylonians who dared to pierce the sky (Plate 12).

In the fortified inner city of Babylon, crowded with palaces and temples, there was no room for natural woods and gardens, so the gardens were man-made. Near one of the palaces of Nebuchad- nezzar were the *Hanging Gardens* created for Amytis, the queen, who grew homesick for the hills of her native land. Supported on a vaulted substructure, this artificial, terraced hill was covered with trees and flowers which were irrigated by water pumped to the summit by ingenious devices. The whole effect is said to have been that of a wooded hill watered by a natural stream.

A traveler journeying to Babylon for the early spring festival could see from afar the seven-staged ziggurat rising above the walls. The varicolored levels represented the sun, the moon, and the five planets that were known in that day. The lowest stage was constructed of black bitumen-coated brick; the succeeding ones were colored respectively orange, red, pale yellow, deep blue, gold for the sun; the topmost one was silver, symbolizing the moon. This magnificent tower with its brilliant hues, dazzling in the noonday sun, must have been impressive to behold. After entering the outer gates of the city, the traveler, proceeding along the dusty roadway to the inner city wall and passing through its gate, would find himself on the famous *Procession Street*, which was paved with limestone and breccia and bordered on either side by the unpierced walls of the king's palaces. These high walls were richly adorned with beautiful glazed bricks. Here upon a field of blue marched rows of animals both mythical and real. Each brick was cast separately in a mold after which it was baked, glazed, and put into place. Procession Street led through the Ishtar Gate to the temple enclosure and the open square where the people gathered.

At this time the city was filled with activities of all kinds. People from all parts of Babylonia, and some from foreign lands, came to the festival either to take part in the ceremonies or to view the pageantry. They brought gifts for the gods and such offerings for the temples as sheep, cattle from their herds, fruits and vegetables from their farms, or articles which they had manufactured in their homes. The cargoes destined for the temple were brought in by boat, unloaded, and packed upon the backs of donkeys. Caravans from distant parts of Babylonia were laden with precious hand-wrought objects, rich fabrics, and fine woods. Numerous rooms in the ziggurat enclosure were set aside for the accommodation of pilgrims and travelers, and tents were pitched in every available place. Priests in pompous processions ascended the central stairway of the ziggurat, and slowly wound their way around the different stages to the summit where the sacred ceremonies were performed. The people used the side stairways to reach the first stage, from which point they could see the various temples of the gods. Although they could not enter the innermost sanctuary, they must have enjoyed the view of the sacred river with its many boats, the city with its palaces, and, beyond the encircling walls, the vast plain dotted with little villages in the midst of palm groves along the canals. The near-by city of Kish was clearly visible, and the dim outlines of more distant cities could be traced. The narrow rooms which could be seen about the ziggurat were the sanctuaries of the great gods, accessible only to the priests and the king. Sacred fires were kept burning in the open court during the festival.

NEBUCHADNEZZAR, LAST GREAT CHALDEAN KING

At this time Nebuchadnezzar held audience and settled grievances which the people might bring before him. He offered sacrifices to the gods and humbled himself before Marduk, the greatest of them all. Although in most cases the will of the king was law, there were times when he had to defer to the powerful priests, the human representatives of Marduk. It has been said that Nebuchadnezzar, whose reign was long, knew when to order and when to obey. He was careful not to anger the priests, for no doubt he remembered the fate of some of his predecessors, especially the Assyrian kings who had been too proud to bow to any authority. Records are still extant of his gifts and temples dedicated to the gods.

In the house of the god near the ziggurat, a statue of the god *Marduk* was shown seated upon a throne, forty feet high. Its outer covering was pure gold. The god's hair and beard were elaborately arranged in many curls fashioned of pieces of lapis lazuli cleverly fitted together. The whites of his eyes were of mother-of-pearl, and the iris of chalcedony ringed with lapis. A crown of feathers rested upon his head, and his rich garment was held by a girdle of gold and agate. Beside him on a stone decorated with wavy lines, stood a dragon, the king's sacred beast. The stars on his shield, the wavy lines, and the beast symbolized the god's power over the heavens above, the waters of the sea, and all the creatures of the earth. The inner chamber which held the statue of the god was equally sumptuous and magnificent.

Nebuchadnezzar was the last of the great Chaldean kings. He was succeeded by his son, who ruled for eight years; then Nabonidus ascended the throne (556 B.C.). Like Ikhnaton of Egypt, Nabonidus was not interested in aggression, conquest, and warfare. Preferring the moon-god to Marduk, he offended the powerful priests who turned against him, gave information to his enemies, and poisoned the minds of the people. The morale of the nation was undermined by this intrigue, and when the Persians under Cyrus stormed her gates the proud old city surrendered without resistance. Thereafter, the imperial city of the great Nebuchadnezzar was subject to the rule of Persian kings, who allowed it slowly to disintegrate until it became a mere village perched upon the ruins of its former glory. But life still clung about it until the twelfth century A.D., when it was finally abandoned.

OUTLINE OF
THE ART OF THE VALLEY OF THE TWO RIVERS

TIME: Sumerian culture—c. 4000-1925 B.C. Sumerian-Semitic Age—cultures united (c. 2650 B.C.). Power oscillated between the two peoples. Later Assyrian-Babylonian ascendancy—c. 885-539 B.C.

BACKGROUND: Sumeria and Babylon in southern part of valley, Assyria in the foothills to the north. Entire valley subject to frequent invasions. Assyria's vast empire finally disintegrated and Babylon again rose to supremacy. Weakened by luxury and internal strife she opened her gates to the enemy and became a part of the vast Persian empire (538 B.C.).

Villages and towns widely separated. Frequent floods. Rich soil. People engaged in commerce and agriculture. Interested in life on this earth, not concerned with life in hereafter. Sumerians laid basis of valley culture. Assyrians warlike, imperialistic; Chaldeans or later Babylonians, luxury-loving.

ARCHITECTURE: Palaces most important structures, temples usually a part of palace complex—tombs insignificant. Ziggurat most conspicuous architectural feature. Stone entirely lacking in southern part of valley, more plentiful in the north, but nowhere found in sufficient quantities for erecting enormous palaces—confined to use in platforms and decorative friezes. Brick, material most extensively employed for building. Imported wood sometimes used for roofing. Arch type of construction combined with lintel. Rooms narrow, walls thick. Rooms grouped about several courts placed in irregular order. All monumental structures erected upon high platforms to avoid damage from floods, and surrounded by thick tower-studded walls pierced by impressive gates—for protection from the enemy. Due to materials used, palaces have disintegrated.

Decorations: sculptured reliefs, multi-colored glazed bricks and fresco painting.

Contribution: development of the arch, increased use of glazed tiles for decoration.

SCULPTURE: Few examples remain of Sumerian sculpture in the round. Example, *Gudea*, 3½ feet high. Guardian animals at gates and entrances to Assyrian palaces are in extremely high relief. Friezes: Low stone reliefs, more naturalistic than Egyptian—found in Assyria where stone was available.

Human figures still conventionalized, muscles exaggerated in both men and beasts. Hunting and battle scenes expressive of cruelty, violence, and energy; glorified might and power of the kings. Excellent and sympathetic portrayal of animals.

Purpose: both narrative and decorative. Assyrian sculpture is full of movement—exciting.

PAINTING: Fresco painting, bands of human and animal figures decorated with rosettes and palmettes. Limited range of colors, outlined in black. In Assyria, flat multi-colored tiles: in Babylon, tile designs both colored and raised.

BIBLIOGRAPHY

BRODEUR, Arthur G., *Pageant of Civilization* (Garden City Publishing Co., Garden City, N. Y., 1931).

JASTROW, Morris, *The Civilization of Babylonia and Assyria* (J. B. Lippincott Co., Philadelphia, 1915).

OLMSTEAD, A. T., *History of Assyria* (Charles Scribner's Sons, N. Y., 1923).

WOOLEY, C. L., *Development of Sumerian Art* (Charles Scribner's Sons, N. Y., 1935).

CHAPTER IV

Pre-Hellenic Art

D URING the Egyptian Middle Kingdom, before Moses led the children of Israel out of the Land of the Pharaohs, the Mediterranean Sea was alive with Phoenician boatmen and merchants, fishermen, and pirates from the islands of the blue Aegean which "lie like stepping stones" between the continents of Europe and Asia. Even then there existed an advanced culture which had its origin in the practically riverless island of Crete. This southernmost and largest island of the Aegean group was within easy sailing distance of three continents, and with the exception of several hundred years immediately following the destruction of its remarkable civilization by barbarian invaders, there was a constant interchange of both products and ideas throughout the eastern Mediterranean world.

Egyptian art of the Amarna period, that is, during the reign of Ikhnaton, strongly reflects the influence of Cretan naturalism, for during that short period it lost some of its formality and conventionalism. The discovery of Cretan wares about the pyramids of the Egyptian kings indicates that even in that remote age colonies of island workmen had been employed there.

Contact with Mesopotamian civilization is evident in certain changes in costume. This fusion of Egyptian and Mesopotamian ideas and customs with the freer spirit of the Sea Peoples culminated in a rich and refined culture which equaled, and in some respects surpassed, that of the older civilizations. Nevertheless, the island folk were not mere copyists; they took what they wanted and made it their own. The more realistic Cretan art was quite different from that produced on the continents of Asia and Africa.

43

LIFE AND HOME OF THE SEA PEOPLES

In appearance the inhabitants of Crete, whom the Egyptians called *Kieftu* or Sea Peoples, were neither like the Semites of the Tigro-Euphrates valley, for they were taller; nor did they closely resemble the darker Egyptians or their successors, the Indo-Europeans. Just where they came from is not quite clear. Probably they migrated from Asia Minor in the Late Stone Age and mixed with other groups coming over from Upper Egypt and Libya before the time of Menes. Although it has been announced that the key to their language has been discovered, scholars have not yet been able to decipher the numerous documents which in time may give valuable information concerning their origin.

The Cretan world was a moving world, restless like the sea. Its merchants and pirates plied their trade on the shores of three continents. Along the coasts they planted colonies for the safety and convenience of their commerce and as bases for the piratical expeditions which terrorized the people of the Mediterranean world. Theirs was an adventurous life. Regimentation such as we found in the river civilizations of Mesopotamia where travel was difficult, or in Egypt with its natural barriers, did not exist in Crete. It has been pointed out that people free to roam the seas do not readily submit to the will of priest or despot. Likewise, their art was not shackled by rigidly imposed conventions. In it there is none of the mysterious and somewhat mystic quality characteristic of that Egyptian art dedicated to funerary purposes, nor the bombastic glorification of the king which characterizes Assyrian art.

On the contrary, Cretan artists represented life as being joyous, exciting, and happy. Appearing frequently on their pottery were wavy lines suggesting the movement of the sea which they knew so well. Naturalistic motifs of the flora and fauna of the islands and the waters about them decorated their vases and weapons. Painted on the walls of their palaces were representations of religious ceremonies and of various sports in which both sexes shared the dangers. Proud men and elegant—if somewhat overdressed —women appeared as spectators. A popular interest in sports also appears on the mainland, in such frescoes as *Hunter with Horse and Dog* (Plate 18), uncovered during the excavation of the pre-Hellenic citadel at Tiryns.

Like the Egyptians, island artists used a dull reddish hue to represent the skin of the men whose bodies were bronzed by exposure to sun and wind during countless days spent at sea; and a lighter color for the women who lived a more sheltered life indoors. The men wore a single garment, a short gayly colored kilt held in place by a wide belt drawn tight about the waist, and high shoes made of soft leather. The costume of the women was more elaborate: bodices, with low necks and short sleeves, were tight fitting; skirts were long and full —some were ruffled from waist to hem, while others had richly embroidered over-skirts. Both sexes wore their hair in long, tight curls falling to the shoulders. Among the relics of this civilization is a brightly painted clay figurine, *Girl in a Swing* (Plate 15).

Profile of a Girl. Fresco fragment. 1500-1350 B.C. Reproduction from the original in the Candia Museum. (Metropolitan Museum of Art)

She wears a tightly laced and gayly decorated bodice.

Some of their activities were more cruel and hazardous than our modern versions. Boxers fought with metal armaments on their hands; and bull-leaping, in which both youths and maidens took part, was even more brutal than the bull-fighting of today. Driven through the gate immediately after the fighter entered the arena, the angry bull with lowered head rushed toward the youth, who nimbly stepped aside and caught his horns. As the animal raised his head, the athlete was tossed high in the air. If he had a good sense of balance and timing, he was able to somersault over the back of the animal, but if he missed and fell forward, he was in danger of being gored to death (Plate 18). It is believed that the Athenian king sent captive youths and maidens to Knossos, where they were trained and sent into the arena on festal days to grapple with the bull. The sport of hunting wild bulls was naturalistically portrayed in repoussé* on the delicately wrought golden cups (Plate 15) found at Vaphio, a city on the mainland.

On the decorative bands of the *Vaphio cups* men and animals are portrayed against lower reliefs suggesting a landscape. One design represents the hunting of wild animals; the other depicts a more peaceful scene in which a cow is used as a decoy to trap the bull. The curving lines of the former produce the effect of wild, rapid movement in contrast to the quieter, more peaceful scene shown on the latter. On both the technical execution is superb. Copies of these famous cups may be seen in almost every large museum. The originals, together with many other objects of the period, were in Greece before World War II.

In the populous towns and cities of Crete, the inhabitants were governed by a benevolent but absolute monarch, a priest-king called the Minos. This title was derived from the name of a legendary king of Knossos who may have been the founder of a dynasty. Through the strength of his navy, the Minos established his power. From his palace crowning the hill of Knossos, Crete's most important city, he ruled the island, dominated the sea-lanes, and exacted tribute from the cities of the Aegean Islands and the European mainland.

In tribute to the legendary Minos, Sir Arthur Evans termed the remarkable culture of the Cretan peoples Minoan. For convenience he divided the period into three categories: Minoan I, Minoan II, and Minoan III, extending from about 3000-1100 B.C. Toward the end of this time the island culture, which had been extended to the islands of the Aegean and the mainland of Greece, reached its climax.

THE PALACE OF THE MINOS

In 1900 Sir Arthur Evans made excavations in the city of Knossos and uncovered the remains of the *Palace of the Minos* (Plate 16). The ground plan shows a haphazard system of grouping of rooms with no symmetrical or orderly system of unification. It seems that a smaller palace had been built first and other parts

* Designs hammered from the back.

were added as needed. When completed it was an enormous rambling structure providing living quarters for the priest-king, his courtiers, craftsmen, servants, and soldiers. There were storage spaces for grains, oil, treasures, and military stores; workshops for artisans; and facilities for merchants to carry on their trade. Little is known of the exterior appearance of the palace, which has been almost completely demolished. Built on hilly terrain, it was several stories high. Conspicuous features of the structure were monumental stone staircases leading to the different levels. The flat roofs of the porticoes were upheld by wooden columns tapering inward toward the stone bases into which they were set. Surmounting the shafts were queer cushion-like capitals bearing a plinth, or square-shaped block.

The discovery of tortuous passageways leading to the innermost rooms of a labyrinth recalls the old Greek legend which tells of Theseus' destruction of the Minotaur, a monster with a human body and the head of a bull. According to the myth, some of the youths and maidens sent annually as tribute by the Athenian king were to be fed to the beast. Theseus, the king's son, who had been granted permission to accompany one group, won the favor of Ariadne, the Cretan king's daughter. She supplied him with a thread; by attaching it to the entrance he was able to penetrate the maze, slay the monster, and find his way back, thereupon releasing the Athenian king from his obligation to offer human tribute to the Minos. If not entirely in accord with fact, the story does reveal that the piratical kings of Crete were feared throughout the Mediterranean world.

Many of the rooms of the palace contained windows; those with few or no outside openings depended upon light wells or openings in the ceilings. Throughout the structure there was a plumbing system almost as effective as our own. This step in sanitary engineering was far in advance of anything that the Europeans of the Middle Ages ever dreamed of.

Although there was no great temple with its mysterious innermost sanctuaries which could be entered only by priest or king, there were megarons—open spaces surrounded by a covered colonnade—with a pool for purification purposes and an altar for sacrifices. Here either the priest or priest-king performed the sacred rites in the presence of the people. The processions and games that are shown in the mural paintings which adorned the palace walls were closely related to their religious ceremonies. Paintings belonging to the later period represented priestly figures wearing long robes and bearing ceremonial axes. The long robes indicate Assyrian influence, and the axe symbolized one of their own most important cults. The Cretans called their palace the *Palace of the Double Axe.*

RELIGION OF THE CRETANS

We actually know very little about the religion of the Sea Peoples. They erected shrines on certain high mountain peaks, and they built altars in rocky caves like that of Kamares on Mount Ida, where many excellent vases known as *Kamares ware* have been found. Their chief deity was the Mother Goddess, usually accompanied by a young person either her son or consort; his identity is not clear. Rocks, springs, and such creatures of the animal world as the lion, dove, raven, and serpent were considered sacred. Perhaps the most important cult symbols were those of the double-axe and the pillar or column. The double-axe appears repeatedly in decorations on palace walls and palace pottery. The pillar, similar in shape to the columns of the porticoes, is found in the sculptured decoration of the *Lion Gate at Mycenae* (Plate 17), which exemplifies Cretan influence on the mainland.

Kamares ware was elaborately decorated in designs that were either floral and naturalistic, or geometric with the spiral a conspicuous feature. Lilies occur frequently in the floral designs. Other examples of Cretan pottery are the *Octopus Vase*, on which is a naturalistic representation of a sprawling denizen of the sea (Plate 17), and the steatite *Harvester Vase* with a sculptured frieze of men marching home, singing as they go. Little *snake goddesses,* some of them made of gold and ivory, have been found. In low-cut bodices and flounced skirts, they stand holding reptiles which are wound about their arms (Plate 16).

DESTRUCTION OF CRETAN CIVILIZATION

About 1400 B.C. a great disturbance in Asia Minor resulted in restless movements of large masses of peoples. During this migratory period a group of semi-barbaric Aryans, the tall, blue-eyed and brown-haired Achaeans, descended from the north, overran the Peloponnese (the southern part of the Greek peninsula), and crossed over to the island of Crete where they wrought havoc and burned the palace of Knossos. Eventually, however, most of them returned to the Greek mainland and established themselves in fortified cities such as Mycenae, Sparta, Corinth, and Tiryns.

Two views of a basket-shaped vase decorated with the double-axe motif. (University of Pennsylvania *Bulletin*)

The palace at Knossos was rebuilt, but later an earthquake, invasion, or some other catastrophe destroyed certain parts of it which were never restored. The Achaean invasion, together with frequent earthquakes, must have discouraged the island people, for many of them left to settle on the European and Asiatic coasts where they mixed with the natives and lost their identity as a separate race. Later (c. 1100 B.C.) came the Dorians, the last of the invading tribes. Bearing iron weapons which were more effective than the bronze swords of the Cretans, they overran the Greek peninsula, completely broke the power of Crete, and utterly destroyed the rich Minoan culture which was to reappear only once again as a faint echo in the art of the beauty-loving Ionians. The Dorians occupied the best lands of the Peloponnese, and for several hundred years little if anything was heard of the brilliant civilization of Crete and Mycenae. The Phoenician and Cretan merchants, fishermen, and pirates were swept from the sea. Intercommunication was reduced to a minimum, and there was a pause in the history of the pre-Hellenic peoples.

TROY: LEGEND AND DISCOVERY

According to Greek legend, the gods who lived on Mt. Olympus descended to earth at times and mingled with mortals. On one occasion Paris, son of Priam, King of Troy, was asked to be judge in a beauty contest. The chief contestants were Hera, the wife of Zeus, who offered him power if he would render a decision in her favor; Athene, who offered him wisdom; and Venus, who promised him the most beautiful woman in all the world for his wife, and thereby won the prize. The goddess in turn helped him to win the love of Helen who was the wife of Menelaus, King of Sparta. Paris took her with him when he returned to Troy and thereby precipitated the Trojan war. To rescue the fair Helen, Menelaus appealed to his brother, Agamemnon, King of Mycenae. A large army composed of the warlike Achaeans and their Greek allies quickly assembled. In the words of the poet, Helen's was "the face that launched a thousand ships and burnt the topless towers of Illium" (Troy). Led by Agamemnon, "King of Men," the armies boarded their black ships and sailed for Troy. Upon arrival they laid seige to the city, and after ten years captured and burned it. In reality, the origin of this conflict might have been jealousy between the rival cities of Troy and Mycenae, or perhaps just another Achaean migration. Whatever the cause, the Trojan war made a deep impression upon the Greeks of later times and furnished much of the subject-matter of their art.

Heinrich Schliemann, later to become a famous traveler and archaeologist, read about the Trojan wars in Homer's *Odyssey* and *Iliad* when he was a schoolboy in Germany. His imagination was so fired by tales of the old Greek heroes that he decided to discover whether or not there had ever been a city named Troy. First he had to acquire the necessary funds to enable him to realize his dream. After many years of hardship and travel to distant lands, he amassed a fortune and his search began. Since he had not been trained in archaeology, he wisely took with him the scholar, Wilhelm Dörpfeld. Following closely the Homeric account, he was able to locate the cities of Mycenae (1876) and Tiryns (1884) on the Greek mainland. He found that these ancient cities were fortified by strong walls made of stones so huge that the ancients thought they were raised by the mythical Cyclops. At one entrance to the city of Mycenae was the famous *Lion Gate* through which

Corbeled gallery of the Citadel at Tiryns. (Perret and Chipiez)

Agamemnon might have led his army of brave Achaeans when they left to recover the beautiful Helen.

Above the *Lion Gate* (Plate 17), which was outlined by two posts with a lintel across the top, was a corbeled arch. The triangular space above the lintel was filled with a sculptured stone on which was represented two lions, on either side of a Cretan pillar. This stone, said to be the oldest piece of monumental sculpture in Europe, is still preserved; only the bronze heads of the animals are missing.

Such a corbeled arch as that over the gate was common in Mycenaean times. It was formed by placing each stone slightly inward above the one below. This type of construction was also used in the "beehive" tombs and the open galleries which were left in the thick stone walls that encircled the cities.

The walls and arches of heavy stone are monuments to the engineering skill and structural genius of the inhabitants of the cities of the Greek mainland. This brilliant civilization, doubtless indebted to that of Crete, was also destroyed by the Dorians. Years of darkness ensued. Then came the Greeks, or Hellenes as they called themselves, the so-called "enlighteners of the world."

OUTLINE OF PRE-HELLENIC ART

TIME: To c.1100 B.C.

BACKGROUND: An advanced island culture centered in Crete. Achaean invaders came down from the Greek peninsula, burned the great palace of the Minos, then withdrew to the mainland, where they established city-states such as Mycenae and Tiryns, and took over culture of the conquered peoples. Cretan palace was rebuilt, but another tribe, the Dorians (c.1100 B.C.), destroyed the island civilization known as Cretan, or Minoan. A seafaring people, the islanders were ruled by a benevolent despot called the Minos; were free and unoppressed. The effect of their contact with Egypt during Ikhnaton's time is reflected in the naturalistic character of Egyptian art of that period. Echoes of their lyrical art appear later in the sculpture of the Ionian Greeks; for some of the Cretans had gone to western Asia after the disturbances in their own country. Their religion comprised various cults among them, those of the Mother Goddess, the Bull, and the Double Axe.

ARCHITECTURE: Confined chiefly to palaces protected only by the sea. Large rambling structures built about courts. Monumental stairways were conspicuous features. Columns of porticoes tapered toward the base. Megarons for religious ceremonies were included in palace complex. Walls were decorated with colorful frescoes. On the mainland, cities were surrounded by walls of heavy stones with corbeled galleries.

SCULPTURE: The triangular stone topping the *Lion Gate of Mycenae* is said to be the oldest monumental sculpture in Europe. Sculpture confined for the most part to carving on vases, such as the steatite *Harvester Vase,* to repoussé work like that of the *Vaphio Cups,* to small porcelains or to ivory statuettes of goddesses or priestesses.

PAINTING: Chiefly frescoes—paintings on wet plaster. Flat spaces of color separated by lines—all enclosed within heavy contour lines, which are sometimes incised. Subject-matter: scenes from everyday life, sports, spectators, and religious ceremonies. The double-axe and other cult symbols, flowers, and marine life together with the spiral and wavy lines suggesting the motion of the sea, furnish motifs for the decoration of palace pottery. Cretan art is narrative, gay, and lively. In the recording of essentials gained from direct observation, it is somewhat akin to the art found in the Spanish caves.

BIBLIOGRAPHY

EVANS, Sir Arthur, *The Palace of Minos,* 4 vols. (The Macmillan Co., N. Y., 1921-35).

FORSDYKE, E. J., *Minoan Art* (Oxford University Press, N. Y., 1931).

PENDLEBURY, J. D. S., *A Handbook to the Palace of Minos at Knossos* (The Macmillan Co., N. Y., 1933).

CHAPTER V

Greek Art

MYCENEAN culture had become but a memory of a golden age when the Greeks, an intelligent, imaginative, and artistic people representing a fusion of barbarian and Aegean stocks, appeared upon the scene about 750 B.C. and developed one of the most remarkable civilizations the world has ever known.

Greece now comprised the Greek peninsula, the islands of the Aegean Sea, and the west coast of the Asiatic mainland where the Ionians had settled. The climate was temperate and the air crystalline clear. The people lived in the small valleys between high mountains and along the narrow strips of land near the numerous bays and inlets which furnished excellent harbors for their small ships. Because their soil was too poor to support the entire population, and because no part of the land was more than forty miles from the sea, the Greeks, like the Cretans, became seafaring folk. In time their trade expanded to include the entire Mediterranean area. Fruits, wines, oils, and manufactured articles such as their famous pottery were exchanged for necessary grains and other foods. They are said to have been the first people to sell their art products.

Enterprising and self-reliant, the Hellenes highly prized their liberty, which was constantly being threatened by their neighbors. Eventually two great city-states emerged: Sparta in the Peloponnese, the southern part of the peninsula; and Athens in Hellas to the north. For protection smaller states were forced to attach themselves to one of the stronger powers. The Spartans, isolationists of the time, were concerned primarily with their own welfare. For many years the union of Sparta and her satellites, known as the Peloponnesian League, was the strongest force in Greece. The more progressive Athenians made several attempts to promote pan-Hellenic unity, but this was a dream never to be quite realized. For some time the history of Greece was the story of the rivalry between Sparta, whose army was dominant on land, and Athens, whose fleet controlled the sea.

When the need for union became acute, the Delian League, a voluntary organization, was formed for the purpose of continuing the war against the Persians until Greece could be liberated from this threat. Each city-state contributed ships or appropriated money to build them. The Athenians, who were the ship-builders of the country, used some of the money to enlarge their own navy and thereby increased their power at the league's expense. Under the leadership of Pericles during the fifth century they even went a step farther and diverted some of the funds to the beautification of their own city. There was, of course, much criticism of this procedure, but the Athenians attempted to justify their actions by saying that after all it was their great navy which had driven the Persians from the homeland. If the means seemed questionable at best, the result was laudable; for Athens became the most beautiful city in all Greece.

After the death of Pericles (429 B.C.), no effective leader arose to take his place; and during the Peloponnesian War the strength of Athens was broken. The Spartans built up a despotic tyranny and attempted to rule the Greeks with an iron hand, but the Hellenes, who could not bring themselves to submit to the rule of other Greeks, rebelled. The city-states continued to wear themselves out with dissension. It was a case of "when Greek meets Greek."

Meanwhile there was strong power rising in Macedon, a minor Greek province inhabited by a tribe of Hellenic stock who nevertheless were regarded as semi-barbarians by the Athenians. With the determination to make his small country the leader of all Hellas, ambitious King Philip marched south at the head of his armies, only to be slain just as he was about to attain success. However, his son, the twenty-year-old Alexander, a former pupil of Aristotle and a youth of great promise, in addition to his scholarly attainments proved himself one of the outstanding military geniuses of all time.

Boldly attacking before the Greeks had time to take advantage of Philip's death, Alexander compelled the Hellenes to submit (338 B.C.). After completing an organization of the Greek city-states, he turned north, crossed the Hellespont (334 B.C.), and landed on the shore of Asia Minor near the site of ancient Troy. Moving east, he met the Persians, fought and won the Battle of the Issus; but he had not yet won the war. After marching on Egypt he returned to Persia. This time his victory was complete; Persepolis, the Persian capital, was sacked and burned. In time Alexander's empire included Greece, Egypt, much of central and western parts of Asia, and the northern part of India. Wherever his armies marched Hellenic culture followed.

The center of civilization now began to shift from Europe back to Asia and Africa. It was centered in the great commercial port of Alexandria, named for the young conqueror. Through its harbor flowed the wealth of India and the East. Greek scholars, along with artists and craftsmen, came in contact with the cultures of the East. The older art forms, imbued with the youthful spirit of the West, developed into a distinct style known as *Hellenistic* ("Greekish," or like the Greek).

ATHENS UNDER PERICLES

During the fifth century, when Hellenic culture reached its height in Athens under the leadership of Pericles, the city had a population of about one hundred thousand inhabitants. The houses of the citizens were insignificant and in all probability insanitary, but her temples, theatres, and other public buildings were magnificent. Athens was taking steps toward the democratic way of life and devoting herself to learning; Sparta was still a military state.

In Athens, as in other Greek cities, only native-born citizens enjoyed the privileges of free government, and it is to these we refer when we speak of the Greeks. Citizens of foreign birth were allowed to conduct their business in the city, but they could not participate in all forms of government. At the lower end of the scale were the poor peasants and the serfs who worked on the farms of the land owners, and finally the slaves whose labor provided the leisure that the upper classes not only enjoyed but also used wisely —in the pursuit of knowledge and the creation of beauty.

RELIGION AND THE OLYMPIC GAMES

The peoples of the older civilizations had depended upon magic to explain natural phenomena. What their priests told them they had accepted without question. According to their ancient myths, the world was in a chaotic state until some particular god appeared to establish order. The Greeks revised the legend to read that "chaos reigned until mind arose and restored order." They found it difficult to believe what they could not understand. This new attitude toward the world colored every aspect of their life: thinking, religion, and art. In the beginning the Greeks believed in many gods, not gods like the monsters and animal-headed beings that are represented in the art of Egypt, but gods who were men and women like themselves, only larger and more beautiful. These gods, immortal and invisible, moved about among the people and took part in their daily activities, even taking sides in conflicts and protecting their favorites when the battle was going against them.

The imaginative Greeks personified everything in nature: they had gods of the sky, air, earth, and sea; each stream had its nymph, each tree its dryad. Mighty Zeus, the sky-god, hurler of thunderbolts, ruled from the home of the gods on Mt. Olympus. Other gods were Juno, the jealous wife of Zeus; Poseidon, lord of the Sea; Apollo, the sun-god, whose "shining arrows always found their mark," the beloved god of the athletes, and also of music and medicine; Mercury, the moon spirit, the swift-footed messenger of the gods and the patron of trade and commerce; Aphrodite, the goddess of love and beauty; Athene, the air-goddess, also patron goddess of Athens, presiding over war and wisdom.

With the coming of the philosophers and the development of intellectualism the Greeks, like the Egyptians, lost their simple faith. Their attitude toward both life and death was fatalistic. They did not fear death. According to their belief, the departed went to a gloomy abode called Hades; but the living were content with a world which they knew and enjoyed perhaps more than any people who came after them. Doubtless recognizing that their beautiful myths were merely figments of their own fertile imaginations, they accepted them as part of their tradition; however, they also were careful to observe the prescribed ritual such as offering sacrifices and taking part in games and celebrations which occurred during the festivals. When these duties were performed, they placed the responsibility for their welfare squarely on the laps of the gods and calmly accepted whatever fate decreed.

The Olympic games, held in honor of the gods, were activities and exercises which the Greeks thoroughly enjoyed. Although they could not effect a lasting political union, the citizens of all of the city-states were held together by tradition, a common language, and religion. The religious festival, of which the games were an important part, was held every four years. At this time any differences, political or otherwise, were set aside. People from the mainland and the provinces traveled for days to reach Olympia in time for the celebration; contestants came from all parts of the country, some arriving a month beforehand to undergo rigid training for competition. The five-day festival ended in general rejoicing, banquets, and the offering of sacrifices. Victorious athletes were celebrated in poetry; sculptured in bronze and marble, and shown at their sports on the painted decorations of the famous Greek vases which are among the best sources of detailed information concerning this phase of Greek life. In 1896 A.D. the Olympic games were revived with the hope that a common interest would promote better understanding among the nations of the world.

Along with the games in which only men were included, there developed a cult of the body; both strength and beauty became the goals. Youths exercised for the symmetrical development of their bodies as well as to achieve victory in competitions. Consequently the pentathlon, comprising a group of activities such as running, jumping, discus throwing, and wrestling designed to promote versatility of performance together with suppleness and beauty, was the most popular event of the festival (Plate 20). Contesting for honor and glory rather than for material award, the victorious athletes received merely a wreath of olive leaves to be placed over a ribbon wound about the head, a branch of palms, or a coveted vase made by one of the famous Attic potters.

This emphasis upon the beauty of the human form created a great demand for athletic sculpture. Countless idealized statues of athletes were created by the sculptors, who had ample opportunity to study the nude bodies of the youths as they were exercising in the gymnasiums or contesting in the games. The changing ideal of physical beauty was reflected in their work.

FORMALISM OF ARCHAIC SCULPTURE

Archaic sculptors concerned themselves mainly with representations of gods and goddesses, whom they conceived in terms of the human form. The goddesses were draped in clinging garments with stiff, angular folds; whereas the male figures appear nude like the athletes whom the sculptors saw at their exercises and games. One early statue, now in the Metropolitan Museum of New York, though known as an Apollo, is now believed to represent an athlete (Plate 23). The first free-standing statues were block-like in form, suggesting Egyptian influence. In accordance with the law of frontality, the body faced straight forward with one foot extended and hands close to the sides in the Egyptian manner; in the Greek work, however, muscles were accentuated, and the faces bore an expression which came to be known as the archaic smile (Plate 23). The true origin of this smile is a controversial subject. The more practical-minded attribute it to a lack of skill on the part of the sculptor, to his clumsiness in making the transition between the planes of the mouth and the cheek. Others, more romantic or imaginative in their viewpoint, believe it to have been the deliberate intention of the sculptor, who was interested in objectifying his idea of a benevolent god rather than merely copying a human form. Whatever the cause, the archaic smile imparts a suggestion of vitality to the face. The eyes of the Dorian gods, devoid of any fleeting, momentary expression, are nevertheless intensely alive. In the Oriental manner, the eyes of some of the Ionic goddesses are almond-shaped and slanting under their thick ribbon-like lids.

Cheek bones are high, and the hair, usually hanging to the shoulders, is plaited or tightly curled.

The Archaic Dorian athletes (Apollos), vigorous and strong, and the feminine Ionic goddesses, gracious and charming, represent respectively the two influences which permeate the best of Greek art. First one is predominant, then the other; when they are subtly fused the strength of the Dorian is tempered with Ionic grace.

If the anatomical knowledge of the Archaic sculptors was meager, their comprehension of formal values was well advanced. Certainly artists are not obliged to copy nature. By attention to the basic structure of the figure and the expression of movement through a rhythmic arrangement of the draperies in which it is clothed, a sculptor can convey an idea and impart life to stone. Judged by these criteria, Archaic sculpture is more than an immature step toward naturalism; it is a distinct style. In the work of the Archaic period the idea was as important as the form through which it was expressed. The sculptor was conscious of the fact that he was giving objective form to the god-idea; the human figure was merely the motif for its construction. Purely naturalistic representations belong to the later years of the Greek period when the true creative urge had worn thin.

TREND TOWARD NATURALISM

To the transitional period belongs the *Charioteer* (Plate 24), an original statue from group created just after the end of the Persian wars. Displaced by an earthquake and buried in debris, this figure has unfortunately lost one of its arms. The statue, made in bronze inlaid with silver and enamel, is an idealized representation. It once belonged to a group dedicated by a young Syracusan aristocrat to commemorate a victory in the chariot races. The *Charioteer* stands straight and tall like a column; and like the flutings of a column are the wide vertical folds of his rigid robe. This garment, fashioned in the usual style worn by the chariot drivers, was held in place by a girdle over which the narrower folds of the waist fall in crisply curving lines. Passing around the arms the folds become narrower still, and the lines more curvilinear. This variety of

rhythm in the different parts of the garment, beginning with the
static lines of the skirt and ending with the curving lines of the
sleeves, creates a subtle sense of life and movement. In contrast
are the feet planted firmly on the base and the immobility of the
features of the face. The head is well poised on the strong neck.
The conventionalized hair, lying close to the top of the head, is
bound by a fillet below which it escapes in less formalized curls.
The only action suggested is in the slightly twisted torso and the
upraised arms. The naturalistic rendering of feet and hands is an
unexpected feature and one which is not immediately apparent,
because the modeling of these forms is subordinated to the figure
as a whole. This step toward naturalism, though timid, forecasts
the direction which Greek art was to follow until the fine early
formalism was replaced first by an almost photographic, and afterwards a melodramatic representation.

Also characteristic of the transitional period is the *Apollo* from
the west pediment of the Temple of Zeus at Olympia (Plate 25).
Though much of the stiffness and conventionality of the Archaic
conception remains, a more accurate rendering of the anatomy,
particularly apparent in the musculature of the body, is definite
evidence of a trend toward naturalism.

Another sculpture produced shortly after the end of the Persian
wars was the so-called *Ludovisi Throne*, discovered in the ruins of
an old Roman villa which had once belonged to the Ludovisi
family (Plate 24). The three-sided block of marble, carved out in
the form of a seat and once considered a throne, is now believed
to be an altar dedicated to the worship of Aphrodite who, according
to legend, rose from the sea. Two nymphs hold a robe to cover her
wet, clinging garments as she rises from the water. The figure on
one side of the altar is supposed to represent a diligent wife at some
daily task either domestic or religious, while on the other side, the
woman playing the flute seems to be devoting herself to a life of
ease and pleasure.

Although the relief of the central panel is low, the sculptor has
succeeded in giving the illusion of depth to the composition. Three
well-rounded arms, one in front of the other, occupy three different
planes; the turned head suggests room for movement; the contrast-

ing detailed pattern of the folds of the robe held before the goddess and the simply modeled figure also serve to convey a sense of intervening space. There is no attempt to indicate a background, but a pebbly shore is suggested by the rocky texture of the base upon which the assisting figures stand. An impression of wetness over the entire composition is produced by the flowing lines about the goddess and the straight, dripping folds of the draperies of the nymphs. This illusion of great depth within a shallow space will again be seen in the great *Panathenaic frieze* of the Parthenon (Plate 26). The same sculptural qualities noted in the central panel are apparent in the two side pieces of the altar.

IDEALIZED NATURALISM

During the fifth century there were three outstanding sculptors: Polyclitus, Myron, and Phidias. The first two specialized in statues of athletes; and Phidias usually portrayed the gods. The former designed their work for casting in bronze, which is more permanent than marble but usually disappears first because it can be quickly melted down for war material. Unfortunately, most of the bronze originals are gone; we know them only through copies made by Roman artisans. Some of the fine quality of the originals has been preserved, however, by the accurate method of duplication.

By the fifth century technical difficulties had been mastered and sculptors were concerning themselves with movement and proportion. Polyclitus created the *Doryphorus,* a figure with proportions so satisfying to his contemporaries that it became the canon or model for male figures (Plate 25). Somewhat shorter and stockier than the *Charioteer,* this figure stands more easily with its weight resting on the right foot. The left knee is bent and the left foot pushed slightly back. There is little action in the easy yet studied pose, but movement is expressed by the rhythmic curving line passing through the head, torso, right leg, and ending in the foot which is free, thus implying a sense of freedom lacking in the more rigid *Charioteer.* The figure has been reduced to a symmetrical pattern with deepened lines marking waist and hips; the pectoral muscles are indicated by well-defined planes. Treated in the conventionalized Archaic manner, the short hair lies close to the square-shaped head. The face has no individualized expression; nevertheless, there is a feeling of inner life. Polyclitus carved also the figure of an *Amazon,* one of a mythical band of female warriors. We find here some of the same qualities observed in his male figures.

Myron, freeing himself completely from the columnar type, created a figure in vigorous action. The *Discobolus,* or *Discus Thrower,* is shown with body tensed just at the moment before the discus leaves the hand (Plate 25). The impression of stenuous action indicated by the almost angular position of the body is heightened by a strong counteracting curve passing from the discus through the arm to the left foot. Despite the energetic movement of the figure, facial expression, like that of the other fifth-century statues, is calm and unruffled. Fluent bronze, which Myron employed for this figure, is an appropriate medium for the expression of vigorous movement. The additional supports required to balance the marble copies of this work detract from the flowing rhythm of the bronze original. A charming *Bronze Maiden,* a nude figure, is attributed to Myron.

Most of the work of Phidias, the third and most celebrated of the sculptors of the Periclean age, was done in connection with the Parthenon. It is not known whether he really completed any of these famous statues, or if he merely drew designs or made terra-cotta models for others to copy; but it is certain that he could not have carved all of them. One of the finest figures is the so-called *Theseus*—also known by various other names, such as Dionysus and Mt. Olympus—a reclining figure from the eastern pediment of the temple (Plate 26). Theseus was one of the favorite Athenian heroes, a sort of demi-god. It was he who slew the Minotaur and sailed away with the fair Ariadne, daughter of the Cretan king. This majestic figure clearly expresses the godlike qualities of austerity, serenity, aloofness, and quiet repose. The planes of the figure are broad and simple; the face is calm, serene, yet alive. The young god seems to be just awakening from sleep or perhaps a dream; slowly his strong body begins to move with easy grace. By a fine arrangement of its parts, the figure fits easily in the triangular space of the eastern pediment of the Parthenon.

Perhaps the most celebrated works of Phidias were the chryselephantine (gold and ivory) statue of *Zeus* made for the temple at Olympia and the thirty-nine-foot figure of *Athene* which stood in the Parthenon. Considering the precious materials of which they were composed, it is small wonder they disappeared in early times. Our sources of information concerning the *Athene* are descriptions by ancient writers and reproductions on coins and vases. The goddess stood with right knee bent. Her heavy golden garment was belted at the waist, and a gold, scaly aegis bearing the deadly Gorgon's head covered her chest. On the crest of her golden helmet was a three-horse chariot, and on each cheek piece, a gold Pegasus in repoussé. In her right hand she held a statue of victory six feet high; her left hand rested on a shield which bore the huge Ericthonius, the coiled snake of the underworld. Depicted on the inside of the shield was the struggle between the gods and giants, and on the outer surface, the battle between the Greeks and Amazons. A representation of the contest between the Greeks and centaurs adorned the soles of her sandals. The three warlike themes are a repetition of the subject-matter of the broken frieze on the exterior of the temple. By introducing on the shield of the goddess the likeness of his friend Pericles in the act of fighting an Amazon, and of himself as an old man throwing a stone, Phidias incurred the wrath of some of the Athenians who held this to be a sacrilege. He also was accused of cheating in the amount of gold used on the statue of Athene, but with great foresight he had fashioned the figure so that the gilded parts might easily be removed and the correct weight ascertained. Doubtless these charges were of a political nature, brought about by the enemies of Pericles who sought to hurt him through the banishment of his favorite sculptor.

Attributed also to Phidias is the *Athene Lemnia,* originally cast in bronze and existing now only in the form of a marble copy (Plate 28). Like many other Greek statues, the marble *Athene* suffered mutilation from an earthquake or other destructive causes; the head was severed. When found, it was taken to Bologna. The body is in Dresden wearing a head copied from the original. The pose of this dignified and noble statue is easy and restful; the facial expression calm and unruffled.

THE GODS BECOME MORE HUMAN

With the beginning of the fourth century a change is noted in the representation of the male figures. No longer godlike and austere, they are more human, softer, more effeminate. The former apparent though consciously controlled movement becomes more exaggerated, and over the face there is a play of fleeting emotion. Texture is emphasized, and the inherent qualities of stone or marble such as rigidity and blockiness are somewhat neglected. In effect, marble has become soft like flesh. This new softness can be seen in the charming *Victory Adjusting Her Sandal,* a fragment of relief from the Temple of Athene Nike dating from the late fifth century (Plate 27).

One of the few Greek statues known to be original is the *Hermes* by Praxiteles, which still bears the sculptor's name (Plate 29). By a stroke of fortune it fell into the mud and was incorporated in the walls of a temple there to remain until it was rediscovered in modern times. The young god, holding the infant Dionysus on his arm, is leaning gracefully against a tree trunk while apparently amusing the child with something held in his now missing right hand. With a hint of a smile on his face and only half conscious of the baby, he gazes dreamily into space. Here surface beauty and facial expression are emphasized above the inner poise and strength which characterized the earlier Greek work. The softness of the flesh is in strong contrast to the rougher texture of the hair and the deep naturalistic folds of the drapery. There is no longer a trace of Archaic stiffness, nor of the clear demarcation of muscular forms. The transition from one plane to another is subtle; the lights, shadows, and half-tones playing across the surface produce something of the quality of painting. However, the superb technical quality of the work and the more human, though still somewhat controlled, expression of godlike beauty contribute to the well-deserved praise of the *Hermes.*

Scopas, who was not primarily a sculptor of athletes, emphasized the trend toward an interest in story-telling and the portrayal of emotions. By such devices as overhanging eyebrows and deep-set eyes he imparted a melancholy expression to his faces. His figures are more realistically modeled, less idealistic than the work of Praxiteles. The figure of *Mausolus* from a group on the Mauso-leum of Halicarnassus, representing an Asiatic ruler, is highly in-dividualized (Plate 30). Wrapped in heavy draperies, Mausolus stands on the roof of the tomb. The folds of his garment are deeply cut, reflecting highlights and imprisoning dark shadows, thereby insuring strong carrying power. The *Niobid series, Meleager,* and *Demeter* (Plate 30) are other statues attributed to the school of Scopas.

Lysippus, favorite sculptor of Alexander the Great, created the *Apoxyomenos,* also a canon of masculine beauty, which reveals the changing ideal of proportions (Plate 29). The athlete, who is scraping oil from his body, is taller and more slender than his fifth-century prototypes; also the head is smaller than the Dorian ideal. Unlike the *Discobolus,* which was conceived in one plane, the *Apoxyomenos* is three dimensional, that is, it may be viewed from all sides.

Belonging to the fourth century are the two best-known statues of women, the *Venus de Milo* (Plate 31)—found on the island of Melos—and the *Winged Victory* (Plate 32), both of which are among the most highly prized possessions of the Louvre in Paris. The *Venus* is placed at the end of a long gallery whose sides are lined by other statues of that goddess; the *Victory* stands on a high base above eye-level. Here both may be seen to advantage. Though made during a later period, the *Venus* still retains some of the impersonal quality characteristic of fifth-century work. With the exception of slightly parted lips, no expression disturbs the calm serenity of the idealized face. The fine relationship of volumes, that is, the head, neck, torso, and legs which are concealed by drapery, contribute to the balance and easy pose of the figure. It is difficult to imagine any position of the arms that would en-hance the beauty of the statue. Many attempts have been made to reconstruct them, but none has proved satisfactory. It may be that the goddess is more beautiful in her present incomplete state than she was in her original form.

The *Winged Victory*, commemorating a naval battle, is extremely dramatic. A powerful suggestion of drive and movement is created by the heavy, windswept folds of the drapery and the tremendous sweep of the outspread wings. Seen from the front, the curves of the wet drapery spiraling around the figure also contribute to the effect of swift movement. Doubtless she too has profited by her misfortune in the loss of head and arms, for often naturalism, which is as limiting as the more formal man-made conventions, is lacking in esthetic power.

Two other statues of Venus or Aphrodite which reveal the fourth-century ideal of softly rounded, full-bodied womanhood are the *Venus of Cyrene* (Plate 33) and the *Venus of Syracuse*.

An appraisal of the comparative merit of fifth and fourth century work will depend largely upon one's concept of beauty. If the formal values of art are preferred to the more realistic copy of nature, the *Charioteer* will be considered more beautiful than the *Hermes*. The work of Phidias is somewhere between the two. During the first part of the fourth century, the strong tendency toward idealized naturalism was still somewhat tempered by the impersonal godlike quality of the fifth-century work, but soon thereafter subject-matter became more intimate and expression more individualized. During the Hellenistic period, Greek sculpture reached its final stage of extreme naturalism verging on the theatrical and melodramatic.

TEMPLE FORMS

In Hellenic times neither a large enclosed space for congregation nor dark rooms with a hint of mystery were requirements of the Greek religion. The priests were merely assistants at the sacrifices or other rituals which were conducted in the open. Only occasionally did an individual or a small group of people enter the temple to ask a particular favor of the gods. The temples dominated the sacred enclosures and furnished a background for the religious ceremonies.

Strange as it may seem, the intellectual Greeks did not bother to invent new structural forms. They were content to use the simple post-and-lintel construction which the Egyptians had em-

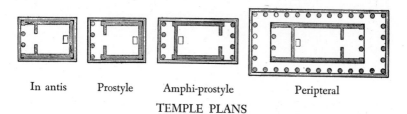

In antis   Prostyle   Amphi-prostyle   Peripteral

TEMPLE PLANS

ployed thousands of years before. In finish and refinement, however, their small temples far surpassed the colossal monuments of the Nile valley which were dependent upon sheer bulk for impressiveness.

Through experimentation with simple box-like forms, constructed first of wood and sun-dried brick and later of stone, the Greeks developed a fine design for their temple. Extending the side wall beyond the *cella* (box) and using columns to support the roof of this extension, a style called *in antis* was created; by building a front porch without lengthening the walls, the *pro-style* came into being; by the addition of a back porch to the pro-style the *amphi-prostyle* was formed; and in the final form, the peripteral, the cella was entirely surrounded by a colonnade. The Parthenon was amphi-prostyle-peripteral. It had two porches and a continuous colonnade.

Especial attention was given to the columns and the entablature which they supported. This led to the development of the three orders: the *Doric, Ionic,* and *Corinthian,* examples of which may be seen in many of the civic buildings of America and also in the houses of the colonial type of architecture.

The *Doric order,* sturdy and strong, was the simplest of the three. Without a base (in some cases) the columns rested directly upon the stylobate. The shaft, usually plain but sometimes fluted, had an entasis or slight bulge near the center. A transition from the vertical shaft of the column to the architrave or crossbeam was made by the horizontal necking and curved echinus, which were

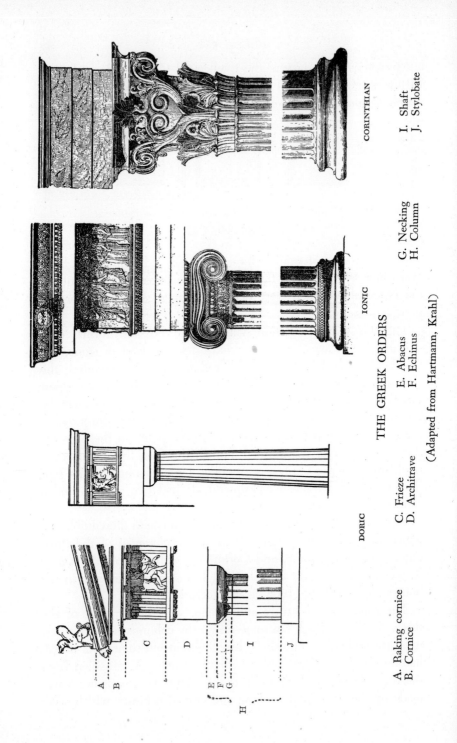

THE GREEK ORDERS

DORIC   IONIC   CORINTHIAN

(Adapted from Hartmann, Krahl)

A. Raking cornice   C. Frieze   E. Abacus   G. Necking   I. Shaft
B. Cornice   D. Architrave   F. Echinus   H. Column   J. Stylobate

topped by a square abacus. In different buildings of the Doric order the height of the shaft ranged from four to six and one-half times the diameter of its base. The Doric column of the Parthenon was comparatively slender, the height being five and one-half times the six-foot diameter of its base. Comparing the measurement of this diameter with that of one of the columns of the *Temple of Karnak,* upon which almost a hundred men could stand, we realize how small the Greek temple would seem if it were placed beside the colossal Egyptian structure.

The *Ionic order,* used extensively during the fourth century, was graceful and more feminine in character than the Doric; an example is the *Erectheum* on the Athenian Acropolis. The more ornate *Corinthian* column, with its inverted bell-shaped capital decorated with acanthus leaves, was more slender still, taller, and more elaborate than the other two. Rarely used in the earlier periods, it was commonly employed by the Greeks of the Hellenistic era and later by the luxury-loving Romans.

Above the unadorned architrave (lintel) which rests directly upon the columns is a frieze or decorative band, either continuous as in the Ionic and Corinthian orders, or broken abruptly by alternating triglyphs (projecting members with two V-shaped grooves) and metopes (square blocks) in the Doric style. A protecting cornice overhangs the frieze and a similar feature, the raking cornice, encloses the triangular space or pediment above the frieze.

The interior of a Greek temple was usually a windowless hall, or *cella.* In the Parthenon (Plate 21), however, a wall separated the space into two parts, a larger room which housed the statue of Athene and a smaller one which contained the treasure. Entrance into both was made through bronze doors which opened upon the eastern and western porches. How the interior was lighted is still a question, since all temple roofs whether of wood, terra-cotta, or marble on wooden supports have disappeared, but it is generally believed that the only source of light was the great bronze doors. No other was necessary since worship was conducted outside and people came in small groups only when they wished to ask some special favor of the goddess.

When the Athenians returned to their homes after the with-

drawal of the Persians (480 B.C.), they found that their shrines
and temples had been razed and their gods destroyed. Under the
leadership of Themistocles they began to rebuild their city. Since
the Acropolis was not clear of buildings, they abandoned the idea
of attempting to salvage any of the wrecked structures. Instead,
they used the sacred ruins to level off and widen the top of the hill
on the southern side, and to prepare foundations for the new
temples. Recently archaeologists have found many broken Archaic
figures of goddesses, which they called the *maidens of the Acropolis,* lying amid the rubbish where they had been thrown by Greek
workmen (Plate 23).

THE ACROPOLIS REBUILT

The remarkable achievements of the Greeks were accomplished
in the time between the Persian and the Peloponnesian wars, a
short space of about fifty years. At this time the *Acropolis* (Plate
19) assumed its final form. The top of the hill was reached by a
winding road terminating in wide marble steps which led up the
rocky slope, giving access to the *Propylaea,* a monumental gateway
with colonnades resting on different levels. To the right, perched
on a high bastion extending outward from the side of the hill, stood
the little *Temple of Nike* (Plate 23), the Wingless Victory, which
balanced the larger left wing of the *Propylaea.* The *Parthenon,*
housing the statue of Athene, was on the southern side just opposite the irregularly-shaped *Erectheum,* with its porch of the maidens,
a small Ionic temple dedicated to several deities (Plates 20, 22).
Towering over all was the colossal statue of *Athene Promachus*
which probably had the same significance to the returning Greek
sailors that the Statue of Liberty holds for homecoming American
travelers. Smaller and less important buildings, statues, and altars
completed the picture.

THE PARTHENON

The most famous of all the Greek temples was the *Parthenon.*
"Like an athlete," well-poised and sturdy, it stands on the most
conspicuous site in Athens. (Plates 19, 20, 21). Pericles selected

Phidias, his favorite sculptor, as superintendent of the works. His assistants were the architects Ictinus and Callicrates. By working together harmoniously; profiting by the experience of former builders; improving the relationships of parts to the whole; refining the respective parts; and wisely subordinating the sculptural decoration to the simple architectural form of the temple they achieved a perfectly proportioned and a completely unified structure.

The horizontal lines of floor and architrave and the contour lines of the supporting columns appear straight to the untrained eye. Nevertheless, accurate measurements have revealed that there is not a straight line in the whole building. The seemingly straight line of the floor rises in a curve eight inches high in the center. With eye at floor-level looking along the stylobate, an experiment that most tourists make, one can not see an object such as a tin can that has been placed at the opposite end. These subtle curves are designed to correct certain optical illusions such as the appearance of sagging when horizontal lines are combined with verticals. However, they are not immediately apparent to the casual observer. In the *Parthenon* the entasis of the column is slighter and more refined than in the shafts of former Doric temples. Axes of the columns which appear vertical are slightly inclined toward the center and also inward toward the walls of the structure, thereby contributing to the appearance of strength and stability. It has been said that if the leaning lines of the axes were extended upward they would meet at a point in the sky directly above the temple. Because the light columns in the center would appear larger than they really are, when seen against the shadowed wall of the portico, they were reduced in size. Conversely, since the proportions of those at either end seen against the brilliant sky are apparently diminished, they were increased in size. Such adjustments of optical relationships, together with carefully considered transitions from one of the various elements to the other and the incomparable workmanship noted in every part of the structure, account for a few of the refinements that give a living quality to the *Parthenon* and make it still beautiful though in ruins.

We know the gable sculpture from drawings made by Jacques Carrey before the Parthenon was wrecked by a shell fired from a

Venetian ship. Morosini, a Venetian general more eager to please his government than he was wise or skillful, attempted to lower the sculpture of the western pediment. The ropes broke and the marbles were smashed to fragments. In the nineteenth century Lord Elgin took most of the remaining eastern gable sculpture and fragments of the Ionic frieze to the British Museum where they still may be seen.

In the eastern and most important pediment of the *Parthenon,* the story of the *Birth of Athene,* goddess of wisdom and patron goddess of the city of Athens, was told in free-standing sculpture. At one end is Apollo, the sun-god, urging his fiery steeds to begin their daily circuit across the sky. The horses' heads are up; energy is expressed in every line. Next comes the monumental figure of Theseus, reclining with easy grace. Goddesses, some of whom seem to be conveying the news of the miraculous birth, occupy the intervening space between Theseus and the place of honor in the center where once stood the throned-figure of Zeus and his newly-born daughter, Athene. To the left of the central figure stands Hephaistos, still bearing the hammer with which, according to the old myth, he smote the head of the mighty god, whereupon Athene sprang forth fully armed. On the right-hand side of the pediment is the group known as the Three Fates; in the corner, Selene, the moon-goddess, with her tired horses is disappearing from sight. Thus the rising of the sun and the setting of the moon indicate that the birth of Athene took place at dawn. In other words, with the coming of the Greeks, "the enlighteners of the world," the darkness of ignorance was dispelled, and the light of wisdom shone upon the earth.

The western pediment presents the story of the *Contest between Athene and Poseidon* for supremacy over the future destiny of Athens. This has been interpreted to mean that the city had come to the parting of the ways. She would have to decide whether to choose Poseidon, the sea-god, and devote herself to commerce with material prosperity as her goal, or whether to follow the goddess of wisdom, develop intellectually, and produce the finest in drama, song, and art. Athene was the victor; and Athens became the center of culture of the ancient world.

Extending around the entire building beneath the pediments and just above the architrave is the broken frieze made up of alternating triglyphs and metopes. On the metopes, all of which were sculptured in high relief, the themes are related to war and conflict; battles between the Greeks and Amazons, centaurs and Lapiths; contests between the gods and giants; hand-to-hand fighting between the Trojans and Achaeans; all symbolical of the destruction of barbarism or the supremacy of intelligence over brute force. These decorations of varying style, size, and merit were done by a group of artists and artisans working within a single plan.

The subject-matter of the inner *Ionic frieze* (3 feet 4 inches high), running along the top of the side walls and above the inner rows of columns at either end of the temple, is man and his relationship to the gods. Peace and harmony are emphasized. To the Greeks man, "the measure of all things," was only slightly lower than the gods. This idea is conveyed through the representation of the Panathenaic procession, the most important feature of the pageantry of the great Athenian festival held on the Acropolis every four years. The different groups taking part in the procession were chosen from the wisest, the strongest, and the most beautiful citizens of Athens. There were young men, the pride of the city, mounting or riding their horses; marching warriors; priests and attendants leading sacrificial animals or bearing jars of wine and oil; matrons; wise old men; and beautiful young maidens who had woven the robe or *peplos* for the ancient wooden statue of Athene that the Greeks had carried with them when the Persians compelled them to leave their city. From both sides of the temple the procession approached the eastern front where the leaders of the groups paused as if in deference to the seated gods who had come down from Mount Olympus to take part in the festivities.

The rhythmic movement of the frieze is produced by the repetition of angular and curving lines apparent in the backs, legs, and necks of men and horses, by the flying garments of the riders, and by the quieter straight lines of the slow-marching figures. The progress of the procession, now slow, now fast, is controlled. Accelerated at the center along the side walls, it becomes less hurried until

Rearing Horse, from the west frieze of the Parthenon.

it is almost halted by a figure, perhaps a marshal, who directs the turning at the corner, and finally ceases on the east front where the figures stand dignified and motionless before the gods. Although the cutting is no deeper than two and a half inches at any one point, the clearly marked contours, the overlapping forms, and the breadth of the modeling contribute to the appearance of a much greater depth. Modern experiments in lighting emphasize the fine linear quality of the frieze, thus permitting the present-day observer to see the beauty of line more clearly than the Greeks who saw it in the shadow of the roof over the portico.

The Greeks who adorned the *Parthenon* solved one of the most difficult problems which had confronted the sculptors, namely, placing groups of figures in that awkward triangular space known as the pediment. Earlier attempts at a solution had been made at the temples of *Aegina* and *Olympia*. At Aegina fallen warriors conveniently fill the sharp corners. A step forward was taken at Olympia where the central figure, the godlike Apollo, stands calm in the midst of a more complex arrangement of fighting Greeks and centaurs. In the *Parthenon* pediment the vigorous movement beginning at the left reaches a climax in the center, continues quietly toward the right, and finally is exhausted in the lowered head of Selene's weary horse which rests upon the cornice (Plate 27).

The Greek temple, as exemplified by the *Parthenon,* is the result of a combination of reasoned order and intuitive taste. We are told that the mathematical proportioning of part to part and the parts to the whole has been so carefully calculated that an entire temple may be reconstructed from a small fragment. The workmanship was so meticulous that the joining of the drums of the columns were practically invisible. The back of the pediment sculpture, which was made to be seen only from the front, was carefully finished. The Greeks carved their marble cornices, doorways, and string-courses with delicate chisel work showing conventional border patterns such as the *Egg and Dart.* The egg and dart, dog's tooth, and the bead and reel designs were so skillfully executed that the sculptors received as much pay for a foot of this carved border as for an entire metope. The ability of the Hellenes to make such fine choices was doubtless due largely to their emphasis upon moderation in all things and to tireless experimentation in their relentless quest for beauty.

Although most of it has disappeared, we know that the Greeks of all periods enhanced both their temples and their statues with vivid hues. Nevertheless, it is believed that their appreciation of color was not so highly developed as their sensitivity to line and form. For the most part they used primary hues, with the addition of black and gilding, which were applied to the upper part of the temple to accent the sculpture and lessen the glare caused by the light of the brilliant sun shining on white marble.

HELLENISTIC PERIOD AND CIVIC PLANNING

Although there was never a sudden break between one period and another, it seems justifiable to make a distinction between Hellenic and Hellenistic art. After the destruction of Athenian power and particularly during that decade when Alexander was establishing his empire in Asia and Northern Africa, the Greeks were in close contact with the Orient. Gradually their world was becoming more cosmopolitan. The Hellenes brought new life to the East; but they in turn were impressed with the opulence of the Orient. Forsaking the simple life, they developed a desire for luxury.

The release of great wealth acquired by the Greeks after Alexander's conquest of Persia had stimulated commerce and promoted utilitarian and domestic as well as religious architecture. Everything was conceived on a grand scale. There was a widespread demand for more luxurious homes for the wealthy. Harbor works facilitating shipping appeared in every port. The *Pharos of Alexandria* was the most famous of the lighthouses. The renowned *Temple of the Ephesians* was dedicated to Diana, twin-sister of Apollo. *The Colossus of Rhodes,* an enormous figure holding a large beacon in his hand, stood across the harbor with feet planted on opposite shores. Marble tombstones like the *Stele of Hegeso,* simple, restrained, and dignified, gave way to massive tombs such as the *Mausoleum of Halicarnassus,* which was adorned by Scopas' statues of *Mausolus* and his wife.

Civic planning became important. The sacred enclosures now comprised temples, treasure houses, council chambers, theatres, stadiums, libraries, and other structures necessary to a more complex mode of life. At the foot of the acropoli lay the cities, with business houses surrounding open squares or market places and beyond which were the residential districts. In Pergamum, one of the most magnificent as well as one of the most powerful of the Asiatic Greek cities, Greek civic planning reached its height. The acropolis rose about a thousand feet above the plain. Every terrace was covered with buildings, both religious and civic. These structures were not designed to be impressive as separate entities like the Parthenon and Erectheum; they were subordinated to the design as a whole. The citizens of Pergamum, unhampered by the necessity of making an adjustment between the new and the old, for their acropolis had not been destroyed like that of the Athenians, were able to achieve a perfectly unified plan.

Among the structures near the top of the hill was the great *Altar of Zeus* (183-179 B.C.), set upon a high base in the center of the square and enclosed on three sides by a basement structure which in turn was topped by a colonnade. Around the upper part of the base was the celebrated frieze depicting the gods warring with the giants, a subject which provided excellent opportunity for the portrayal of violent combat and melodramatic expressions such as fright, pain, or victory (Plate 34). When seen from a distance the decorative play of light and shadow on the high relief of the over-life-size figures was most impressive. Here the ornamentation dominated the structure.

HELLENISTIC SCULPTURE

By this time Hellenistic sculptors had learned a great deal about anatomy, and since there was a demand for more naturalistic representation, they concerned themselves chiefly with reproducing the outward visual aspects of the human form shown in scenes from everyday life. Such subjects as a boy struggling with a goose, a youth extracting a thorn from his foot, or an old woman replaced the earlier idealized statues of the gods and athletes. Earlier the athletes always had been shown at the height of their strength and intellectual powers, whereas the Hellenistic sculptors did not hesitate to depict older men with exaggerated muscles like the *Boxer* (Plate 34) or with bodies bent by the burdens which they bore. The heads and faces, more individualized, were not subordinated to the figure as a whole as in fifth-century work. Sculpture now tended toward the theatrical, melodramatic, and personal; portraiture became popular.

The tendency toward a more literal realism is well portrayed in the statue of the *Dying Gaul,* a fine example of Hellenistic work (Plate 30). The beard and torque about the neck of the figure indicate his nationality. A tragic mood is created both by the expression of pain on the face and the drooping pose of the body, which is losing strength as the life blood flows from a wound in his side. The *Laocoon* group and the *Farnese Bull,* both full of restless action, are skillfully executed and highly dramatic. Michelangelo was so impressed with the movement of the twisting bodies that a spiraling movement became an outstanding characteristic of his own work. The *Dying Gaul* shows more restraint than the two groups which have just been mentioned.

The *Tanagra Figurine of Dancer* is a typical example of late Greek genre art (Plate 35). Delightful grace and coquetry are expressed in the clay modeling and enhanced by the application of color and gilding. Thousands of clay figurines which reveal the everyday life of the people of that time have been found in graves.

GREEK PAINTING

Few Greek paintings are left. We know them mostly through stories, the decorations of the Greek vases that reflect the styles and indicate the subject-matter of the murals, and the Graeco-Roman wall paintings found at Herculaneum and Pompeii which probably are copies of earlier Greek works. The *Aldobrandini Wedding* and the *Initiation into the Mysteries* (Plate 37) are among the latter. Such vase painting as *Women Putting Away Their Clothes* by Douris (Plate 36), and *Hunter with Dog* by the Pan Painter (Plate 33), both early fifth-century red-figured Attic ware, depict scenes from daily life with vigorous clarity. Gods and goddesses, wars, and every aspect of Greek life were used as subject-matter by the vase painters.

A well-known example of an ancient Greek painting copied in another medium is the *Alexander Mosaic* * (Plate 36), which once decorated the floor of the House of the Faun, one of the most ancient dwellings in Pompeii. It depicts the meeting of Darius the Persian and Alexander the Great at the Battle of the Issus. Here is a fine portrait of Alexander in pursuit of the fleeing Darius, who turns backward just in time to see one of his men fall from a horse. An old tree against a wide expanse of sky suggests a landscape. In the general confusion horses are racing in different directions. Some are rearing, others falling. Nevertheless, the conflicting lines of men, animals, and spears are all gathered in the general sweep of movement toward the right, the direction in which the army is fleeing, thus imparting unity to the composition. The contrast

---

* A mosaic is made of *tesserae*, small blocks of varicolored glass or stone, set in cement. Marble tesserae were used in the *Alexander Mosaic*.

of dark and light is striking and the general effect is quite realistic. Unrivalled realism is shown in the *Rabbit Mosaic* made of glass in the period of the Roman Empire (Plate 35). Of special interest is the artist's careful representation of animal, reptile and vegetable forms.

The Greek ideal of moderation was lost after the fourth century, and the newly acquired interest in size which was conspicuously lacking in the earlier period increased. The massive Hellenistic architecture especially appealed to the Romans who, being better engineers, surpassed the Greeks in the

Potter at Wheel. Drawing from a vase painting. (Museum of Fine Arts, Boston)

construction of buildings notable for sheer size, magnificence, and grandeur. Roman architecture did not, however, show the subtle refinement of the fifth-century Greek temples.

OUTLINE OF GREEK ART

TIME: Archaic Period—c. 750-470 B.C. Hellenic Period—c. 470-338 B.C. Hellenistic Period—338-146 B.C.

BACKGROUND: Mountainous terrain, soil poor, excellent harbors—all conducive to making a seafaring people. Greek world held together by a common language and religion. During Age of Pericles, scholars and philosophers became skeptical. Middle class respected myths and religious rites for traditional reasons. Illiterate and superstitious group probably retained their faith in the gods. First attempts to form a democracy. City-state most important unit in government. Athens intellectual and artistic. Sparta militaristic—constant conflict between the two. Slaves did the manual labor.

ARCHITECTURE: Marble and stone plentiful—wood scarce. Post and lintel chief structural element. Masonry construction for walls. Columnar temples rectangular in shape, with tile roofs. Small in size. Purpose: to house cult statue. Sculptural decorations characterized by refinement and restraint. Doric, Ionic, and Corinthian orders (the last named seldom employed by the Greeks) invented. Color applied to top part of temple. Other civic structures were theatres, porticoes, gateways. Homes unimportant. Chief contribution: the three orders. Examples: Doric, Parthenon; Ionic, Erectheum; Corinthian, Choragic Monument to Lysicrates—all in Athens.

SCULPTURE: Materials, marble and bronze. Both relief and free-standing statues. Subject-matter: athletes, heroes, gods. *Archaic* period, nude athletes or Apollos posed in Egyptian manner with arms close to sides and one foot advanced. Prominent eyes, high cheek bones, and archaic smile. Expression ingratiating, charming. Goddesses, same facial characteristics, garments follow stiff lines of figure. *Transitional* period (480-450 B.C.), easier pose. *Later fifth century,* tendency toward idealized naturalism, freer movement. Faces expressionless but alive. *Fourth century and Hellenistic* periods, athletes become soft, gods less austere, more human. Increasing number of statutes of women, both clothed and in the nude. Early reliefs, fine spatial design—later, full of action, melodramatic.

PAINTING: Vase painting: subject-matter, deeds of heroes, athletic games, processions, genre. Murals: show that the Greeks understood perspective and employed light and shadow.

BIBLIOGRAPHY

CARPENTER, RHYS, *The Esthetic Basis of Greek Art* (Longmans, Green & Co., N. Y., 1921).

GARDNER, E. A., *The Art of Greece* (Boni & Gaer, N. Y., 1925).

McCLEES, Helen, *Daily Life of the Greeks and Romans* (Metropolitan Museum, N. Y., 1933).

RICHTER, G. M. A., *The Sculpture and Sculptors of the Greeks* (Yale University Press, New Haven, 1930).

STOBART, J. C., *The Glory That Was Greece* (D. Appleton-Century Co., Inc., N. Y., 1935).

SWINDLER, M. H., *Ancient Painting* (Yale University Press, New Haven, 1929).

CHAPTER VI

Roman Art

To the west of Greece lies Italy, that familiar boot-shaped peninsula with toe pointing toward Sicily. The majestic snow-capped Alps frown down upon its northern border, while the Apennines extending from north to south divide the country almost in half. Although its coast line is long it has few good harbors; on the other hand, its soil is highly productive. Naturally under such conditions the early inhabitants became farmers rather than seafaring folk.

During the great Indo-European migrations (c. 1600-800 B.C.), some of the tribes sailed past many lands to settle in western Italy. In his *Aeneid* Virgil recounted some of the adventures of these restless peoples who found a home on the Italian coast, just as Homer compiled the legends of the pre-Hellenic Greeks.

THE ETRUSCANS

After much warring with each other various tribes merged to form a small agricultural settlement on the banks of the Tiber less than twenty miles from the sea. From this humble beginning sprang the proud city of Rome. During the ninth century B.C. the most cultured of these wandering tribes, the Etruscans, a people of a different race and speaking a different language, came from the Asiatic coast to settle on the rugged hilly land between the Arno and the Tiber. At first they lived in strongly-fortified dwellings perched high upon the hilltops, but in time they established hill towns with fortified acropoli similar to those of the Greek cities. By the sixth century B.C. they had forced their way into the small settlement along the banks of the river and occupied two of the

seven hills upon which Rome was built. Upon one of these, the
Capitoline, they erected altars to their gods, chief among whom
were Jupiter, the god of gods; Juno, his wife, who protected the
home; and Minerva, the goddess of war and wisdom. These deities
later became the favorite gods of the Romans, and the Capitoline
the most revered place in Rome.

Not content to be merely farmers, the enterprising Etruscans
built ships and sailed down the Tiber into the Tyrrhenian Sea.
They carried on commerce with the near-by coasts and harried
their strongest competitors, the Greeks and Phoenicians. Among
their imports were the famous Greek vases, which the Etruscans
brought home in great quantities. Like the other Mediterranean
peoples, they valued them highly. In fact, it is recorded that most
of the Greek vases now in the museums of the world have been
discovered in tombs, placed there by the Etruscans for funerary
purposes.

Since the language of these people has not yet been deciphered,
historians have depended largely upon their art for information
concerning their character and customs. Their sculpture and the
decorations on the walls of their tombs and temples seem to indicate that the intelligent though emotional Etruscans were a restless
and warlike tribe. Characteristic of their sculpture is the vigorous
Striding Warrior (Plate 38), an eight-foot terra-cotta figure. The
paintings on the walls of their tombs, showing them drinking at
banquets while musicians and dancers entertained them (Plate
38), have a distinctive style somewhat similar to that found in the
decorations of early Greek vases. Apparently the Etruscans had
acquired many skills from older peoples before they journeyed
westward.

THE ETRUSCANS EMPLOY THE ARCH

By making wide use of the arch and the barrel vault—which is
merely a continuous arch—the Etruscans were able to construct
subterranean tombs, bridges, sewers, and monumental gateways at
the entrances of their cities. Their temples were somewhat like
those of the Greeks though more nearly square in shape. The

wider wooden eaves were supported by wider-spaced columns in a style resembling the Greek-Doric. The wooden beams and roof were covered with terra-cotta facings, and terra-cotta sculptures adorned the pediment and entablature.

Few of their monumental structures have withstood the ravages of time; nevertheless, the Etruscans made an important contribution to architecture and its related arts. They taught the Romans how to build vaulted sewers for sanitation; how to erect walls by inserting a combination of mud and small stones between stone or brick facings—a method of construction which eliminated much of the skill and labor required in stone-cutting. Etruscan city gates were the prototypes of the Roman triumphal arches, and no doubt their round tombs suggested the circular peripteral temple which became a distinctive Roman feature. As time went on, the Romans began to fear these aggressive people from whom they had learned so much and eventually they conquered them (290 B.C.).

THE ROMANS AS EMPIRE BUILDERS

It has been recorded that the Roman thought of himself as a man with a mission—to bring order to the world. He carried out this mission peacefully in the beginning, demanding only that his neighbors coöperate with the Roman state and keep the Roman peace. It was along the southern shores of Italy and the eastern coast of Sicily that the Romans first encountered the Greeks, who were quarreling among themselves. The Romans intervened and established order. Realizing that the Greeks had a superior culture, they determined to learn more about the country from which these Hellenes came. But first there were other matters to settle.

Just across from Sicily on the African coast was the rich commercial city of Carthage, Mistress of the Mediterranean. Seeing in her a potential enemy, the Romans attacked. Finally, after long drawn out wars they captured and completely destroyed Carthage in 146 B.C. Inheriting the vast Carthaginian empire, Rome now became Mistress of the Sea.

From this time onward the Romans, having had a taste of conquest, began to think in terms of empire. To this end they built

their famous roads for extending trade and expediting the movements of their well-trained armies. So well constructed were these
roads that our soldiers traveled over some of them during World
War II.

Turning again to settle dissensions which arose among the Hellenes of Greece, the Romans, unsuccessful in the beginning, took
sterner measures. Finally the Greek city-states, one by one, were
reduced to Roman provinces, and the liberty-loving Greeks irrevocably lost their highly prized freedom. Among the conquered
Greeks sent to Rome were scholars, writers, artists, and craftsmen
whom the Romans employed either as slaves or freedmen to edu-
cate the Roman children, to elevate the culture of their newly rich
masters, or to beautify the Imperial City. The Greeks respected
the superior might of the Romans, who in turn took great pains to
acquire the culture of the Greeks.

The art of the Greeks met with a fate similar to that of the people themselves. When the city of Corinth was destroyed, her art
treasures were carefully collected by the victorious Romans and
carried off to be displayed in the triumphal procession. A figure
representing Roma, the goddess who personified the city, rode in a
chariot at the head of the procession comprising returning soldiers,
captives, and military booty which moved along the Sacra Via to
the Capitoline Hill. A conspicuous place was devoted to confiscated
works of art—both sculpture and paintings—which afterwards were
taken to a temple where they were dedicated in an impressive ceremony. The Eternal City is still an important custodian of art
objects.

In brief, after she had won the coöperation of her allies on the
Italian peninsula, accomplished the destruction of Carthage, subjugated the Greek provinces on the mainland, and defeated the
Ptolemies in Egypt, Rome emerged as the capital city of the greatest empire the world had ever known. Having proved her ability
in military affairs, she now became such a successful organizer of
her vast possessions that one of her poets was moved to write that
she had "made the world a single city."

The realistic Romans did not possess the vivid imagination or the
artistic ability of the Greeks. Instead they excelled in law, admin-

istration, business, military affairs, and engineering skill which they displayed in the building of aqueducts, roads, and bridges. Typical of their vast utilitarian projects is the *Pont du Gard* aqueduct (Plate 41). This soundly constructed bridge had three colonnaded tiers with the water conduit running through the upper one. Here function is united with beauty of form, for the rhythmic arrangement of well-spaced stories and arches enhances the appearance of this utilitarian structure.

THE IMPERIAL CITY

By the end of the Republic, however, these people who had become conquerors and rulers of others had lost control over themselves. Trouble broke out on the home front. The strong took advantage of the confusion to promote their own interests. A standing army of volunteers or mercenaries replaced the citizen legions who had grown tired of serving in foreign wars while their own farms were neglected. It was in midst of such upset conditions that Julius Caesar, with his victorious legions, returned from the west to restore order in the Imperial City. Following Caesar's untimely death (44 B.C.), his nephew Augustus (31 B.C.-14 A.D.) became the first of the "good emperors." The Republic had definitely come to an end; Rome had lost her opportunity to become a democracy; she had submitted to a one-man rule. Nevertheless, for two hundred years there was outward peace and prosperity.

During the first century A.D. Rome became increasingly cosmopolitan; about half of her population were foreigners. The Greeks and other prisoners of war who were reduced to slavery did the necessary work, thus releasing the wealthy Roman to devote himself to a life of pleasure, to own a stable for the popular sport of chariot racing, to maintain gladiators for fighting in the arena, or to plan the famous naval combats in the Colosseum which could be sufficiently flooded to serve as a miniature sea.

The great public works program furnished jobs for many of the people who had flocked to the city, but there were countless others who were unemployed. In order to keep them more or less contented with their miserable lot, the emperors put on such extrav-

agant entertainments as the gladiatorial shows in the arenas and
chariot races held in the circuses especially designed for that sport.
On such occasions food was provided for all. Many of the enormous Roman structures had a distinct political function.

With the coming of prosperity, due to the increase of power
and growth of empire, the Romans departed from the earlier austere traditions, and gradually succumbed to the more sensual
of Greek culture around 200 B.C. Some of the frescoes on the walls
influences derived from contact with the Hellenistic Greeks, particularly those whom they had encountered at Alexandria, the center
of the houses unearthed at Pompeii depict the luxurious life of
the Nile valley. From this time Roman architecture was to become
increasingly impressive and its decorations exceedingly ornate.
During the reigns of Augustus and his immediate successors Rome
became a magnificent city. Wide symmetric forums or market
places, surrounded by porticoes, adjoined the public buildings.
Usually a triumphal arch spanned the entrance of each forum.
Thermae or baths were clubs, libraries, and gymnasiums all in one;
basilicas were both civic meeting places and law courts; temples
were dedicated to the gods; central heating plants made houses
comfortable; aqueducts brought water from the mountains; a fine
drainage system emptied into the Etruscan-built *Cloca Maxima*—
which still receives the water from the low valley of the old forum;
excellent roads led to the city from all directions. The wealthy had
residences in the city and palatial villas on their country estates,
but most of the people lived in houses in the midst of the city or in
simple dwellings along its fringes. Replicas of the capital city in
all its grandeur dotted the empire from its extreme eastern border
to the countries lying along the shores of the Atlantic in the west.

By the application of cement to the rubble which the Etruscans
had used for filling in between the stone facings of the walls, the
Romans perfected a method of building which great gangs of unskilled laborers could handle successfully. By crossing two barrel
vaults they produced the groined vault—the sharp intersections of
these vaults were called *groins*. With increased support at the
four corners where the groins converged, the walls between the
supports could be lightened, an advantage over the old barrel vault

which required uniformly thick walls. In the baths such extra support was supplied by placing the walls of the small rooms, surrounding the central area, at right angles to the corners of the vault where the greatest pressure was exerted.

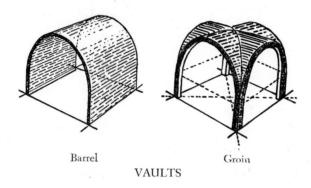

Barrel   Groin

VAULTS

With the growing need of vast structures, the Romans became space conscious. The Egyptians had erected colossal buildings dedicated to religion, but their great halls were filled with a forest of massive columns. The Assyrians had constructed enormous palaces for their kings, but their wall-enclosed areas were divided into many narrow rooms and corridors. The Greeks, spending most of their time out-of-doors, seemed to have little need for a large amount of enclosed space. The daring Roman engineers, employing the Etruscan arch as a basic structural element, spanned vast areas of unobstructed space with high vaulted roofs and domes such as those which covered the baths, accommodating several thousand people, and the Pantheon, with a rotunda 142 feet in diameter. Thus the Romans solved their structural and spatial problems by the use of new materials suitably adapted to unskilled workmanship; excellent organization of labor; and a hitherto unsurpassed engineering skill. From those ancient times to the present day space has become an increasingly important element in architectural design. From the Greeks the Romans had inherited the three orders: the Doric, Ionic, and Corinthian. Modifying the columns to fit the larger scale of their buildings and the extravagance of their taste, they employed them not only for structural purposes but also as decorations in the form of engaged or half-columns—a device the Greeks would never have employed.

TEMPLES

During the empire the Roman temple was employed for civic as well as religious purposes. In addition to the cult statue, it housed the gifts donated by the wealthy and art objects taken in by the victorious armies or presented by the emperor. Functioning as a museum as well as a place of worship, the temples of the empire were necessarily much larger than those of Greece.

Some of the temples were dedicated to emperor-worship. Because of its unifying influence, this cult, which the ancient Romans inherited from earlier civilizations, had a strong political significance; and they sought to perpetuate it for that purpose. Doubtless varying degrees of coercion were responsible for its widespread acceptance. Some of the Roman emperors dressed like gods and sat enthroned in their temples to receive the homage of the people. Julius Caesar erected a temple to Venus, whom he claimed to be his ancestress; but the Greeks, we are told, laughed when Alexander proclaimed himself a god.

One of the best-preserved and the most satisfying of the Greek-inspired temples is the *Maison-Carrée* in Nîmes, France. Of particular interest is the delicate carving of decorations on the frieze and pediment. Among the circular types, the *Temple of Vesta* is small and well-proportioned; but the most imposing of all is the *Pantheon* (Plate 39), built by Hadrian near the site of Agrippa's baths. Some historians state that the foundation of this temple, a part of its portico, and some of its columns are remains of these earlier structures.

The exterior of the *Pantheon* is impressive, but it is the vast spaciousness of the interior that stirs the imagination and compels the wonder and attention of the spectator. Beyond the portico is the deep-set entrance guarded by magnificent bronze doors said to be the originals, placed there in Hadrian's time. Light streams through a circular opening in the dome, illuminates the floors and the windowless walls, and penetrates the shadowy niches. Also reflected upon the ceiling of the dome, it emphasizes the immensity of the great void and imparts an illusion of lightness to the heavy roof. The smooth marble-veneered walls on the interior are interrupted by three large semicircular niches alternating with smaller rectangular ones. The former, which are flanked and screened by columns, once contained statues of the principal Roman gods; but during the early years of the Christian era, when the *Pantheon* became a Christian church, these niches were modified to serve as chapels. The smaller ones are now shrines, where noted Italian statesmen and other important persons, including the famous artist Raphael, are buried. Above the niches is a continuous entablature surmounted by the drum which supports the cupola. This dome is richly coffered; that is, it is honeycombed with set-back panels which both lighten its weight and ornament its surface. Still in use, the *Pantheon,* dedicated to all the gods as its name implies, is the best preserved of all the ancient Greek or Roman monuments.

ARENAS, ARCHES, BATHS, AND COLUMNS

The *Colosseum,* begun in the first century and completed in the third, is the best-known and the most imposing of the great arenas (Plate 40). Elliptical in shape, with thick walls of concrete faced with travertine (a limestone), it is a four-story building over six hundred feet long. The ground story is pierced by eighty successive arches, between which are engaged columns of the heavier Doric style. There are similar arches on the second and third stories, with corresponding half-columns of the Ionic and Corinthian styles in the order named. To some observers, this combination of arch and column—the latter being used for decoration only —is a pleasing innovation; to others, the rhythmic recurrence of the mighty arch, the basic structural feature, is sufficiently satisfying and impressive without further adornment. Such unadorned "businesslike" arches as those of the magnificent bridges and aqueducts that span the rivers or stride across the Italian landscape seem almost modern in their stark simplicity.

In the interior there were receding tiers of seats, elevated on a podium raised high enough to discourage the wild beasts from joining the spectators (Plate 40). When not performing, the animals were confined below in dens connected with the arena by long tunnels. Concrete stairways leading up from the eighty arched entrances on the ground floor, provided easy access to the radiating aisles that divided the seats into sections and facilitated the rapid exit of sixty to eighty thousand spectators.

For ten centuries the *Colosseum* was used as a quarry to supply building material for Roman houses. Still retaining its original form despite centuries of multilation and deliberate wreckage, it is a great monument to the excellent building skills of the ancient engineers and by far the most impressive of the Roman ruins. Standing amid these ruins, one can easily see in imagination the population of the entire city gathered to view a gladitorial spectacle, and can almost hear the shouts of the people as they applaud their favorites, or see them turning thumbs down to condemn other contestants to death.

Extending over a wide area, the baths were laid out in symmetrical order. The central feature, often round in shape, was the general meeting place. Wide steps led to a pool in the center which was surrounded by couches and other lounging equipment. On either side of the central axis, as in the *Baths of Caracalla,* the most famous if not the largest, were the *frigidarium* and the *calidarium* (Plate 39). Surrounding this central core were extra rooms for private baths, dressing rooms, lecture halls, libraries, entrance halls, and open peristyles. These enormous Roman baths served as patterns for the huge railway stations in our own country which are also characterized by expansive spaciousness.

Of the triumphal arches, one of the finest in the proportion of its parts to the whole, in the balance of weight to support and in the extraordinary beauty of its inscription, is the *Arch of Titus,* commemorating that Emperor's victory over the Palestinian Jews (81 A.D.). On the interior of the arch is a sculptured frieze depicting in part the triumphal entry of the victorious soldiers. Here attendants are bearing the sacred ark and the seven-branched candlesticks from the temple at Jerusalem. On the opposite side the emperor is shown in his chariot preceded by the goddess Roma

(Plate 41). The marble *quadriga*—a four-horse chariot driven by an emperor—that once topped this arch, over the entrance of the old Roman forum, has long since disappeared.

Tall columns rose in a conspicuous place in the different forums. The one erected by Emperor Trajan, which was literally covered with sculptured reliefs, depicted one hundred and fifteen different episodes of his reign. Most of these monuments, however, are conspicuous for their historical rather than artistic value. The naturalistic figures on *Trajan's Column,* rather crowded, restless, and confusing, lack the welcome rest spaces or "silent passages" of the Greek reliefs.

THE ROMAN HOUSE

Since the Romans conducted much of their business, worshipped their gods, and entertained their friends at home, their houses were more pretentious than the simple dwellings of the Greeks, who had lavished most of their skill on civic and religious buildings. A Roman house, which often occupied an area equal to a small city block, was built around an *atrium* or central hall which contained the altar and the sacred fire. The father, acting as priest, conducted the religious rites; his power was supreme even over the life and death of his family and other members of the household. The mother also was highly respected and revered. It was Roma, the mother-goddess, who personified the city. The household gods, the Lares and the Penates, were taken wherever the family went.

Connected with the house and facing the streets were small shops, some of which were used by the owner; others were rented. The more public rooms of the dwelling were grouped around the atrium, which had an opening in the roof to admit rain and light. Directly below it was an *impluvium* or sunken pool to collect the rain water, which was conducted to underground cisterns and stored for future use. These rooms were lighted only by doors. A large part of the unbroken wall space was decorated with figures set against a black, red, or white background; or it was divided vertically by painted columns or other architectural devices to enclose representations of a garden or distant landscape. It seems that the ancient Romans, like the architects of today, strove to bring their gardens into their houses.

Even the homes of the average well-to-do family had central heating and sanitary facilities connected with the public system. The city residences and the magnificent villas of the emperors and the wealthy Romans were similar but more complex. Their gardens contained flowers, statues, and fountains. Usually the villas were built upon heights commanding fine views of sea or landscape. Well-preserved city residences were found in the excavated ruins of Pompeii and Herculaneum, the two cities buried under ash and lava during the eruption of Vesuvius in 79 A.D. Remains of palatial country places may still be seen in Europe and along the northern coast of Africa. Homes of wealthy Romans, such as the *House of the Vettii,* have been found at Pompeii buried and preserved in volcanic debris and lava. These Roman dwellings contain beautiful frescoes with lifelike figures rendered in a remarkably impressionistic style. The *Villa Livia,* presumably the home of an adviser of the emperor, was located on the Palatine. It is famous for the richly decorated interior walls, showing beautiful paintings designed from natural forms. Some walls have heavy garlands of leaves, flowers, and fruit; while others represent a garden with trees, vines, fountains, flowers, and birds in typical mural design. Fine mosaics decorated the floors.

Masks of Comedy and Tragedy. From Pompeii. (Dyer)

ROMAN SCULPTURE

Greek statues of both Hellenic and Hellenistic times were brought to Rome where copies were made to adorn the great baths. Friezes of intricately carved garlands or naturalistic fruits and flowers appeared frequently upon stone altars and embellished the marble sarcophagi of important personages who, while still alive, had their tombs decorated with carvings depicting some outstanding event of their career. The Greek sculptors were not able to supply the extravagant demands of their masters, so the Romans themselves expedited matters by inventing a system of casting—a practical, though not a creative process—by means of which they could make reproductions in great quantities. Headless statues of citizens, senators, soldiers and emperors, with the proper symbols for their respective ranks, were turned out in mass production. When an order was given, the sculptor had only to carve the head of the sitter and screw it to the shoulders of the ready-made body. We have obtained most of our information concerning the lost Greek originals from Roman copies.

Surpassing the Greeks in the portrayal of children, which the Hellenes rarely attempted, the Romans have left some remarkable and charming works showing a sympathetic understanding of childhood (Plate 42). Nevertheless, their most significant contribution to sculpture was the realistic portraiture of Roman citizens, soldiers, senators, and emperors (Plate 42). In the hands of the Roman sculptor, marble became living flesh and the bony structure underneath was clearly indicated. Including every wrinkle and blemish, line for line, features were copied without any attempt to soften or flatter. So clearly did the artist report exactly what his discerning eye had seen, that one not only could easily recognize the subject, he could learn something about his character as well.

Portraiture was an innovation in sculptured processional friezes such as that of *Ara Pacis* (Altar of Peace) erected by Augustus (Plate 42). In one portion of the frieze the Emperor, his family, and some of his followers may be identified. An effect of deep space is produced by the overlapping of many figures and by making the nearer ones larger than the ones in the distance. All are set either against an urban background indicated by houses or in a rural landscape suggested by trees. The figures, clothed in minutely detailed garments, are naturalistic. Roman reliefs are visual representations of both episode and allegory. Roman portraits are ruthless records of a people who rose to the heights of military and political eminence, established the greatest empire of ancient times, and then weakened by luxury, extravagance and self-indulgence fell before a more vigorous race.

By the third century A.D. a great financial depression, combined with class struggle and civil wars, had weakened the western part of the empire. Finally Constantine (who ruled from 324-337 A.D.) began to recognize the growing power of Christianity and encouraged the religion for which people had formerly been persecuted, but to what extent is a point of disagreement among authorities. When the Emperor moved his capital to Byzantium on the Bosporus the center of civilization shifted back to the East. With the fall of Rome (476 A.D.) to the barbarians who had been constantly knocking at her gates, the ancient world came to an end.

The great art dedicated to the service of the Christian church, was not to flower in Rome, although it had some of its beginnings there, but in the eastern half of the Empire, which remained Greek at heart and later became known as the Byzantine Empire—but that is a subject for another chapter.

OUTLINE OF ROMAN ART

TIME: Republic—early times-27 B.C. Empire—27 B.C.-313 A.D.

BACKGROUND: Mountains in central part. Few harbors. Soil productive. Early Romans, farmers. Religion similar to Greek—centered in the home. Rome strong city-state. When vast empire grew unwieldly, it was divided into two sections, East and West. Constantine moved capital to Constantinople. Rome fell. Romans of republic hardy, self-reliant, practical; later became luxury-loving and weak. Law-givers, engineers, soldiers. Brought order to the world.

ARCHITECTURE: Stone, colored marbles, wood, clay found near Rome. The arch chief structural element. Strong thick walls supported the barrel and groined vaults which covered vast spaces. Columnar style in rectangular and round temples. Homes important. Other types of structures: arenas, aqueducts, sewers, triumphal arches, tombs, bridges, baths, palaces, basilicas, and civic buildings. Greatest contribution: fine engineering and development of vault construction.

SCULPTURE: Materials: marble, bronze. Influences: Etruscan and Greek. Many copies of Greek statues. Roman work more realistic. Character portraiture. Individual, powerful. Uncompromising realism in contrast to Greek idealism. Relief decorations tend toward illusionism and suggest depth and to a certain extent, perspective—not purely decorative. Often crowded and confusing in design. Sculpture lavishly employed as decoration of buildings to the extent of detracting from the fine engineering of the enormous Roman structures.

PAINTING: Influence: Greek. Types: mural and portraits. Subject-matter: architectural borders enclosing a figure or group of figures. Naturalistic gardens, cupids on black and red grounds, all used as decoration for walls of houses. Wax portraits such as those found on Egyptian mummy cases (Graeco-Roman).

BIBLIOGRAPHY

ANDERSON, W. S., SPIERS, R. P., and ASHBY, Thomas, *Architecture of Ancient Rome* (Charles Scribner's Sons, N. Y., 1927).
STOBART, J. C., *The Grandeur That Was Rome,* rev. ed. (London, 1934).
SWINDLER, M. H., *Ancient Painting* (Yale University Press, New Haven, 1929).
WALTERS, H. B., *The Art of the Romans* (London, 1911).

CHAPTER VII

Mohammedan and Ancient Persian Art

IN THE fourth and fifth centuries A.D. Arabia was surrounded by the two great empires of the world. To the north and east was the Sassanian-Persian, a revival of the ancient Persian Empire which had fallen under the furious assault of Alexander the Great. The Roman Empire, called Byzantine in the East, lay to the north and west. The Arabs, living on barren lands suited only to nomadic habitation, were not directly affected by the constant conflict between the two. Nevertheless, since fighting was second nature to the sons of the desert, both powers were able to increase their ranks by recruiting these poor but free nomads as mercenaries.

The Arabs, who had already come in contact with the religions of the Jews and Christians, remained unimpressed by either Judaism or Christianity and continued to practice their tribal ritual. The belief in one God was not a new idea, as we have seen. It had been promoted by Ikhnaton in Egypt and by the philosophers in Greece; the Jews had proclaimed Yahweh as the one and only God; later Christianity originated in Palestine. In the sixth century there appeared in Arabia a lowly camel driver, Mohammed, who was to formulate another monotheistic religion.

MOHAMMED AND ISLAM

Mohammed (570-632 A.D.) was born in the little city of Mecca, a typical commercial center about fifty miles from the Red Sea. It was inhabited by a number of Arabs, a few Christians, a smaller proportion of Jews, and at certain times it was teeming with nomads from the desert. Little is known of Mohammed's life there except that he was early left an orphan and had to fend for himself; consequently he had no opportunity to gain an education. He was of a nervous temperament subject to visions and dreams, we are told, but he was unusually gifted and exceedingly ambitious to improve his lot. Eventually he married a well-to-do widow, thus relieving himself of financial worries and acquiring leisure for contemplation. After having experienced the distressing hardships of a life of extreme poverty in his early years, it is small wonder that he would be keenly aware of social injustice.

In Mecca there was a black stone, a meteorite, which the Arabs believed had been sent to them by heaven. Together with other sacred objects it was housed in a cubicle building known as the Kaaba. At certain times it was the custom to postpone all feuds in the Arab world, and merchants and pilgrims from far and near came to worship the stone. To these and any others who would listen, Mohammed told the spiritual thoughts which constantly raced through his mind, and he tried to bring about better living conditions for the poor and destitute. His teachings appealed to the lower classes, but on the whole his efforts proved to be unsuccessful, for he provoked the disapproval of the ruling groups who feared an upset in the existing social structure and also the loss of business if the Arabs should cease to come to worship the stone. Finally Mohammed was forced to seek a more hospitable center for his activities.

Not far from Mecca was the small town of Medina, which had a large Jewish population. At this time the Arabs, also present in large numbers, were in the midst of one of their frequent disputes, and they were looking for an arbitrator strong enough to cope with the situation. Having heard about Mohammed, they appealed to him for help. He decided to go to their aid, and in spite of those who, for various reasons, attempted to prevent his leaving the city, he managed to depart secretly. His flight, known as the Hegira, occurred in 622 A.D., and from that date the Arabs reckon their years, just as we count ours from the birth of Christ.

Before leaving Mecca, Mohammed had been greatly impressed by the teachings of St. Paul, and when he later encountered the Jews at Medina he became interested in the life of Moses. Borrowing from both Christianity and Judaism he formulated a new religion called Islam, similar to the two older creeds in many respects, but differing conspicuously in form.

Mohammed's beliefs together with some of his sayings, are recorded in the Koran, the Mohammedan bible. He regarded some of the Old Testament characters, such as Adam, Noah, Abraham, Isaiah, and even Jesus, as prophets who had received revelations from God; and he identified himself as the last of the prophets, for he also had a vision in which an angel appeared to him and commanded him to preach.

The followers of Islam were promised life after death in a paradise of shady, rose-filled gardens, brooks with cool running water, and beautiful dark-eyed maidens to serve them—all sensual pleasures highly desirable to nomads of the desert who spent most of their time under the heat of the burning sun. The Moslems were told that if they died fighting to spread their faith to the infidel they would immediately enter such a heaven. In their palaces, particularly those in India and Spain, they came close to an earthly realization of their imaginary visions of paradise.

Islam, like Christianity, stood for the brotherhood of man and frowned upon race prejudice, but it also had a militant aspect. The code of the Arabs had always permitted fighting for booty against any peoples other than their own clan. Mohammed himself, in the earlier days when it was difficult for the members of the new sect to support themselves, sanctioned and even promoted this practice. In Islam, as in the Christian and Jewish religions, there were certain prohibitions or restraints. The Mohammedans were forbidden to drink wine, to eat pork, or to worship idols. On the positive side they were instructed to believe in one god, Allah, and in Mohammed as his prophet; to pray five times a day with face turned toward Mecca; to fast at stated intervals; to give alms to the poor; and to make at least one pilgrimage to the Holy City, Mecca. The prophet also commanded the Moslems to spread their religion, by persuasion when they could, or by the might of the sword when gentler methods failed.

ARABS AS CONQUERORS

It is doubtful that the ambitious Mohammed himself ever dreamed of world conquest, but after his death Abu Bekr proclaimed a holy war; and in the unsettled Arabian world there arose a mighty leader, Khalid, "the sword of Allah." Successful in pillaging raids conducted chiefly for the acquisition of booty, he conquered the eastern part of the land as far as the Persian Gulf. Small raids soon developed into extensive campaigns with a twofold purpose: the spiritual desire to spread the faith; and the materialistic expectation of reward from booty.

Thus fired with a tremendous energy aroused by religious zeal and the hope of material gain, the Arabs mounted on swift steeds and launched the *blitzkrieg* of their time. Their success depended upon the speed and fury of their attack. At full gallop they came, "each separate Moslem appearing like a missile loosed from the desert and charged with an inward momentum which irresistibly drove him on." Without regard for such things as lines of communications and organization of transport and supplies, their armies, composed entirely of cavalry, swiftly overran Syria and the Sassanian-Persian Empire. After this taste of victory they sought other worlds to conquer. In an incredibly short time they swept over the northern coast of Africa and crossed the Mediterranean Sea into Spain, leaving death and destruction in their wake. Finally they were stopped by Charles Martel and his Frankish army. Thus most of Europe was spared and the symbol of European religion was still the cross instead of the crescent to which the peoples of western Asia and northern Africa were compelled to bow.

The Arabs seem to have been a romantic, emotional, and sentimental people, fond of poetry and masters of the art of story-telling. The *Rubáiyát* of Omar Khayyám is a well-known example of the former, and the *Thousand and One Nights* of the latter. These nomads were also fanatical, capable of daring deeds and impulsive sacrifices, as these stories will testify. Their home was wherever they happened to pitch their tents. Semi-civilized when they began their conquests, they had no well-developed culture of their own, but both by nature and mode of life they were unusually

adaptable and ready to learn from the peoples whom they conquered.

Artists and scholars who had been expelled from the city of
Athens took refuge in the luxurious capital of the Sassanian-Persian Empire, and when the Arabs became masters of Persia (Iran),
they came in contact with the knowledge of the Western cultures
which had been salvaged from a decaying world. Their caliphs
were instrumental in opening new universities in which such subjects as geometry, geography, and medicine were taught and alge-
bra was devised. Although the nomads enjoyed the luxuries and
other advantages of their conquest, they found it difficult to settle
down. As a result, they became world travelers, acquiring knowledge and conveying it to the different peoples of their vast empire.
If as conquerors they were ruthlessly destructive of life and property, it is to their credit that much of the classic literature of the
ancient world has been preserved.

The western Moslems were orthodox, but the Mohammedans in
the East, including Persia, did not literally follow the teachings of
the Koran, which forbade the representation of any living thing.
When Mohammed ordered his followers to convert the infidel to
the Islamic faith, he excluded those people who had sacred books,
thus the Jews and Christians who had the Bible were spared. In
their rush to conquer, the Arabs did not trouble to find out whether
the Persians too had a sacred book, so they forced all of them (with
the exception of the above-mentioned sects) to become Mohammedans. The book of the Persians was the Shah-nama or Book
of Kings.

PERSIAN ART IN THE ACHAEMENIAN DYNASTY

Under the Achaemenian dynasty (558-330 B.C.) Persia had
become a mighty empire with vast domains reaching from the
Indus to the Nile, from Ethiopia to Mesopotamia; likewise her art
had had a long and illustrious background. With such widespread
possessions, it is but natural that Persian art would eventually
assume something of a cosmopolitan air. Through a successful
combination of native forms and borrowed motifs tastefully rear-

ranged, the Persians achieved a new style characterized by a heightened elegance, a clear-cut precision of line, harmonious color, and superb technical skill.

Pre-Achaemenian pottery with geometric and stylized animal decorations has been found in Susa and other ancient cities. Some of it has been dated as early as 1000 B.C. A branch of Iranian nomads known as Scythians produced fine bronze vessels during the sixth and fourth centuries B.C. The originality and inventiveness of their abstract and conventionalized animal designs indicated a great degree of sensitivity to rhythmic line and fine pattern. Bodies of animals, highly stylized and frequently reduced to extremely simplified forms, were elongated or condensed to serve as handles for vessels or for some other utilitarian purpose. An example of Scytho-Persian sculptured animal art, is the *Reindeer Ornament* on a gold plaque, which shows boldly vigorous movement and a fine decorative treatment of the horns (Plate 44).

THE PALACES OF DARIUS AND XERXES

The palaces which Darius and Xerxes erected at Persepolis and Susa were great columned halls set upon high platforms reached by monumental stairways adorned with figures and animal sculpture (Plate 45). The columns terminated in capitals composed of conventionalized animal forms set back to back in a crouching position. In Susa glazed bricks similar to those employed by the Assyrians and Babylonians produced a brilliant colorful effect on the exterior of the palaces, and like the sculpture of the Mesopotamian cities, the Persian carvings glorified the might and prowess of the kings.

The political power of Persia, crushed for a time by the conquest of Alexander, was restored by the Sassanian dynasty (226-642 A.D.). Under this feudalistic system of government, there was an increased demand for art. It now served the nobles as well as the king. The Oriental character of Iranian art, which had been preserved in some localities remote from the Greek centers, was revived.

The sumptuous brick palaces of the Sassanian kings followed

the Mesopotamian rather than the columnar style employed by the Achaemenians. The vast halls were vaulted. Ruins such as the arched structure of *Ctesiphon* give some idea of the extent and magnificence of these royal residences which had important constructional as well as ornamental features (Plate 44). The interior ivory-white walls of the palaces usually were covered with stucco embellished with vigorous designs and occasionally varied with dadoes of multi-colored tile mosaics, luxurious wall hangings, and jewel-studded rugs which are known to have been prized possessions of both kings and nobles. This great dynasty came to an end with the conquest of Persia by the Arabs.

The nomads found the more ancient palaces at Persepolis in ruins, but the vast vaulted halls of the Sassanians still remained. Fortunately the Arabs were wise enough to utilize the rich Persian culture as a basis for their own. The Persian craftsmen, who had now become Mohammedans, did not forget their ancient heritage, and the Sassanian style of pottery, metal work, and decorations for buildings, largely Oriental in character, persisted long after the dynasty had fallen.

MOSQUES IN AFRICA, IRAN, AND SPAIN

Living in tents, the Moslems naturally knew little about the construction of buildings; therefore they were content to leave structural problems to the natives of the various countries which they invaded. Activated by the tremendous amount of enthusiasm which Islam communicated to its adherents, these native builders became as fanatical as the nomads, and in time, mosques, palaces, and caravanseries sprang up throughout the conquered territory. On every oasis that dotted the desert there arose white cities with fantastic domes and slender minarets, which must have seemed more like a mirage than a reality to the nomads returning from a long journey over the hot sands.

During their relentless sweep across northern Africa and parts of Europe and Asia, the Arabs were in too great a hurry to stop to build. Instead, they seized churches or temples wherever they found them and converted them into mosques by erecting minarets, hollowing out a niche, raising a pulpit, and installing a basin or fountain. Among the structures thus adapted to their use were the Greek *Parthenon* and Justinian's church, *Hagia Sophia*.

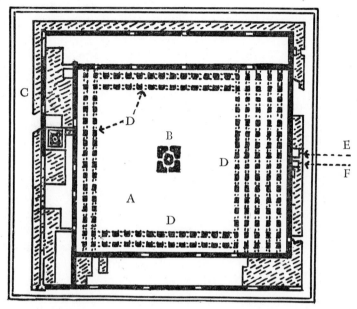

PLAN OF A MOHAMMEDAN MOSQUE

A. Court
B. Fountain
C. Girdle wall

D. Covered arcades
E. Niche (mihrab), pointing
    toward Mecca
F. Pulpit (nimbar)

Although the main purpose of the mosque was to provide a secluded place for daily prayer and a weekly sermon, some of the larger ones, like the Christian monasteries of the middle ages, provided living quarters for caretakers and travelers; hospitals; rooms or courts for schools; and storage space for provisions. Smaller mosques, meeting every requirement of the simple Mohammedan ritual, were usually rectangular or square in shape like the one of *Ibn Tulun* at Cairo. The court was surrounded on three sides by a plain wall pierced by an inconspicuous gate. The fourth wall was oriented toward Mecca. Within the walls there was an open court which contained a basin or fountain for the rite of purification before prayer. Surrounding this court on three sides were parallel rows of arcades covered with the flat roofs which are found in most countries with warm climates. For the comfort of the worshippers the arcades in front of the fourth wall were several rows deep. In the center of this wall was the *mihrab*, a niche, indicating the direction of the Holy City. Upon this niche the ecstatic gaze of the worshippers was fixed when they knelt to pray. To the right of the mihrab was the *nimbar*, a pulpit set upon a high platform approached by steps and covered by a small dome supported by columns. Here the Koran was read and the sermon preached.

The stone *Mosque of Sultan Hassan* at Cairo, built in the fourteenth century, was a more complex structure (Plate 46). Though a great dome over the mausoleum of the founder identified it as a tomb-mosque, it also contained numerous rooms for lodging, schools, and other purposes.

Perhaps the most characteristic features of the Moslem mosques were the minarets, slender square, octagonal, or cylindrical towers usually set at the four corners of the structure. Each had one or two balconies from which the *muezzin* called the people to prayer five times a day, a rite observed even when the Arabs were in the desert. They simply spread their *prayer rugs* (Plate 48) upon the sand and knelt down, bowing their heads to the ground. These prayer rugs were distinguished from the Oriental carpets which lined their tents by the niche-like shape woven in the center of the design. When they prayed they always turned the point toward Mecca. In the West, particularly in Spain, the simple arrangement of small courts surrounded by parallel arcades was superseded by enormous halls with multiple aisles, producing the effect of a forest of columns. *The Mosque of Cordova* is an example of this type (Plate 48). Columns for many of the arcades were taken from old Roman buildings which existed in profusion throughout the empire, notably in the northern part of Africa. If the column was too long the Arabs cut it off; if it happened to be too short, they built it up by inserting wedges of wood or brick. In either case the work was usually crude and hasty. Sometimes the column was turned upside down and the highly ornamented Corinthian capital favored by the Romans was found resting on the base. The flat wooden roofs over the arcades of the smaller mosques seemed too low for the greater width of these larger structures, many of which were entirely covered by vaults or domes. To increase the height as well as to support the vaulted roofs, the Moslems simply super-posed vertically one arcade upon another and, in some cases, they added a third row of columns.

The purely structural round arch which the Romans had em-ployed to support aqueducts or to pierce the thick walls of arenas now became pointed, cusped, or bent into horseshoe shape for decorative purposes. The wedge-shaped blocks of the arch were frequently painted in black and white or in alternating colors. Again, the inner surfaces of the arches were honeycombed with stalactite ornamentation made of molded or stamped plaster. Wooden or iron rods were used as ties near the springing to coun-teract the outward pressure of weakened arches. These rods, which became a common feature of a mosque, were still retained long after the Arabs had learned to construct a strong arch; they served as supports for the hanging lamps.

Due to such structural practices and the use of inferior materials, the meticulous precision of stone cutting and fitting which char-acterized the Greek temples and the strength and seeming inde-structibility of the Roman structures are not found in Moslem architecture. Greek and Roman buildings are still impressive though in ruins, whereas the ruins of the mosques and palaces of the Arabs remind one of the temporary buildings constructed for a movie set or a world's fair which, after a short span of usefulness, have been left to disintegrate. The nomadic Arabs were not con-cerned with erecting "houses of eternity."

Ornamentation was not confined to the interior of the mosques. Glazed tile decoration covered much of the exterior surface of the *Mosque of Isfahan* in Persia; but it was kept flat, leaving the clear-cut geometric silhouette of the structure unbroken by pro-jecting ornament (Plate 46). The entrance was a great arched portal flanked by tall minarets decorated with polychrome glazed bricks—some in relief, others flat like the wall tiles of ancient Babylon. In the windows were plaster frames filled with jewel-like colored glass.

In the eleventh century A.D., a Moslem Turkish tribe who captured Bagdad, the seat of the Mohammedan caliphate, also proved to be great patrons of art and learning. To their cities came scholars, scientists, poets, and artists from all parts of the Mohammedan empire. At this time Islamic art began to assume its final form. The Mohammedans continued to be more concerned with ornamentation than with structural problems, and the art of all the Mohammedan countries was influenced by the Persian predilection for purely decorative color combinations, the use of stylized human figures and animal forms, calligraphic inscriptions, floral decoration, and arabesques. *Arabesques* were at times a combination of calligraphy with floral forms, again intricate interlacings of geometric patterns without beginning or end. The geometric arabesque was a distinctive contribution of the Arabs, who are said to have been the greatest geometricians of their time. One can easily imagine that the star pattern so frequently encountered in Islamic design might have been suggested during long nights spent upon the desert with only the sky as a roof. These motifs were employed in the embellishment of brass objects inlaid with copper and silver, luxurious textiles, stucco wall decorations, and the famous Rhages pottery which was painted in gold-brown lustre.

PERSIAN MINIATURES

With such a rich inheritance, and unhampered by the restrictions of the Koran, it was to be expected that Persia also would have produced an important school of painting. For the most part Persian painting was small in scale: used as illustrations for books, as miniature portraits, and figures shown singly or in compositions designed to decorate the leaves of albums. The themes portrayed were usually hunts, games, drinking scenes, and romantic episodes, all highly decorative and intricately detailed, with an emphasis upon striking color effects (Plate 48). The areas between clear-cut lines, usually of uniform width, were filled with flat washes of color, thus producing the general effect of a mosaic. All figures were equally important regardless of their position in the composition. Garments were patterned and extremely decorative. Persian architecture, paintings, and industrial arts were enhanced by rich designs of gorgeous hues. Persian art was introduced into India by the Mogul descendants of Tamerlane, who had made a famous raid into that country in the sixteenth century. There art became even more imaginative than in Iran itself.

THE TAJ MAHAL

It would seem that the Moslem's dream of heaven finally materialized in two structures of incomparable beauty; one a tomb-mosque in India and the other, a palatial "castle in Spain." One of the great Moghuls, Shah Jehan, located his capital at Delhi in India, where on state occasions he occupied the famous peacock throne, but his favorite place of residence was Agra, on the right bank of the Jumna River. Although there are several fine examples of Mogul architecture within that city's limits, none can compare with the celebrated *Taj Mahal*, Crown of the Palace, so-called for the Shah's favorite wife, Mumtaz-i-Mahal, who bore that title (Plate 43). Upon this magnificent structure which became her tomb the Shah spared neither time nor expense.* For seventeen years the finest workmen, artists, and artisans alike toiled to make the *Taj Mahal* the most beautiful building in the world. For himself the Shah had planned to erect another larger tomb across the river which was to be connected with the *Taj* by a marble bridge in a corresponding style, but his sons revolted, made him a prisoner, and confined him to the Pearl Mosque of the fort from which he could look across the river and see the tomb of his wife. When he died, they buried him in a smaller tomb beside that of Mumtaz-i-Mahal.

Ustad Isa is said to have been the architect who planned the *Taj Mahal* (1631-1648 A.D.). Some say that he came from Turkey, others believe that he was a native of Shiraz in Persia, but all agree that he was an Asiatic, for his work is unmistakably Oriental in character. His plan for the *Taj* included the usual high square

---

* The cost has been estimated to be about thirty million dollars.

terrace or basement common to most Oriental structures. Rising from each angle of the square was a slender minaret. In the center of the terrace was an octagonal domed structure of white marble enhanced with the most intricate and delicate ornamentation which, however, was kept subservient to its simple structural shape. The spandrels around the arches and the most important architectural details were enriched by floral designs and arabesques, together with verses from the Koran in beautiful Mohammedan calligraphy. These decorations, made of semi-precious stones such as agate, bloodstone, turquoise, and jasper, were inlaid in the dazzling white marble. A shadowy ethereal appearance was produced by the deep-set arched doors, and windows screened with perforated marble carvings softened the glare of the brilliant sunlight.

Under the great central dome was placed the sarcophagus of Muntaz-i-Mahal and beside it the smaller tomb of the Shah. According to Mohammedan custom, the bodies were buried beneath the earth. Stairs led down to a basement or crypt in which there were tombs duplicating those above. It is said that every Friday when the Shah visited the tomb of his wife a coverlet of pearls was spread over her sarcophagus, but that has long since disappeared, as has the gold and silver screen that formerly surrounded her tomb. Today both tombs are enclosed by a marble screen so delicately carved that it resembles lace.

When the *Taj* was completed the Shah, according to legend, looked upon it and straightway ordered that the eyes of the architect should be put out; no other person, he said, could plan such a beautiful building, and among all buildings he wished the *Taj Mahal* to remain supreme. The remarkable beauty of the tomb is largely due to its fine proportions, its perfect symmetry, precious materials, exquisite carvings, colorful inlays, and the subordination of excessive ornamentation to its structural beauty. The central dome is flanked on either side by two smaller domes. Two smaller buildings, one of which may be seen on the right and the other on the left as one approaches from the main entrance, echo in miniature the larger structure just as the two smaller domes on either side complement the larger dome. Each façade has a great recessed doorway between deep-set windows—two on either side, placed one above the other. There are also two windows on the four narrower sides of the octagon. Like all Oriental buildings of great beauty, the *Taj* owes much to its setting. Spreading out to the principal gateway is a large garden with cypress-bordered lagoons. The central one, which is marble-lined and set with bronze fountains, reflects the loveliness of the tomb. Seen in the moonlight, which enhances its ethereal beauty, this shrine dedicated to the beloved wife of the Shah is most impressive.

THE ALHAMBRA

Perched high upon a wooded eminence overlooking the Spanish city of Granada was the *Alhambra,* the fortress-palace of the Moors, begun in the twelfth and completed in the thirteenth century. The top of the plateau, comprising about thirty-five acres, was entirely surrounded by reddish-brown crenelated walls studded with thirteen great towers. Since the *Alhambra* was a fort as well as a royal residence, there were ample quarters for soldiers, courtiers, retainers, and attendants in addition to the centrally located palace. The latter was partially destroyed in later times to make way for a residence which Charles V began and later abandoned because of an earthquake. However, upon the foundation which he had constructed, a Renaissance palace was subsequently built and still remains an eyesore to many who visit the *Alhambra.* Despite neglect, vandalism, earthquakes, wars, and time this stronghold of the Moors is still fairly well preserved. Parts of it have been carefully restored by a young Spanish architect, so one may still get at least a vague idea of its former splendor.

The palace itself, of the same reddish-brown stone with roofs of tile, was plain on the exterior in the Oriental manner. In contrast to its severe outward appearance, the light and airy interior was like a palace in a fairy-tale. Everywhere there were decorations rhythmic in line and gorgeous in color; ceilings were gilded; arabesques covered the upper walls; and many of the wainscotings were tiled. Impressive halls and miniature rooms of dream-like beauty were built about two large, and a number of smaller, courts. The largest was the *Court of Myrtles* and the most famous, the

Court of the Lions (Plate 47). A fountain in the latter court contained an alabaster basin mounted on twelve conventionalized marble lions, and about the walls were galleries similar to those in the *Court of Myrtles*. The galleries, screened with open-work marble carvings, permitted the women to take exercise and to view the gardens and courts below while remaining unseen themselves.

Aqueducts brought cool water from the mountains to service the fountains, luxurious baths, and the most important rooms of the palace. The overflow from the fountains was conducted through marble-lined channels to water the gardens of roses, myrtles, oleanders, and orange trees. Everywhere there was the sound of rippling water flowing through conduits both above the ground and under the floors. To the nomads, accustomed to life on the desert, water was a most highly-prized possession. The song birds of the *Alhambra*, particularly the nightingales, are famous. Amid this magnificent setting with the snow-capped Sierra Nevadas in the distance the Moors lived a life of langorous ease and Oriental luxury, until the armies of Ferdinand and Isabella drove them out of Spain (1492 A.D.). It is said that tears came to the eyes of the departing Moorish monarch as he turned to look for the last time at his lost paradise. His mother, noticing this evidence of emotion, unsympathetically asked, "Why do you cry like a woman for what you could not hold like a man?"

ARCHES, DOMES, AND COLORFUL TILES

The styles of mosques, tombs, and palaces varied in different localities, but curiously enough there was a great similarity in Mohammedan architecture. Pointed and horseshoe arches, domes either pointed or round, colorful arabesques, and intricate carvings were to be found in all parts of the empire. Although the Arab himself may not have taken part in the actual construction, the imprint of his taste makes it quite apparent that he has passed that way. It was in the exotic type of decoration that his mind found its fullest imaginative expression. He decorated his wainscotings with multi-colored tiles set in geometric patterns; the upper walls with arabesques (intricate interlaced conventionalized floral, or geometric patterns including angular Kufic or the more cursive Mohammedan calligraphy) which were either stamped or carved in plaster; and divided many of the ceilings and arches into cells

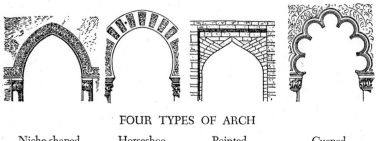

FOUR TYPES OF ARCH

Niche-shaped   Horseshoe   Pointed   Cusped

(Hartmann)

dripping with gilded stalactite ornamentation. In the best of his architecture this ornamentation is to a greater degree subordinated to the structural forms.

The nomad created an empire by conquering many separate countries, and his religion united the different peoples. Over his vast empire he spread his art like a beautiful dream, and, like a dream, much of it has vanished. The Arab himself has shed his rôle of conqueror and returned to that obscurity from whence he came. In recent times, however, with "black gold" flowing in from the oil wells of Iraq and Arabia, wealth has come again to the Arabian world, and disturbances in India and Palestine have once more aroused the militant spirit of the Mohammedans.

OUTLINE OF MOHAMMEDAN AND ANCIENT PERSIAN ART

PLACE: Arabia, Persia, India, Northern Africa, Southeastern Europe—Spain.

TIME: Sassanian-Persian—226-642 A.D. Mohammedan-Persian, etc.—641-1736 A.D.

BACKGROUND: The Mohammedans, a people with no real nation, were held together by religion. Arabs were quick to learn from the inhabitants of the countries they conquered. Universities were soon established in the East and the West as far as Spain. The restless nomads, after converting the natives of conquered countries to Mohammedanism, often moved on leaving them in charge, thus weakening their empire until the Mohammedans were reduced to a second-rate power; but Islam is still one of the most widespread religions of the world. Mohammedan art, beautiful in its own way, has had no lasting influence in the western world.

ARCHITECTURE: Mosques, tombs, palaces—plain geometric structures overlaid with complex and detailed surface decorations, especially on the interior walls. Distinctive features: domes with flame-like lines (called lotus, bulbous, or onion domes) pointed and "eccentric arches," arcades, galleries, minarets. Materials: usually brick, but some stone and marble. Decorations: glazed brick and tiles, inlaid semi-precious stones or colored marbles, and arabesques stamped or modeled on plaster. Style varied in different localities. Contribution: original devices for supporting octagonal and round domes over a square space (not discussed in text).

SCULPTURE: Very little monumental sculpture. The nearest approach was the conventionalized lions of the fountain in the Alhambra.

PAINTING: Chiefly notable in India and Persia. *Persian painting:* subject-matter included romantic scenes, hunts, games. Clearly outlined figures. Flat colors laid mosaic-like between the lines. Accessory figures given the same importance as those of central interest. Detailed, colorful, decorative. Later under Chinese influence lines became freer and more rhythmic and drawing in general was more naturalistic. As a rule lines remained uniform in width. Their lines never attained the expressive power found in Chinese paintings.

BIBLIOGRAPHY

ARNOLD, Sir T. W., *Painting in Islam* (Oxford University Press, N. Y., 1928).
——, and Guillaume, Alfred (eds.), *The Legacy of Islam* (Oxford University Press, N. Y., 1931).
DIMAND, M. S., *A Handbook of Mohammedan Decorative Arts* (Metropolitan Museum, N. Y., 1930).
GROUSSET, René, *The Civilizations of the East,* Vol I. (Alfred A. Knopf, Inc., N. Y., 1931).
IRVING, Washington, *The Alhambra* (Thomas Y. Crowell, N. Y., 1911).
POPE, A. U., *An Introduction to Persian Art Since the Seventh Century* (Charles Scribner's Sons, N. Y., 1931).
Ross, Sir E. D. (ed.), *Persian Art* (London, 1930).

CHAPTER VIII

Byzantine and Early Christian Art

LEAVING the blue waters of the Aegean, sailing northward, one passes through the Dardanelles (the famous Hellespont of ancient times), the Sea of Marmora, and the Bosporus to reach the Black Sea. Overlooking the Bosporus at a point where Europe and Asia almost meet is the fascinating city of Istanbul. Its harbor, the Golden Horn, is one of the finest in the world. Thus favorably situated, it has long been the gateway to the East through which have come the silks of China, the magnificent textiles and rugs of Persia and objects of silver, ivory, and gold from Africa and Asia Minor. Here the Western world came in close contact with Oriental culture.

Istanbul was formerly the ancient Greek city of Byzantium, which the Roman Emperor, Constantine, chose for his capital and renamed Constantinople. He rebuilt the city in the Roman way, and by 331 A.D. this "New Rome" which, like the ancient capital on the banks of the Tiber, was set on seven hills, was magnificent and luxurious. During Justinian's reign (527-565) it had a population of a million inhabitants.

The *Great Palace* was a fortified city within itself, comprising fourteen palaces, many smaller mansions and private baths, a university, theatres, and basilica. These buildings were connected and adorned with porticoes, marble steps, and Hellenistic bronze and marble statues brought from Asia Minor, Greece, and Sicily. Beyond the palaces upon a high promontory rose the *Forum Augusteum,* and near-by to the west was the *Great Hippodrome.* Here over the emperor's box stood the *bronze horses* which the Greek Lysippus had made for the city of Chios. These "much traveled horses" were subsequently taken by a conquering Venetian general to adorn the church of St. Mark's, that imposing Byzantine church of his native city (Plate 52). Later Napoleon, looking upon them with a covetous eye, included them in the loot of art treasures which he took to Paris and housed in the Louvre. However, they afterwards were restored to Venice and there they may still be seen above the central portal of St. Mark's.

Despite the appearance of imperialistic splendor reflecting that of Rome, the luxurious life of the ruling classes was patterned after that of the decaying Greek cities of Antioch and Alexandria; consequently the general character of Constantinople was more Hellenistic than Roman. The intellectual curiosity which had its beginnings in Greece persisted. A great library was established, and here for a thousand years while the Western world was more or less in a state of chaos the writings of the early church fathers as well as the remains of classical literature were preserved.

The population of Constantinople, part Oriental, part barbarian, part Greek and part Latin, was as cosmopolitan as that of imperial Rome. Christian churches were set beside pagan temples, and, as in the ancient city on the Tiber, there were as many different creeds as nationalities. Christianity grew in power until its ascendancy was established throughout the entire empire. The Emperor and his court, a few favored families, and the dignitaries of the church lived in Oriental luxury at the expense of the people, who were heavily taxed. In order to divert the minds of the populace from their constant state of poverty the Eastern rulers, like their predecessors in the West, planned chariot races, games, contests, and other amusements which were held at the great Hippodrome.

JUSTINIAN AND THEODORA RULE IN CONSTANTINOPLE

It was at the Hippodrome that Justinian first saw Theodora, the daughter of a wild-animal trainer who had taken her there at an early age to appear in the mimes of the circus. The actor's profession was not highly regarded in those days and certainly it was far beneath the rank of one who some day would ascend the throne. Though born a barbarian, Justinian was highly educated and had rendered valuable service to his ignorant uncle whom he was to succeed. In return for these favors the latter by a special dispensation raised Theodora to patrician rank so that his nephew might marry her. After a stormy and eventful life, Theodora at the age of twenty became the wife of Justinian and Empress of the Roman Empire, and by the consent of the Emperor her power was equal to his own. She soon became versed in the formalities of the court, surrounded herself with many attendants, and ruled like any haughty empress who had been born to the purple. Under their administration the arts flourished and *Hagia Sophia,* the finest church in Christendom, was erected.

Justinian's reign was especially notable for his recovery of parts of Italy and the north African provinces which had been lost to the barbarians, for his contribution to jurisprudence, and for his extensive building activities. Although a lawmaker himself, in the opinion of some of his biographers, he, like most of his immediate predecessors, was not always wise or just. His inordinate vanity led him to such extravagancies in his building program, his personal life, and the elaborate ceremonies of his court that the resources of his empire were severely taxed.

The tremendous amount of building activity beginning in Constantine's time and increasing during Justinian's administration attracted many artists from Asia Minor. These Hellenistic sculptors and architects had been too long in contact with the luxury of the Orient to retain the austere simplicity and calm serenity which characterized the Greek work of the fifth and fourth centuries B.C. Furthermore, art at this time was subservient to a powerful Christian church which had become authoritative and dogmatic. Religious edifices now matched imperial palaces in magnificence. The Byzantine builders, however, still retained the Greek admiration for structural clarity. The luxurious appearance was manifested almost entirely on the "enveloping skin" of the building which comprised the glittering mosaics on the walls, the patterned marbles covering the floors, and the lace-like carvings of the capitals of columns and framework of the windows. There were elaborate enamel and gem-encrusted screens about the altar. Byzantine architects made wide use of mosaic in their murals. Composed of small pieces of colored stone or glass set in cement, these mosaics brought vibrant color to the dim interior. This difficult medium necessitated the use of a flat, unrealistic design as shown in *The Empress Theodora and Her Retinue* at St. Vitale, Ravenna and in *Making Wine* at Santa Costanza in Rome (Plates 50 and 51). Decoration on the pagan temples, when employed at all, was done with restraint, whereas the adornment of churches bespoke a taste for extravagant display. This was partly due to increased wealth, partly to the impact of Oriental culture, and for the most part to the imperialistic attitude of the powerful Christian church.

CHRISTIANITY EAST AND WEST

From the beginning we have seen that art has been inseparably linked with religion. The Byzantine Empire, so-called from Byzantium, the ancient town, succeeded the Roman Empire and marked the end of the city-state which had produced the art and literature known to us as classical. The pagan religion of the Greeks and Romans was likewise destined to disappear gradually, and henceforth the Christian religion would be dominant in the Western world. Since it would also be the chief inspiration of art until the end of the Italian Renaissance, it might be well to consider more carefully the rise to power of the Christian church.

Simultaneously with the decline of the power of Rome and the transfer of the imperial capital to the East, the church was growing in temporal as well as spiritual power, and even the barbarians of the West were accepting the new faith. Churches had been built in Syria, and both monasteries and churches had been established in Egypt and northern Africa. Constantinople, because of its strategic position, early became the center from which missions were sent out to western Europe.

Asiatic in origin like most of the great religions of the world, Christianity had its beginnings in Palestine among the Jewish people in a part of the world which had already felt the influence of Hellenistic culture. To the Mosaic law and the chronicles of the Old Testament of the Hebrews the Christians added the four accepted Gospels recounting events in the life of Christ. These, together with letters and other literature, made the Christian Bible, in which the harsher commandments of the ancient Hebraic scriptures were tempered by the doctrine of brotherly love as set forth in the New Testament.

Christianity was only one of a number of Oriental religions introduced into Rome in the early centuries of this era. Paganism still persisted, although it was slowly dying out. The intellectuals had accepted the teachings of the Stoics and Epicurean philosophers who also were stressing the brotherhood of man, but the inimitable personality of Jesus had a special appeal to the lower classes, for His teachings held out the hope of future happiness to those who had been oppressed. They were also impressed by the fact that the twelve disciples of Christ gave up their worldly goods, went forth penniless to preach the gospel, and lived in circumstances somewhat comparable to their own. This idea of poverty and humility exerted a great influence upon the spiritual thought of the Middle Ages. In the beginning, the wealthy were more hesitant to accept a religion which stressed the idea that it was "easier for a camel to go through the eye of a needle than for a rich man to enter into the kingdom of heaven," for they were not yet quite prepared to relinquish their many possessions.

The first Christians in Rome attracted little attention from the ruling classes, who merely considered them rather strange until they refused to worship the emperor on feast days or bow down before any god other than their own. Like the Jews, they held themselves separate and apart from the populace. Emperor worship was not strictly enforced, however, until the emperors began to feel less sure of their power and more fearful of a popular revolt. Then they began to take certain measures to protect themselves, such as passing a law to prohibit anyone from becoming a Christian. Notwithstanding, the Christians continued to meet in secret, thereby making themselves still more unpopular with the government. Much unfavorable propaganda, including tales of atrocities and sedition, was circulated by their enemies, and persecution began in earnest. It reached its height in the reign of the infamous Nero who, so it has been recorded, had the Colosseum lighted at night by torches made of bodies of burning Christians. Although this is probably an exaggeration, such incidents doubtless did occur, if on a smaller scale. The emperor Valens legalized their religion and ceased to persecute the Christians, for he observed that when one martyr died many new converts were added to the church.

In the early Christian communities, founded by different missionaries each of whom had his own interpretation of the meaning of the new religion, conflicting beliefs naturally sprang up, prophets claimed to have divine revelations, and in some localities the people still practiced the rites of the old religions. So-called heresies arose, and there were heated discussions concerning beliefs or doctrines. One of the most conspicuous of these dissensions during the Roman Empire period was that of Arianism. The Arians held that Christ occupied a position secondary to that of God the Father, and that He was not equal with Him as the orthodox Christians believed him to be. In order to settle these and similar disputes and to bring about some semblance of unity in the church the leaders began to organize the different communities scattered about the entire Mediterranean area. Important centers such as Alexandria and Antioch were among those chosen to settle all controversies and serve as models for others to follow. The church at Rome, of which St. Peter was reputed to be the first bishop, was early selected as the foremost authority in doctrine. The head of this church was the Pope. His decision became final. Archbishops presided over the churches of important cities and bishops over those of smaller communities. Under them were lesser officials, the clergy. The people were designated as the laity. The organization of the church became so effective in time that it began to assume a monarchical character.

As the church grew in wealth and temporal power, the bishops considered themselves equals of the rulers of the Empire. They dressed themselves in costly garments which rivaled imperial robes and sat at the same table with the emperors themselves. Though the Pope of Rome nominally became head of the entire church, he never exercised complete dominion over its eastern branch.

In the first centuries the Roman Christians worshipped in a room of the house of some one of the more affluent members of the group. This arrangement seemed adequate in the beginning, for Jesus had said that "Where two or three are gathered together in My Name, there shall I be also." Nevertheless, as persecution increased it became necessary to find a burial place for the many martyrs. Since the members of the flock desired to be close together in death, they followed the old Roman custom of forming an organization to furnish and finance a common mausoleum. Outside of the walls of the city were large abandoned quarries which the Romans had used as a source for procuring limestone, useful in the making of cement. These subterranean galleries, with a few necessary changes such as the straightening of a wall here and there and the reinforcement of roofs where needed, served for both burial purposes and places of worship.

At intervals intersecting galleries formed spaces which were enlarged and converted into chapels. Here the tomb of a famous martyr or an important church official served as the altar. In some rare cases these chapels were lighted by means of a carefully concealed shaft which extended above ground, but for the most part the passages were dark and damp with only artificial lighting. The Christians overlooked these inconveniences because here they could worship in peace. The *catacombs*, containing the bodies of the martyrs and many of their venerated relics, attracted numerous visitors during the first five centuries of the Middle Ages, and some of the pilgrims have left valuable manuscripts describing these journeys. Eventually churches were built over the entrances to the underground chambers where the saints had been interred.

Oriental artists who had come to the Imperial City, together with the Romans, decorated the walls of the catacombs with paintings, such as *Christian at Prayer* (Plate 51). Naturally, since the Christians had no traditions of their own other than the Oriental and pagan themes and styles to which they were accustomed, the catacomb paintings reflected both pagan and Oriental influences. During the first century Old Testament themes furnished the subject-matter. Classical themes persisted, but they were imbued with a new meaning. Orpheus, taming the wild beast with the music of his lyre, came to represent Christ in an unbelieving world. It was not until after the first four centuries that artists began to depict scenes of the Crucifixion and to represent Christ as the bearded figure which has become the characteristic ideal of all subsequent Christian art. In earlier sculpture in the round, and also in painting, Christ was represented as a beardless youth. Such

Two Doves and a Vase. Design from a catacomb painting. (Perret)

figures as the calf-bearer, a young man carrying an animal on his shoulders, had been common in Greek art since Archaic times. A similar youthful figure clothed in the garments of a shepherd now represented *Christ as the Good Shepherd* (Plate 51). These are only a few of the themes employed in the art of the early Christian era, but they serve to give some idea of the beginnings of the development of Christian art.

Since their ritual was quite different from the rites of the religions of Greece and Rome, the old temples were not suited to Christian use; furthermore the new sect had gradually become prejudiced against anything pagan. As usual, when a need arose for a structure to fit a new purpose the builders sought the most suitable one of those already in existence. The old Roman basilicas with the round apse at one end seemed best to meet the needs of the Christians. The large central aisle which they called the nave housed the congregation and the terminating apse contained the altar. Here the drama of the mass was performed and undisturbed by outside noises, the people listened to sermons and the reading of the Bible.

The environs of Rome furnished building material. The old pagan temples no longer in use provided polished stones and carved columns and became a chief source of supply for the new churches. In some cases the columns were not of equal heights, but that seemed to make little difference to the builders who raised or lowered a base at will and proceeded with their work. If in some part of the church a marble facing was needed the older structures supplied it.

The Christians in the West concentrated their interest on the altar located in the apse; therefore they preferred the basilica with a ground floor plan shaped like a Latin cross with one arm longer than the other. The eastern church, with interest focused on the center, assumed the shape of a Greek cross with a dome over the intersection of the arms which usually were of equal length. *Hagia Sophia* was a combination of the two.

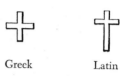

Greek   Latin

CROSSES

JUSTINIAN BUILDS HAGIA SOPHIA

It has been related that when Justinian began the erection of the great church he established temporary quarters near the site of the building where he could personally supervise the daily progress of construction. He appointed Anthemius of Tralles, both a noted mathematician and an architect, as master of the works and Isodorus of Miletus as his assistant. Ten thousand workers labored for six years (532-537) to produce this magnificent church (Plate 49).

Permanent building material in the vicinity of Constantinople was scarce; consequently bricks were used for the main part of the structure. But for its decoration Justinian commanded the governors of the provinces to furnish the finest marbles and most precious materials, including stones such as porphyry, marble, and jasper, gold for ornaments and backgrounds of the mosaics, and precious stones for the decorations of the furnishings. Both materials and transportation were costly but the emperor spared no expense.* Indeed, the result of his efforts was so satisfying that when the church was dedicated with ceremonial pomp and feasting Justinian is said to have raised his arms to heaven and cried, "I have surpassed thee, O Solomon!"

The plan of the church, like that of the Roman basilica, provided for a large central nave and side aisles. There was an atrium or open court and a double narthex or columned porch at the en-

* A modern writer has estimated that the cost of the church would amount to about seventy-five million dollars in our currency.

trance, and the opposite wall was interrupted by the apse. The
most striking difference between *Hagia Sophia* and the old Roman
basilica is that a circular dome spanned most of the long nave.

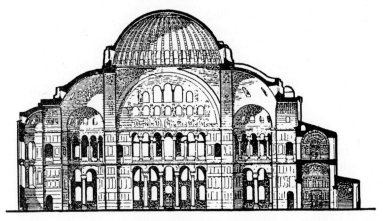

Cross-section of Hagia Sophia (Reber)

Constructing a dome over a complicated structure with nave and
side aisles was a far more difficult problem than erecting a round
dome over the thick walls of a circular building, as in the case of
the Pantheon. Fortunately Anthemius was a mathematician as
well as an architect. He solved the problem by the application of
geometry. Geometrically stated, "the four pendentives at the angles
of a square filling the triangular spaces between the square of the
sub-structure and the inscribed circle of the base of the dome are
segments of a hemisphere whose diameter is equal to the diameter
of the square." The problem was solved architecturally as follows:
Heavy piers were erected at the corners of the square. These piers
were connected by enormous arches paralleling the sides of the
square. Curvilinear triangles (pendentives), resting on the piers,
rose upward to the height of the crowns of the arches, thus forming
a circular opening which could easily be covered with a separate
dome. The dome of *Hagia Sophia* was 107 feet in diameter and
180 feet high. On the east and west sides of the central space the
semi-domes covered the remainder of the nave and counteracted

some of the outward thrust of the great dome. On the north and south heavy exterior buttresses served as reinforcements.

The Egyptians had known the arch but seldom employed it. The Romans had attained grandiose ef- fects with it, although they often ren- dered it lifeless by moulding it in concrete; but the Byzantine builders reached still greater heights by the use of this dynamic type of construction.

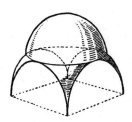

Dome on pendentives

Hagia Sophia on the exterior is not un- usually impressive. Its walls are plain and unadorned either with carving or mosaic. We have been told that the western wall, which contains the central portal known as the Golden Gate, was at one time sheathed with colored marble. In modern times the entire exterior has been covered with a background of yellow paint upon which horizontal reddish brown stripes have been laid. Fortunately these have been toned by time and the weather so that they are not quite so pro- nounced. Rising above the flat walls in the square center part of the building is the low circular dome with its semi-domes. The upper walls are broken by semi-cylindrical forms which appear be- neath the semi-domes which they support.

In Justinian's time one entering the atrium of *Hagia Sophia*, then passing into the dimly lighted double narthex adorned with colorful mosaics and fine veined marbles, and through the Golden Gate, must have been overcome by the magnificence of the shining interior (Plate 49). Through the forty windows set close together in the base of the dome brilliant sunlight poured unobstructed. The entire nave was a great light space enclosed by walls inter- rupted by the arcades of the lower story. The direct light flowing in from the windows of the dome and tympana of the north and south arches, together with the indirect lighting of aisles and gal- leries, gave an ethereal aspect to the interior. The light from its close-set windows tended to dematerialize the drum, and according to the old writers "the dome seemed to flare." The darkest of the mosaics concentrated at the top, together with the light drum, made the dome seem as if it were floating in air. The shadowy aisles were the only parts of the church which suggested a dim religious light. By optical illusion the walls and even the four great piers no longer appeared to function as supports. As in a theatre with artificial lighting objects may be made to disappear entirely, so here with natural lighting piers became merely decorated surfaces, and, walls, glowing curtains which enclosed brilliant space.

The lower parts of the walls of *Hagia Sophia* were covered with richly-hued veined marbles. The upper spaces, the roofs, and the great dome were adorned with multi-colored mosaics resplendent upon backgrounds of gold. These mosaics were made of little cubes of *tesserae,* glass, marble, or semi-precious stones set upon a cement base. Pure gold leaf, which covered the stones used in the gold background, caught and reflected the light that poured through the windows. The galleries of the second floor were set apart for the women, who sat behind loosely woven curtains of cloth of gold which afforded privacy, yet permitted them to observe the ceremonies.

The sanctuary was separated from the nave by a silver barrier. We are told that the altar and the bishop's chair were of gold encrusted with gems. Upon and about the altar were thousands of candlesticks of pure gold. Elaborately designed golden censers, crosses, enameled statues, reliquaries, tiaras, and diadems were used in the ritual. The emperor and the patriarch were clothed in robes so heavily adorned with metal and other precious materials that they could hardly move. It is recorded that spectators moving along beside them attempted to read the legends pictured in the colorful embroidery of their garments which were stiff and storied like the mosaic walls of their churches. Such robes may be seen upon the immobile figures shown in the mosaics of a church in Ravenna where *Justinian* and *Theodora* are represented with their attendants. Plate 50 shows the Empress with her group.

Still in good repair, considering its extreme age and the shocks of many earthquakes, this church has stood for centuries while around it empires rose and fell. The city itself had been repeatedly stormed by the barbarians, but it held firm until it was captured and pillaged by the crusaders (1204) and finally fell to the Turks (1453). Most of *Hagia Sophia's* treasure was confiscated.

The Turks converted the church into a Mohammedan mosque by adding minarets from which the muezzin called the faithful to prayer. They also covered the interior decorations symbolic of the Christian religion, with matting, plaster, and whitewash. Over this they hung huge circular plaques bearing the name of Allah. The patterned marble floor was covered with carpets and prayer rugs pointing toward the *mihrab,* a niche which was erected off center and oriented with respect to the Holy City of Mecca. In recent years the Turkish government has permitted archaeologists and scholars to uncover some of the original mosaics for scientific study, and in 1935 they stripped the building of some of its Mohammedan symbols and transformed it into a national monument. Now, no longer a mosque into which only the faithful may enter, its doors are open and the former glory of the fine mosaics on its walls is gradually being revealed by the efforts of skilled and patient workmen under the direction of Professor Whittemore, an American scholar.

Hagia Sophia, one of the most impressive domed structures of the world, is so tremendous in scale and so luxurious in its appointments that human beings inside its walls are dwarfed into insignificance and all but lost in the brilliance of the light from the dome, which is reflected by the glowing mosaics.

OUTLINE OF BYZANTINE AND EARLY CHRISTIAN ART

TIME: Early Christian art in the West: 4th to 6th centuries. Byzantine art centered in the East: 4th to 15th centuries.

BACKGROUND: Roman Empire divided into eastern and western sections. Decline and fall of Rome. In West: widespread poverty, confusion, and unrest. Barbarians converted to Christianity and, in time, assimilated by Latins. Church rose to power. Pope became preëminent. *In the East* power centered in Constantinople. Government, absolute monarchy. Influence extended over Asia Minor, Syria, Egypt, Greece, Ravenna, and other cities of Eastern Italy. People heavily taxed to support luxurious court and build magnificent churches in Constantinople. Church—both wealthy and powerful—like the empire was split into two factions: the Roman Catholic church in the West, and the Greek church in the East. Both still exist. After 7th century, constant conflict between Christians and Mohammedans.

ARCHITECTURE: *Early Christian:* most popular style was basilican. Central type (shape of Greek cross) also employed. Structural elements: post and lintel combined with arcades and vaulting, the latter usually confined to side aisles and semicircular dome over apse. Additions to old basilica form: atrium —an enclosed court; narthex—a vestibule; and transepts—cross aisles between nave and apse. The atrium and narthex are reminiscent of the Roman house. Decorations: translucent marbles, from pagan temples and mosaics. *Byzantine:* churches of central type or combination of the two like Hagia Sophia. Use of dome and vault of eastern origin. Most conspicuous contribution, the pendentive, invented to enable builders to cover square space with round dome. Windows in lower part of dome or in drum, which supports dome. Unimpressive on exterior, glowing with color on interior.

SCULPTURE: *In the Catacombs,* pagan sculpture imbued with new meaning. Classical figure with animal slung across shoulder represented Christ, the Good Shepherd. Bas-reliefs on sarcophagi were filled with emblems, such as peacocks symbolizing eternal life. *In the East:* Semitic and Islamic prejudice, the former against graven images and the latter against representation of living things, brought about the destruction of sculpture during the iconoclastic controversy. Carving restricted to small ivories such as those used for book covers or other church furnishings, to capitals of columns either adorned with patterns of basket-like weavings and raised patterns with undercut backgrounds, or variations of the Romanized Corinthian order.

PAINTING: *In the Catacombs,* paintings on walls and ceilings contained pagan forms adapted to Christian symbolism. In style, a somewhat crude reflection of Roman painting. *In the East:* encaustic—wax—paintings with strongly outlined figures and faces with large dark eyes. Portable icons— sacred pictures—painted on wooden panels or enameled on metal were hung on screens about the altar or placed on walls of homes. Like the sculpture of the early times, paintings were designed to instruct the illiterate. In both sections of the Empire manuscripts of excellent quality were produced. Mosaics, brilliant masses of flat color—flat decorative style. Symbols give literary meaning to stiff figure compositions.

BIBLIOGRAPHY

DALTON, O. M., *Byzantine Art and Archaeology* (Oxford University Press, N. Y., 1911).

LETHABY, W. R., and SWAINSON, Harold, *The Church of Sancta Sophia at Constantinople* (The Macmillan Co., N. Y., 1894).

MOREY, C. R., *Christian Art* (Longmans, Green & Co., N. Y., 1935).

SWIFT, Emerson H., *Hagia Sophia* (Columbia University Press, N. Y., 1940).

TALBOT RICE, David, *Byzantine Art* (Oxford University Press, N. Y., 1935).

WHITTEMORE, Thomas, *The Mosaics of St. Sophia at Istanbul* (Oxford University Press, N. Y., 1933).

CHAPTER IX

Medieval Art—Romanesque

W HILE the Byzantine empire was prospering in the East,
western Europe (500-1000 A.D.) was overrun by German
barbarians who ravaged the countryside and plundered the un-
fortified Roman cities. After creating havoc they collected a large
amount of booty and moved on, for as yet they had no desire for a
settled existence. Later, other barbarians, coveting the luxuries enjoyed by Mediterranean peoples, forsook the wild roving life, acquired land, and became a part of the aristocratic landholding
group. Since their huge estates were maintained by servile tenants
and dependents, they could still indulge in their favorite activities:
hunting and fighting.

By the seventh century the invaders had gained control of most
of western Europe. Out of the mingling of the barbarians, natives,
and Romans, all speaking different dialects, came the modern
Romance languages which were to become important factors in
determining the boundaries of the European states in the West.
The architecture of the period, also akin to the Roman, after having
been subjected to barbarian influence finally developed into a distinctive style called Romanesque.

In the provinces where the barbarian element predominated
government was unstable, but in sections where numbers of
Romans remained some order was established by giving the invaders responsible positions. During the ninth and tenth centuries
conditions went from bad to worse. The last, but not least destructive, of the barbarians were the Norsemen or Vikings from the
Scandinavian peninsula. These hardy pirates, coming in swift long
boats with multi-colored sails, burned the towns and devastated the
country, sparing neither church nor monastery. As early as the

ninth century they had challenged the power of Charlemagne and sailed the Mediterranean as far as Constantinople.

THE NORSEMEN

We are particularly concerned with the Norsemen who finally settled in Normandy, adopted the customs, religion, and languages of that province, and left the imprint of their boundless energy and fanciful imagery upon the great Romanesque churches and Gothic cathedrals of France.

Shrewd traders as well as hard fighters, some of the Northmen became merchants and carried on commerce with other lands from which they brought new ideas as well as new goods to people of the backward West. Others became landholders and employed serfs and vassals. Fortunately these barbarians displayed a greater capacity for organization than some of their predecessors. Impelled by their tremendous energy and inspired by aggressive leadership, they embarked upon military conquests both on the continent and in Britain. In 1066 A.D. England fell to William the Conqueror, who introduced the Romanesque way of building into the land across the Channel. He and his wife Matilda erected the two great churches, *La Trinité*, the Abbaye-aux-Dames, and *St. Etienne*, the Abbaye-aux-Hommes, in the city of Caen in northern France.

The Norsemen, like other nomadic peoples, confined their possessions to animals or movable things. They liked fine horses, effective weapons adorned with intricately wrought designs, luxurious garments, and ornate jewelry. Coming originally from the steppes of Asia, they had become acquainted with the arts of the older civilizations and had acquired great skill in metal-work. To the church they gave gifts of metal set with semi-precious stones. Kings and queens donated crowns. The iron crown which the Pope placed upon the head of Charlemagne, was really made of gold; inside was an iron ring said to have been fashioned from a nail of the true cross. Altars were encased in a gem-set sheath of gold and silver or covered with a priceless textile or oriental carpet. This barbaric love of richness partly accounts for the magnificent furnishings of medieval churches which were dedicated to

Christianity, a religion springing from humble beginnings. Like the Greeks, who dedicated to their gods the games which they themselves enjoyed, the barbarians gave to their churches the richly decorated ornaments and articles which they most valued.

DIVISION WITHIN THE CHURCH

The different denominations of the Christian church that we have today did not exist at that time. The medieval church was the Catholic church with its two divisions: the eastern Orthodox with its authority centered in Byzantium; and the Roman Catholic headed by the Pope in the West. The two factions arose from differences in interpretation of the Christian doctrine.

During the eighth and ninth centuries much of the ancient Greek art as well as the early Byzantine, was deliberately destroyed. The iconoclastic party which was strong in the East objected to human likenesses of Christ and other sacred persons, contending that they were idols. They were also opposed to relic worship, but after long controversy, the Western Christians still continued to adorn their churches with sculptural representations of Christ, apostles, and saints as well as kings and church dignitaries. Furthermore, the imaginative and superstitious Normans who believed in wizards, ghosts, sorcerers, and other supernatural forces could easily attribute miraculous powers to sacred objects such as the bones of saints or a nail from the cross on which Christ was crucified, so relic worship was continued in the West.

The rich ecclesiastical art of medieval Russia retained the other-worldliness characteristic of Eastern Christianity. In the earlier Russian icons, large eyes dominate the thin faces of ascetic saints and emaciated figures are clothed in drapery arranged in angular folds. In the *Vladimir Madonna* an enamel-like purity and brilliance of color, combined with the suave curves of the composition, induce an emotional effect (Plate 57). The Eastern church depended almost entirely upon color for emotional appeal, whereas the Roman Catholics still retained their love of form.

CHARLEMAGNE'S EMPIRE

Eventually in 800 A.D., the Pope summoned Charlemagne to Rome and crowned him Successor of the Caesars and Emperor of the Holy Roman Empire, thereby uniting church and state. Charlemagne's inland empire was essentially an agricultural state and life was chiefly rural. Many of the unprotected Roman cities had been destroyed. Even Aix-la-Chapelle (the modern Aachen), where the emperor established his capital, was only a small settlement. Though an international organization, the court of Charlemagne was still predominantly barbarian. Charlemagne, at heart a barbarian chieftain, had not mastered the arts of reading and writing, but he respected Roman culture and was wise enough to surround himself with missionaries, learned men from the monasteries, and also artists and scholars from Rome, Ravenna, and Byzantium. Apparently he thought that some of them, under his direction, of course, could attend to matters of state, promote the arts, and superintend education, thus leaving him free to give most of his time to military affairs and the extension of his empire.

Preferring the Eastern style of architecture, he modeled his *palace at Aix* after St. Vitale, a Christian church in Ravenna, an outpost of the Byzantine empire. Surrounded by an ambulatory, it was octagonal in shape and covered with a central dome supported on piers in the Byzantine manner. Although by this time the destructive practice of denuding older churches and temples in order to procure materials for the newer ones had been prohibited by law, the Pope gave the Emperor special permission to import columns and decorative marbles from Rome and Ravenna.

FEUDALISM AND THE CASTLES

Out of the heretofore unsurpassed disorder following Charlemagne's reign there eventually emerged that political state known as feudalism, which for a time was a stabilizing influence. The people sought protection by becoming farmers or serfs and living on the land of the strong and wealthy landowners or on the great estates which the church had acquired by gift or purchase. The latter were managed by the abbots in the monasteries or the bishops from the towns. Although by feudalistic law, the serf—and a large proportion of the people belonged to this class—could not leave the land upon which he worked, he was not a slave in the strictest sense of the word; however, under the existing conditions there was little incentive for him to improve his lot. He had his own crude hut and lived on what was left of his produce after the owner had taken his share.

Very soon the prosperous landholders found it to their advantage to divide their estates and grant fiefs, either portions of land or some other source of income, to vassals who would swear allegiance to them and render military aid when needed. The vassal might himself become a lord by subdividing his fief. Through subdivision, marriage, and inheritance ownership became increasingly complicated. Many quarrels or "feuds" arose. Feudalism, based both on "destructive war and productive agriculture," ceased to function effectively when money came into common use and when the invention of gunpowder brought about a change in warfare. Many of the people moved to the towns and became self-supporting. Nevertheless, through all of these and other changes the church retained its supremacy.

With feudalism we associate its most important monuments, the great stone castles perched high on a rocky cliff commanding a magnificent view or set upon a plain and surrounded by a protective moat which could be crossed only by lowering the draw-bridge. Familiar to all are its crenelated walls furnishing protection for the defenders, its square or round towers with flat or conical roofs, and the openings or trap doors through which boiling pitch or molten lead could be poured upon attackers. These massive castles with their forbidding exteriors were romantic settings for the songs and stories of the days of chivalry.

MEDIEVAL BELIEFS

In medieval days when travel was perilous nobles and their ladies had to spend most of their time within the castles where life was gay after a fashion, if rather uncomfortable according to our

standards. There was little or no privacy and the great halls were
cold and draughty. For the common people, life was not so pleasant. With frequent invasions, wars, famines, plagues, and pesti-
lence, all were constantly haunted by the fear of sudden death.
Their only hope was a reward in the hereafter for which they
believed this life was only a preparation, but after the year 1000
the general outlook began to improve.

The medievalists interpreted the Bible literally and were greatly
impressed with the references to the Millennium found in the Book
of Revelations. Many of them were convinced that on the first day
of the year 1000 the world would come to an end and Christ
would begin His reign on earth. The wealthy gave their vast
possessions to the church, for in the glorious Millennium there
would be no need of worldly goods; furthermore, gifts might help
to atone for one's past sins. Those who could, went to the tops of
high mountains or climbed up the hills to get a better view of the
coming of Christ. The long anticipated day came and went, but
the old world still remained. With a collective breath of relief
everybody returned to the business of living imbued with a spirit
of thankfulness to God, a tremendous energy, and an unbounded
enthusiasm. How widespread was this belief in the coming of the
end of the world we do not really know. Some modern historians
discredit its importance as a factor in the betterment of conditions;
but all agree that during the early part of the eleventh century
there were improved economic and cultural changes. The building
of roads facilitated travel. Markets were developed and towns grew.
There was increased interest in learning, a great revival of construction, chiefly ecclesiastical, and the arts and crafts flourished.
Life in general became more pleasant.

THE MONASTERIES

Standing out against a background of unstable government and
the almost intolerable social conditions of early medieval times
were the monasteries, oases of peace and protection. Practically
self-supporting, they were a refuge for philosophers, leading
scholars, artists, and educators, or any others who wished to live in

peace and quietude. Kings came to rest there from perilous journeys; but equally welcome were the poor, the unfortunate, sick,
or disgraced.

Originating in Africa, the monastic system was introduced first
in Asia Minor and spread from there to the West. The early
fathers taught that existence on this earth was of no value except
as a preparation for the future life in the hereafter where the godly
would receive their reward; on the other hand, those who failed to
abide by the rules of the church would be condemned to everlasting punishment. So eloquent were their representations of the
sufferings of the lost souls that some individuals living in the sup-
posedly iniquitous city of Alexandria or some other Graeco-Roman
town in northern Africa retired to the mountains bordering the
desert on the eastern side of the Nile. There, in order to save their
souls, they lived a peaceful contemplative life in solitary asceticism.
With emaciated bodies clothed only in a hair-cloth tunic, they must
have been a strange sight when they made infrequent appearances
upon the streets of the refined Graeco-Egyptian city of Alexandria.
Here the hermits talked to all who would listen, endeavoring to
convert them. Sometimes, upon returning to solitary haunts, the
monks were accompanied by a group who had been attracted by
their persuasive discourse. Upon arrival all agreed upon certain
rules and elected one of their members as head. Each built his
little cell about a chosen place of worship and there they lived
together. Gradually larger groups with common interests came to
reside under one roof with an abbot in charge. Such a community
became a monastery. The two most famous monastic systems in the
West were the Benedictine and the Cluniac. The latter, by a
revival of monastic ideals, brought about a much needed reform
in the church.

The monasteries were modeled somewhat on the general plan
of the Roman house, that is, the different parts were grouped about
an open space surrounded by a covered walk, now called a cloister.
This colonnaded porch connected some of the buildings. According
to one plan, on the north side of the square court was the church
facing west. Store-rooms for provisions were on the west side. To
the east of the court were the sleeping quarters, which adjoined

the church. On the south side was the refectory or dining-hall and a near-by living room. Outside this group of buildings were gardens, fields, orchards, mills, shops of various kinds, and also a fish-pond.

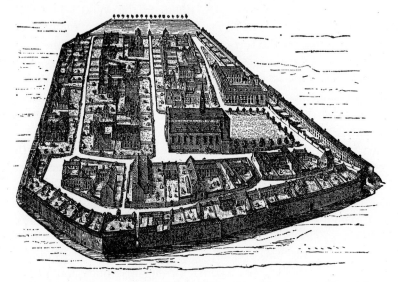

Panorama, cloister at Gand. Founded in the 12th century. (Lacroix)

In the beginning the monks took the vows of chastity, poverty, and obedience. Later a fourth, industry, was added. The monks were ordered to work with their hands seven hours a day; they were urged to put forth their best efforts to make their work acceptable to the Lord and worthy of a reward in heaven. Discipline differed in the various monasteries, but in all a premium was put upon work.

Some of the monks became missionaries and went out to convert the barbarians. One of the most famous, Gregory the Great, became a pope. Some did the necessary chores about the monastery. Others were builders, painters, illuminators, or craftsmen. Copies of the *Book of Kells*, a notable example of the work of the Irish monks, can be seen in many of our large libraries (Plate 56). It is conspicuous for its finely decorated initial letters. The sculptors and painters who decorated the Romanesque churches drew much of their inspiration from the work of these illuminators rather than from nature. Although sculptured in stone, the lines of the hems and the many folds of the garments of the figures of Christ and the saints are as freely flowing as if they had been drawn by the pen of the monks who decorated the manuscripts. Because of their similarity to handwriting, these rhythmic lines, quite characteristic of Romanesque sculpture, are referred to as *calligraphic lines*. These are shown in the relief in the tympanum of St. Pierre. The Bible was the book most often illustrated by the monks, but they also made copies of some of the classical literature of Greece and Rome, and the English monks in particular recorded medieval beliefs concerning science and medicine. Dynamic linear movement characterizes the page paintings in the *Winchester Bible* of twelfth-century England. In the *Death of Absalom*, the figures and faces display nervous agitation (Plate 57). Effective use of gestures is also achieved by a restless linear quality in the positions of heads, hands, and fingers. These early illuminators produced some of the finest calligraphy the world has ever known.

Although the monastic structures were not uniform in appearance, many features were sufficiently common to mark the Romanesque as a distinct style. Some, as the Cathedral of Pisa in Italy, had a dome over the crossing. In Italy the bell towers were free standing. In Germany there was a tendency to place another apse at the entrance opposite the usual one at the western end. In England the churches built by the Normans were longer, lower, and narrower than those in France. Norman towers flanked the entrances or rose above the crossing. Nowhere do we find such emphasis on naturalistic sculptural decoration as was common on the temples of Rome. The nearest approach to it are the sculptures on the churches of southern France. In the West, Norman fantasy expressed in the form of queer birds and animals is interwoven with formalized classical features in the ornamentation of capitals of the columns.

ROMANESQUE CHURCHES

The new Christian churches had to meet the requirements of an increasing elaboration of the Christian ritual. A crypt beneath the altar for burial purposes became necessary. Also the church had to be large enough not only to take care of the usual congregation, but also to accommodate the ever increasing bands of pilgrims

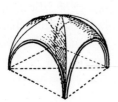 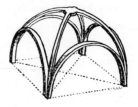

GROINED VAULT

Left, groined vault, square bay. Right, ribs of a
groined vault.

who, having formerly limited their journeys to the sacred cities of Rome and Jerusalem, were now beginning to travel westward to view the sacred relics of the monastic churches.

In general plan the Romanesque churches followed the T-shape of the basilica, but with increased emphasis upon the altar; the apse was enlarged, and longer wings (transepts) were set at right angles to nave and side aisles. As a result the plan became cruciform. The people congregated in the nave. They were also permitted to stand in the transepts so that they could be nearer the altar. The monks who assisted with the ritual and furnished the music were accommodated in a choir, formed by the extension of the space between the apse and the crossing (the intersection of nave and transepts). Around apse and choir were special ambulatories (small aisles) with numerous adjoining chapels, each with its own altar and sometimes its own special relic, either wrapped in a rare textile or placed in a reliquary richly enameled and set with precious stones. Other monks presided over the altars in these small apsidal chapels. Using the processional path formed by ambulatories curving around choir and apse, pilgrims were able to view the relics without interrupting the sermon or disturbing the ceremonies about the main altar.

With the special needs of the church in mind, the monks were faced with the problem of constructing a fireproof building with walls thick enough to support a heavy stone roof without sacrificing light. Some attempted to solve the problem by placing a Byzantine dome over the crossing; others used the barrel, the groin, and later the ribbed vault. The Romans had understood the groin and barrel vaults, but few examples of their work remained in the West, particularly in the northern sections where the Normans had settled. The Lombards in Italy had experimented to some extent with the rib vault, but it was left to the architects of the Middle Ages to develop ribs which could both sustain the webbing (stone covering) and gather the thrusts of the vault to points of support which could be reinforced by buttressing (a strengthening of the support).

Barrel vaults required a large amount of centering. To reduce this the Normans erected transverse arches at regular intervals across the nave, thus dividing it into squares or bays. In this case the outer walls had to be very thick. Usually a second story was added over the side aisles to counteract the outward thrust of the nave vault. Later they learned that by extending other arches diagonally across the squared segment of the nave they could subdivide the bay into four parts. Such an arrangement made it possible to erect centering for only one part of the bay at a time. After the stone webbing was in place the wooden centering could be removed and used again, thus saving time, expense and labor. Furthermore, if one part was damaged the entire vault would not necessarily be affected. At the point of convergence the arches rested upon large piers. The thrust of the vault was thus gathered and transferred to piers set at each corner of the square. In some of the earlier churches the pillars were monoliths, but later, particularly in the Gothic period, flat pilasters or semi-circular engaged columns were added to a square core, resulting in a complicated support known as a compound or clustered pier, clearly shown in the view of the twelfth-century *Abbey Church of Fontevrault* (Plate 53). Each additional element strengthened the pier.

During the Romanesque period the problem of construction of a fireproof roof over the side aisles, at least, had been solved, but the churches were still low and dark. In the West the adventurous and enterprising Normans raised the walls of the nave high above

the roofs of the side aisles to form a clerestory for the admission of
light. Some of the members of the compound piers were extended
above the second story. Other smaller columns carried the weight
of the arches of the arcade which separated the nave from the side
aisles. In the later Norman churches such as the *Abbaye-aux-Hommes* and the *Abbaye-aux-Dames* at Caen, the strong outward thrust
of the clerestory wall was met by a half-barrel vault springing from
the heavy outer wall, and extending across the side aisle to that
part of the nave wall which adjoined the clustered pier. Romanesque massive solidity reminiscent of Roman architectural forms is
seen in the *Chapter House of Notre Dame de Pontaut* (Plate 55).

A famous example of a series of cupolas forming the chief feature of the church is seen in *St. Front at Périgueux,* where five
high stone cupolas are supported by pendentives (Plate 55). Although St. Front resembles the brick Byzantine edifices in general
plan, it exemplifies a variation of the Romanesque style. Thus
Norman builders were beginning to solve the problem of lighting, but the churches still had thick walls, few doors and small
windows. The arches over the doors, windows, and the ribs of the
vaulting were still the round arches used by the Romans; and the
rudimentary flying buttress was still concealed within the outer
walls of the structure. In Romanesque architecture the only support found outside the thick walls was an occasional pier buttress,
that is, a thickening of the walls by additional masonry construction
placed at strategic points. In these churches equilibrium was maintained by using sheer mass to counteract the thrust of the vault.
The Gothic builders were later to discover that thick walls were
not a necessity.

On the exterior, the Romanesque churches were rather plain
and heavy in appearance. The triple façade with the three doorways indicated the interior vertical divisions—the nave and side
aisles. Horizontal moldings (string-courses) suggested the divisions
of the three stories: the ground story; the *triforium,* a sort of second
story balcony separated from the nave by an arcade; and the third,
a *clerestory.* Usually there were two bell towers flanking the façade.
Many features of the Romanesque churches built, or at least super-

vised, by the monks were retained by the builders of the great Gothic cathedrals.

SCULPTURAL DECORATION

Sculpture, concentrated chiefly about the portals, had a twofold purpose: to decorate and to instruct. In the north, where barbarian influence was strongest, geometric ornament, sawtooth edges, or spiral patterns were roughly hewn out of stone. Elsewhere there was the closely carved patterning of Oriental origin which the barbarians had brought with them from the East. In the southern part of France, Roman influence, tempered by the new elements of the West, is shown in the quieter sculptured figures which more nearly approach naturalistic forms, such as those on the façade of *St. Trophime* at Arles (Plate 53).

The placement of certain subjects was rigidly ordered by the church, but within this limitation, the sculptors were given a great deal of freedom. The *Abbey of Vézelay* is embellished with an elaborately sculptured tympanum above the central portal (Plate 54). The subject of this carving is the descent of the Holy Spirit, who sends rays down upon the apostles. In the center, God the Father is represented larger than other figures and is surrounded by an almond-shaped nimbus. This twelfth-century Burgundian abbey, said to contain the preserved relics of St. Magdalene, attracts countless visitors.

As in other periods of history, learning was confined to the priesthood. Books were rare or non-existent, and the laity was wholly unlettered. Romanesque sculpture, therefore, became a means of visual education. Augmented by an extensive iconography, it served to indoctrinate the people and to familiarize them with the teachings of the Bible, especially that part of it known as the New Testament.

At no other time in Western world history was architecture more preoccupied with religion than in the eleventh and twelfth centuries. The "storied capitals" at the top of columns in the twelfth-century Romanesque churches show such scenes from the Bible as *"Samson and the Lion"* (Plate 56). Characterized by realism and vigorous movement, the designs of the capitals are purely decorative. Some show deeply chiseled hollows behind the intertwining foliage. The various motifs of the capitals are always subordinated to create an integral part of the masonry. Since both art and religion belong to the spiritual side of life, though neither is entirely dependent upon the other, a close relationship exists between the two. When such a union occurs a great and highly productive period of art may be expected. Then art is thoroughly understood by the people and becomes an integral part of everyday life.

The calm, intelligent Greeks had been concerned with the world they knew and enjoyed, with little thought of a future life. Their sculpture was based upon the physical man, the known. It was realistic, idealized, well-proportioned, and more or less static. In contrast, the imaginative, non-realistic style of Romanesque sculpture communicates something of the religious fervor of the energetic people of the Middle Ages who "set spirit above flesh." This emotional exuberance is expressed by exciting linear rhythms and ecstatic elongated figures twisted in unnatural positions, with legs crossed, garments fluttering, and feet barely touching the ground—as in a dance. With literal translations of the visions of St. John recorded in Revelations as a point of departure, the Romanesque sculptors peopled their mystic world with objective representations of Christ, angels, symbolical beasts and terrifying unseen monsters, and demons. Romanesque sculpture was vigorous, dynamic, naïve, and charming—in direct contrast to the quiet and down-to-earth appearance of the churches themselves. Despite its highly exciting character, it is always subordinated to the architecture. Forms are composed to fit the spaces as in the tympana, or elongated to either replace the column or become an integral part of it.

In the sculptural representation of the *Vision of the Apocalypse*, on the tympanum of the church of St. Pierre at Moissac, the central group of figures about Christ enthroned are enclosed in an imaginary circular form and are emphasized by contrast in size (Plate 54). The horizontal spaces marked by sculptured line divisions suggest a quietude in strong contrast to the agitated moving figures which they contain. Calligraphic lines sharpen the folds and edges of the garments, and a strong linear pattern throughout contributes to the agitated, dynamic style of expression characteristic of Romanesque sculpture.

The Romanesque builders had solved many of the problems and had at least introduced the most conspicuous features which the Gothic builders were to perfect. Most of the painting of the Romanesque period has been entirely lost or "restored." In fact, few of the churches themselves exist in their original state. Romanesque sculpture belongs to the great sculpture of all time. Romanesque art, stimulated to activity by the inspiration of Christianity, prepared the way for the building of the Gothic cathedrals.

OUTLINE OF MEDIEVAL ART—ROMANESQUE

PLACE: Italy, France, England and other countries in western Europe.

TIME: "Dark Ages"—500 A.D.-1000 A.D. Romanesque Style—c.1000-1200 A.D.

BACKGROUND: Barbarian invasion. Fusion of races. Feudalism 9th to 14th centuries. Life chiefly rural, agricultural. Conditions improved after 1000 A.D. Catholic church only unified institution. Power of church increased, allied with state during Charlemagne's reign. Monastery important. Learning confined chiefly to monks and other churchmen. Religious orders supervised work in artistic fields, such as: painting, manuscript illumination, sculpture and the "sacred science of architecture."

ARCHITECTURE: Chiefly ecclesiastical. Style varied with locality (diversified in France). Churches—sense of heaviness, massive. Space enclosed by thick walls. Only a few small apertures. Round arches. Dome or tower over transepts. Barrel and groin vaults, resting on heavy piers. Vault thrusts met by thick walls, semi-vaults over side aisles, and static buttresses. *Horizontality.* String-courses on façade strongly marked.

In *northern France:* naves protected by wooden roofs—aisles by stone vaulting. Decorative carving—chevron (zig-zag), dog tooth, and other geometrical designs used on mouldings and archivolts (Norman influence). Churches higher (clerestory for light) in this section.

In *southern France:* barrel vaults and domes used.

Chief contribution: development of rib vaulting.

SCULPTURE: Found on different parts of structure, usually concentrated about portals, most important in tympana. Highly conventionalized. Mystic, moving, imaginative forms clad in garments with rhythmic calligraphic lines are shown in relief. Classical influence: acanthus, ivy, and laurel together with variations of other classical forms on capitals of columns. Animals, both conventionalized and naturalistic, also human figures on capitals of columns—all formed to fit space assigned to them.

PAINTING: Other than manuscript painting, most has disappeared. Only a few examples in Italy. Technique, fresco. Some mosaic work. Colorful marble on floors of some of the churches.

Bibliography follows Chapter X.

CHAPTER X

Medieval Art—Gothic

TRAVELING in northern France, one is impressed with the massive stone structures which dominate the landscape for miles around. These great monuments, the Gothic cathedrals topped by towers and spires, dwarf the small houses of the towns that cluster about them. They are the crowning glory of the Middle Ages and may be called the greatest objective contribution to civilization by the people of those times.

The term *Gothic* was applied to this architectural style by the men of the Renaissance who, interested only in the rediscovered art of Greek and Roman antiquity, considered everything of the Middle Ages to be barbaric and uncivilized. In later times we have learned to see the beauty and importance of the Gothic style and the term has become one of respect instead of contempt.

The Gothic, or Pointed style as it is sometimes called, had its beginning in northern France about the middle of the twelfth century. It reached its height in the thirteenth century and spread to England, Germany, Spain, and other countries, continuing as late as the fifteenth century in some localities. It dominated not only church and other ecclesiastical buildings, but civic and domestic architecture as well—notably the town halls of Flanders and the houses of Germany. Costume and furniture designers went to the cathedral for inspiration, and their creations reflected the elongated and perpendicular lines characteristic of Gothic architecture. Tall chairs had backs topped by gable-shaped forms set between supports terminating in pinnacle-like ornaments. Gothic designs like the *trefoil*, the *quatrefoil*, and *lance-shaped* open work decorated the lower parts. Men's shoes, beginning with a conservative pointed toe, gradually became so elongated that they had to be chained to a jeweled garter worn just below the knee. Women's dresses had V-necks and long pointed sleeves. Their hats were high and pointed. In the end the most extreme style, the hennin, soared to a height of three feet.

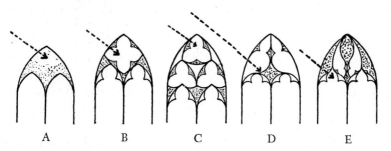

Gothic design motifs as used in windows. A. Lance-shaped; B. Quatrefoil; C. Trefoil; D. Double curve; E. Flamboyant, based on double-curved or ogee arch.

DECLINE OF FEUDALISM; RISE OF TOWNS

The later Middle Ages saw the decline of feudalism and the emergence of national states. Many people moved to the towns and cities and allied themselves with the national monarchs who, with their help, were able to defy the feudal barons. For a time the common people enjoyed a greater degree of freedom than they had ever before experienced. They were no longer under the thumbs of the barons; the Church had not yet grown tyrannical; and the power of the kings had not become absolute. Coincident with the great changes in government and the status of the workmen was a change in architecture. The monastic Romanesque developed into the communal Gothic which, relatively speaking, was the free creation of a free people.

UNREST AND MASS MOVEMENTS

Along with the new freedom, however, went a feeling of unrest, as is always the case when great masses of the population are exposed to new ideas and a new social system. People were moving about the continent of Europe in large numbers. Students wan-

dered from one university to another, to study with the great
teachers and scholars of the time. Merchants from all parts of
Europe attended the fairs, such as the famous ones of Flanders or
the one at Leipsig, to visit with friends, to find entertainment, and
to develop new markets. Troubadours and jongleurs, itinerant
musicians, and other entertainers traveled from town to town and
from castle to castle. Bands of pilgrims in ever increasing numbers
visited the churches and shrines where sacred relics were preserved.
Besides legitimate travelers, bands of robbers roamed the countryside, and unfrocked monks and other charlatans preyed upon the
ignorant populace by selling false relics and pretending to work
miracles upon the sick and distressed.

The most conspicuous of the great mass movements were the
Crusades, which occurred at intervals between the years 1096 and
1270. These organized bands drew many civilians as well as
knights and soldiers to Palestine and Constantinople. They
brought back precious objects of gold and silver and ivory, sumptuous silks and satins, spices and rare perfumes. More than that,
they returned with tales of the mysterious Orient, of buildings of
marble and alabaster, of walls covered with glittering mosaics, and
of Persian edifices with pointed arches; in fact, the whole rich
pageantry of the Levant. All of which served to fire the imaginations of the Gothic craftsmen in western Europe and to enrich the
quality of their workmanship.

THE CATHEDRAL A COMMUNAL PROJECT

The love of building was one of the outstanding characteristics
of the people of the Middle Ages. Beginning with the year 1000
A.D., church building continued with increasing enthusiasm until
the end of the Gothic period. It would seem that the descendants
of the barbarians, now civilized and mixed with the older inhabitants of France and England, were trying to rebuild what their
forefathers had so ruthlessly destroyed.

Towns competed with one another to build the most beautiful
cathedral. Plans were kept secret, but certain elements were common
to all. Looking at the façades of the four major French cathedrals, one

will see the two great towers, the three portals with recessed arches, a row of statues called the *row of kings,* an arcade, and a huge circular window known as the *rose window.* The arrangement of these features is different in each case, and variety in the ornamentation gives to each its peculiar character. The façade of *Notre Dame* is the most fortress-like of the four major cathedrals (Plate 58). The upward-soaring quality is most apparent at *Rheims.* The towers of *Chartres* are topped by dissimilar spires. At *Amiens* the height of the towers has been sacrificed for the vast spaciousness of the interior. Its nave is said to be equal in height to an eighteen-story building.

The workmen of the towns organized themselves into guilds, somewhat like the unions of today; however, the guilds of the Middle Ages not only set the prices for work and guaranteed compensation for the workman, but they also guaranteed that the product would meet the high standard set by the guilds. Each guild operated a sort of school for the training of their members who began as apprentices, became journeymen traveling about to gain experience, finally were admitted to membership in the guild, and allowed to share in its privileges and protection. The builders belonged to the masons' guild and were permitted to go wherever there was an important building program. The best craftsman of the group was selected as the master mason; he probably did the planning, as there were no professional architects at that time. Certainly some master mind made the fine calculations which resulted in the balance of thrust and counter-thrust. The cathedrals were built and decorated by the members of the masons' guild, the sculptors, the glaziers, and the zealous people who worked together to make the cathedral a bit of heaven on earth.

Musicians of the day composed beautiful music for the church service. The *Te Deum* was first sung in Rheims Cathedral. The liturgical writers endeavored to give beautiful form to the ritual. Everyone strove to make the cathedral as nearly perfect as possible, for these great churches were all dedicated to the Virgin Mary, Mother of Christ, who was looked upon by the people as a tender and loving woman who would understand their troubles and intercede for them, as they did not feel worthy to approach God directly.

All of the four major cathedrals were called *Notre Dame* (Our Lady), but only the church in Paris still is known by that name. The others are distinguished by the name of the town or city in which they are located.

It is difficult for people of modern times who have separate buildings for each of their activities to realize what the cathedral meant to the people of the Middle Ages. It was not only church but town hall and theatre all in one. There all of the important events of one's life occurred. It even affected the styles of the day. We still build cathedrals, huge and imposing ones such as those in Washington, D.C., and New York City. Handsome and stately as these are, however, they are in a large degree merely an imitation of the old European cathedrals. The Gothic churches filled a deeply-felt need of the people and the shapes they assumed grew out of a communal need, a communal religious spirit, and a communal artistic effort. The wealthy contributed money but the poor people of the French villages, fired by religious zeal, worked on the construction often without pay or the desire for pay. We are told that the builders worked almost unceasingly during the long days, and that at night the people lighted candles on carts around the church over which they kept watch, singing songs and hymns. Somehow this mass enthusiasm has transmitted itself into the very fabric of these buildings and will continue to be felt as long as the buildings endure.

CHARTRES CATHEDRAL

Perhaps the most representative and, in many respects, the most beautiful of the French Gothic cathedrals is at Chartres, a small town some fifty miles southwest of Paris. To show with what loyalty and intrepid spirit the people of medieval France labored through generations and centuries in the face of fires, ravages of time, and other obstacles to produce these great monuments, let us glance briefly at the history of *Chartres Cathedral*.

As long ago as the ninth century there was a church at Chartres, and Saint Frobold was the bishop when the town was besieged by Northmen who pleaded for admittance, pretending that they desired to be baptized as Christians. No sooner were they within the walls than they began to sack the city; they plundered and then set fire to all the buildings. The bishop and the people fled to the church for protection, but the invaders set fire to that also, and it was destroyed (879 A.D.). Undaunted, the inhabitants erected a new church which also was destroyed, this time by lightning (1020 A.D.).

King Canute set aside a sum of money to be used in rebuilding the church, and in 1026 the foundations were laid. This was the first stone structure, but it had a wooden roof. In 1099 Queen Matilda provided funds for covering the roofs with lead and for the purchase of a set of bells. In 1037 the high altar was dedicated though the church was not yet complete. In 1115 foundations for the two towers were laid. Another disastrous fire occurred in 1134, leaving only the west façade, including the two towers and the crypt. To enlarge the nave this façade, which had been built behind the towers, was by 1150 moved forward in its entirety to a position flush with the western or outer side of the towers. By 1194 the south tower was completed and the north tower half-way up, when still another destructive fire left only the two towers, the west façade, and the crypt which of course was below ground level. Still undaunted, the villagers again set to work to rebuild. Kings and queens of France contributed money, church dignitaries gave revenue, and the ordinary people gave their labor. It is recorded that prince and pauper alike hitched themselves to carts and helped drag stones from the quarries six miles away.

Finally in the year 1260, nearly four hundred years after the destruction of the original church by the Northmen, the cathedral assumed what is substantially its present form and was consecrated by St. Louis, the Crusader (King Louis IX of France). But other things still had to be done. In the fourteenth century the sculptured porches and the gables were completed. In the early years of the sixteenth century the lead-covered wooden northern spire burned down and was replaced by 1513 with the present one. A change in style during the three hundred years which had elapsed since the construction of the southern spire accounts for the different design of the newer one, with its more ornate and flamboyant appearance. The transition from the older sturdier base to the delicate tracery of the spire is carried out so skillfully, however, that one does not regret the lack of symmetry between the two towers. Rather, the sturdy southern one and the graceful northern one seem to complement each other like man and woman.

Yet another disastrous fire occurred in 1836 A.D., but fortunately the vaulting remained intact and repairs could be made. Considering the havoc wrought by many fires and the wanton destruction of its sculpture during the French Revolution, it is amazing that *Chartres Cathedral* still stands. Fortunately, with due respect for antiquity, historical significance, and importance as works of art which could not be duplicated in the machine age, both Axis and Allied fliers of World War II sought to spare the great cathedrals, monuments to the religious zeal of the people of the Middle Ages. Although some close to military targets, notably *Cologne Cathedral* in Germany (which is near a large railroad station) were damaged, not one of the most important cathedrals was entirely destroyed.

PLAN OF THE GOTHIC CATHEDRAL

The ground plans of the cathedrals varied, but all were based on the cruciform shape developed by the late Romanesque builders (Plate 59). The Gothic choir was elongated and the apse was elaborated by the addition of ambulatories and many projecting chapels. This complicated arrangement is known as the chêvet. The central longitudinal division of the church still consisted of a high-roofed central nave paralleled by two low-roofed side aisles.

In the western, or frontal, façade are the three main entrances: a large portal in the center opening into the nave and two smaller portals opening into the side aisles. The façade as a whole, like the interior, is three-storied. In *Chartres Cathedral* the first story is defined by the portals; the second, which is low in comparison with the first and third, by an arcade or colonnade; the third by the rose window.

The two towers of the French cathedrals rise either directly above the side portals, as in *Notre Dame* at Paris, or they flank the façade as in *Chartres*. The original architects' plans usually called for the towers to be surmounted by spires as at *Chartres*, but often the spires were never completed and the builders decided to leave the tops square, finishing them off with small pinnacles to relieve the abruptness of the termination of the perpendicular tower. This procedure came to be intentional in many cases, especially in the English cathedrals, and in our day has become common in the United States where the Gothic style has been adapted to churches and university buildings.

Upon entering the nave of a cathedral we are overwhelmed by the impression of great height, as if we were standing in a vast northern forest whose tall pines with interlocking branches tower above us in the dimness. We cannot see the sky, but sunlight filters through the foliage on either side, slanting downward in long, shimmering beams. The human being is dwarfed, and we feel ourselves in the presence of the infinite.

STRUCTURE OF THE CATHEDRAL

The Gothic cathedral, unlike the earlier churches of Graeco-Latin derivation, was conceived not in the image of physical man, but in terms of the great dynamic forces of the natural world. The stone skeleton, made of arches supported on piers and brought to equilibrium by a finely calculated system of thrusts and counter-thrusts, was a living organism. Like the human body or a modern machine, both of which must be kept in good condition in order to function properly, the living arches of perishable stone which constantly exerted a force downward and outward, had to be kept in constant repair. If any part of such a skeleton is damaged, all of the parts are affected, because they are interdependent. Upon this stone skeleton the builders supported the heavy stone vaults which, half lost in the mysterious shadows high above the floor of the nave, seem to rest lightly upon their supporting stone ribs and piers.

Like the trunks of trees are the towering clustered stone piers, with engaged columns terminating at different levels where the pointed arches of the bays and the vaults of the roof branch off. Let us examine the structure of these branches. From the engaged columns at the right and left of the pier spring the arches which support the lower wall of the nave and divide the nave from the side aisles. On the opposite side of the pier the engaged column supports the arch which forms part of the vaulting of the side

aisle. The remaining column continues straight up, inter-rupted only by string-courses (horizontal moldings) to a point about half-way up the clerestory, from which point spring the arches or ribs which support the vaulted roof of the nave and transept.

Just as the Greek builders by the subtle refinements of their marble temples had perfected the post-and-lintel type of architecture, so the Gothic builders, employing to ad-vantage all the structural knowledge acquired by their predecessors, the Etruscans, Romans, Lombards, and Romanesque builders, gave to the arcuated or arch type of structure its highest expression in their great cathedrals. After their time there would be many variations of both of these structural types; during the Renaissance, the Gothic principle would be applied to the erection of high domes, but there would be

Cross-section through nave and aisle of Cathedral of Amiens. Note flying buttresses at upper left. (After Krahl)

no other conspicuous structural development until the advent of steel. The Gothic builders had accomplished all that could be done with stone, the material which the ancient Egyptians had skillfully cut and employed in the building of their indestructible pyramids.

In contrast to the sunny climate of the Mediterranean region, the gray skies of northern France required that more window space must be provided. This was achieved by making the clerestory very high and piercing it with many tall windows. The use of the pointed arch (Plate 60) instead of the round arch of the Roman-esque structures, enabled the builder to achieve greater height by raising the apex of the lateral and longitudinal arches to the level of the crown of the diagonal rib within each vault. This skeleton-like form of construction required additional buttressing at and above the clerestory level, and this problem was solved by use of the open half-arch buttress, or, as it is called, the flying buttress.

First are the massive pier buttresses, rising from the ground and placed in alignment with each set of piers. Above them are the open or flying buttresses, carrying the thrust of the vaulting diagon-ally down to the pier buttresses on the exterior of the building and through them to the ground itself. Since the space between the flying buttresses is not roofed over, and since they themselves are open instead of being solid, there is plenty of room for daylight to penetrate the clerestory windows. The same characteristics of these buttresses permit of lighter weight in the construction without loss of structural strength, so that the interior vaulting can be carried very high without becoming top-heavy. The flying buttresses, struc-tural features frankly expressed in Gothic construction, become decorative features as well. They tie together or unify the different parts of the cathedral—particularly notable in the apse. In Roman-esque churches each chapel has its own roof and the general effect is a number of volumes grouped around a central core. There is an effect of "manyness" in contrast to the "oneness" of the Gothic.

The three stories indicated on the façade are the ground arcade, the triforium (a low-roofed balcony), and the clerestory, a skeleton wall filled almost entirely with glass. In France the simplest Gothic architectural style, exemplified in *Chartres Cathedral,* was called Rayonnant (radiating) and the later more elaborate style was termed Flamboyant (flame-like). These terms were derived from the types of stone tracery employed in the great rose windows. In *Notre Dame* the window has radiating stone spokes like a wheel. In *Amiens* the tracery is of the more elaborate double-curved Flam-boyant style.

STAINED GLASS

Stained glass in Gothic times took the place of the earlier mural paintings as the chief decorative element of the interiors of the churches. The open-work wall construction, or rather, the lack of large areas of interior wall surfaces suitable for mural paintings, consequently turned designers' attention to the possibilities of the windows themselves. The result was that the art of designing in colored glass was carried to its highest point. The Gothic cathedrals of northern France represent history's supreme achievement in this medium.

Stained-Glass Maker at Work. Jost Amman. (Bates)

The stained glass of the Middle Ages must not be confused with the painted glass of more modern times. This older glass was made of simple materials—sand and other silicates such as quartz, with an alkali like soda and a metallic compound. The coloring, usually some metal oxide, was added while the glass was in a molten state so that it became fused into it, permeating its whole thickness. In painted glass the light has to pass only through a thin film of color, whereas in true stained glass it has to traverse a heavy translucent layer perhaps half an inch thick, thereby becoming thoroughly saturated with color.

Near every cathedral was a glazier's shop where new windows were made and older ones were repaired. After the measurement of the window had been obtained, the craftsman drew his design in full size upon the whitened boards which formed his table or work-bench. He drew heavy black lines to indicate the iron bars which were necessary to support the window, and lighter lines to show the thin lead strips which were to hold the pieces of glass together.

The next step was to cut the sheets of colored glass to the proper sizes and shapes to fit his design. These pieces were very small, hardly ever more than six inches in the longest dimension. The cutting had to be done very carefully with a hot iron or a diamond point. The pieces were held together by lead strips attached by means of soldered wires to an iron framework. The latter was of course necessary on account of the large size of the window surface; without the iron bars these great areas of glass and thin lead strips could not resist the pressure of a high wind.

In the beginning of the Gothic period these iron bars were merely vertical and horizontal strips. Little if any attention was given to their relation to the general design of the glass. A bar might cut across the middle of a face or a hand, giving the figure a rather disturbed appearance. Soon, however, the craftsmen learned to adapt the pattern of the iron framework to the design of the glass, and beautiful hand-forged iron came to be an important part of the window's ornamentation as well as a part of its physical structure.

These excellent workmen never lost sight of the fact that they were making, first of all, a window which must function as such, that is, admit daylight and conform to its architectural setting. They were willing to submit to the natural limitations imposed upon them by the structure of the building and the nature of their material. At the same time they realized the esthetic possibilities of their medium and developed them to the full. The rich, glowing colors obtainable by direct sunlight transmitted through stained glass surpassed in intensity anything previously attained either by painting upon an opaque surface, such as a wall or a piece of wood, or by the mosaic technique where colors are seen only by reflected light. Furthermore, the use of transmitted light of different hues in juxtaposition with each other produces the phenomenon of "additive color mixing," the fusion of hues taking place in the eye of the beholder instead of on the surface of the picture as in fresco or in most easel painting. Without going into a technical discussion of the matter of "additive" and "subtractive" color-mixtures, let us say that the effect of the former phenomenon in the case of stained glass windows is to produce a sparkling, jewel-like luminosity unobtainable in any other artistic medium.

The finest French Gothic glass, which dates mostly from the twelfth century, has very few colors. Red and blue were dominant, with smaller quantities of green, yellow, and a few other hues. The designs of the best period were in some ways comparable to the Early Christian mosaics in that naturalistic drawing and a third-dimensional illusion were not considered important; rather, the object was to create a harmonious flat pattern wherein natural forms and natural colors were altered to suit the design as a whole, and the small pieces of glass, like the tesserae of the mosaics, were juxtaposed primarily for the sake of color effectiveness.

In the later Gothic glass we see a greater variety of color and a tendency toward naturalistic representation. There is a legend that one day a workman accidentally dropped a silver button into some molten glass, and to his great surprise the glass turned silver-yellow. It was found that silver oxide produced varying shades of yellow, thereby increasing the range of hues. Brown, purple, rose, and yellow-green came to be used more and more. The process of etching the glass came into practice also. Later Gothic craftsmen, however, seemed to possess a less refined color sense than their predecessors (or perhaps they were trying to harmonize too many different colors at high intensity within each window), and this, together with their increasing interest in realistic representation of natural objects at the sacrifice of spatial pattern, brought about a decline in the art.

In the fourteenth century glass became lighter and was used for secular as well as religious buildings. It adorned town halls and guild halls, and was used to make coats of arms for the windows of private dwellings. It was also used privately to depict marriages and baptisms of wealthy citizens. These panels were set into the walls of the family's private chapel in the local church.

The usual shape of the Gothic cathedral windows in the side walls of the clerestory and elsewhere was that of the *lancet*, a tall, narrow rectangle culminating in a pointed arch at the top. However, the principal windows at the front of the building and at the ends of the transept were circular, and were called *rose windows* because of the form of the stone tracery which radiates from the center like the petals of a rose (Plate 61). The larger windows of both shapes employed stone tracery. This stonework in the flamboyant Gothic era came to be extremely elaborate, as in the great rose window in the west façade of Amiens Cathedral.

Many of these windows depicted some legendary incident in the life of Mary. The *Tree of Jesse* at Chartres records the ancestry of Christ. Other windows relate some of the popular tales of chivalry. A great favorite was the *Song of Roland*, recounting the brave exploits of the nephew of Charlemagne. If a window was donated by a guild, the "signature" would appear in the lower part. In the corner of one window the cloth-makers were shown weaving the cloth. In the opposite corner a guild member was displaying the material to a prospective customer. In others, bakers would be making bread and putting it into the oven, or the glaziers might be busy making the glass.

The jewel-like quality of Gothic stained glass and its universal appeal to the esthetic sense are illustrated in a story told by an American ambulance driver in the first World War. After the German bombardment of Rheims (August, 1914) which shattered the beautiful windows and almost demolished the cathedral, many French soldiers picked up the fragments of stained glass from the ground and had them set into rings, brooches, and similar ornaments to send to their loved ones at home.

CATHEDRAL SCULPTURE

Although the most important statutes are concentrated about the portals, stone sculpture adorns almost every part of the cathedral. Calendars carved of stone representing the signs of the zodiac or the months of the year with occupations appropriate to each appear on the lower part or basement of the cathedrals. Elongated stone statues decorate the columns. Grotesque figments of the sculptor's imagination appear in the most unexpected places. Gargoyles, or waterspouts, which conduct the water from the roofs to protect the stone masonry, project from the gutters of roof and flying buttress. Stone tracery frames the glowing stained glass of the windows. In some instances—notably the façade of Rheims—the rough hard stone seems to be dematerialized. So intricate is the carving of the delicate tracery and the elaborate canopies, one feels that by the magic of the sculptor's art stone has been turned to lace.

The sculpture of the Gothic cathedral, like that of the Romanesque church, served two purposes: that of decoration and religious instruction. Books in that time were few; they were still laboriously lettered by the hands of painstaking monks, for printing with movable type had not yet been invented. Indeed, books were considered as valuable as precious jewels and as carefully guarded. In the churches they were actually chained to the reading desks, and their covers were kept locked when not in use. Certainly one could not own one unless he belonged to the clergy or the nobility. In all probability the ordinary person's education would have been imparted by word of mouth, supplemented by illustrations in the stained glass windows or the stone sculptural decorations of the cathedrals.

The most popular book of that time—and ours—was the Bible. The stories of the Old and New Testaments, together with the lives of the saints, formed most of the subject matter of the cathedral sculpture, so that the portals and porches of these churches were really books of stone. Here, in the words of Dante, "sculpture is visible speech."

To a medieval observer the statues about the portals of the cathedrals would be more than mere sculptural decorations. To him they would take the place of living dramas. As he entered the church, just above him in position as they were in life, were elongated figures of kings, queens, saints, prophets, crusaders. As at *Chartres* these figures, with feet barely touching their supports, seem to step forth in a gesture of greeting. They do not bear the burden of a roof like the Greek caryatides, nor are they placed in niches in the Roman manner. Their long lines, soaring upward like the columns to which they are attached, direct the spectator's eye upward and turn his thoughts toward heaven. At Amiens, the celebrated Vierge Dorée, or *Gilded Virgin* (Plate 64) graces the southern portal where her figure gleams with dramatic joyousness when the sun shines on it. Above her head, three smiling angels support the nimbus which completes this typically late Gothic sculpture.

Some of the best-loved stories were: the *Annunciation,* wherein the angel Gabriel comes to announce to Mary that she is destined to become the mother of Christ; the *Visitation,* in which Mary goes to tell the news to Elizabeth; the *Nativity,* or birth of Christ; the *Presentation in the Temple,* where the infant Christ is blessed by Simeon; the *Flight into Egypt,* after the Holy Family learns that King Herod seeks to destroy the Child; the *Death of the Virgin;* the *Coronation of the Virgin* as Queen of Heaven; the *Crucifixion;* the *Last Judgment,* the joys of the blessed and the horrors of those souls damned to perdition. An amusing story-telling group in the *Strasbourg Cathedral* shows the *Foolish Virgins* with their seducer (Plate 62). Despite the stiff, stylized treatment, these stone figures with their fixed, almost silly smiles, evoke a continuing human response.

The most sacred subjects were usually carved in the tympanums of the church's portals—the space within the pointed arch but above the lintel or horizontal top of the doorway. The *Coronation of the Virgin* is depicted on the central portal of Rheims; *Christ in Majesty,* surrounded by the four beasts of the Apocalypse, adorns a similar space at *Chartres* (Plate 64).

With sensitive skill, the sculptor of the *Last Judgment* scene on the tympanum of the central doorway of *Bourges Cathedral* (Plate 63) portrays the violent emotions of the dead as they rise from their graves. On the great central portal of *Amiens Cathedral* are people excitedly rising from their graves amid angels blowing trumpets. Christ is seated in judgment and kneeling beside him are the Virgin and John the Baptist. Below them, one panel shows the souls of the blessed being led by angels into paradise. Another panel shows the souls of the doomed chained together, walking toward a boiling cauldron where grinning devils with pitchforks await them. Below these panels appears St. Michael with the scales in which he weighs the souls. On the *voussoirs* (the wedge-shaped stones) of the arch are carved the figures of guardian angels bearing souls, martyrs, saints, confessors, and others related to the theme of the Last Judgment.

Although most of the sculpture of the Gothic cathedral was concentrated in and around the recessed portals on the exterior of the building, it also occurred in many other places, as on the capitals of the interior piers, on the string-courses, in a band across the façade above the portals as at *Notre Dame* in Paris, the latter being known as the Gallery of Kings. The water-spouts at the corners of the roof-gutters were often carved into grotesque forms—part animal, part human—called *gargoyles*. The meaning or symbolism of grotesques which appear at various places on the exteriors of cathedrals has long been a subject of speculation. Some think they represent evil spirits that were exorcised by the Church and condemned to be eternally frozen into stone. Others believe them to be manifestations of a sort of spiritual let-down or reaction from the deeply religious mood in which the sculptors were absorbed during their work on the serious sculpture of the church—just a human tendency to revert from the sublime to the ridiculous, from the beautiful to the horrible. Perhaps a few may be merely caricatures of the sculptors' personal enemies. This type of figure should not be confused with the gargoyles or water-spouts which had a definite function. The grotesque appears at various places on the exteriors of the cathedrals. Perhaps the most famous one, perched high upon the parapet of *Notre Dame* in Paris, is the *Devil Looking over His City* (Plate 61) depicted in an etching by Meryon.

The human figures in the portals and galleries, as for example at *Chartres,* are elongated to conform to the verticality of the whole cathedral structure, and they are swathed in heavy draperies so that there is little indication of the body itself. The faces of the saints show a considerable degree of individual characterization. Here and there we find a smiling queen, gracious and charming, a bishop, grave and serious, or a young crusader with a challenge in his facial expression.

Naturalism is carried to a greater degree in the plant and flower forms that overflow the capitals, the string-courses, and the archivolts (the moldings of the arches). One may imagine the sculptor, on his way to work in the morning, stopping now and then to examine carefully the plants that grow along the wayside. Then, with their shapes in mind, he proceeds to the cathedral where he carves a capital or a molding into a pattern based on the natural appearance of the plant but adapted to conform to the particular shape of the surface on which he is working. Earlier craftsmen employed plant forms in architectural decoration in a highly formalized manner. It is not until Gothic times that we find this type of ornament carried out with an attempt to preserve a feeling of the organic growth of vegetation. The nature of the vine as a whole is considered, not merely the individual leaf.

Thus we see that as the Gothic style in art emerges from the earlier forms of the Middle Ages, it reflects a growing interest in natural growth, in the whole vast outdoor world, in contrast to the Graeco-Roman exaltation of the physical human being, and to the Early Christian and Romanesque conception that the material world is nothing, the after-life everything. Indeed it would seem as if the cathedral-builders turned for inspiration to the living forces of nature—for their sculptured ornament to the growing plants and flowers, for their vast naves to the towering forests, and for the rich illumination of their windows to the very sunshine iself.

OUTLINE OF MEDIEVAL ART—GOTHIC

PLACE: Western Europe.

TIME: 12th to 16th centuries (c.1150-1500 A.D.) French: 13th century—Early Gothic, 14th century—Rayonnant, 15th century—Flamboyant. Gothic reached its height in 12th and 13th centuries.

BACKGROUND: Decline of feudalism and the monastery. People moved back to towns and cities. Religious zeal and civic pride stimulated erection of ecclesiastical buildings. Church still united. Worship of Mary became increasingly popular. Legends of life of Mary furnished subject-matter for the arts. Universities founded: Eton College, and Oxford and Cambridge universities in England; University of Paris in France. Learning more widespread. Guilds prominent—members belonged to laity. Expansion of trade. Great activity—mass movement—crusades, etc. Arts flourished.

ARCHITECTURE: Based on skeleton construction of arches supported by lighter piers than those in Romanesque churches. Thrusts stabilized by pier buttresses and flying buttresses. Pointed arch. Thin walls. Many apertures. In some cases walls consist almost entirely of glass (windows). Walls no longer needed for support. Effect of limitless space. Recessed portals highly ornamented with sculptural decoration—figures, naturalistic, foliage, etc. Rose and lancet windows. Accent on *verticality*. Every tower, lancet (window), spire, and pinnacle points toward heaven.

Chief contribution: Development of pointed arch and flying buttress.

SCULPTURE: Concentrated chiefly about the portals, but used extensively elsewhere. Figures first formalized and architectural, later more naturalistic. Facial expression important. Sculpture subordinated to architecture—much of it symbolical—some grotesque. English cathedrals also profusely decorated.

PAINTING: Little wall space, but painting used decoratively on structural parts of churches. Color obtained by introduction of stained glass windows. Stained glass of Gothic period unsurpassed.

BIBLIOGRAPHY (CHAPTERS IX AND X)

ADAMS, Henry, *Mont-Saint-Michel and Chartres* (Houghton Mifflin Co., Boston, 1930).

BAUM, Julius (ed.), *Romanesque Architecture in France* (E. P. Dutton & Co., N. Y., 1912).

BUMPUS, L. Francis, *The Cathedrals of France* (London, 1927).

BUSHNELL, A. J., *Storied Windows* (The Macmillan Co., N. Y., 1914).

GARDNER, Arthur, *Medieval Sculpture in France* (The Macmillan Co., N. Y., 1931).

LETHABY, W. R., *Medieval Art* (Charles Scribner's Sons, N. Y., 1913).

MOORE, C. H., *Development and Character of Gothic Architecture* (The Macmillan Co., N. Y., 1899).

PARKHURST, Helen Huss, *Cathedral* (Houghton Mifflin Co., Boston, 1936).

RAYNER, Edwin, *Famous Cathedrals and Their Stories* (Grosset & Dunlap, Inc., N. Y., 1935).

WORRINGER, Wilhelm, *Form in Gothic*, tr. by Herbert Read (London, 1927).

STONEHENGE. Cromlechs. Salisbury Plain, England. (Ewing Galloway)

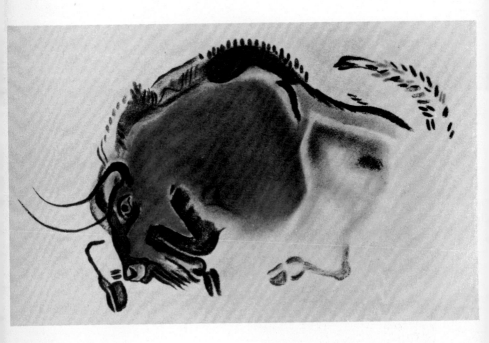

GIZEH. Sphinx and Great Pyramids.

Opposite page
Upper. FONT DE GAUME CAVE, France.
        Galloping Horse. (drawn by Breuil)

Lower. ALTAMIRA CAVE, Spain.
        Bison at Rest. (drawn by Breuil)

EGYPTIAN ART

3

ABU-SIMEL. Rock-cut temple. Statues of Ramses II. 66 ft. high.

DEIR-EL-BAHRI. Temple of Queen Hatshepsut, from southwest

KARNAK. Reconstruction of hypostyle hall, Temple of Karnak. The two styles of capitals represent the bud and opened flower of the papyrus plant.
Metropolitan Museum of Art.

KARNAK. Columns of hypostyle hall.

SHEIKH EL-BELED. Wooden statue.
5th Dynasty. Cairo Museum, Egypt.

PRINCE AS SCRIBE. Portrait statue. About 2800 B.C. 4th dynasty.

Museum of Fine Arts, Boston.

Opposite page

Upper left. QUEEN NOFRETETE. Painted limestone with rock
crystal eyes. Life-size. Reconstructed after original in
the Berlin Museum. (Metropolitan Museum of Art)

Lower left. RAMSES II wearing a war helmet. Brown quartzite.
Broken from a life-size statue. 19th Dynasty.

Metropolitan Museum of Art.

HATSHEPSUT
as king offering jars of
wine to the god Amon.
From   Deir-el-Bahri,
Thebes.
Metropolitan Museum
of Art.

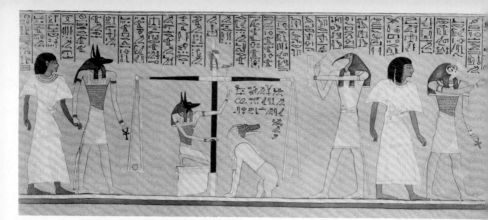

BOOK OF THE DEAD. Detail from the Papyrus of Hunefer. The jackal-headed god Anubis presides over the weighing of the conscience (heart). British Museum.

OFFERING BEARER. Painted wooden funerary figure from a Theban tomb. Basket on head contains models of meats and a wild duck.

Metropolitan Museum of Art

CAT. Bronze. 22nd Dynasty or later.
University Museum, Philadelphia.

Opposite page
STELE OF
IKHNATON
Relief showing Ikhnaton and his wife, Nofretete, playing with their daughters. From El Amarna.
Berlin Museum.

NAKHT HUNTING
Detail from a wall painting of Nakht and his family hunting fish and fowl. He holds fowling stick in his raised hand. Tomb of Nakht, Thebes.

CAT EATING FISH
Detail from a wall painting. Tomb of Nakht, Thebes.

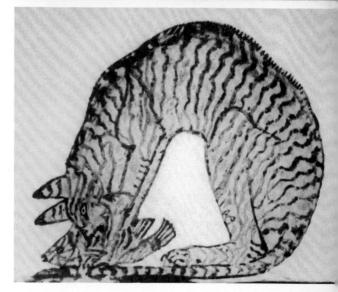

BABYLON in the days of Nebuchadnezzar (605-562 B.C.). Note ziggurat
at upper left. Painting by Bardin after
Unger.

SUMERIAN NOBLE. Limestone statuette from Khafaje.
University Museum, Philadelphia.

Upper
PALACE OF SARGON (722-705 B.C.),
Khorsabad. Reconstruction of façade, after
Place.

Lower
DYING LIONESS. Relief from the Pal-
ace of Ashurbanipal (669-626 B.C.) a
Nineveh. British Museum.

ASHURBANIPAL DINING WITH
QUEEN, attended by servants, fan bearers,
and musicians. Severed head of his enemy
hangs in tree at left. A cast made from a relief in the British Museum.
(Oriental Institute, University of Chicago)

GUDEA. Sumerian head carved from diorite.
Museum of Fine Arts, Boston.

VAPHIO CUPS. Gold repoussé, decorated with bulls and men. 3½ in. About 1600-1100 B.C. Reproductions from originals in the National Museum, Athens. (Metropolitan Museum of Art)

Opposite page
ASHURBANIPAL
HUNTING. Ashurbanipal, drawing his bow, rides ahead of his attendants. Relief.
British Museum.

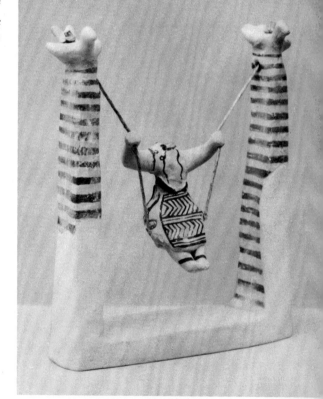

GIRL IN A SWING. Painted clay. 5½ in. high. About 1600 B.C. Reproduction of original found at Hagia Triada. (Metropolitan Museum of Art)

PALACE OF THE MINOS. Knossos. Queen's Megaron, restored view. (From Sir Arthur Evans, *Palace of Minos*, Macmillan Company, London)

SNAKE GODDESS. Gold and ivory statuette. 6 in. high. About 1500 B.C.

Museum of Fine Arts, Boston.

LION GATE. Mycenae.
Late Minoan period.

OCTOPUS VASE, false necked.
About 8 in. high. Reproduction
from original in the Candia Museum.
(Metropolitan Museum of Art)

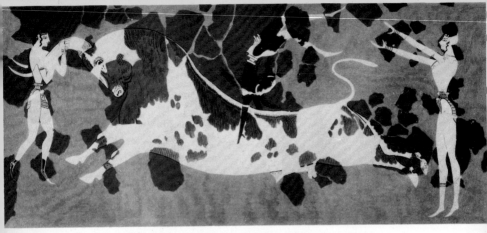

ACROBATS WITH A BULL. Fresco from Knossos. About 1500 B.C. Reproduced from original in the Candia Museum.
(Metropolitan Museum of Art)

ACROPOLIS. Athens. The Erectheum is at left, the Parthenon on the right. View from west.

Opposite page

Lower. HUNTER WITH HORSE AND DOG. Fresco
from Tiryns. Restored copy.
(University Museum, Philadelphia)

PARTHENON. Acropolis, Athens. Southwest corner.

ATHLETES. Palaestra scene. Ball players, jumpers, wrestlers, spear throwers. Frieze. 510 B.C.   (Clarence Kennedy)

PARTHENON. Restored
model. Northeast view.
Metropolitan Museum of Art.

PARTHENON. Restored
model of the interior.
Metropolitan Museum of Art.

PORCH OF MAIDENS. Erectheum. Acropolis, Athens. Southwest corner.

Opposite page
TEMPLE OF NIKE. Acropolis, Athens. West façade.

MAIDEN FROM THE ACROPOLIS.
6th cent. B.C. Cast made from the
marble original.
(Metropolitan Museum of Art)

APOLLO. Greek youth of the Apollo
type. 6 ft. 4 in. high. End of 6th cent.
B.C. Metropolitan Museum of Art.

LUDOVISI THRONE. Center panel of a three-sided relief. 40 in. high. Marble. 480 B.C. Terme Museum, Rome.

CHARIOTEER. Part of a chariot group. Bronze. 6 ft. high. Museum, Delphi.
(Clarence Kennedy)

Opposite page
Left. DISCOBOLUS by Myron. Composite reconstruction. Torso after marble copy in the Terme Museum, Rome; head after Lancelotti bronze.
(Metropolitan Museum of Art)

Right. DORYPHORUS. Attributed to Polyclitus. National Museum, Naples.

APOLLO. West pediment. Temple of Zeus at Olympia.

Museum, Olympia.

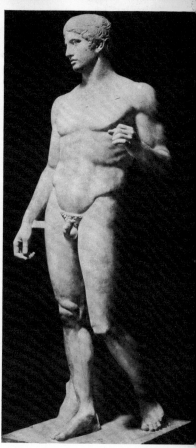

HORSE OF SELENE. East pediment.
Parthenon. British Museum.

VICTORY ADJUSTING
HER SANDAL
421-415 B.C.
Acropolis Museum,
                    Athens.

Opposite page
Upper. THESEUS. East pediment of
the Parthenon. Pentelic marble. 3 ft.
10 in. high. 447-432 B.C.
                    British Museum.

Lower. PARTHENON FRIEZE
North side. Pentelic marble. 40 in.
high. 447-432 B.C. British Museum.

ATHENE LEMNIA. After Phidias. Museo Civica, Bologna.
(Clarence Kennedy)

APOXYOMENOS. After Lysippus. 4th cent. B.C., last half. Vatican Museum, Rome.

HERMES, with infant Dionysus. By Praxiteles. 7 ft. high. 350 B.C. Museum, Olympia.
(Clarence Kennedy)

DEMETER. School of Scopas. Head of the statue from Cnidus. Marble. About 350 B.C. *Marbles and Bronzes*, edited by Walters (British Museum)

MAUSOLUS. Head from the cast of the colossal statue found at Halicarnassus. Original in the British Museum. 4th cent.
(Metropolitan Museum of Art)

DYING GAUL. Hellenistic period. Capitoline Museum, Rome.

VENUS DE MILO. Marble.
C. 300 B.C. Louvre.

VENUS. Found at Cyrene. Hellenistic copy of a 4th
cent. type. Terme Museum, Rome.

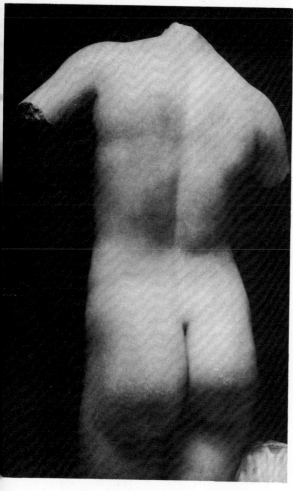

HUNTER WITH DOG. Red-figured
Attic vase, lekythos. By the Pan
Painter, 500-475 B.C.
Metropolitan Museum of Art.

Opposite page
WINGED VICTORY OF
SAMOTHRACE. 306 B.C. Louvre.

ATHENE SLAYING A GIANT
Frieze from the altar at Pergamum.
2nd cent. B.C. Pergamum Museum,
Berlin.

BOXER. Bronze.
Hellenistic period.
Terme Museum, Rome.

RABBIT, LIZARD, AND
MUSHROOMS. Glass mosaic. 1st
cent. A.D. Graeco-Roman.
    Metropolitan Museum of Art.

DANCER.   Terra-cotta   figurine.
4th-3rd cent. B.C.
    Walters Art Gallery, Baltimore.

BATTLE OF ISSUS. Alexander and Darius. Mosaic from Pompeii, detail. 17 ft. long.

Naples Museum.

WOMEN PUTTING
AWAY CLOTHES
Red-figured Attic vase
painting by Douris
About 470 B.C.
Metropolitan Museum
of Art

INITIATION INTO THE MYSTERIES. Fresco in the House of Mysteries at Pompeii.

STRIDING WARRIOR. Etrus-
can. Terra-cotta. C. 500 B.C.
Metropolitan Museum of Art.

BANQUET SCENE, with
dancers and musicians. Etruscan wall painting. 5th cent. B.C.
Tomb of the Leopards, Corneto.

PANTHEON. Rome. Reconstructed model. C. 120 A.D. Metropolitan Museum of Art.

BATHS OF CARACALLA. Rome. 3rd cent. A.D. Restored by Spiers.

COLOSSEUM. Rome. 70-82 A.D.

INTERIOR OF COLOSSEUM

THE PONT DU GARD. 160 ft. high. Nimes, France

TRIUMPH OF TITUS. Relief inside the Arch of Titus, Rome. 81 A.D. (Philip Gendreau

ARA PACIS FRIEZE. Procession detail. 13-9 B.C. Uffizi Gallery, Florence.

EMPEROR AUGUSTUS. Marble.

PORTRAIT OF CHILD. 1st cent. A.D.
Both above, Museum of Fine Arts, Boston.

TAJ MAHAL. Agra, India. 1632-53 A.D. (Vic Kayfetz)

ARCH AT CTESIPHON. Iraq. 83 ft. wide and 100 ft. high. C. 129 A.D. by Parthians.
(Philip Gendreau)

REINDEER. Gold shield ornament. From Kuban. 7th cent. B.C. Hermitage Museum, Leningrad.

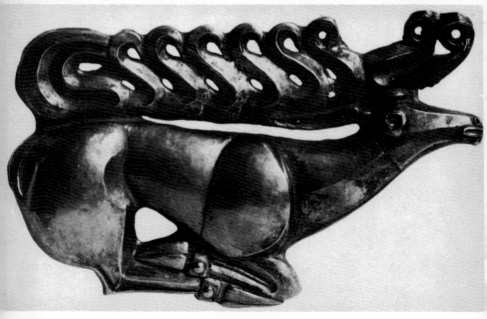

MOHAMMEDAN AND ANCIENT PERSIAN ART

PERSEPOLIS. Iran. Stairway to Audience Hall of Palace of Darius and Xerxes. 13 columns remain of 72 which once supported the roof.

LION ATTACKING BULL. Detail of relief seen on stairway above.

MOSQUE OF THE SHAH
Isfahan, Iran. 1612. Entrance
façade with minarets.
(Eric R. Schmidt)

**MOSQUE OF SULTAN
HASSAN.** Cairo, Egypt. 1356.
Dome shows that it is a tomb
mosque.

ALHAMBRA. Granada, Spain. 1248-1354. Court of Lions.

ALHAMBRA. Court of Myrtles.

GREAT MOSQUE OF CORDOVA, Spain. Interior. (Ewing Galloway)

BAHRAM HUNTING WILD ASSES. Persian miniature painting. About 1310.
Worcester Art Museum.

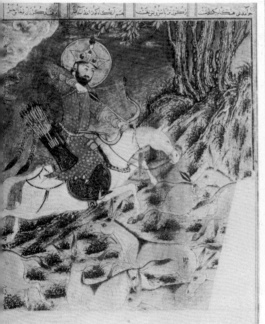

PRAYER RUG. North Persian. 16th cent. Note Arabic script woven into design.
Metropolitan Museum of Art.

MOHAMMEDAN AND ANCIENT PERSIAN ART

HAGIA SOPHIA. Istanbul, Turkey. 532-537.

HAGIA SOPHIA. Interior. Recently uncovered mosaics may be
seen decorating the upper portions
of the walls.

EMPRESS THEODORA AND HER RETINUE. Mosaic. Copy of the original in the Church of San Vitale, Ravenna, Italy. Detail. (Metropolitan Museum of Art)

MAKING WINE. Mosaic detail. Church of Santa Costanza, Rome. Early Christian.

CHRISTIAN AT PRAYER. Copy of a painting in the Cata comb of St. Pretextat.

CHRIST AS THE GOOD SHEPHERD. Early Christian. 2nd cent.
     Lateran Museum, Rome.

ST. MARK'S CATHEDRAL. Venice. Begun 1063 A.D. (Lillian Christensen)

HORSES OF ST. MARK'S
Close-up view of the horses over the entrance to the Cathedral.

(Lillian Christensen)

CHURCH OF ST. TROPHIME
Arles. Early 12th cent. Façade sculptures.

ABBEY CHURCH OF FONTEVRAULT
1101-1119. Note square bay.

VEZELAY. Abbey Church. 1132-1142. Tympanum over north portal. Scenes from everyday life surround central panel. From a cast.

MOISSAC. Church of St. Pierre. C. 1100. Tympanum over south portal. Christ in majesty and the twenty-four elders. From a cast.

CATHEDRAL OF
ST. FRONT. Péri-
gueux. Apse side.

NOTRE DAME DE
PONTAUT. Chapter
house of Abbey. From
Pontaut, France.
Ribbed vault may be
seen. The Cloisters,
Metropolitan Museum
of Art.

BOOK OF KELLS. Celtic. 8th-9th cent. Detail from a page.
Trinity College, Dublin.

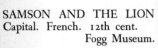

SAMSON AND THE LION
Capital. French. 12th cent.
Fogg Museum.

VLADIMIR MADONNA
Copy by Bryagine. 11th
cent. Russian.
Historical Museum, Moscow.

DEATH OF ABSOLOM
Miniature painting in the
Winchester Bible. English.
12th cent.
Pierpont Morgan Library.

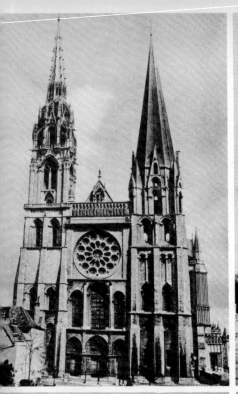

CHARTRES CATHEDRAL, seen from the air. Note cruciform shape. (Philip Gendreau)

Opposite page: Façades of four principal French Gothic cathedrals.

Upper left. CHARTRES. 12th-13th cent.

Upper right. AMIENS. 12th-13th cent.

Lower left. RHEIMS. 1221-1288. (Ewing Galloway)

Lower right. PARIS. Notre Dame. 1163-1235.

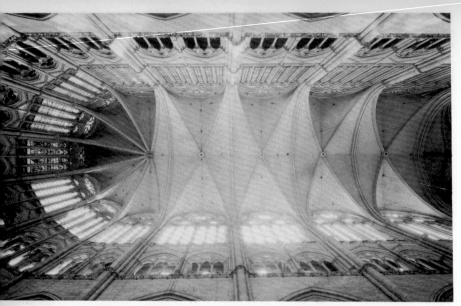

AMIENS CATHEDRAL. Ceiling detail. Apse end. Plan of rectangular bay may be seen. Below. Looking toward apse. (Clarence Ward—both photos)

ROSE WINDOW. Chartres
Cathedral. With five smaller
stained glass windows below.
13th cent. (Ewing Galloway)

"THE DEVIL LOOKING
OVER HIS CITY." Etching by
Charles Meryon (1821-1868)
showing a gargoyle of Notre
Dame Cathedral, Paris.
New York Public Library.

THE FOOLISH VIRGINS AND THEIR SEDUCER. Sculptured figures from the south portal.
Strasbourg Cathedral.

THE DEAD RISING FROM THEIR GRAVES. Details from the Last Judgment panel on the
tympanum of the central doorway. Bourges Cathedral.

CHRIST IN MAJESTY, surrounded by the
four beasts of the Apocalypse. Chartres Cathedral.
Tympanum over center door, the Porte Royal.

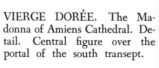

VIERGE DORÉE. The Ma-
donna of Amiens Cathedral. Detail. Central figure over the
portal of the south transept.

SANCHI STUPA GATE. 3rd cent. B.C. (Cohn-Weiner)

BORO BUDUR TEMPLE. Java. About 8th-9th cent.

STUPAS. Atop Boro Budur Temple. Close-up view.

KARLI CAVE TEMPLE. Bombay. 1st cent. B.C. Assembly Hall. 125 ft. long, 46 ft. high, 46 ft. wide. Buddhist. (Ewing Galloway)

ANGKOR VAT TEMPLE. Cambodia. 12th cent. Upper tier of structure.

Above. DANCING SIVA. Bronze. 14th
cent. 33½ in. high.
William Rockhill Nelson Gallery,
                Kansas City, Missouri.

Right. UDAY SHAN-KAR, modern Indian dancer, and his partner, reinterpret
classic gestures in their dances.

AVALOKITESHVARA.   Ceylonese.   8th
cent. Bronze. 3⅝ in. high.
            Museum of Fine Arts, Boston.

DEVI or deified queen. South India. Late 11th or early 12th cent.
Bronze processional figure.
            Freer Gallery, Washington.

THE MINISTER HIRU LANDS IN
HIRUKA. Relief from Boro Budur Temple.

AJANTA CAVES. The Questions to Sāriputra. Fresco. Cave XVII. C. 5th cent.

ANGKOR THOM. Small Buddhist sanctuary now completely overgrown and encircled by the roots and trunk of a tropical tree.

TEMPLE OF HEAVEN. Peiping. 12th cent.

CHIMERA. Stone. 5th-6th cent. Colossal size. University Museum, Philadelphia.

AILOU. Western gate to Ming tombs. 1420. Marble. Upper detail.

THE FORBIDDEN CITY. Peiping. Air view.

SIDDHARTHA IN MEDITATION. From the Lungmen Caves. Northern Wei period.
Museum of Fine Arts, Boston

LAO-TZU ON WATER BUFFALO. Bronze statuette. Sung Dynasty (960-1279). Worcester Art Museum.

KUAN-YIN. Sung Dynasty (960-1279).
Polychrome wood. Art Institute of Chicago.

LUTE PLAYER. Tomb figure.
T'ang Dynasty (618-906). Red
painted unglazed clay.
      Art Institute of Chicago.

Opposite page
Left. ADORING BODHISATTVA. Chinese Buddhist. 8th cent. Polychrome clay.
      Fogg Museum, Harvard University.

Right. STANDING WOMAN. Terra-cotta.
Early T'ang Dynasty. 7th-8th cent.
      Yale University Art Gallery.

LANDSCAPE. Scroll painting by Tung Yuan. Sung Dynasty (960-1279). Detail.

Museum of Fine Arts, Boston.

馬
遠
松
陰
玩
月

LANDSCAPE. Attributed to Ma Yuan. Active 1190-1224. Metropolitan Museum of Art.

LADIES PLAYING "DOUBLE SIXES," a game. Style of Chou Fang. Sung Dynasty or earlier. Scroll painting, color on silk. Freer Gallery, Washington.

BUDDHA OF KAMAKURA
Bronze. 1252.
(Mrs. Gertrude Emerson Sen)

PAGODA OF HOKKIJI. 706.
Oldest extant three-storied pagoda.

YUMEDOMO. Monastery at Horiuji. 607.

GUARDIAN SHIKKONGOJIN
Unbaked clay with drapery supported by copper wire.
(From Langdon Warner, *Craft of the Japanese Sculptor*)

KWANNON. Head of wooden sculpture in the Yumedomo of Horiuji Temple, Nara. Detail. The crown is made of pierced copper. Early 7th cent.
(From Langdon Warner, *Sculpture of the Suiko Period*)

THE WAVE. Ogata Korin (1653?-1716). Detail of two-fold paper screen painted on gold ground.
Metropolitan Museum of Art.

THE BURNING OF SANJO PALACE.
Heiji Monogatari. 13th cent. Detail.
Museum of Fine Arts, Boston.

MIROKU, so-called Hokei Ny-
oirin Kwannon. Wood and lacquered leather. Hairdo is copied
from typical Chinese T'ang
style. Kyoto Imperial Museum.
(From Langdon Warner,
Sculpture of the Suiko Period)

SOGA SHOHAKU (1730-1783).
Three Laughers. Detail of a two-pan-
eled painted screen.
      Museum of Fine Arts, Boston.

Opposite page
GIOTTO (c. 1276-1337). Fresc
Massacre of the Innocents. Deta
Arena Chapel, Padua.

ORCAGNA (c. 1308-1368). T
Triumph of Death. Detail.
Camposanto, Pisa.

HARUNOBU (c. 1718-1770). A
Windy Day. Colored wood-block
print. Art Institute of Chicago.

SASSETTA (1392-1450). St. Anthony Tormented by Demons. Yale University Gallery of Art.

DUCCIO (1260-c.1320). Three Marys at the Tomb.
Cathedral Museum, Siena.

SIMONE MARTINI (1284-1344).
St. Anthony, the Abbot.
Church of St. Francis, Assissi.

ANTONIO POLLAIUOLO
(1433-1496). Battle of Nude
Men. Engraving.
Metropolitan Museum of Art.

GOZZOLI (1420-1497). Journey of the Magi. Fresco, detail.
Medici-Riccardi Palace, Florence.

MANTEGNA (1431-1506). Tarquin and the Cumaean Sibyl.
Cincinnati Art Museum.

GHIRLANDAJO (1449-1494). Birth of the Virgin. Detail.
St. Maria Novella, Florence.

MASACCIO (1401-1428)
Adam and Eve Expelled
from the Garden of Eden
Fresco panel.
Brancacci Chapel, Florence

FRA FILIPPO LIPPI (c. 1406-1469). The Annunciation. 40½ x 64 in. National Gallery.

FRA ANGELICO (1387-1455). The Annunciation. San Marco Museum, Florence.

BOTTICELLI (1444-1510). Jethro's Daughters. Fresco, detail. Sistine Chapel, Rome.

Lower. BOTTICELLI. Birth of Venus. Uffizi Gallery, Florence.

LEONARDO DA VINCI (1452-1519). Madonna of the Rocks. Louvre.

LEONARDO DA VINCI. Last
Supper. Fresco. St. Maria delle
Grazie, Milan.

LEONARDO DA VINCI
Mona Lisa, or La Gioconda.
Louvre.

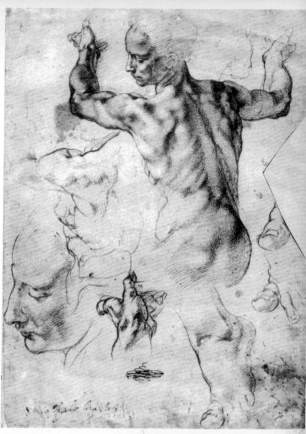

MICHELANGELO (1475-1564).
Studies in red chalk for the Libyan
Sibyl on the Sistine Chapel ceiling.
Metropolitan Museum of Art.

MICHELANGELO. Creation of
Adam. Fresco panel. Sistine
Chapel ceiling, Rome.

RAPHAEL (1483-1520). School of Athens. Vatican, Rome.

MICHELANGELO. Sistine Chapel ceiling frescos. Rome.

MICHELANGELO. Drunkenness of Noah. Fresco panel. Sistine Chapel, Rome.

RAPHAEL. Pope Julius II.
Detail. Uffizi Gallery, Florence.

GENTILE BELLINI (1429-
1507). A Turkish Artist. Isabella Stewart Gardner Museum,
Boston.

ANDREA DEL SARTO
(1486-1531). Madonna and
Child with Infant St. John.
National Gallery.

CORREGGIO (1494-1534).
Madonna with St. Jerome.
Detail. Pinacoteca, Parma.

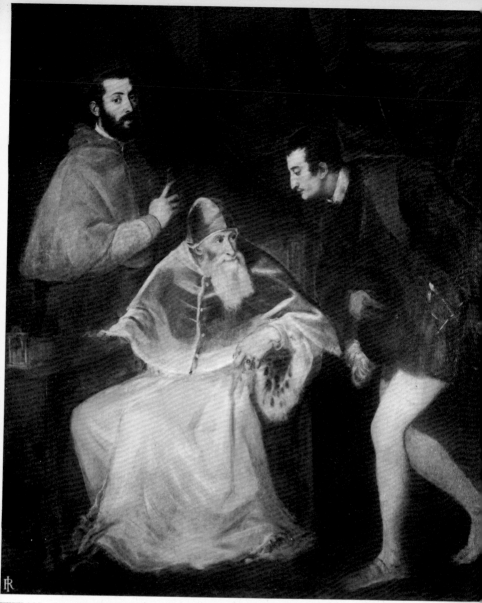

TITIAN. Pope Paul III of Farnese, his nephew Luigi, and a cardinal. National Museum, Naples.

Opposite page
Upper. TITIAN (1477-1576). Venus and the Lute Player.
Metropolitan Museum of Art.

Lower. CARPACCIO (c. 1455-1526). Vision of St. Ursula.
Academy, Venice.

Opposite page
Upper. TINTORETTO (1518-1594).
Bacchus and Ariadne Crowned by
Venus. Figures slightly above life-size.

Lower. VERONESE (1528-1588).
The Finding of Moses. Detail. 22¾ x
17½ in.
National Gallery, Washington.

Right. JACOPO DELLA QUERCIA
(c. 1367-1438). Madonna and Child.
Louvre.

Below. GIORGIONE (1478-1510).
Fête Champêtre. Louvre.

DONATELLO (1386-1466).
Niccolo da Uzzano.
National Museum, Florence.

BRUNELLESCHI (1377-
1446). Sacrifice of Isaac.
Bronze panel submitted in
competition for North Door
of the Baptistery, Florence.

VERROCCHIO (1435-1488). Colleoni. Venice.

GHIBERTI (1378-1455). Sacrifice of Isaac. Bronze. Panel of East Door of the Baptistery (Gates of Paradise). Florence.

MICHELANGELO (1475-1564)
Tomb of Guiliano de Medici. New
Sacristy, San Lorenzo. Florence.
Below. Detail. "Day" from tomb
sculpture.

MICHELANGELO. Moses. Rome.

MICHELANGELO. Pietà. Ba-
ilica of St. Peter, Rome.

ANDREA DELLA ROBBIA
(1435-1525). Head of a Youth.
Medallion. Glazed terra-cotta.
Metropolitan Museum of Art.

BERNINI (1598-1680). St. Theresa in Ecstasy. Detail. St. Maria della Vittoria, Rome.

CELLINI (1500-1571).
Cup of gold, enamel, pearls.
Metropolitan Museum of Art.

ITALIAN RENAISSANCE ART 107

FLORENCE. Cathedral, Santa Maria del Fiore. 1296-1462. Dome by Brunelleschi.

(Ewing Galloway)

VENICE. Ducal Palace. (Lillian Christensen)

ROME. St. Peter's.

FLORENCE. Medici-Riccardi Palace. 1444.

HUBERT AND JAN VAN EYCK (1366-1426—1385-1441). Adoration of the Mystic Lamb. Center detail. Church of St. Bavon, Ghent. Copyright, Huntington Library and Gallery, San Marino.

VAN DER WEYDEN (1399-1464).
Madonna and Child.
Copyright, Huntington Library and
Gallery, San Marino.

MEMLING (c. 1430-1494). Portrait
of a Lady.
      Metropolitan Museum of Art.

MASSYS (1465/6-1530). Man with
Pink. Art Institute of Chicago.

BOSCH (c. 1450-1516). Mocking of Christ. Before painting was cleaned.

Art Museum, Princeton University

Opposite page
Upper. PIETER BRUEGHEL the Elder (1520-1569). The Wedding Dance. Detail.

Detroit Institute of Ar

Lower. PIETER BRUEGHEL the Elder. Unfaithful Shepherd.

John G. Johnson Collection, Philadelph

RUBENS (1577-1640). Suzanne Fourmont, in a straw hat.
National Gallery, London.

VAN DYCK (1599-1641). James Stuart, Duke of Lennox.
Metropolitan Museum of Art.

DE HOOCH (1629-c. 1683). In the Pantry. 27 in. high. Rijksmuseum, Amsterdam.

STEEN (c. 1626-1679). Fair at Oestgeest. Detail. Detroit Institute of Arts.

TER BORCH (1617-1681). A Music Party. Detail.
Cincinnati Art Museum.

RUISDAEL (c. 1628-1682). Jewish Cemetery.
Detroit Institute of Arts.

HALS (1580-1666). Yonker Ramp and His Sweetheart.

Metropolitan Museum of Art.

VERMEER (1632-1675). Young Girl with a Flute. 7 x 7⅞ in.

National Gallery, Washington.

REMBRANDT (1606-1669).
Girl at Open Half Door.
Art Institute of Chicago.

REMBRANDT. Woman Carry-
ing a Child Downstairs. Pen
and wash drawing.
Pierpont Morgan Library.

REMBRANDT. Descent from the Cross by Torchlight. Etching.

Metropolitan Museum of Art.

REMBRANDT. Supper at Emmaus. Louvre.

LUCAS CRANACH the Elder (1472-1553). Judgment of Paris.
City Art Museum, St. Louis.

DÜRER (1471-1528). Madonna and Child with St. Anne. Metropolitan Museum of Art.

HOLBEIN (1497-1543). Catherine Howard. Toledo Museum of Art.

DÜRER. Knight, Death, and the Devil. Engraving.
   Metropolitan Museum of Art.

EL GRECO (1541-1614). The Holy Family. Cleveland Museum of Art.

EL GRECO. View of Toledo. Metropolitan Museum of Art.

GOYA (1746-1828). From
the "Disasters of War"—And
There Is No Remedy. Aqua-
tint.
Metropolitan Museum of Art.

VELAZQUEZ (1599-1660).
Don Baltazar Carlos.
Prado, Madrid.

Opposite page
VELAZQUEZ. Philip IV of
Spain. Copyright,
Frick Collection.

GOYA. Family of Charles
IV. Detail. Note portrait of
artist at left. Prado, Madrid.

GOYA. Duchess of Alba. Hispanic Society, N. Y.

MURILLO (1617-1682). The
Virgin and St. Anne.
Prado, Madrid.

SEVILLE. La Giralda Tower,
Cathedral. C. 1190. From
Orange Court.
(Philip Gendreau)

WREN (1632-1723).
Hampton Court Palace.
Middlesex, England.

GAINSBOROUGH (1727-
1788). The Blue Boy. Copyright, Huntington Library
and Gallery, San Marino

REYNOLDS (1723-1792). Jane, Countess of Harrington.
Copyright, Huntington Library and Gallery, San Marino.

GAINSBOROUGH. The
Artist's Daughters.
Worcester Art Museum.

CONSTABLE (1776-
1837). Stoke-by-Nayland.
49 x 66 in.
Art Institute of Chicago.

HOGARTH (1697-1764). The Shrimp Girl. National Gallery, London.

TURNER (1775-1851). Antwerp: Van Goyen Looking Out for a Subject. Copyright, Frick Collection.

BLAKE (1757-1827). Christ and the Woman Taken in Adultery. Water-color.

Museum of Fine Arts, Boston

EL CASTILLO. Mayan Pyramid at Chichen Itza, Yucatan. 13th or 14th cent. 105 ft. high. Base covers an acre.

AXE-SHAPED STONE
Human face with tatooing.
Totonac.
Cranbrook Academy,
Bloomfield Hills.

MAIZE GOD. Mayan. C. 300 A.D. Peabody Museum, Harvard University.

RIVERA (1886-   ). Zapatá, the Agrarian Leader, 1931. Fresco panel adapted from a fresco in the Ministry of Education, Mexico City. 93¾ x 74 in. Museum of Modern Art.

PYRAMID OF QUETZALCOATL. San Juan Teotihuacan, Mexico. Sculpture details. Toltec culture.

OROZCO (1883-   ). Table of Universal Brotherhood: Book of Peace—blank pages. Those who will write on it on equal terms include all the races of the world. Fresco panel. New School for Social Research, New York City.

PORTRAIT VASE. Pottery. Early Chimu, Peru. American Museum of Natural History, New York.

PAINTED SHIELD COVER. Sioux, from South Dakota.
Museum of the American Indian, New York.

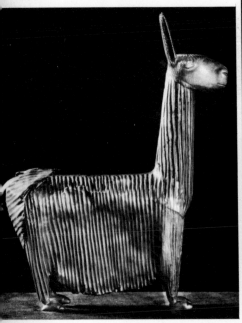

ALPACA. Silver. 9 in. high. Inca. Peru. American Museum of Natural History, New York.

HAIDA WOMAN. Wooden mask. From British Columbia. American Museum of Natural History, New York.

TAXCO, Mexico. Cathedral. (Hu Watson from Philip Gendreau)

BABY IN RED HIGH CHAIR. Artist unknown. C. 1790. 22 x 15¼ in.
Museum of Modern Art.

BY THE FIRESIDE. Artist unknown. 19th cent. 19 x 16 in. Museum of Modern Art.

WEST (1738-1820). Death of Wolfe. Detail. 60½ x 84 in. National Gallery of Canada, Ottawa.

TRUMBULL (1756-1843). Battle of Bunker Hill. Yale University Art Gallery.

PEALE (1741-1827). Benjamin Franklin. Pennsylvania Academy of Fine Arts, Philadelphia.

COPLEY (1737-1815). Mrs. Seymour Fort. 40 x 50 in. Wadsworth Atheneum, Hartford.

STUART (1755-1828). Mrs. Perez Morton. Worcester Art Museum.

Opposite page
INNESS (1825-1894). Home of the Heron. 1893.
30 x 45 in. Art Institute of Chicago.

ALLSTON (1779-1843). Elijah Fed by the Ravens. Museum of Fine Arts, Boston.

BINGHAM (1811-1879). Fur Traders Descending the Missouri. Metropolitan Museum of Art.

AUDUBON (1785-1851). Wild Turkey. Water-color. New York Historical Society.

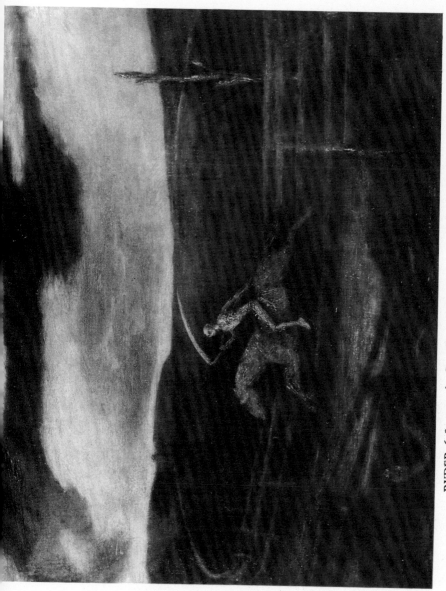

RYDER (1847-1917). Death on a Pale Horse. Cleveland Museum of Art.

SARGENT (1856-1925).
Madame X.
Metropolitan Museum
of Art.

EAKINS (1844-1916). Portrait of a Lady (Mrs. Eakins) with a Setter Dog.
Metropolitan Museum of Art.

WHISTLER (1834-1903). The Pacific. Copyright, Frick Collection.

BELLOWS (1882-1925). The Circus.
Addison Gallery of American Art, Phillips Academy, Andover.

SLOAN (1871-   ).
Old Clown Making
Up. Phillips Gallery,
Washington.

HOMER   (1836-
1910).   Herring Net.
1885. 29½ x 47½ in.
Art Institute of
            Chicago.

WOOD (1892-1942). American Gothic. 1930. 29⅞ x 25 in.
Art Institute of Chicago.

BURCHFIELD (1893-). Ice Glare. 1933. 30 x 24 in. Watercolor. Whitney Museum.

CASSATT (1845-1926).
In the Loge. National
Gallery, Washington.
(Chester Dale Collection
loan).

BENTON (1889-1947).
The Meal. 1926. 33 x
27 in. Tempera.
Whitney Museum.

MARIN (1875-   ). On Morse Mountain, Small Point, Maine.
Philip Goodwin Collection.

MT. VERNON. Arlington, Va. 1743. Home of Washington. (Samuel Chamberlain)

INDEPENDENCE HALL. Philadelphia. 1734. (Webb)

ART OF THE UNITED STATES

NEBRASKA STATE CAPITOL. Lincoln. Designed by Goodhue. Completed 1926.

UNIVERSITY OF VIRGINIA. Charlottesville. Designed by Jefferson. Late 18th cent.

ART OF THE UNITED STATES

VERSAILLES.   (1805-
1836).

ARC DE TRIOMPHE
Paris. (1806-1836).

BARYE (1796-1875).
Theseus and the Min-
otaur. Bronze.
Brooklyn Museum.

GOUJON (1510?-1568). Fountain of the Innocents. Paris. Nymph of the Seine panel.

RODIN (1840-1917). By the Sea. Marble statuette. Metropolitan Museum of Art.

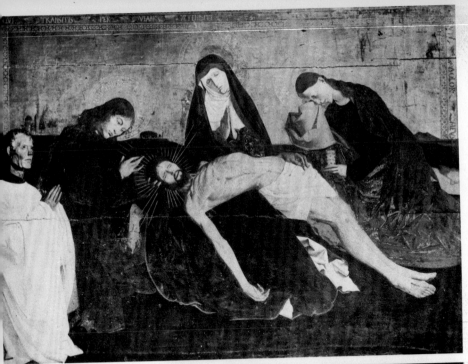

PIETÀ. Virgin Mary, Mary Magdalene, St. John, and a donor. About 1475. Louvre.

JEAN CLOUET (fl. c. 1516-1546). Charlotte of France. Max and Leola Epstein Collection.

POUSSIN (1594-1665). Shepherds of Arcadia. Louvre.
CLAUDE LORRAINE (1600-1682). Figures on the Bank of a Stream. Water-color.
British Museum.

INGRES (1780-1867). Portrait
of a Gentleman.
Metropolitan Museum of Art.

CHARDIN (1699-1779). House
of Cards. National Gallery.

DAVID (1748-1825). Youth with a Horse. Detroit Institute of Arts.

GÉRICAULT (1791-1824). Riderless Races at Rome. Walters Art Gallery, Baltimore.

DAUMIER (1808-1879). Rue
Transnonain. Lithograph.

MILLET (1814-1875). Sower.
Museum of Fine Arts, Boston.

DELACROIX (1789-1863). July 28, 1830. Liberty Leading the People. Louvre.

COURBET (1819-1877). Mère
Gregoire. 50½ x 38 in.
Art Institute of Chicago.

MONET (1840-1926). Gladi-
olas. Detroit Institute of Arts.

SEURAT (1859-1891). Sunday on the Island of La Grande Jatte. 1886. 81 x 120⅜ in.
Art Institute of Chicag

MANET (1832-1883). Luncheon on the Grass. Louvre.

COROT (1796-1875). Portrait of a Girl, 1859. Chester Dale Collection.

MANET. Madame Michel-Levy. 1882.
    National Gallery, Washington. (Chester Dale Collection loan)

CÉZANNE (1839-1906). Village of Gardanne. Water-color. Brooklyn Museum.

CÉZANNE. Still Life with Apples. 1890-1900. 27 x 36½ in. Museum of Modern Art.

CÉZANNE. Card Players. Stephen C. Clark Collection.

Opposite page
Upper. DEGAS (1834-1917). The Rehearsal.
Copyright,
          Frick Collection.

Lower. TOULOUSE-LAUTREC (1864-1901). Au Moulin Rouge: Detail. The dance. H. P. McIlhenny Collection. Philadelphia Museum of Art.

RENOIR (1841-1919). La Bal à Bougival. Museum of Fine Arts, Boston.

GAUGUIN (1848-1903). The Moon and the Earth. 1893. Oil on burlap. 44¼ x 24 in. Museum of Modern Art.

ROUSSEAU (1844-1910). The
Sleeping Gypsy. 1897. 51 x 79 in.
Museum of Modern Art.

REDON (1840-1916). Mystery.
The Phillips Gallery, Washington.

VAN GOGH (1853-1890).
The Postman Roulin.
Museum of Fine Arts,
Boston.

VAN GOGH. Stairway at
Auvers.
City Art Museum, St. Louis.

AFRICAN SCULPTURE. Wooden
head from the Gabun district.
University Museum, Philadelphia.

DERAIN (1880-   ). Window on
the Park. 1912. 51½ x 34¼ in.
Museum of Modern Art.

DUCHAMP (1887-   ). Nude Descending a Staircase. 1912. 58⅜ x
35⅜ in. Mr. and Mrs. Walter C. Arensberg Collection.

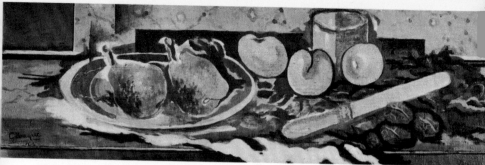

BRAQUE (1882-   ). Plums, Pears, Nuts, and Knife. Phillips Gallery, Washington.

PICASSO (1881-   ). Three Musicians. 1921. Philadelphia Museum of Art.

PICASSO. Guernica. Mural on canvas. May, 1937. 25 ft. 3 in. x 11 ft. 6 in. Owned by the artist, courtesy of the Museum of Modern Art.

MOORE (1898-   ). Reclining Figure. Elmwood. 1935-36. 19 in. high, 35 in. long. Albright Art Gallery, Buffalo.

MATISSE (1869-   ). Woman in White Dress. 1946.

PICASSO. Woman in White. 1923. 39 x 31½ in. Museum of Modern Art.

HIRICO (1888-   ). Delights of the Poet. C. 1913. 27⅜ x 34 in.
Museum of Modern Art.

FEININGER (1887-   ). Side-Wheeler. Detroit Institute of Arts.

SEVERINI (1883-). Pan-pan in Monaco.

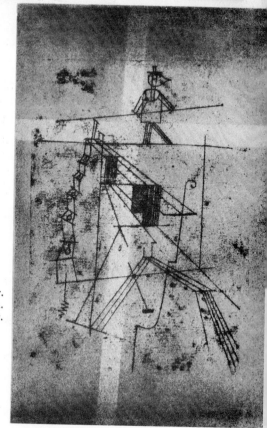

KLEE (1879-1940). Tight-Rope Walker. Color lithograph. 1923. 17½ x 10½ in. Museum of Modern Art.

KANDINSKY (1866-1944). Calm. 1926. 19 x 18 in. Museum of Non-Objective Painting.

MONDRIAN (1872-1944). Composition in white, black, and red. 1936. 40¼ x 41 in. Museum of Modern Art.

REBAY (1890-   ). Animation.
1941-2. 71½ x 71½ in.
Museum of Non-Objective Painting.

BAUER. Red Square. 1931.
17⅛ x 12½ in. Water-color,
tempera, and ink.
Museum of Non-Objective
                    Painting.

ROUAULT (1871-   ). The Old Clown. 1917. 44½ x 29⅜ in.
Edward G. Robinson Collection.

MODIGLIANI (1884-1920). Chanteuse de Café. Philadelphia Museum
of Art. (Chester Dale Collection loan)

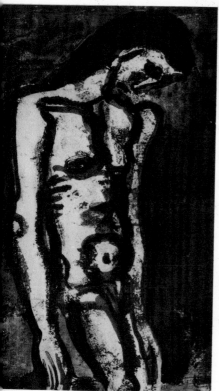

ROUAULT (1871-   ). Christ Forever Flagellated. Detail. Etching.
1922. 19 x 14⅜ in. On extended loan
to the Museum of Modern Art.

NEW YORK street scene with elevated railroad. (Berenice Abbott for the Federal Art Project.) Museum of the City of New York.

LEGER (1881-   ). Le Treillage Noir. 1943-44. 44 x 50 in.
Museum of Non-Objective Painting.

DAVIS (1894-   ). House and Street. 1940. 26 x 42⅖ in. Whitney Museum. A translation of a scene similar to the photograph opposite in terms of a semi-abstract composition.

DALI (1904-   ). Paranoic-Astral Image. 1934. 8⅝ x 6½ in.
Wadsworth Atheneum, Hartford.

ART OF THE TWENTIETH CENTURY   197

O'KEEFFE (1887-   ).
Long Island Sunset. International Business Machines Corporation.

Opposite page
Upper. WEBER (1881-
). Music.
        Brooklyn Museum.

Lower. MIRO (1893-
). Person Throwing
a Stone at a Bird. 1926.
29 x 36¼ in.
Museum of Modern Art.

CHAGALL (1889-   ).
I and My Village. 1911.
75⅝ x 59⅝ in.
Museum of Modern Art.

SHAHN (1898-   ). We Want
Peace. Poster.
        Museum of Modern Art.

MAILLOL (1861-1944). Seated
Woman. Paris. Garden of the
Tuileries.

EPSTEIN (1880-).
Mademoiselle Gabrielle
Soene.
    Toledo Museum of Art.

MILLES (1875-). Fountain of the Tritons. 1931. Bronze. Art Institute of Chicago.

LACHAISE (1882-1935). Floating Figure. 1927. Bronze. 53 in. high.
Museum of Modern Art.

ARCHIPENKO (1887-   ). Reclining Torso. Brooklyn Museum.

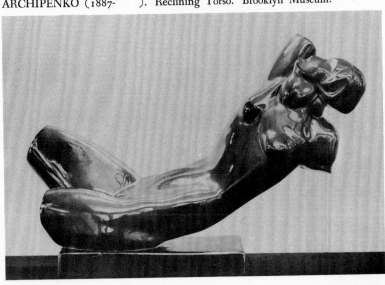

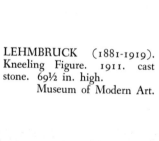

LEHMBRUCK (1881-1919). Kneeling Figure. 1911. cast stone. 69½ in. high.
Museum of Modern Art.

ZORACH (1887-   ).
Affection. York fossil.
Munson Williams Proctor Institute.

MOHOLY-NAGY (1895-1946). Space Modulator in
Plexi-glass. 1940. Mrs. Sybil Moholy-Nagy.

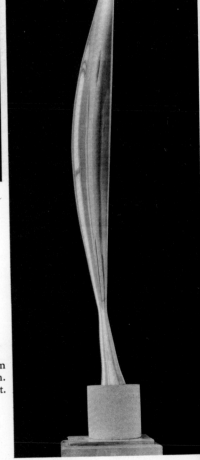

BRANCUSI (1876-   ). Bird in
Space. Bronze. 1919. 54 in. high.
Museum of Modern Art.

GROPIUS. The Bauhaus. Dessau, Germany. Students Building. Built 1925.

J. J. P. OUD. Workmen's houses, 1926-7. Hook of Holland.

WRIGHT (1869-   ). Above. Falling Water house. Bear Run, Pennsylvania. 1939. Owned
by Mr. and Mrs. Edgar J. Kauffman.
    Below. S. C. Johnson & Son Inc. Racine, Wisconsin. 1936-37. Administration Building.

LOW-COST HOUSING PROJECT. Westfield Acres, New Jersey. Built with PWA funds, 1942.
Hettel, Stonorov, & Associates. (Latham Studio)

MUNICIPAL ASPHALT PLANT. Borough of Manhattan, New York City. Exterior design.
Kahn and Jacobs.

R. C. A. BUILDING. Rockefeller Center. 1932. 850 ft. high. New York City. Corbett, Harrison & MacMurray; Hood & Fouilhoux; Reinhard & Hofmeister; architects.

CHAPTER XI

Art of India

INTERRUPTING the story of the progress of Christian art for a moment of time, we turn again to the Orient—India first, and then China and Japan. At this point Christian architecture in western Europe had reached its height, structurally speaking, with the Gothic style. Sculpture was already turning from the intensely spiritual manifestation of the Romanesque and early Gothic periods toward the naturalism or realism which was to be developed during the Italian Renaissance, when painting, too, become most important.

INDIA, A LAND OF CONTRASTS

India has often been described as a land of contrasts and extremes. Her northern snow-capped mountains are believed to be the highest in the world and with the exception of those in the Antarctic regions, the whitest and coldest. Below the frozen Himalayas the country is sub-tropical, but a changeable monsoon climate varying from extreme heat to frosty winters largely controls man's activities. In certain parts of the country, the rainfall is too heavy; elsewhere, it is too light. Great areas are covered with jungle, other areas are desert lands. Gold and the most precious stones as well as the more ordinary metals, copper and iron, are found together with such building materials as limestone and marble; here the forests produce sandal wood, teak wood, and ebony. India's population is equaled in density only by that of China. Within her borders at the present time live the wealthiest men on earth; although the greater proportion of her inhabitants exist in direst poverty. Her cities contain the finest palaces and the most miserable slums. Her culture is one of the oldest of all the nations and her inhabitants among the most peace-loving. She has adopted the outward forms of Western culture; but remains aloof and indifferent to many Western ideas. It has been said that the Indians have given more attention to spiritual thought than any other people on the globe. For their worship they have created some of the most amazing, the most highly decorated, and the most fanciful architecture the world has known. Their art, infused with both the joy of living and the spirit of contemplation, is perhaps the most difficult for an Occidental to understand. Whereas the Romanesque and Gothic sculptors denied the physical to emphasize the spiritual, the Indians seemed to have considered physical beauty a part of the great plan of existence.

The sub-continent of India, surrounded on three sides by water—the Indian Ocean, the Bay of Bengal, and the Arabian Sea—and separated from the remainder of Asia by the high Himalayas, deserts, and almost impenetrable forests, is as isolated as if it were an island instead of a peninsula. Only a few passes break through India's mountain barrier. Even in these modern times there are no railroads connecting her with the outside world. Bound for China, airplanes fly over the dangerous "hump" and in many cases ships unload their cargoes to lighters while still at sea, for there are few natural harbors to facilitate transportation. Easy access to the interior by water routes is further impeded by the sheer cliff-like edges of the vast plateaus which rise sharply from the narrow coastal plains. However, the rivers flowing east and west, especially those in the northern part of the country, do furnish fairly good highways for travel. Railroads now radiate from her most important cities: Calcutta, situated on one of the mouths of the Ganges River; Bombay, on the one fine harbor in India; Delhi, the city of fabulous wealth which was the old capital of the Mogul Empire and more recently (since 1912) the center of the English government while it was in India.

In the days of the Moguls, Delhi was made a city of fairy-like splendor. Here the monarchs sat upon the famous *Peacock Throne* which was made of gold and covered with a canopy upheld by pillars of the same precious metal. On it two peacocks on either side of a life-sized parrot were carved from a single emerald.

Palaces and other governmental structures were magnificent. Near by was the city of Agra where Shah Jehan erected the *Taj Mahal,* "the pearl of India," which has been described in a previous chapter.

EARLY DAYS IN INDIA

Despite the forbidding barriers of mountains, deserts, and sea, foreigners filtered in through the mountain passes. Among them were the nomadic Aryans (c. 1400 B.C.), the Persians (520 B.C.), the Greeks led by Alexander the Great (326 B.C.), successive waves of Mohammedans, and finally the Moguls who came to establish an empire in the 16th century A.D. The Aryans drove the native Dravidians south of the Ganges. These ancient inhabitants are thought to have been a carefree people who looked to their thirty-three Vedic gods for the personal satisfactions which are obtained from physical comfort and worldly pleasures. To them heaven seemed but a continuation of earthly joys. To obtain the favor of the gods, ancestral worship and the sacrificial ritual were practiced as in other Oriental countries. As time went on the Aryan invaders developed a caste system based largely on race differences—doubtless for their own preservation, since they were fewer in number than the conquered peoples. The old Vedic pantheon was multiplied and their gods were numbered by the hundreds. In time iconography and ritual became too complicated for the people to understand and the father of the household could no longer conduct the elaborate ceremonies which had replaced the simple sacrifice. With the advent of the belief that the gods were required to grant the petitions of the worshippers—that is, if they were properly approached—great power accrued to intermediaries, the Aryan priests. Because of this prestige the Brahmins eventually became the highest caste in the entire system, for the people were induced to believe that these priests alone could deal with Indra, the national god of the Indo-Aryans. Next in rank to the priests, in the order named, were the soldiers, the merchants, craftsmen, those who performed menial tasks, and below all the "untouchables," who lived outside the system.

It naturally followed that under such circumstances the religion of the learned would be quite different from that of the masses. As a result the people chose the path of devotional worship which was the only one they could understand while the intellectuals, who sought the way of knowledge, gathered together the sacred works and wrote them in Sanskrit, which became the language of the learned. The old Dravidian transmigration-reincarnation theory which was still accepted had posed a question—how to circumvent the fate of endless reincarnation over which one had little control. According to belief, it seemed that after death the soul enjoyed a brief sojourn in another form. If it could show a former life filled with good works the soul might reappear in the form of a prince or even a Brahmin; on the other hand, if good deeds were found wanting it could be forced to return as a lowly insect or plant. Some men attempted to solve the question by living an ascetic life spent in meditation. Through withdrawal from the world or self-inflicted suffering they sought to avoid evil and thereby insure themselves a better life in the next reincarnation.

BUDDHA AND THE DOCTRINE OF NON-SELF

During the sixth century a great wave of spiritual thought swept over all Asia and there was increased activity in art. Numerous cults appeared, among them Buddhism. About the middle of the century, there was born an Indian prince, Siddharta Gautama (563-483 B.C.), who was to be greatly affected by this spiritual intensification. Preceding the medieval monk St. Francis by more than fifteen centuries, this high-born nobleman likewise relinquished his princely estate and devoted his time to spreading the humanistic gospel of love and kindness to all living things. Before the thirtieth year of his life, Siddharta had drunk deeply of earthly pleasures only to find that they did not satisfy the yearnings of the spirit. Brooding long over the sorrows and sufferings of humanity, he decided to give up his inheritance, abandon his young wife and their small son, and seek the way of the spirit. Like St. Francis, he exchanged his princely robes for the garments of a vagrant and thus attired set forth in search of salvation.

For a while he resided with a number of philosophers who also were seeking the truth and attempting to discover how one might avoid reincarnation. After much time spent in long discussions, he left these hermits and sat alone under a banyan tree where, by excluding from his mind all thoughts of external phenomena and remaining inactive day after day, he was able to direct his thoughts inward. After remaining in this receptive state for six years the truth suddenly appeared to him in the form of a great illumination. From this time onward he was known as Buddha, the "Enlightened One."

Buddha believed that one could not find ultimate happiness in this worldly life, nor could one attain it by the opposite practice of self-torture. There must be, so he thought, a "golden mean" conducive to Nirvana, a state of mind devoid of all desire. Having attained enlightenment, he spent the remainder of his life spreading his newly discovered doctrine of the non-self and showing how the state of no-desire could be achieved through the proper concentrated mental effort. He also preached friendliness, forgiveness of enemies, and kindness to all living things. Buddhism was essentially an ascetic system combined with highly developed ethical ideals; its humanistic teachings were designed to promote a universal tolerance. One can readily understand how such a religion, dependent upon personal efforts rather than upon intermediaries, would not be popular with the priests.

Under the reign of the Emperor Asoka (272-236 B.C.) Buddhism reached its zenith. It spread over India, and missionaries carried it to various parts of Asia. All the while the priests were awaiting an opportunity to turn the thought of the people backward to the old gods of the Vedic religion. During the successive reigns of weak or indifferent emperors Buddhism became partially merged in Hinduism and in the country where it was born it eventually died out (c. 8th century A.D.) as a separate religion.

The Indians who then returned to the old gods now worshipped them under different names. Brahma, the Creator; Vishnu, the Preserver of Heaven and Earth; and Siva, the Destroyer were at this time deemed more important than Indra. Whatever their belief, most of the people followed, as Indians still do, the way of Hinduism.

HINDUISM, A "WAY OF LIFE"

During the hundreds of years of its existence Buddhism had failed to shake the caste system that had been enforced by the Aryans. Buddha did not set out to reform the world; his mission was rather to teach how one could attain his soul's salvation and circumvent the law of reincarnation. When the priests came back into power the caste system was gradually strengthened and each of the four original castes were broken down into separate categories. Although the priests had triumphed and Brahmanism returned, Buddhism had left its impression in forms of kindness and tolerance. The old Dravidian theory of transmigration-reincarnation was and still is accepted. All have become fused in Hinduism, which is more a "way of life" than a religion. Relying as it does upon behavior and not upon faith, Hinduism encourages an attitude of gentleness and non-injury toward living things.

Through the contemplative way of life the Hindu is encouraged to value the spiritual above the material, to acquire tolerance, and to respect the holy man or saint. This latter was exemplified in the attitude of the present-day Hindu toward Gandhi, the late spiritual leader. The Hindu may be an atheist, a monotheist, or he may worship many gods; for according to his belief it is conduct, not creed, that counts. Thus Hinduism, despite the caste system, is today considered to be the most unifying principle in India. On the other hand, the Mohammedans, who have no caste system and are therefore more socially democratic, are military minded and fanatically religious, in which respect they are less tolerant than the Hindus. The clash of ideas of the two seemingly irreconcilable groups largely accounts for the slow progress in the modern attempt to achieve the coöperation of all forces in India.

ASOKA BUILDS SHRINES TO BUDDHA

After Asoka, backed with powerful armies, had waged successful war over India, he was overcome with remorse when he saw the destruction which he had inflicted upon humanity and the suffering which his successes had caused. Adopting Buddhism as his religion, he set about to make restitution for the wrongs he had committed. Opening the mound which contained the body of Buddha, he took such remains as a tooth, a lock of hair, or a bit of his garment and distributed them over the various parts of his empire. To house the sacred relics solid brick or stone shrines, known as *stupas,* were erected; and steles, containing Buddhist symbols, were placed on the flattened tops. The entire structure was mounted upon a base which in turn was surrounded by a balustrade. At the four points of the compass were four gates, more decorative than functional.

Near each stupa there was a *viharra,* or cell, for the monk who kept lonely vigil. As time went on pilgrims from all parts of India and even from Tibet and China came to visit the shrines; other hermits came to spend their time in quietude and philosophical study. Extra accommodations for travelers and cells for monks became necessary. The cells, built about a court facing the enclosed stupa, were afterwards converted into chapels, and separate buildings were added to house the guardians of the shrine. Thus were formed monasteries similar to those of Europe during the Middle Ages. Some of these had gables and columns reminiscent, though not exactly replicas, of the Greek temples—the result of Hellenistic influence brought in the train of Alexander's armies. The *Stupa of Sanchi* is a notable example. Its gate (Plate 65) shows sculptured scenes from the life of Buddha, depicting stories from other incarnations when he appeared in the form of an elephant or a bird, as well as episodes of his life as a prince and later as the "Enlightened One." At each end of the lintels were spirals. Here symbolism and realism have been combined.

The Greek scholars who came with Alexander report that many buildings which they saw were covered with gold, but that the structures themselves were made of wood. Most of these structures have disappeared, for the climate of India is not, like that of Egypt, conducive to preservation. For centuries great temples and palaces such as those of *Angkor Vat* (Plate 67) and *Angkor Thom* (Plate 70) in Cambodia were entirely concealed by a thick jungle growth. In comparatively recent years these structures have been revealed by the Dutch and French authorities. *Angkor Vat* is perhaps the most renowned of the Brahmin temples.

SOUTHERN TEMPLES

In the Dravidian south the temple complex, similar to that of *Angkor Vat* in Indo-China, is something like a stepped pyramid in shape. Resting on a square base, each succeeding story decreases in size. Steps lead to the great stupa at the top and smaller echoing stupas stand at the corners of the various stages. Great ceremonial gates surmounted by intricately carved roof combs are set at the cardinal points, and ceremonial balustrades encircle the different terraces. Every inch of these stupas, which are divided into horizontal bands, is covered with elaborate ornamentation.

CAVE TEMPLES

Temples were also carved of rock, and such a one is found at *Karli* (Plate 67). Here the interior of the assembly hall is divided by columns into a nave with side aisles. In a rounded recess in the back of the cave comparable to the Gothic apse stands the stupa. Over it is an umbrella, the symbol of royalty. About the stupa was an ambulatory. The columns and arched roof of the hall were designed in imitation of earlier wooden buildings. The wooden ceiling must have been attached to the rock, for the columns—with highly decorated carved capitals—were not employed as supports. These cave structures afforded welcome relief from the tropical heat and heavy rains.

A TEMPLE IN JAVA

The magnificent Buddhist temple of *Boro Budur* (c.8th-9th century) in Java is built around a low hill (Plate 66). This temple assumes the general appearance of a stepped pyramid. About the lower stages are relief carvings in black stone which, from an artistic point of view, are considered to be the most important feature of the temple (Plate 69). Over two hundred miles of

these reliefs are spread stories of the different incarnations of the
life of Buddha. Here the sculptors let their imaginations run riot.
They did not confine themselves to the representation of the "En-

Javanese shadow hand-puppet.

lightened One," but included musicians, dancing girls, and animals which belonged to his princely life on earth. All combined
to produce a rich vibration of light and shadow. On one of the
three topmost circular stages there are said to be over seventy
smaller stupas, similar in shape to the crowning one, which have
elaborately carved niches that serve as shrines for about five hundred statues of Buddha. Regardless of such a wealth of sculptural
ornamentation, the simple outline of the general pyramidal shape
is still apparent.

SCULPTURE THE MOST IMPORTANT ART

Usually sculpture, though considered the most important art in
India, was treated as an integral part of architecture. Spread over

the walls, columns and gates of chapel and temple in jungle-like
profusion, it is enclosed in horizontal bands. Among the carvings
representing rocks, mountains, forests, animals and plants, man—
though not in a dominating rôle—has found his place. He is shown
engaged in all of the activities of life. Also sculptured in stone are
the legends of his heroes and his gods, together with the stories
of beasts. A free-standing bronze sculpture of the twelfth century
from South India shows a processional image of a *Deified Queen*
(Plate 69). An example of sculpture from Angkor Thom, French
Indo-China, is the *God on a Brahmin Temple,* which is deeply
chiseled from the stone background (Plate 70). The god is placed
in frontal position, showing bi-lateral symmetry. Throughout the
decorative bands in which the sculpture is confined, a rhythmic
line movement as well as a rich play of light and shadow imparts
life to the sheath that covers the entire temple. Like that of the
Romanesque and Gothic periods, Indian sculpture is didactic as
well as decorative.

The free-standing images usually represented Buddha or a Bodhisattva—a being who one day might become a Buddha. The In-
donesians particularly favored the compassionate *Avalokiteshvara*
who, even though he had earned the right to become a Buddha,
determined never to leave the earth until the whole world had
found salvation. All of these statues are imbued with that outward
quietness and repose which is conducive to the vibrant inner life
of the spirit. It was not until the second century B.C. that an image
of Buddha was permitted; a symbol, the stupa, was used instead,
for Buddha never claimed to be a god. Indeed, according to his
teaching the individual should lose himself in the universal. After
this time, however, images of him multiplied until there were literally hundreds of them, such as those found on the elaborately
carved shrines of *Boro Budur.*

Presented as a Yogi deep in meditation the motionless Buddha,
seated with body erect and eyes half closed, legs crossed and hands
lying quietly in his lap, is a perfect objective expression of the
soul in search of salvation through contemplation. The distinguishing attributes of the Buddha are the protuberances of wisdom on
top of his head; the small mound on his forehead which is referred

to alternately as a jewel, a mole, or again as the inner eye; and
the ears, elongated by the weight of the heavy jewels which he
wore while still a prince. His robe with its rhythmic folds is
slightly reminiscent of Greek drapery.

Among the statues of the gods, *Siva,* the Destroyer, is shown as
the Lord of the Dance (Plate 68). In one of his hands he holds
the drum with which he "awakens all nature to life"; in another he
holds the fire with which he destroys it. One foot is touching the
broken back of an inimical dwarf. In India the gestures of the
hands are particularly significant in both art and the dance (Plate
68). Here they are symbolical of the god's activities as he creates
the forces of life and then destroys them. Usually about his head a
cobra is entwined; his thin garments cling close to his body. The
whole figure is enclosed in a flaming wreath, which in this case
has been lost. This violently active figure, said to be symbolic of
cosmic energy, is in direct contrast to that of the immobile Buddha.

Looking down in pity upon suffering humanity the merciful
Avalokiteshvara sits with erect body, resting on one arm (Plate
69). The right leg is drawn up in the traditional fashion to support the right arm raised in the symbolic gesture of teaching; the
left leg is pendent. Through the relaxed and graceful pose of body
and the flowing lines of drapery the sculptor has achieved a fine
pattern that is quite well suited to the bronze material of which it
is made. It has been pointed out that such images as the enlightened Buddha or the Avalokiteshvara were employed as a "bridge
to contemplation."

FRESCOES IN THE AJANTA CAVES

Although painting was not the major art of India, impressive
frescoes have been found in the *Ajanta caves* (1st-7th centuries
A.D.) The subject-matter is similar to that of the sculptured reliefs
mentioned above. Like the sculpture, these friezes are sometimes
overcrowded; nevertheless, some of the strongly outlined individual
figures, rendered in clear colors, are of exceptional beauty (Plate
70). Few other monumental paintings have survived. After the
middle of the 16th century A.D., with the coming of the Moham-

medans, there appeared a number of miniatures reminiscent in style of the Mohammedan-Persian illustrations.

EAST MEETS WEST

East met West when Alexander the Great and his conquering army descended upon India. In his train he brought all of the pageantry of the Hellenistic world. Competing in the games, chariot races and contests of various kinds were the nude young Greek athletes who exercised to acquire symmetry of form as well as strength and skill. Here was a frank display of physical beauty. One of the most conspicuous examples of the Greek ideal was Alexander himself, who resembled "a shining Greek god." The Indians who watched all of this activity with its emphasis upon bodily perfection must have been unimpressed, for they looked upon the soul, not the body, as the ultimate reality. The Greeks were content to enjoy the life they knew, whereas the Indians, believing that they must return in other forms, were more concerned with the progress of the soul. In India the individual strove to lose himself in the universal while in Greece "man was the measure of all things."

When Alexander turned homeward, he left a Greek garrison near the borders of Afghanistan and thus communication with the Indians was kept open. As a result the art of India, to a certain extent at least, was affected by that of the Greeks. In the northwest particularly, Greek drapery on some of the religious figures and a trace of Greek influence may be seen in the hair and facial expression. The viharras, with their pedimented entrances and columns, have a hint of classical influence, testifying that the Greeks had been there.

In the Western world until the twentieth century—with a short interval during medieval times—man continued to be the center of the universe and art as well, just as he was in the Golden Age of Greece; but Eastern art as in India—or that part of it which is not under Mohammedan influence—has been concerned with the inward satisfaction of the soul or spirit. Recent events—particularly notable in the activities of the late Gandhi, who was largely re-

sponsible for freeing India from British rule without recourse to
warfare—have demonstrated the power of the contemplative spiritual life.

OUTLINE OF THE ART OF INDIA

TIME: C.1400 B.C. Aryan invasion. 6th to 8th centuries—Buddhist influence.
Reign of Asoka (c.250 B.C.). 4th to 9th centuries—"Golden Age" of Hindu
civilization. 1526-1761—Mogul Empire.

BACKGROUND: India a sub-continent—climate sub-tropical. Varied topography: high mountains, rich river valleys, arid deserts, and thick jungles. Recent excavations seem to indicate a culture paralleling in both time and
quality, the civilization of Egypt and Mesopotamia. Chief religions: Brahmanism, Buddhism, Islam—Hinduism (a Way).

ARCHITECTURE: Masonry laid in corbeled system. Material: limestone,
sandstone, and marble. Monasteries and temples: structures set upon high platforms, which resembled stepped pyramids, were topped by a stupa. Smaller
echoing stupas set at the corners. Each stage surrounded by railing. Decoration profuse. Steps leading from ornamental sculptured gates to the central
stupa. Other type: Sikara forms echoed by smaller ones. Assembly hall
attached to principal tower. Usually most profuse decoration concentrated
about the base of temple. Few lofty interiors. Assembly halls of cave temples
as at Karli divided by columns into nave and side aisles. Columns non-
functional.

SCULPTURE: Horizontal bands of sculptured reliefs decorated the walls of
caves and exteriors of temples. Somewhat crowded at times, but full of
rhythmic vitality. Single figures of Buddhas, Bodhisattvas or the gods. Subject-
matter of reliefs: the whole of life including figures, plants and animals—at
times symbolic, grotesque, or again convincing though non-imitative representation of all living things.

PAINTING: Not a major art in India. Best examples found in the thirty-nine
caves of Ajanta. In Mogul period: miniatures similar to Mohammedan-Persian
paintings.

Bibliography follows Chapter XIII.

CHAPTER XII

Art in the Far East—China

IN THE Far East, half a world away, lies China. Now that the airplane is covering vast distances in an ever decreasing amount of time, China, like other far-flung nations of the world, is becoming our neighbor. Nevertheless, in terms of customs, philosophy and religions—or "ways of life"—the yawning chasm that separates East and West is yet to be spanned by a bridge of understanding. For the solution of China's most obvious social and economic problems, the West offers modern technology and industrialization as a substitute for the Oriental doctrine of contentment with one's lot through self-adjustment; and the modern scientific approach as an alternative for the Oriental intuitive method of arriving at conclusions. When the restless impatient Westerner pauses long enough to think, he probably will realize that the philosophy of the ancient East in turn has something of a spiritual nature to offer the newer West—among other things, an inner poise and a deeply grounded love of peace.

While European countries still were inhabited by barbarians of the most primitive types, China had a rich culture, ancient yet not quite as old as that of Egypt or Mesopotamia. Many times her country has been invaded by warlike nations, but eventually the conquerors have either been assimilated or rejected. She still remains a country of promise while the glories of Nineveh, Babylon, Egypt, Greece, and Rome have waned.

China proper, which is now about half the size of the United States, is one of the most densely populated countries of the world. In social prestige the early inhabitants were divided into four groups in the order named: the aristocrats, who were the scholars; the farmers and others dependent upon the land—by far the largest class; the artisans, who worked with their hands; and lowest of all, the traders or merchants.

Like the United States, China has a varied climate and topography. In the north winters are long and cold and the summers are hot and dry. The Yellow River is both a menace and a blessing; rising in the snow-capped mountains of Tibet, it brings down silt to enrich the valleys; yet it is constantly changing its course, overflowing the land, destroying crops, killing hundreds of people, and causing the terrible famines that frequently occur. In the south there are rich green valleys, excellent harbors along the coast, natural streams, and a network of canals. Here life seems gayer and more pleasant.

For ages China, like Egypt, was an isolated country. Her natural barriers are great deserts and icy plateaus to the north and west; and the Pacific Ocean, the high mountains, and almost inpenetrable forests of Indo-China and Burma on the east and south. To reinforce these the great man-made wall was erected as a defense against the Mongols. This, however, proved to be a futile undertaking, for the Mongols penetrated it and for a time ruled over China.

As early as the first centuries of the Christian era there were peaceful trade relations, both overland and by sea, especially with those nations of the Graeco-Roman world and later with the Byzantines. Chinese silks were in such great demand that the main highway leading westward through Turkestan to the Mediterranean was known as the Silk Road.

CHINA'S SPIRITUAL LEADERS

Like India, China felt the impact of the strong current of religious thought which swept over Asia in the sixth century B.C. About this time there appeared three great leaders: Confucius (551-478 B.C.); Lao Tzu (or Laotse), a contemporary of Confucius; and Buddha (570-490 B.C.). These men formulated the religions and philosophies which have had the greatest influence upon Chinese culture. Literally speaking, the first two are "ways of life" rather than religions, but all are humanizing and spiritually significant.

Since Confucius and Lao-Tzu spoke in paradoxes, parables, or maxims—for fear of uttering half truths, it has been said—their devoted disciples endeavored to record and explain their teachings. Maxims removed either from the content or the situation that produced them may mean different things to different people. Therefore, it is small wonder that in the course of time some inferences drawn from the sayings of the great leaders have become so diametrically opposed to the implication of their original utterances that the authors themselves would not have recognized them. Furthermore, for practical purposes, the "ways"—like the Christian religion—have been somewhat modified to meet the needs of a changing world.

None of the leaders claimed to be of divine origin, yet after their death all except Confucius were worshipped as gods. Dissatisfied with a worldly life, each in his own way sought that inner satisfaction which only the spiritual life can provide. Confucius, a great scholar, turned to the past and became an insatiable student of the Chinese classics. Laying no claim to being an innovator, he described himself as being merely a transmitter of the wisdom of the ages. For years he applied himself diligently to collecting, classifying, and editing the ancient lore of great scholars who had long since joined their ancestors. It has been estimated that he compiled three hundred "points of ritual or ceremony and three thousand points of behavior" which fixed for all time the rules applying to conduct, morals, government, and human relationships. Nothing in daily life was too trivial to command his attention. He told the people how they should eat their rice, how they should lie in bed, and advised them not to pick their teeth. Since he taught by example as well as by precept, he was careful to practice what he preached, and perhaps therein lay his power.

When asked how a country should be governed, Confucius replied that reform should begin in the home and the individual should make himself as nearly perfect as Man can be. If children would be obedient to their parents, parents to the village officials who in turn would obey the laws of the central government, then, he said, there would be a perfect government. Confucianism had a socialistic tendency, with the family as the most important unit in the scheme. Within the family filial piety was exalted above all else. This reverence and respect for parents and elders is, in a sense, tied up with ancestor worship.

The ancestors of the Chinese were revered and honored almost like gods. Through ritual and ceremony the people sought to obtain their blessing and to avoid their enmity. The customs of their forefathers, until recent times at least, were adhered to because it was thought to be disrespectful, even bad luck, to alter them. Many superstitions were connected with this worship. Spirit gates were placed in front of the temples to prevent the entrance of unfriendly spirits. Little bells hung from roofs of pagodas to attract friendly spirits and to repel those bent upon mischief. Such beliefs seem strange to us, but superstitions have crept into the religions of all nations.

While uncompromising rules usually bring about order, they may also impede progress. Confucianism, looking backward toward the past and demanding that everything be done according to rule, did not appeal to such free creative souls as poets and painters. However, with the exception of a few intervals, it remained the state philosophy and "way of life" until China became a republic (1911 A.D.) under the leadership of Sun-Yat-Sen. Even to this day Confucianism is a strong factor in molding the life and thought of Chinese intellectuals. Nevertheless, its effect upon creative art was not so strong as that of either Taoism or Buddhism.

Little is known about Lao-Tzu, but he must have been a liberty-loving soul who abhorred rules and regulations. An amusing bronze statuette shows this carefree philosopher seated upon a water buffalo (Plate 74). According to his followers, the Taoists, Nature was ordered not by rule but by an unseen eternal force or energy which was working constantly for the good of man and all living things. In such a belief there is nothing clear-cut or static; everything is changing—"in a state of becoming."

Caring little for books, the Taoists left the dust and noise of the cities and the "locked-inness" of family life in an overpopulated community to go into the country where they could experience individual freedom and sit for hours inactive in contemplation of nature. In this manner, so they believed, man could find the Tao (Way or Path) within himself, and thus close to nature he could realize the inner harmony he sought. This love of solitude and contemplation is reflected in the quietude of Chinese landscape paintings.

Taoism, like Confucianism, was a "this worldly" system. It discarded rigid rules of conduct and ethics and even stressed the futility of reforming the world. To the Taoists, Confucianism was rather prosaic. The three jewels of Taoism were contemplation, humility, and frugality. According to such philosophy, man accomplishes little through restlessness, being too ambitious, or striving for material wealth; instead he should adjust himself to his environment and be content. Individuality was respected; however, the Taoists taught that since man was only one element in the over-all scheme of the universe, he should be aware of his proper relationship to Nature and attempt to unify himself with that mystical force which orders it. Under the influence of Taoism, landscape painting received a great stimulus and became the preferred medium of religious expression, the outward expression of the inner self. If figures were introduced in the "mountain-water" pictures, as these paintings were called, Man was shown in his due proportion; he neither dominated the scene nor was he lost in it.

By the first century A.D., Buddhism, which came from India, was becoming widespread; monasteries were being erected and worship conducted openly. Nevertheless, the original teaching of the imported religion was destined to undergo great changes before it was acceptable to the Chinese, who by nature were neither inclined to pessimism nor to a complete withdrawal from life. In its final stage it came to be known as *Zen* or *Zennism* as the Japanese called it. According to Zen the worldly life was as important as the spiritual, and there was less withdrawal from life than in earlier Buddhism. As in Taoism so in Zen the individual was considered important. In both there were differences of opinions resulting in many sects, just as there are different denominations in Christianity. However, there were similarities as well as differences in the three Ways or religions. During the Sung dynasty, after a number of modifications had been made, a synthesis was sought and attained to such an extent that it was possible for a Chinese to accept all three without uniting himself exclusively with any one of them; just as it was possible for Gandhi to be a follower of Christ and still remain a Hindu. Chinese philosophy molded the temper of the people and taught them to value knowledge above material wealth, kindness above force. The ideal of contemplation led the artists to turn their eyes inward to seek the meaning of nature instead of imitating its outward appearance. It is not surprising, then, that their art is unlike that of the West.

FOUR IMPORTANT DYNASTIES

In this short chapter on Chinese art we shall consider only the four dynasties most notable for the highest achievement in art: the Han (206 B.C.-220 A.D.), T'ang (618-906 A.D.), Sung (960-1279 A.D.), and Ming (1368-1644 A.D.). The Han dynasty parallels the rise of the Roman Empire in the West. During T'ang, Charlemagne was bringing order to a large section of Europe and Chinese art was reaching its first golden age. During Sung and the following Mongol dynasty (Yüan, 1279-1368 A.D.), the Romanesque and Gothic cathedrals were being erected in western Europe and Byzantine art was still flourishing in the East. Two hundred years were to elapse between the end of Sung, when Chinese painting reached its height, and the arrival of Columbus upon the shores of America.

During the Han dynasty China extended her boundaries westward and increased her commerce with the Western world both by land and sea. This era was distinguished by great progress in learning. Also it must be remembered that the excellent art created at this time was preceded by long preparation and fine accomplishment. Among the finest achievements in the earlier art were the famous bronze mirrors, bells, and ceremonial vessels, as well as bronze and stone sculpture—both free-standing and in relief. Also, the pattern for architecture had been set. Buddhism, through its highly formalized ritual, broadening of the horizons of Chinese thinking, emphasis upon other-worldliness, and promise of entrance into a real heaven, held the interest of many of the philosophers and furnished stimulating subject-matter for the arts.

Civilization under T'ang was far superior to that of western Europe during the corresponding centuries. Indeed, China at that time was the most highly civilized nation in the whole world. The extension of boundaries and the constant movement of Buddhist monks and pilgrims back and forth from India, China, and other parts of the Buddhist world resulted in a certain amount of cultural unity throughout most of Asia. Other religions including Christianity were introduced into China, though Confucianism, "the cult of the learned" with its practicality, its "this worldly" aspect and social emphasis, retained its importance and encouraged portrait paintings of great men together with both sculpture and painting of a moralistic character. Largely due to Buddhist influence, sculpture reached its height about the middle of the period when it became well rounded, less rigid, and more graceful in pose. Bronze Buddhas with drooping eyelids, completely withdrawn from all mundane affairs and lost in contemplation, appeared together with smaller bronze figures of the Trinity, usually placed against a sculptured screen. Glazed figurines were excellent, and both poetry and painting were highly developed. T'ang is known as the golden age of all the arts.

In Sung the Mongols, ever a constant menace, eventually conquered the provinces north of the Yangtze Kiang. However, the Emperor and his court were allowed to retire to "Southern Sung" which in time fell to Kublai Khan and became a part of the Mongol Empire; but culturally this section remained pure Chinese, for Kublai was educated in China. In Sung, art, particularly painting, pottery, and porcelain reached a second golden age.

The Mongol Yüan was followed by the Ming Dynasty when art, displaying great technical skill but less originality than that of T'ang or Sung, lost some of its vitality and began to decline. Many of the paintings of the time were copies of those of the two preceding eras. Nevertheless, the ceramics or porcelain ware of both Sung and Ming attained high pinnacles unparalleled at any other time. These wares, the first expressions of Chinese art to reach Europe, were introduced during the reign of Queen Elizabeth.

TEMPLES, PALACES, AND DWELLINGS

With the exception of pagodas, some as high as ten or twelve stories, Chinese architecture was kept close to the "good earth." There were no lofty spires such as the Gothic builders pointed toward heaven. Seldom did the monumental temples and palaces rise more than three stories above the high basements upon which they were usually placed. The equable calmness of the people is reflected in the symmetry and horizontality of their buildings.

Both palace and temple were symmetrical and formal, comprising a series of structures set horizontally upon a straight-line axis and separated by open spaces which were enclosed by subsidiary buildings. The latter connected the larger units, thus forming intervening closed courts. Such courts could be easily multiplied when it became necessary to enlarge the structure. In some respects the plan, as may be seen in the air view of the Forbidden City of Peiping (Plate 72), resembles that of a Roman house with rooms built about a number of courts, or the symmetrical plan of an Egyptian temple with rooms set upon a straight-line axis; but in both house and temple the long sides of the different rooms or units were parallel to the axis, whereas in the Chinese plan they were set at right angles to it, thus doubly emphasizing the feeling of horizontality and nearness to earth. The entrance to a Chinese palace or house was invariably placed in the middle of the long side of the rectangular unit, and to insure privacy the exit to the court at the rear was often placed slightly to the side rather than directly opposite the entrance. All faced south. Nevertheless, in outward appearance Chinese architecture was not even slightly reminiscent of either Roman house or Egyptian temple.

Wood was the material which determined the general stylistic character of Chinese architecture. The high basements were made of packed earth faced with brick or stone walls. To this day the style is copied throughout the entire country, regardless of climate or the availability of different materials.

All types of roofs were upheld by two rows of wooden pillars, one visible on the interior, and the other on the exterior. The spaces in between were either filled in by walls—usually of brick or plaster—or left open to form a gallery. The wide eaves were supported by elaborate brackets. Posts and beams were ingeniously tied together. No nails were used.

Notable features of the temples were the drum tower and the pagoda or bell tower. The latter always had an odd number of stories, each with its own tilted roof. Small bells hung from the eaves and emitted musical sounds when swayed by the breeze. In shape these pagodas are square, polygonal, or circular, and in some cases each successive story decreases in size as the structure soars upward. Monumental stairways lead from the high basement to the temples. Appropriately circular in shape, the *Temple of Heaven* is entirely surrounded by marble terraces with ceremonial balustrades and triple staircases set at the four points of the compass (Plate 71). The altar is ninety feet in diameter. Supplementary buildings stand near by. Here the emperor came once a year to offer sacrifices.

The entire complex of temple, important house, or palace was surrounded by a plain high wall of brick or stone masonry pierced by one or more carved or brightly painted gates. Although the lintel system was commonly used, the Chinese understood the arch and vault and employed them for the gateways and tunnels which ran through the tremendous basements.

A Westerner accustomed to the enormous unadorned structures of the Machine Age is usually impressed with the unlimited amount of time and labor expended upon the decoration of the Chinese temples, which were erected with only the simplest of primitive machines. In our world the spirited pace of modern life leaves no time to contemplate the beauties of decoration; but the older Chinese, like the Gothic builders, were unhurried, and they understood and appreciated the instructional and esthetic values of the intricate carvings and brilliant hues symbolic of their respective religions.

Temples, palaces, and the dwellings of the wealthy were usually set in the midst of a park or surrounded by gardens. However, the high enclosing walls were not conducive to a fine appearance of the city as a whole. Many of the roofs of Chinese temples, whether of wood or glazed tile, were a golden yellow, the royal color of China.

Touches of blue, gold, green, and white enlivened the bracket work of the eaves, and the ridgepoles were ornamented with fantastic and colorful dragons, phoenixes, and grotesques.

The *Pailou, or Ceremonial Gateway to the Ming Tomb Area,* Peiping, is ranked among the world's great monuments (Plate 72). It was built by the Emperor Yung Lo about 1420 and represents a place for the entrance of a spirit into the next world. This beautiful symmetrical structure, fifty feet high and one hundred feet in length, stands in harmonious relation to the mountainous landscape behind it. Its five ornamental roofs, which are made of colored porcelain, rise gradually to the central level which is higher. The superstructure is supported by six marble pillars connected by broad stone sections bearing designs of Buddhist symbolism. Six sculptured crouching lions are mounted on bases where square plinths are ornamented with carved designs.

Due to the perishability of wood, wars, fires, and other destructive forces there remains in China little if any architecture produced before the Ming period; but since the style did not change, one may still get a very good idea of the general appearance of it from the structures of a later time. The most ancient, and therefore the most important archaeologically, are the Chinese structures still extant in Japan.

CHINESE SCULPTURE

Reliefs for informative or symbolic as well as decorative purposes appear on the backgrounds of screens behind the bronze Buddhas and attendant Bodhisattvas which comprise the Buddhist trinity. But generally speaking, monumental sculpture was not used so extensively in the architecture of the East as it was during the Romanesque and Gothic periods in the West. There were, nevertheless, the great stone animals which guarded the gates of temples, occupied the niches of pagodas, or stood in pairs along the "spirit paths" leading southward from the tombs of emperors or other important persons. Some of these animals recall the fierce winged bulls of Nineveh, Babylon, and Persia; others are quietly watchful, like the rams and sphinxes which guard the roadways to the Egyptian temples. When seen either pictured in a book or standing alone in a

museum far from their original setting, these animal guards lose
much of their former significance. Those who have seen them tell
us that when they are suddenly encountered as they rise up from
the grass-covered plains or stand starkly against the wide horizon of
the desert, they are impressive to behold. Here, out in the open
where their inherent strength and vitality are intensified by the
ever changing play of light and shadow, they actually seem to be
alive. Among these dromedaries, elephants, chimeras (Plate 71),
and other conventionalized forms there are short-maned lions with
powerful bodies. The strong curves of their necks, ending in wide-
open mouths with tongues extended, are so expressive of ferocity
that they must have struck terror to the hearts of superstitious
people. There also were strange mythical beings decorated with
scales and feathers suggestive of swift motion through sea, land,
or air.

Within the tomb were both glazed terra-cotta statuettes, like the
Standing Woman of the T'ang dynasty, and unglazed figurines,
exemplified by the *Adoring Bodhisattva* (Plate 74). Represented
also were servants, dancing girls, members of the family, horses,
camels, and other domestic animals, together with objects serving
the same purpose as the funerary sculpture of Egypt. Although
more naturalistic than the monumental sculpture in stone or
bronze, these images were not individualized. Instead, they were
generalized representations of a particular class or type, such as
dancers, servants, or musicians like the *Lute Player* (Plate 75) of
the T'ang dynasty.

The Chinese, unlike the Greeks who regarded "man as the
measure of all things," considered man to be only one manifestation
of Nature. They were more concerned with spiritual beauty and
inner vitality than with idealized physical beauty and bodily movement. The withdrawn Buddhist figures, either standing quietly or
seated as if in meditation, personified the brooding contemplation
of the soul seeking harmony with the universe. Such figures are
sometimes accompanied with other symbolic representations of
deities and semi-divine beings. The Oriental sculptor did not attempt to create highly original forms; instead he was content to
work within the limits of a conventionalism, imposed by Buddhist

iconography, which the artist had to accept if he wished to be understood. Nevertheless, he found an outlet for his individual feeling and decorative ability in the rhythmic expression of the

Stags. Jade ornaments, Chou dynasty. (Metropolitan Museum of Art)

folds of garments, jewelry, or other appurtenances, and by variations of the composition when several figures were united in a group.

Siddhartha in Meditation (Plate 73), a highly realistic portrait carving in limestone, is an example of early Chinese sculpture (c. 534 A.D.).

There are also variations in the statues of seated Buddha, who is usually shown with legs crossed, either with one hand extended in a gesture symbolic of teaching or again with both hands folded quietly in his lap, and eyes half closed as if in contemplation. Some are carved directly from the living rock of cave temples, others are made of wood. Usually the stone statues are near the entrance of the cave where they are seen in a mysterious half-light. Others fashioned of wood stand in open spaces. The smile spreading over the faces of the bronze or wooden Bodhisattvas imbued them with a benign expression similar to that found in Archaic Greek sculpture, and the calligraphic lines of the wing-like draperies impart a sense of vitality and rhythmic movement to the still figures.

As time went on the elegant slender figures of the Buddhist pantheon gave way to representations of more solid forms and a more naturalistic but still rhythmic type of drapery. The figures became well-rounded in contrast to the thin figures which were meant to be viewed from one position only. Enhanced by icono-graphic symbols which made the sculpture more intelligible to the initiated, many of the smaller figures are integral parts of an elabo-rate composition. Decorative haloes are usually placed behind the Buddha and the two flanking Bodhisattvas who complete the trinity. All are usually set against a background adorned with sculp-tured reliefs. Some of the haloes have flame-like edges symbolic of "the enlightenment" and inward intensity of religious fervor. In contrast to the moving lines of screen and haloes is the motionless figure of Buddha, the "Enlightened One" who has attained Nir-vana, that state of mind freed from all desire.

In Chinese art, the compassionate Avalokiteshvara of the Indians became the merciful *Kuan Yin* (Plate 75). Represented first as a sexless being, this Bodhisattva gradually assumed a feminine form. Seated in the relaxed "pose of royal ease" with head erect and body partially resting on the left arm, left leg pendent and right arm supported by the right knee which is raised and bent, this figure has great dignity. It is made of wood over-laid with gesso and painted. The folds of the flowing garment, the ornamental belt, elaborate head-dress, gold chain, and other jewels which are either carved or modeled in relief, all contribute to a richly decorative effect.

CALLIGRAPHY AND PAINTING

The Han and T'ang dynasties were especially noted for their sculpture and architecture; Sung for its painting; Ming for its pottery; and both of the latter for their porcelain which became so well known that the word *china*, meaning porcelain, has become a part of the English language. Nevertheless, the major arts of the Chinese were the related arts of calligraphy and painting. The Chinese painter used the familiar materials to which he had been accustomed since he learned to write, namely, the brush and a block or stick of ink made of soot which he moistened by rubbing on a wet stone. According to the amount of water used, the tones could be made dark or light. The brush was similar to those which are known to us as Japanese brushes.

The characters of an expert calligrapher are judged by their unity and rhythm which are also distinctive art qualities. We are told that a calligrapher does not do any manual work, for he considers it important to keep his hands supple as well as strong. Like the painter, he must be perfectly calm and untroubled by mundane affairs. Moving not only his wrist but his entire body as well, he induces the rhythm of his inner being to flow freely through the lightly-held brush onto the paper.

A Chinese painter has left a record of his manner of working. He says that after he has spent days in contemplation before the scene, then he begins to paint from memory. If he makes an error, he must begin painting again on another piece of silk. When viewing a *makimono*, a horizontal rolled picture several feet in length, we marvel at the unique skill of the artist. The Chinese artist does not give a detailed photographic appearance of a scene at a certain time of day nor does he suggest a particular point of view. When viewing a Chinese painting the observer is led into the landscape with its valleys, mountains, rivers, and trees. Space is the important element in Chinese paintings. Laurence Binyon records the story of an artist who could represent "ten thousand miles of space on a single fan."

No-tan, a Japanese word which refers to various proportions of flat areas of light and dark, was employed for the sake of design or pictorial quality only. The use of cast shadow or of light and shade for photographic representation was not employed in the more important periods of Chinese painting. Usually working from memory, the artist was concerned with the non-transitory, the general character, and shape of things rather than with the accidental light and shade which changes with every movement, varies with the time of day, and sometimes even destroys the appearance of form itself.

The early style of Chou Fang, eighth and ninth centuries, comes down to us in figure paintings such as *Ladies Playing Double Sixes* (Plate 77). These high-bred ladies at their game are painted with delicacy and charm. They are an interesting version of the genre painting, the scene of everyday living, which painters of every period have felt the need to reproduce.

Tung Yuan's *Landscape Scroll* of the early Sung Dynasty, late tenth century, is representative of the many beautiful "mountain and water" pictures which show mastery of technique in the use of brush and Chinese ink (Plate 76). Here is portrayed an enchanted and mystical setting expressive of nature's grandeur—steep mountain ledges, hazy depths of canyons far below, lonely roads leading to secluded caves and grottoes with waterfalls and quiet distant waters. Near the corner of the painting is a fisherman's hut which contrasts with the high mountain, the whole symbolizing the immensity of nature and the humble position of man.

Oriental artists understood aërial perspective, but they either did not understand or deliberately did not often employ linear perspective. When they did lines were apt to open in the distance instead of coming to a point on the horizon. Sung painters knew how to make one object stand behind another with an indication of space between the two. This was done by tone instead of line. Looking out upon a landscape on a foggy day when a mist covers everything, it is very easy to see that objects near-by are darker and more detailed in tone than those in the distance. The Chinese also operated upon the assumption that a mountain seems higher if you are unable to see all of it; distances seem greater if some of the intervening space is lost in a mist; and a small branch of leaves or flowers entering a picture from without can suggest a tree or plant growing outside the picture, thus extending the spectator's vision, or leaving something to his imagination.

Portrait painting was either commemorative or moralistic in character. We are told that many Chinese painters, like the Dutch Rembrandt, preferred to portray the lined faces and calm expressions of philosophers or wise old scholars.

The frescoes in early Buddhist temples which were related to the life of Buddha and his followers on earth or in the Western Paradise included symbols of the different phases of Buddhist belief.

Genre painting (scenes of everyday life) was common, but the landscape paintings or "mountain and water" pictures, as the Chinese called them, were most expressive of the contemplative life and religious thought of the time.

Rejecting the sharp contrasts of light and shadow, the Chinese artist chooses to paint a scene with mists rising here and there or to give the effect of a cloudy day. On such a day the outer vision is not so clear, but the inner vision is intensified and the artist becomes more deeply aware of the mystery, the grandeur, and the all-powerful vastness of nature. A mood of contemplation pervades *Landscape* by Ma Yuang, an artist of the Sung period (Plate 76).

In China artists, poets, or scholars liked to build retreats in some secluded spot where they might sit in solitary contemplation and strive through introspection to identify themselves with the Tao, that universal force underlying all nature, which they "loved for its beauty and respected for its power." While their art does not mirror nature, everything in it retains its proper character. The branches of the pine tree are gnarled, the limbs of graceful willows sway in the wind, mountains are angular or wooded, and water dashes over the rocks or flows quietly along. Man also takes his proper place in the scene. Chinese painting is closely akin to the arts of poetry and music.

OUTLINE OF ART IN THE FAR EAST—CHINA

TIME: Han—206 B.C.-220 A.D.; T'ang—618-906 A.D.; Sung—960-1280 A.D.; Ming—1368-1644 A.D.

BACKGROUND: Diversified climate and topography. Densely populated. For centuries, little outside influence. Later trade routes established to West. Communication with India. *T'ang*: great progress in the arts—particularly sculpture, poetry, and music. Painting and block-printing also practiced. Philosophers, scholars, religious leaders, numerous. Foreigners welcomed. China then most highly civilized nation in the world. *Sung*: progress in literature, "golden age" of painting. From 6th century B.C. Confucianism, Taoism and Buddhism, most prominent "Ways" or religions. The two last named had the greatest effect on art. In all periods the family, chief unit of social structure. Filial piety stressed. Ancestor worship continues to present day—although not practiced by all.

ARCHITECTURE: *Palaces and temples*: complex of separate rectangular units set along a north-south axis. Longest side of unit set at right angles to axis. Subsidiary units parallel to axis, connect central units to form intervening courts. All set upon high platforms, covered with upward tilted roofs and enclosed by gate-pierced walls. Horizontality stressed. Structures usually two, sometimes three stories high. Pagoda, conspicuous feature. *Materials:* wood, brick, marble. *Structural element:* post and lintel. Arch known and used in basement. *Decorations:* rich colorful tiles and profuse carving. Little change in general structure through the ages. Oldest example of this type is to be found in Japan. Great wall outstanding feat in engineering.

SCULPTURE: *Materials:* bronze, wood, stone, lacquer, ceramics. *Subject-matter:* figures and animals used for burial purposes and religious rites. Characteristics: early figures flat made to be seen from one viewpoint. Clad in garments with folds indicated by rhythmic calligraphic lines. Later figures well rounded. Most are conventionalized or symbolic—non-imitative.

PAINTING: Frescoes, hanging scrolls *(kakemonos)* or long scrolls *(makimonos).* Frescoes have disappeared. In Sung landscape painting highest form of religious expression—suggestive, non-imitative. Linear perspective, if employed, was reverse of Western idea; lines opened out in background space instead of converging to a point on the horizon. Aerial perspective expressed by masterly use of the plastic elements, line, and dark-light. Little concern with predetermined or restricted space and three dimensional objects which might occupy it. Space limitless—form suggested, not always definitely expressed.

Bibliography follows Chapter XIII.

CHAPTER XIII

Art in the Far East—Japan

IN THE Far East China held the same position in relation to her Asiatic neighbors that ancient Greece occupied in Europe. She was both mentor and source of inspiration for the art and culture which came through Korea to Japan. The Japanese, like the Romans eager and quick to learn, took over China's fully developed arts and culture and wove them into a fabric of their own by gradually adapting the Chinese pattern to their own needs and temperament.

Before the advent of the Christian era, the Japanese had been living in virtual isolation on their crescent-shaped islands off the coast of Asia. They were still in the stone age when the Chinese were in the middle of Han, an age which was one of the high points in the advancement of China's remarkable civilization.

During the first six centuries A.D. Japanese development was continuous and steady. The Chinese written language appeared; and Buddhist monks came over from Korea and China, bringing with them a new religion which proved to be a great stimulus to civilization in backward Japan.

Just as the Chinese adapted Buddhism to their way of life, so the Japanese again revised it to make it practicable for themselves. That aspect of Buddhism which stressed a withdrawal from the world and the relinquishment of all desire, wholly acceptable to the people of India and in a lesser degree to the Chinese, had little appeal to the energetic Japanese. Nevertheless, other principles such as bodily control and endurance struck such a responsive chord in Japanese character that they have remained a strong influence even to the present day.

SHINTO, THE "WAY OF THE GODS"

Underlying the foreign Buddhist religion was the native primitive cult more recently termed *Shintō*, "the Way of the Gods," which is based upon love of nature, family, and country. There seems to have been no well-defined moral code. If its teachings concerning life after death were rather vague, ancestor worship was the very core of the cult. Prayers were offered for material prosperity or happiness, blessings which the departed spirits could bestow upon the living. Purification or bodily cleansing with water was one of the most important rites.

According to Shintō legend, the earth was first peopled by the direct descendants of the gods, thus making Japan the "Land of the Gods." The grandson of the Sun-goddess Amaterasu is said to have been the first Emperor of Japan, and his descendants have ruled in undisputed recognition of their divine origin until recently when Hirohito publicly renounced his claim to divinity. Difficult to define, Shintōism is, according to a Japanese, "not so much in books, rites, or commandments but in the heart of the nation."

The extremely nationalistic character of Shintōism always asserted itself when foreign influence threatened to absorb the native culture or when a foreign people sought to invade the homeland. The Japanese refused to submit to the demands of the Mongols who conquered China at the end of Sung when, with the assistance of a convenient typhoon, they turned the invaders from their shores.

For many years Buddhism and Shintōism were rival religions. For a time Shintō was absorbed in Buddhism, but with the development of nationalism it finally emerged as the state religion; nevertheless, Buddhism still remains a vital force.

THE ASUKA PERIOD (552-646)

The middle of the sixth century is generally regarded as the starting point for a consideration of Japanese art, for it was at this time that Buddhism found its way into the minds and hearts of the Japanese people. Requiring for its observance thousands of temples, monasteries, and the attendant decoration, Buddhism was a tremendous spur to the development of art. Largely responsible for the development of this new religion in Japan were the famous Empress Suiko, who ascended the throne upon the death of her husband in 593 A.D., and her son, Shotoku Taishi (Sage Virtue), who served her as regent.

As an expression of their faith in the new religion, the empress and her son planned to erect a great monastical structure. From Korea they brought architects, masons, sculptors, artists, and other workmen skilled in building and decoration. In preparation for this undertaking, Shotoku devoted years to the study of architecture and the related arts, and it was under his personal supervision that the famous *Monastery of Horiuji* (607 A.D.) was erected in the foothills not far from the imperial palace (Plate 79). In 670 A.D. a disastrous fire destroyed all but three units of the monastery. The gate, pagoda, and Kondo (Golden Hall) which still remain not only antedate any architecture in China, but are considered to be the oldest wooden buildings in the world. Hence, in addition to being artistically beautiful, they are archaeologically valuable; from them the early Chinese style can be reconstructed.

Following the Chinese classical style of the sixth century, the tiled roofs of these structures, straight on the long sides with slightly upturned corners, are upheld by columns and further supported by frankly expressed structural brackets. Each unit rests upon a high base. Proportions have been carefully considered and the curves of the roofs highly refined. Woodwork is colored with a red of rather low intensity, while the plaster of the walls is left white; the tiles of the roofs are a soft gray-green in hue. The lower galleries of temple and pagoda, added during the sixteenth or seventeenth century, detract from the unity of the whole.

In arrangement, the monastery followed the usual Buddhist pattern: temple, pagoda, and lecture hall stood in the midst of a spacious cloister with an elaborate two-storied gateway at the entrance. Connected with it were other subordinate buildings about additional cloisters.

Another of the few surviving architectural relics of the Asuka period is the three-storied *Pagoda of Hokkiji* (Plate 78), near the

Horiuji both in time and in location. Although the Hokkiji pagoda is the taller in proportion to width, it is identical in most details with the Horiuji structures.

The sculpture of this early period was created to enhance the temples and monasteries and quite naturally expounds a religious theme. Stone, the medium most employed in China, gives way to wood, bronze, and dry lacquer in Japan. The Chinese had made statues of lacquer, light in weight and highly resistant to the destructive forces which attack wood, stone, or even bronze. But it was the Japanese who developed this medium and employed it extensively in the making of figures, some of which were larger than life. Briefly, the method of construction was this: Over an armature or central core of wood or clay were placed layers of hemp cloth soaked in the juice from the lacquer tree. Over the outer layers of cloth there were layers of powdered wood mixed with glue; it is this layer which could be modeled or carved. As the juice dried, the outer layers stiffened, so that when the core was removed, a hard form remained. Lacquer, which could be colored easily, was long a favorite medium for portraiture, although later it was abandoned in favor of wood.

The *Kudara Miroku* (Plate 81), gilded dry lacquer over wood, depicts a gentle, thoughtful figure, delicately poised; and represents the Buddhist messiah. Heavily lacquered leather straps, simulating textile, hang from shoulder to lap. The hairdo of this figure is typical of the Chinese. The wooden image of the *Kwannon* in the Yumedono (Plate 80) is a much venerated piece of work. It has been considered the largest, best-preserved, and one of the most beautiful relics of Asuka art. Once it was covered with gold leaf, now gone. It is believed to have been done shortly after the death of Shotoku (621 A.D.). The dry-lacquer *Miroku* and the wooden *Kwannon* are representative of a high point in Japanese sculpture, which subsequently moves toward the naturalistic at the expense of vitality and spirit.

THE NARA PERIOD (646-794)

The early Nara period was marked by great strides in Japanese art. Then, for the first time, there was direct and easy interchange of culture between the Japanese and the then existing T'ang dynasty on the mainland.

The building of a new capital at Nara (710 A.D.), from whence the period derives its name, proved a great spur to architecture: countless temples and dwelling places, now gone, were erected. The most important relic of the architecture of the period is the *Pagoda of the Yakushiji Monastery*, built in the new city of Nara in 718 A.D. The pagoda is characterized by a softening of the Chinese classical model, with additional emphasis upon height, consummate grace, elaboration of bracket work, and an increased richness of ornamentation and detail. This insistence upon richness of detail was to grow until decoration almost completely obscured the structural elements of Japanese architecture. Most of the palaces of this time, owing to the perishability of wood, constant warfare, and the Japanese custom of moving court and capital at the beginning of each new dynasty, have disappeared, and their magnificence can only be imagined.

Early Nara sculpture reveals strong Chinese T'ang influence, and as before is concerned with Buddhistic images. The increase of technical mastery can be easily seen by comparing Asuka figures with an outstanding bronze of this later period: the *Sho-Kwannon* at Yakushiji. This larger than life-size impressive figure is swathed in clinging draperies which contrast with the stiff folds in the gown of the *Kudara Miroku*.

The last half of the eighth century is generally considered the golden age of Japanese Buddhist art. The city of Nara becomes a fountain of art work; not only are new monasteries erected, but older ones are moved in to embellish the imperial scene. Characteristic is the *Todaiji* (Great Eastern Monastery), enclosing within its area two miles square. One of the monastery's largest and most magnificent buildings was the *Hall of the Great Buddha*. Little remains of the monastery today, but some of the statuary which

adorned it remains to indicate the wealth and beauty of this huge
construction.

The Todaiji figures, along with other sculpture of this second
half of the eighth century, show that Japanese sculptors were
ready to leave the Chinese nest. Naturally there remains T'ang
influence, for Buddhism imposes restrictions of theme and treatment, but a mature Japanese craftsmanship is now evident. In the
clay image of *Bonten* (Brahma) in the Lotus Hall of Todaiji there
may be seen the marks of a new secularism, a new naturalism,
operating within the Buddhist tradition. Fierce warlike figures
guarded the gates of temple and shrine. The *Shikkongojin* (Plate
79), a martial figure of mildly terrifying aspect, also belongs to the
Todaiji. It is fashioned of unbaked clay.

TRANSITION (794-894)

Between the end of the Nara period and the beginning of the
Fujiwara period is a time of transition in the arts. There are signs
of increasing interest in secular art, although Buddhism remains
the chief concern. Monasteries which in the Nara Period were constructed on level ground, usually near the imperial courts, now became retreats built on the tops, or sides, of mountains. There is a
tendency toward overelaboration in their decoration. The inner
strength and spiritual quality of earlier sculpture is lost; a new
iconography of the now popular mystical sects of Buddhism replaces it. Buddhas or Amidas are depicted seated on birds and other
animals symbolically important. Sculpture in general is more mythological and fairy-like than spiritual. Wood replaces clay, bronze,
and lacquer.

THE FUJIWARA PERIOD (894-1185)

The year 894 marks a break in the relations between Japan and
the T'ang court, a further waning of Chinese influence, and the
beginnings of a new national Japanese art. The Fujiwara period,
which corresponds roughly to the Chinese Sung, opened inauspi-
ciously with civil conflict, but toward the start of the tenth century

the Fujiwara family gained political ascendancy. For a while there was peace in the land. Kyoto, the capital, had a population numbering a million. The society of the court and ruling family was sophisticated, refined, intellectual, and gay. Japanese civilization had now reached a height hitherto unattained. Arts were encouraged. We are told that music was so highly appreciated that a minister of state was appointed to supervise it. Dancing also came within his province. Almost everyone was trained in the art of writing poetry. Art was created to satisfy the great demands of both religious and court purposes. Famous women novelists of the time have described current customs, recounted the everyday happenings and romantic and political intrigues of court life. The members of the court and ruling family dwelt in magnificent palaces surrounded by beautiful gardens. They were dressed in garments of silks of the most gorgeous hues and finest textures. It has been said that the nobility spent much time in acquiring elegant manners to correspond with their fine palaces and rich garments. Men and women of the upper classes were educated alike and they were almost socially equal.

In time there arose a strong military caste or *samurai*, as they were called, who literally lived by the sword, disdaining any other occupation by means of which they might earn a livelihood. Thus, the sword became a symbol of rank and power and it was worn constantly by every member of the samurai until the custom was abolished in 1868.

As in Europe at about the same time, these were the days of chivalry, and a code of honor somewhat comparable to that of the medieval knights was adopted. There were frequent wars between clans or between religious sects, and defensive foreign wars also occurred at rare intervals.

Social, political, and religious aspects of life were closely interwoven. Priest and emperor, the leaders of spiritual and temporal power, worked in harmony. If many of the priests were also artists when occasion demanded, they were no less prepared and ready to defend the government with the swords they wore under their priestly robes. In turn the Emperor bowed low before the gods and deferred to the High Priest. Frequently emperors were prevailed upon to renounce their thrones, shave their heads, and retire to a monastery, leaving the crown prince and his ministers in control. This duality of temporal and spiritual power is reflected in the art of the time. The artists were now housed in castles as well as monasteries and there was a demand for secular as well as religious art. Paintings of flowers, animals, and objects became popular.

In the little town of Uji just a few miles from Kyōto, the Ho-o-do or *Phoenix Hall,* originally a pleasure palace but later a temple, is one of the finest architectural examples of this great art period. The approach is through a pavilion connected with the shrine by a long, open corridor. In the opinion of Mr. Cram, the architect, "in delicacy, proportion, and refinement of composition, the *Ho-o-do* marks the culmination of Japanese architecture." He considers it quite worthy of comparison with the Taj Mahal. The roof is not so high as some of the more extravagant styles of later times when roofs were steep and ridgepoles excessively heavy. The curves are still restrained and subtle, reflecting the influence of the more restrained classical style, and ornamentation is still subordinated to fine structural qualities. Although wrecked by time and neglect, traces of the former glory of the magnificent interior can still be seen. From the remains it has been found that the ceiling was covered with black lacquer inlaid with mother-of-pearl ivory and silver, while walls and the woodwork were covered with gilding relieved by multicolored decorations.

Later Japanese temples were larger and more magnificent but their proportions and decorations were not so highly refined. Some of the interiors, covered with gold and accented with black and red lacquer, were most impressive. In others the varicolored walls and ceilings were reflected in the floors of shining black lacquer. All were highly ornamented with precious materials and brilliant hues.

The rise of the new secular art did not by any means displace Buddhist art. As the monasteries grew in wealth and influence much money was spent on buildings and religious statuary. But a new style in sculpture, foreshadowed in the preceding periods, is evident. This is most apparent in the figures of Amida of the time, in which the god is depicted as a gentle and compassionate being. Eventually, manual dexterity degenerates into decadent facility.

THE KAMAKURA PERIOD (1185-1392)

During the twelfth century the Fujiwara power was broken and for a while there was a period of confusion. At the end of these civil disturbances, many palaces, temples, books and priceless art treasures had been utterly destroyed. The Minamoto clan rose to power and ushered in the Kamakura period (1185-1392). In contrast to the ultra-refined Fujiwari, weakened by centuries of ease and luxurious living, they were uncultured and cared little for scholastic attainments, but they were alert, energetic, and physically strong. Like the Romans, they borrowed their culture from their defeated foe.

Buddhism was again modified to suit the minds of the new ruling clan. The mystic sects had made each individual personally responsible for his salvation. Now there was a new trend requiring less thought and not too much time and effort. Amida, clothed in the garments of a Bodhisattva, was the central deity. Faith was exalted over works. One had only to believe in him to attain salvation. Thus restless armored knights were spared the effort of listening to long prayers and sermons, and of following any established ritual other than kneeling before the statue of Amida, and eventually the ritual consisted only in repeating his name.

The change in religion brought about a new style in architecture. In earlier days a worshipper might go to the temple alone, or he could worship in his home or by a wayside shrine. Formerly priests habitually conducted the necessary ceremonies and looked after the needs of the great pantheon of gods regardless of whether or not a congregation was present. Now the temples must be large enough to house congregations. Altars and all interior furnishings were much less ornate. The demand for religious art decreased.

In this militaristic and romantic Japanese period there were fortified structures of wood built upon high stone foundations. Towering above the walls which surrounded the living quarters and subsidiary structures provided for munitions, they were as common to the Japanese scene as were the frowning stone castles to the hills and valleys of medieval Europe. Although the people were serfs who tilled the land, anyone who was strong enough to gather about him a powerful following could rise to the castle class. "Might was right."

When relations with China were resumed, Chinese influence was again felt in the arts. But it was the works of the older Sung which appealed to the taste and imagination of the now-sophisticated Japanese scholars and artists, who at this time collected many of the best paintings of the Sung period. Most of them are still preserved in the finest art collections of Japan.

The rise of feudalism was not without benefit to Japanese art; in fact the culture of Kyoto, somewhat decadent, needed the new vigor which accompanied political changes. Temple building continues to reflect the Fujiwara period, but in sculpture there is a sort of renaissance. The best of Kamakuran sculpture, though highly realistic, shows something of the energy apparent in early sculpture. The great bronze statue known as the *Buddha of Kamakura* (1252), is of colossal size (Plate 78). This impressive and tranquil figure, with legs crossed in characteristic attitude, is seated in contemplation.

JAPANESE PAINTING

Painting as a national art in Japan dates from the Fujiwara period and reaches its high point in the Kamakura and succeeding Ashikaga ages. Painting is largely a secular art; though religious themes are employed, they do not dominate. A characteristic love of nature is asserted; landscape painting appears early.

To the late Fujiwaran period belongs Toba Sojo (1053-1114), priest and painter, who caricatured the uncultured ruling class then coming into power. As a medium for his satirical sallies he chose various animals, such as horses, frogs, goats, dogs, and bulls, which he represented as having the same foibles and weaknesses possessed by humans.

At the same time *makimonos*, colored picture scrolls, became popular. These depicted continuous scenes of crowds in the streets, horse-races, cock-fights, caricatures of monks, camp life, and scenes of warfare. We are told that the emperors especially enjoyed looking at these records of the activities of their subjects, for it was their only glimpse into a world in which they were forbidden to participate. Not all *makimonos* dealt with popular subjects, however; most of the monasteries of the time had scrolls picturing the origin of their particular buildings, or perhaps a recounting of the life of the founder. Some of these became objects of reverence. A number of these scrolls, painted during Kamakuran times, are extant.

Portrait painting is widely popular in the late Kamakuran age; portraits not exclusively of humans, but also of favorite animals. Oversize colored portraits on silk screens are done by contemporary artists.

In the fifteenth century unrivalled ink drawings appear, and Chinese Sung influence is noticeable. During Ming, Sesshu (1420-1506) journeyed to China to find a teacher. He was disappointed in his quest, for he discovered his skill and dexterity exceeded that of any Chinese artist of the time. He did, however, learn a great deal from the earlier Sung paintings which he studied there. We are told of Sesshu that once, during a command performance at court, he painted a dragon among clouds with a single stroke. His landscape scrolls are famous.

The well-known Japanese print came into being in the seventeenth century. These prints, made by artists and artisans especially for the people, were reproduced in quantities by the wood-block printing method, and sold at a price the people could pay. Some of the best painters of the time made designs for this process. Kiyonobu (1664-1729), painter and printer, is largely responsible for the popularity of wood-blocks, which he used to portray actors and theater scenes. Kiyonaga, Utamaro, and Hiroshige were among the excellent print designers of the seventeenth and eighteenth centuries. The last is more famous for his albums of landscape painting. Originally reproduced in black on white, some colored by hand, wood engravings were printed by a polychrome process in the late eighteenth century. Harunobu, who specialized in feminine subjects, is credited with this invention (Plate 82).

Screen painting, a popular form of Japanese pictorial art, had as its principal exponent Ogata Korin. This artist was noted for his decorative interpretation of dashing waves (Plate 80). He succeeded in combining Chinese feeling for spaciousness with Japanese conventions of design.

Crows. Painted screen. 17th cent. (Seattle Art Museum)

The *Three Laughers* by Soga Shohaku, an eighteenth-century painting, shows a genre subject treated in a vivacious and gay style (Plate 82). An overhanging gnarled pine twig, drawn with definite lines, fills the upper part of the composition. The bridge and pathway with jutting edges show the rock formation and make a strikingly angular pattern of asymmetrical balance of which the Japanese artists were masters. The painters of secular subjects of this period added bright color and gold to their lively scenes.

A new style of painting is represented by a set of Tokanobu's paintings in the Boston Art Museum, which deal with the life of *Shōtoku Taishi*, the son of Suikō. Fierce action and moving crowds of people are shown with each figure meticulously represented even to the minutest detail. His portraits are purely Japanese in character. Some of the figures are clothed in the costume of Tokanobu's day, while others are idealized representations of men of a former time. All are highly individualized and executed with the greatest economy of means. The same characteristics may be observed in the *Burning of Sanjo Palace,* by Heiji Monogatari (Plate 81).

The Japanese considered design more important than actual representation. If perspective was understood, it was not employed; a diagonal line scheme, conspicuous in the Fujiwara and Kamakura paintings and in eighteenth-century Japanese prints, suggested spatial depth and served to guide the eye into and through the picture. In many pictures of interiors the observer looks down

Dog Barking at a Man in a Pantomime Mask. Brush drawing by Hokusai (1760-1849). (Barry, *Art for Children*, Studio Publications, Inc.)

upon the scene as if through a transparent roof. Diagonals lead the eye from foreground to background and form a striking contrast with the usual curving lines of garments and figures. *No-tan*, that is, dark and light, was employed for pattern, not as light and shade. Merely suggesting form, the Japanese painter emphasized line, *no-tan*, and color. Figures symbolizing militaristic force and power appeared frequently especially during the later periods. Symbolism was even more important than in Chinese art. Like most Oriental art, Japanese painting is the product of contemplation and memory.

The Japanese, like the Chinese, painted with ink and watercolors on silk or absorbent paper. One Japanese, we are told, said that when armed with a sword he felt invincible, but he deplored the fact that he was not equally confident when wielding a brush. Japanese connoisseurs speak of symbolic and decorative quality and the excellence of brushwork when they are judging a picture. Their wood-block prints exerted a great influence upon the Western painters of the nineteenth century.

OUTLINE OF ART IN THE FAR EAST–JAPAN

TIME: 552 A.D. to 18th century.

BACKGROUND: Japanese still in stone age when Chinese were in the middle of Han. Lived in practical isolation before Christian era. Development continuous and steady during first six centuries A.D. Buddhist monks introduced Chinese religion and culture. Shintō, the primitive religion which later became nationalistic in character, still persists. Japanese more militarily inclined than Chinese. They are noted for their energy, accuracy, orderliness, skill, and dexterity.

ARCHITECTURE: Monastery, temple, and palaces of early period showed Chinese influence. Later architecture became more ornate, more curvilinear, more brilliant in hue than Chinese. Elaboration of bracket work. In many cases decoration almost obscured structure. Wood principal material. Choice of beautiful setting and designing of a harmonious garden considered no less important than architecture itself.

SCULPTURE: Skillfully executed. As in Chinese work, former rhythmic linear style gave way to more realistic—at times militaristic—expression. Imaginative and symbolic, formalistic. *Materials:* bronze, stone, clay, wood, lacquer.

PAINTINGS: Types: frescoes, brush, and ink paintings on silk or absorbent paper, screen painting, wood-block printing. Movement and action in much of their work. Product of imagination and memory. Attention to detail. Design considered more important than naturalistic representation.

BIBLIOGRAPHY (CHAPTERS XI, XII, XIII)

ANAND Mulk Raj, *The Hindu View of Art* (London, 1933).

BACHHOFER, Ludwig, *A Short History of Chinese Art* (Pantheon Books, N. Y., 1946).

BINYON, Lawrence, *Painting in the Far East* (Longmans, Green & Co., N. Y., 1934).

——, *The Flight of the Dragon* (E. P. Dutton & Co., N. Y., 1922).

——, *The Spirit of Man in Asian Art* (Harvard University Press, Cambridge, Mass., 1935).

BROWN, Percy, *Indian Painting* (Oxford University Press, N. Y., 1929).

CARTER, Dagny, *China Magnificent: Five Thousand Years of Chinese Art* (John Day Co., Inc., N. Y., 1935).

CRESSY, George B., *Asia's Lands and Peoples* (Whittlesey House, McGraw-Hill Book Co., Inc., N. Y., 1944).

COOMARASWAMY, A. K., *History of Indian and Indonesian Art* (Weyhe, 1927).

——, *The Dance of Siva*, new ed. (Sunwise Turn, Inc., N. Y., 1925).

CRAIN, R. A., *Impressions of Japanese Architecture and the Allied Arts* (N. Y., Baker & Taylor Co., 1911).

DRISCOLL, Lucy, and Toda, Kenji, *Chinese Calligraphy* (University of Chicago Press, Chicago, 1935).

FERGUSON, J. C., *Chinese Painting* (University of Chicago Press, Chicago, 1927).

FRY, Roger, and others, *Chinese Art: An Introductory Hand Book to Painting, Sculpture, Ceramics, Textiles, Bronzes and Minor Arts* (London, 1935).

FUJII, Koji, *The Japanese Dwelling-house* (Tokyo, 1930).

HAVELL, E. B., *The Ancient and Medieval Architecture of India* (Charles Scribner's Sons, N. Y., 1915).

——, *A Handbook of Indian Art* (London, 1921).

HOBSON, R. L., *Chinese Art* (The Macmillan Co., N. Y., 1927).

LATOURETTE, Kenneth Scott, *The Chinese, Their History and Culture* (The Macmillan Co., N. Y., 1946).

LIN Yutang (ed.), *The Wisdom of China and India* (Random House, Inc., N. Y., 1942).

Museum of Fine Arts, Boston, *Portfolio of Chinese Paintings in the Museum*, text by Kojiro Tomita (Harvard University Press, Cambridge, Mass., 1933).

OKAKURO, Kakuzo, *The Book of Tea* (Duffield, Duffield & Co., N. Y., 1906).

SILCOCK, Arnold, *An Introduction to Chinese Art and History* (Oxford University Press, N. Y., 1936).

SIREN, Oswald, and others, *The Romance of Chinese Art: How to Appreciate and Enjoy It* (Garden City Publishing Co., Encyclopoedia Britannica).

SPENCER, Cornelia, *The Story of Chinese Expression* (Alfred A. Knopf, Inc., N. Y., 1943).

TODA, Kenji, *Japanese Scroll Painting* (University of Chicago Press, Chicago, 1935).

TSUDA, Noritake, *Hand Book of Japanese Art* (Dodd, Mead & Co., N. Y., 1935).

WARNER, Langdon, *Japanese Sculpture of Suiko Period* (Yale University Press, New Haven, 1923).

CHAPTER XIV

Art of the Italian Renaissance

LEAVING Asia and turning again to Europe, one finds a new era dawning in the West, where there is an intense activity of those forces that heralded the beginning of the modern world. In the central part of the continent Gothic influences had met and mingled with Byzantine traditions. This interweaving of Western and Eastern trends, further conditioned by new ideas and the new ways of life peculiar to the times, was to produce an art distinctively different from that of the preceding periods. Broadly considered, in contrast to the formalistic, decorative, and symbolic art of the Orient, it was based upon a fresh and direct observation of nature, a renewed interest in man as an individual and in the environment in which he lived.

The new movement came earliest to Italy. Literally speaking, the term *Renaissance*—meaning re-birth—is a misnomer since it applies to only one phase of development in that dynamic era, namely, the rediscovery of classical learning. But like the term *Gothic* it has been sanctioned by long usage.

Politically, the early Renaissance (fourteenth and fifteenth centuries) was a period of complexity and confusion in Italy. Constant strife among the city-states or so-called republics such as Florence, Pisa, and Siena opened the way for bold individuals to obtain power through wealth, diplomacy, or intrigue and to establish dynasties, some of which lasted over a hundred years. Among them were the Sforza of Milan and the most famous of all, the Medici of Florence. The latter, who were benevolent despots, became the most powerful bankers of Europe and generous patrons of the arts. With the introduction of gunpowder (c. 14th century) warfare changed. Standing armies now comprised professional soldiers who sold their services to the highest bidder for pay and the hope of plunder. The prince frequently employed these mercenaries to further his own ambitions or to satisfy personal greed.

Someone has pointed out that the Renaissance, covering the latter half of the thirteenth through the sixteenth centuries, should be thought of not merely as a period of time but as a way of thinking. During the Middle Ages the common man was dependent upon the church both for his religious and secular knowledge. In the thirteenth century St. Francis of Assisi (1182-1286), who renounced his wealth to devote his life to service, introduced a new spirit of human kindness and taught man to observe and appreciate the beauties of the earth about him. The democratic and kindly spirit of the Franciscan Order resulting from his teachings differed from that of the autocratic Dominican Order which was organized for the purpose of stamping out heresy. In art, this new appreciation of the beauty of the outer world is exemplified in the detailed recordings of animals, trees, shrubs, and flowers which are scattered in profusion over the background surfaces of paintings of the earlier centuries.

SCIENTIFIC INQUIRY; TRAVEL; INVENTION

With the introduction of scientific inquiry and first-hand contacts with the world, men became interested in themselves, and in time individualism superseded the medieval conception of collectivism. Travel, first promoted by the Crusades and later by world trade, broadened men's interests, stirred their imaginations, and stimulated a spirit of adventure. Columbus braved unknown seas to find lands which he believed to exist beyond the western sun, discovered a new continent, enlarged the geographical boundaries of the earth, and opened the pages of American history. Activated by a tremendous energy and an insatiable curiosity about every phase of life, gifted men also extended the limits of scientific investigation. Copernicus announced that the earth and other planets revolved around the sun. Galileo (1564-1642), while watching the swaying of a lamp in the cathedral of Pisa, discovered the law of the pendulum. Leonardo da Vinci (1452-1519), possessing the many-faceted mind typical of the geniuses of the period, solved intricate problems in engineering and anticipated many inventions, among them the tank, submarine, and airplane that

Wood-block illustration from Colonna's *Hypterotomacchia*.
Aldus Press, Venice. 1499. (Metropolitan Museum of Art)

were not to be perfected until recent times. Had he lived today he probably would have become more renowned as a scientist and inventor than as an artist.

No distinct break occurred between medieval and Renaissance times, for many of the aspects of the new movement had their origin in previous centuries. Universities had already been established, but with the advent of the printing press books became more numerous and knowledge more widely disseminated. The publication of the Bible (in 1456) and other books as well enabled men to read the Scriptures and works of their own great writers, such as Petrarch, Dante, and Boccaccio. Bookmaking became a great art. Among the most illustrious of the early printers was Aldus Manutius of Venice, whose work was known for beauty of typography. The illustration for Colonna's *Hypterotomacchia Poliphili,* printed by Aldus in 1499, shows one of the wood-cut illustrations with which these bookmakers embellished their editions. Treatises on botany, geology, astronomy, chemistry, medicine, and anatomy appeared. Cellini, a goldsmith and sculptor, wrote one of the most famous autobiographies of all time. An outstanding individual, a braggart, and something of a scoundrel as well, he considered the most insignificant details of his life worth recording.

REVIVAL OF CLASSICAL LEARNING

Many scholars of the Renaissance, who either erroneously depreciated the cultural contribution of the Middle Ages or ignored it entirely, sought to recapture the glories of their ancient past. To do this they learned to speak, read, and write both Latin and Greek. Through the literature and philosophy of antiquity they became familiar with the personalities, manners, and customs of the men of those early times. This revival of classical learning, known as Humanism, was one of the strong motivating forces of the Renaissance.

About the middle of the fifteenth century the Italians discovered and excavated a vast heritage of long-buried ancient coins, marble urns, sarcophagi, and statues which proved to be a great inspiration to the artists. In Florence the Medici collected such works of art together with manuscripts and other relics, housed them in libraries and museums, and made them available to students. They invited young artists, including Michelangelo and Botticelli, to their court where they could study antique sculpture and listen to the discourse of intellectuals.

Popes and princes employed classical scholars as secretaries and teachers. Thus, both church and state became permeated with Humanism. As a result of the impact of ancient philosophical ideas, together with disillusionment occasioned by deplorable practices that had crept into the church itself, heresy was widespread. Humanists became neo-paganists and tried to recapture the carefree spirit of the Greeks whose religion was a joyous cult; others remained faithful to the doctrines of the church. That institution, however, finally lost the spiritual unity which it had retained throughout the Middle Ages. The church was divided, and eventually Protestantism found a stronghold in the north.

The Dominican friar Savonarola, a dynamic reformer, tried to stem the tide of disintegration of religious faith by thundering against the iniquities of the times in general, and the sins of the neo-pagan court of the Medici in particular. Many masterpieces of art were destroyed when the monk ordered the "burning of the vanities," which included pictures showing nudes or lightly-clad figures. These Savonarola denounced as works of the devil. Artists who disagreed with the now powerful friar left Florence and went to Rome. In the end he became deeply involved in politics, lost his prestige, and suffered martyrdom in the public square.

AGE OF GENIUSES

It is recorded that more geniuses were born in Italy during the fifteenth century than in a comparable period of time in any other country. Since many of them were artists, it is not surprising that art was one of the leading manifestations of that remarkable period. The demand for portraiture was great in this age when men avidly sought everlasting fame. The artist, through his ability to record the likeness of an individual, could in a sense immortalize him; for such an image carved in marble, cast in bronze, or painted on wood, wall, or canvas would exist long after the man himself had passed away.

Three-quarter length likenesses of members of the ruling families adorned the walls of palaces. Donors of paintings of the Holy Family, designed for the church, had their own portraits included, usually in a kneeling or other humble position. Whole families were represented in everyday activities. Young Florentine women appeared as Raphael's Madonnas and as attendants in pictures such as Ghirlandajo's *Birth of the Virgin* (Plate 87). Artists were employed to plan the parades and processions that were important features of carnivals, weddings, military and hunting expeditions, or any other activities of a ceremonial nature. For these they designed gorgeous costumes, colorful banners, and rich trappings. Such processions may still be seen painted on the walls of churches, chapels, and palaces. *The Journey of the Magi,* painted by Bennozzo Gozzoli (1420-1497), represents the visit of the Wise Men bearing gifts to the Christ Child and shows a long cavalcade set against a background reminiscent of a Tuscan landscape (Plate 86). The figures of the three kings, mounted on horses in fine trappings, are actually portraits of Lorenzo, Cosimo, and Piero de Medici. The artist also included himself in the crowd. The entire fresco, painted in the gay Florentine spirit, is filled with multitudinous detail.

In the early years of the period a symbolic background of rocky hills, trees, animals, and shrubs replaced the flat gold of Byzantine mosaics and religious pictures. Later the Florentines, who viewed the outer world objectively, opened a window to give a mere glimpse of a naturalistic landscape in the distance. During the sixteenth century the Venetians, especially in their secular scenes, set groups of figures in the midst of realistic surroundings. Then landscape became almost as important as the figures themselves. But generally speaking Renaissance painting was primarily figure painting.

The training of the earlier artists was similar to that received by the craftsmen of the Middle Ages. Apprenticed when very young, they were sent to work in the *bottegas* (shops) of professional artists until, qualified by study and subsequent travel, they could maintain a shop of their own. Later, academic training was introduced. Among other things copying antique works and studying from live models were included. At this time artists established studios, surrounded themselves with promising pupils, and worked on commissions from church, state, or wealthy patrons.

The cities of Herculaneum and Pompeii had not yet been excavated, and there were few classical examples to inspire the early painters. They had only the paintings in the catacombs, Byzantine mosaics, religious pictures or ikons such as those which were made in Russia until recent times, and altar-pieces (paintings placed back of the altar). These were usually stiff, conventionalized treatments of dignified and coldly formal human figures whose faces had long sharp noses and large staring dark eyes, representing unseen biblical or legendary beings of the heavenly or supernatural world. The transition from the medieval style to that of the fourteenth century, when artists directed their observation to the world of reality, was so gradual that paintings which would seem conventional and formalized to modern eyes were hailed as triumphs of realism by the people of the early Renaissance.

SIENESE PAINTING

In Siena, where medieval traditions still persisted, Duccio de Buoninsegna (1260-c.1320) was the leader of a group of painters including Simone Martini (1284-1344), the Lorenzetti, and Sassetta (1392-1450). Most of these artists employed the method known as *tempera painting*. First the colors were mixed with water. A glutinous medium acting as a binder, such as white of egg, was added. The paint was then applied thickly to wood panels previously treated with successive layers of fine plaster of Paris rubbed to a smooth surface and covered with pure gold leaf.

An unaccustomed naturalism appears in Duccio's panel *Three Marys at the Tomb* (Plate 85). Like most of his work, this painting is characterized by a mystic religious feeling. The stiffness of the figures is modified by curving contours, slightly more flexible postures, and gestures which he had seen in life, such as a turn of the head or a movement of the hand. The faces have a tender, though rather sad, expression. Although the heavy gold background of the Byzantine tradition persists, Duccio's art introduced greater feeling into art expression.

Ambrogio Lorenzetti (c. 1323-1348) and his elder brother Pietro, important fresco painters, applied their colors to fresh plaster into which the paint penetrated to become a part of the wall itself. Only as much plaster was laid in place as the painter could finish in a working day. If a mistake was made the plaster had to be scraped off and relaid before repainting could be done. Since fresco painters were compelled to work with speed, their designs necessarily were simple and their style quite free. Such paintings last as long as the plastered surface endures—in central Italy, for hundreds of years. Among the works of the brothers Lorenzetti is *The Triumph of Death*, a work intended to represent the grim hazards of life, the end of which is death and judgment.

Simone Martini's *Majesty of the Virgin* shows the Madonna

elevated on a picturesque throne covered by a rich canopy. The Christ Child now begins to look more like a human being than a small divinity. Human feeling also infuses the sombre figure of St. Anthony, the Abbot (Plate 85). The painting has individuality and the appearance of being a study of an actual character, despite the stylized, formal tooled-gold halo of the period. Sassetta, in his St. Anthony Tormented by Demons, discarded the gold background for a symbolical landscape (Plate 84).

Continuing well into the fifteenth century, Sienese painting was spiritual, highly emotional, subjective; Florentine art, influenced by classicism and informed by a direct observation of nature, was objective, naturalistic. If the Sienese heralded the dawn of realism, it was the Florentines who pointed the way toward naturalism which their art was to follow over a period of six hundred years.

GIOTTO, ORCAGNA, AND MASACCIO

When Italy had become the cultural center of Europe, by the latter part of the thirteenth century, there was a changing attitude toward life and religion. Asceticism and the seeking after things of the spirit gave way to a growing interest in the outer world and physical pleasures. To the Florentines in particular the world was a pleasant place in which to live, and being full of vitality and energy, they were prepared to enjoy it. Cimabue was the first Florentine artist of note, but it was his famous pupil Giotto di Bondone (c.1276-1337) who was to lay the groundwork for Western art.

A masterly story-teller, Giotto divested his frescoes of all distracting details and made every figure, every line, every gesture contribute both to the clarity of meaning and the unity of design. Like stage settings, his architectural forms, enclosing a box-like space, were subordinated to the figures which enacted the dramatic scenes. By giving solidity to his bulky forms and by employing bodily posture, gesture and facial expression to heighten emotional intensity, Giotto achieved a dramatic effect and hastened the end of the non-realistic, symbolic painting practiced by the Sienese artists.

Giotto's frescoes on the walls of the upper Church of St. Francis of Assisi are sympathetic interpretations of the miracles, sermons, penance, and death of the saint. It was at Padua however, in a small chapel erected on the site of an old Roman Arena—and for that reason called the *Arena Chapel*—that Giotto reached the heights of his ability, for here he left one of the noblest cycles of pictures known to religious art. The thirty-eight frescoes, representing episodes in the lives of St. Anne, Mary, and Jesus, and charged with emotion, depict such universal feelings of joy, pain, longing, or deep sorrow, and give life and meaning to the biblical scenes. Among them is the *Massacre of the Innocents* (Plate 83).

Notable among the followers of Giotto was Orcagna (c. 1308-1368), Florentine architect, sculptor, goldsmith, and painter. Orcagna's paintings closely resemble Giotto's both in style and subject. *Triumph of Death* (Plate 83) is characteristic of his work.

For almost a hundred years artists had continued to copy the style of Giotto, but Tommaso Guidi, better known as Masaccio (1401-1428), accomplished a complete mastery of the painting of naturalistic form. He used light and shadow to give form to his figures, and his outlines were not so sharply defined as Giotto's. Distant objects were made smaller and lighter in tone than those in the foreground, thus producing the effect of atmosphere about his figures. *The Expulsion*, on the walls of the Brancacci Chapel in Florence, shows three-dimensional figures in deep space (Plate 88). Here Masaccio achieved the first full realization of pictorial representation. The artist added to the great naturalistic advances inaugurated by his predecessor, Giotto. Masaccio's skillful use of light and shade and thorough knowledge of human anatomy helped him interpret this dramatic biblical scene with complete naturalism. Evidences of the devastating grief of Adam and Eve are seen in Adam's hand-covered face and the despair on Eve's upturned countenance. In Masaccio's painting of the well-proportioned figures he placed full bodily weight on the legs and feet. His knowledge of perspective, foreshortening, and his skillful use of light and shadow enabled him to create an illusion of a third dimension.

THE PAINTER MONKS

Fra Giovanni (1387-1455), known as Fra Angelico (the angelic one) because of his holiness, came to Florence at the age of twenty. There he labored for nine years to complete—with the aid of his assistants—forty-three frescoes for the convent of San Marco. They are spread over the walls, cloisters, corridors, and cells of that famous shrine. Although he was a member of the Dominican Order, Fra Angelico's paintings were suffused with the spirit of St. Francis. It is recorded that he prayed long and earnestly before beginning to paint and thereafter made no alterations in his work because he thought the Lord had directed him.

The Annunciation, of which the artist painted several versions, shows the Angel Gabriel appearing to Mary to tell her that she is to be the mother of Christ (Plate 89). Here are the usual exquisite colors and detailed decorations that are generally found in Fra Angelico's work. There is also a sweetness of expression on the faces of his figures and a mystic beauty that the gentle monk imparted to everything which he painted. Nevertheless, underlying the sentimental and emotional qualities a fine linear pattern and excellent design prove that he was master of his craft.

Another painter-monk, Fra Filippo Lippi (c. 1406-1469), or Fra Lippo as he is sometimes called, was left to fend for himself when he was still a small boy. Tired and hungry, with no other choice left him, so the story goes, he was persuaded to join the Carmelite order. Under the tutelage of the monks he became an artist and developed a graceful narrative style characterized by beautiful line arrangements and the informal charm of his feminine figures. Fra Lippo was the first to use the ordinary people of Florence as models for religious paintings. It is said that he escaped from the monastery at night and took great delight in mingling with the crowds. His religious works, such as *The Annunciation,* are strongly imbued with human interest (Plate 89).

THE SCIENTIFIC PAINTERS

The spirit of scientific discovery was represented in the works of Paolo Uccello (1397-1475) and Antonio Pollaiuolo (1433-1496). Uccello, meaning "Bird-man," was a nickname given to Paolo because of his fondness for painting birds, although his most absorbing interest was the solution of complicated problems in linear perspective and foreshortening. It is recorded that he succeeded in making a perfect representation of a seventy-two sided polyhedron. Pollaiuolo's *The Battle of Nude Men,* a copper engraving, is chiefly notable for the anatomical construction of nude figures shown in violent movement (Plate 86). His drawings of figures in action were used as models to instruct young artists in the study of anatomy.

BOTTICELLI; MANTEGNA; PERUGINO

Sandro Botticelli (1444-1510), a solitary, temperamental genius who had courage to follow the promptings of his highly imaginative spirit, departed from the naturalistic representation which was foremost in the minds of Renaissance artists. Entering Fra Lippo's studio at the age of fourteen, he worked there for seven years, after which he became a protégé of Lorenzo de Medici and was included in his immediate circle of friends. Although he painted such prominent Florentines as the Medici and the aristocratic Florentine beauties who enjoyed their favor, Botticelli is primarily an interpreter of classic myths and allegories. After the death of Lorenzo in 1492 the artist, who had been deeply affected by the admonitions of Savonarola, turned his attentions to religious painting and thereafter worked under papal patronage. When he was twenty-five years old, he was summoned by the Pope to paint frescoes on the walls of the Sistine Chapel. It was during this decade that he also made his famous illustrations in silverpoint for Dante's *Divine Comedy.* When Savonarola met his tragic fate Botticelli, who had been greatly moved by his fiery warnings, lapsed into melancholia from which he never recovered.

Botticelli saw a mystic beauty in nature and represented it in idyllic scenes of woods, meadows, sea, and moving wind. In the *Allegory of Spring* the foreground is strewn with flowers and figures are shown against a background of orange trees. In the center, Venus, the goddess of Love, awaits the coming of Spring, while Cupid hovers over her as he aims his arrow toward the three Graces. Lorenzo de Medici is represented as Mercury, the messenger of the gods. Spring, blown in by the west wind, enters in a playful mood while Flora scatters blossoms in her path. This poetic conception designed for the Medici Villa is a decorative arrangement of gracefully moving forms against a static background.

In the *Birth of Venus* * (Plate 90) Botticelli again abandoned naturalism to heighten the poetic quality of his linear rhythms. Venus, born of the Sea, stands on a shell which two Zephyrs blow to the water's edge as Spring hurries forward to fold her in a flower-spangled garment. Posed in the manner of a Greek statue and bending with the wind which blows the coiling strands of her long golden hair about her, the figure of the goddess is modeled in the nervous rhythmic lines which Botticelli loved. Her eyes are fixed in the wistful, melancholy gaze that is characteristic of his faces. The entire composition is based upon concentric curves radiating, like the inner lines of the shell itself, from a point just beneath the feet of goddess. The larger curve passes through the forms which hover about her on either side, and the smaller one is formed by the contour line of the shell on which the lithe figure is lightly poised. This line scheme forms the basic design which underlies the story interest, the decorative pattern, and the melancholy charm of the picture. On the faces of Botticelli's Madonnas and biblical characters, as in the painting of *Jethro's Daughters* in the Sistine Chapel (Plate 90), is the same dreamy expression as that of his pagan goddesses. Their long hair is arranged in the same intricate coils, and their garments and other accessories are likewise drawn in minute detail.

An outstanding artist of northern Italy was Andrea Mantegna (1431-1506). He was influenced by the classical sculpture which he had studied in Squarcione's studio in Padua, a city geograph-

---

* This picture was included in the loan collection sent to America as a goodwill gesture by the Italian government before World War II.

ically near Venice but intellectually and spiritually more akin to
Florence. Later he went to Venice and worked with the Bellini
family. Placed against complicated architectural backgrounds, his
sculpturesque figures are sometimes elevated on stage-like platforms placed close to the lower edge of the picture. In such daring
arrangements the characters enacting the dramatic scene are shown
above the eye-level of the spectator, an angle of vision frequently
employed in modern photography which was nevertheless an innovation in his day. While decorating the palace of the *Gonzaga
Family of Mantua*, he painted the interior of a dome on the ceiling
of the bridal chamber to create the illusion of increased architectural space—a trick copied by other artists. The figures of cupids
and attendants looking down over a balustrade at the base of the
dome show his high technical proficiency in perspective and foreshortening. *Tarquin and the Cumaean Sibyl* is typical of his best
work (Plate 87).

Pietro Vannucci, better known as Perugino (1445-1523), left
his birthplace, Perugia, and came to Florence where he worked in
the studio of Verrocchio. Later, like Botticelli and others, he went
to Rome to paint frescoes on the walls of the Sistine Chapel.
Among them is *Giving the Keys to St. Peter*. In 1508, Julius II
dismissed him and engaged his assistant Raphael to complete the
murals. Feeling that he had outlived his fame, the older painter
retired to Perugia where he died of the plague at the age of sev-
enty-eight. Perugino's chief contribution to the general development of art was the introduction of spatial relationships in his quiet
symmetrical compositions. In contrast to Botticelli's flat decorative
backgrounds and Giotto's architectural devices which were like
stage scenery, Perugino gave the illusion of different depths in vast
space—distinguishing between foreground, middle distance, and
background. Distances were established by the strategic placing
of massed groups of figures in their proper planes. Thus, the figure groups served a structural purpose in the painter's compositions
similar to that which masses of material occupy in the architect's
designs for buildings. For this reason they are said to be *architectonic*; they have a functional purpose in the spatial design of the
picture.

LEONARDO DA VINCI

Leonardo da Vinci (1452-1519), painter, sculptor, engineer, mathematician, inventor, musician, and scientist was born in Vinci near Florence. Endowed with great beauty, amazing strength, many talents, an intellect capable of encompassing all of the knowledge of his age, and an insatiable intellectual curiosity which persisted throughout his life, he was one of the most fascinating personalities of all time. At the age of thirteen he was apprenticed to Verrocchio, painter, sculptor, and the eminent art teacher of Florence. During the several years he spent there, he painted and modeled in clay, wrote verses, and worked on his many inventions. As his pupils advanced Verrocchio entrusted them with more important tasks, and Leonardo was allowed to

Caricature drawn by Leonardo da Vinci. (Metropolitan Museum of Art)

paint an angel in one of Verrocchio's pictures. It is recorded that when the master saw the charming figure he exclaimed in effect, "The pupil has surpassed his teacher; henceforth I paint no more." True to his words, he afterwards confined his efforts to sculpture.

Leaving Florence, Leonardo went to Milan where he was employed by Duke Ludovico Sforza to design architectural plans, weapons of war, and to supervise practical engineering projects. His numerous manuscripts, plans, note books, and drawings show that he envisioned mechanical appliances and machines which were three hundred years in advance of his time. While there he painted the renowned *Last Supper* on the wall of the refectory or dining room of the Dominican Church of Santa Maria delle Grazie (Plate 92).

This great mural has been damaged by the moisture of the low damp room. Unfortunately, instead of using the fresco technique

usually employed for such large works, Leonardo, always the ex-
perimenter, painted in tempera on a dry wall with the result that
much of the painted surface has flaked away. In later times various artists have retouched the masterpiece to its detriment. A
doorway has been cut through the lower part of the painting, and
during subsequent wars soldiers who were billeted in the refectory
contributed to the destruction. Nevertheless, even in its deteriorated form, the tremendous conception of Leonardo's painting—
which occupies an entire wall—excites the admiration of the spectator. Christ is seated directly in front of the largest of three
windows through which a distant landscape is seen. The perspective lines of table and walls converge at a point on or behind his
face. Also, a wave-like motion of the heads and hands of his disciples directs the attention toward the resigned and forgiving
Master who has just announced, "One of you will betray me."
With revealing expressions of intense excitement, grief, dismay,
and inquiry, the disciples simultaneously ask, "Lord, is it I?"—that
is, all except Judas who, leaning upon the table in front of them,
sits apart grasping the money bag containing the thirty pieces of
silver, his price for the betrayal of his Master. Startled by the ac-
cusation he suddenly moves and spills the salt over the tablecloth.
For three years Leonardo worked on the *Last Supper*, sometimes
painting feverishly, again spending hours before it lost in concentration, without so much as lifting a brush. This composition
shows his supreme skill in the grouping of figures and his ability
to convey the character of each one by facial expression, gesture,
and attitude.

In both *Madonna of the Rocks* and the *Virgin with St. Anne*
Leonardo has used a pyramidal composition. In the former the
Christ Child and His Mother with St. John and an angel are
placed against a background of dark rocky caves, a waterfall, green
ferns, and other plants (Plate 91). By a subtle treatment of pulsating lights and shadows he created the illusion of air and deep
space and imbued the entire painting with a feeling of mystery.
The *Virgin with St. Anne* shows the two principal figures with
the Christ Child who is amusing himself with a playful lamb. The
background here is a distant landscape.

When the French captured Milan in 1499, Leonardo returned to Florence and afterwards went to Rome. Finally accepting the invitation of Francis I he went to France and remained until his death. The *Mona Lisa* which he took with him is now one of the prized possessions of the Louvre in Paris (Plate 92).

The widespread fame of Leonardo's *Mona Lisa* or *La Gioconda* is due rather to the haunting expression and enigmatic smile of the lady than to a noble conception such as that achieved in the *Last Supper*. Upon viewing the picture the spectator usually feels impelled to interpret her mood, which seems to be a combination of various emotions difficult to identify. Posed to fit into Leonardo's usual pyramidal composition, she sits quietly with hands folded across the arm of a chair. Behind her a landscape background that does not suggest any particular place shows a meandering river which contributes to the general air of mystery that pervades the entire painting. A strong light falls on hands, neck, and face of the figure, clearly outlining these features. Sharp flickering lights appear on the folds of the sleeves and lights more subtly toned fall upon the rich garments revealing the salient forms of the figure beneath. Spreading across the face is the faint smile induced, we are told, by musicians and other entertainers employed to dispel her usual sad expression. About her chin, cheeks, and eyes there are upward curving shadows which are counter-balanced by the downward curve of her folded hands. The curves of the figure echoed in the landscape, together with the vibrating lights and shadows, enhance the pictorial effect and give form, life, and movement to the painting. In this portrait, Leonardo attempts to penetrate the depths of a baffling personality.

RAPHAEL

The climax of a long development in Italian painting was reached in the achievement of Raphael Sanzio (1483-1520), known to the Florentines as Youthful Master. Raphael, born in Urbino amid the picturesque Apennine Mountains, inherited a gift for art from his father who was a second-rate poet and painter. At an early age he entered Perugino's studio and became the master's assistant when he was only seventeen. Perugino's influence is seen in his early works such as *The Marriage of the Virgin,* which is strongly reminiscent of the master's *Giving of the Keys to St. Peter.* The faces of the figures have the same dreamy expression.

Dancing Children and Cupids. By Marcantonio, after a drawing by Raphael.
(Metropolitan Museum of Art)

Raphael was already famous for his paintings of sweet-faced and gracious Madonnas and spacious compositions in Perugino's style when he appeared in Florence to set up a studio of his own. Upon arrival he found the city in great excitement over a competition between the two geniuses Michelangelo and Leonardo, who were making designs, or *cartoons* as they were called, for a battle-piece to decorate the Prior's Palace. He soon increased his knowledge and assimilated new ideas from both a study of the older frescoes in the city and the current fashion as exemplified by the two great masters. Retaining the clarity, simplicity, and spaciousness of his early master, he amplified his designs and concentrated upon the arrangement of many figures in small groups unified by curving lines of bodily movement or gesture of strategically placed figures such as the Diogenes lying on the steps in the *School of Athens.* This accent upon composition or structure, rather than con- spicuous individual achievement in any one aspect of painting such as the palpitating light and shadow of Leonardo's work or the tempestuous movement of Michelangelo's great forms is the outstanding characteristic of his work.

When he was only twenty-five Raphael was summoned to Rome to paint a portrait of *Pope Julius II* (Plate 96) and to decorate his apartments in the Vatican. While in Rome he displayed a remarkable ability to compose many figures and to create the illusion of infinite space. In the *School of Athens,* painted on the left wall of the *Segnatura*—the room in which the Pope affixed his name to documents, there are said to be fifty-two figures symbolizing the wise teachers of ancient Greece (Plate 94). All are set before a long vaulted hall reaching far back into space, thus completely denying the flatness of the wall. In the center of the elevation reached by a stair stand two figures: one is Plato, the philosopher, an old man who holds a book and points upward, for he is concerned with the things of the spirit; the other, pointing downward, represents a man in the prime of life, Aristotle, whose scientific mind is more concerned with earthly practical affairs. Together they symbolize two phases of thought which occupied the minds of the men of the Renaissance. The group on the left is taught by Socrates. Diogenes the cynic is alone on the stairs. In the midst of a group of geometricians, astronomers, and musicians Pythagoras is writing on a tablet. In the lower right-hand corner is a self portrait of the artist, and the beautiful youth standing straight and tall amid the kneeling or seated figures to the left is said to be a member of the Rovere family. A fine unity and space relationship exists between the numerous groups of life-size figures and the architectural background.

It has been estimated that Raphael left two hundred and eighty-seven paintings. Naturally no one man in so short space of time— for he died at the age of thirty-seven—could accomplish all the work represented by his murals alone. The artist drew the cartoons (designs) and left much of the painting to his numerous assistants. In addition to Raphael's murals are portraits of famous people and paintings of the Holy Family and Madonnas. Raphael's work, which reflects his serene and untroubled personality, is notable for lofty sentiment and remarkable skill in composition.

MICHELANGELO

Dominating the sixteenth century was one of the most creative
geniuses of the Italian Renaissance, Michelangelo Buonarroti
(1475-1564), born in Caprese. An austere and imperious intellect,
combined with the highest imaginative power and reinforced by
consummate skill, enabled him to produce masterpieces which are
expressive of the tempestuous spirit of the energetic men of the
Renaissance and the outward turmoil of their times. Attaining a
measure of success in architecture, he rose to supreme heights in
sculpture, and is no less remarkable for his painting. His place in
the history of art is both conspicuous and unique.

Like Leonardo, Michelangelo made his own standards and his
art was a law unto itself. His mastery of anatomy, which he acquired from dissecting cadavers, enabled him to portray the most
exaggerated movements of human form. Considering this special
ability and his passionate enthusiasm for antique sculpture which
he had studied in the Medici gardens, it is small wonder that the
human figure would become his most expressive symbol.

At the age of thirteen Michelangelo entered the shop of Ghirlandajo, but through his marked ability he soon gained entrance
to the academy supported by Lorenzo de Medici where he, like
other artists, had unusual opportunities to improve his education
and develop his talents. After Lorenzo's death he went to Rome to
design and construct an enormous tomb for Pope Julius II. The
old St. Peter's basilica had been razed and the new St. Peter's
church was being erected. After finishing a few of the statues,
Michelangelo went to Carrara to procure more marble to complete
the project, only to find upon his return that the Pope had abandoned the whole project.* The disgusted sculptor returned to
Florence where he obstinately remained despite orders from the
Pope to return to Rome. When he realized that his stubbornness
was about to precipitate war between the two cities he reluctantly
returned. We are told that it was at the request of a jealous archi-

---

* The *Moses*, sculptured for this project, now stands by the small tomb of
the Pope, who was not buried in St. Peter's after all, but in a smaller church
known as St. Peter in Chains.

tect, who believed that a sculptor could not possibly accomplish such a stupendous task, that the Pope commissioned Michelangelo to paint the ceiling of the *Sistine Chapel*, a long narrow barrel-vaulted structure (Plate 94). Protesting that he was a sculptor, not a painter, Michelangelo unwillingly assumed the task, and completed it alone, for the most part. Unlike the even-tempered Raphael who had as many as fifty assistants, the irascible Michelangelo could not work well with one. It is said that he never entirely recovered from the effects of strain upon the muscles of his neck and eyes caused from the four years spent in painting the ceiling while lying on his back on the scaffold or looking up with his head thrown back.

With a painted architectural framework Michelangelo divided the entire space of the vault into oblong, triangular, and half-circular sections *(lunettes)*. In the lunettes over the windows are figures representing the ancestors of Christ. In the spaces between are figures of prophets (Hebrew) and sibyls (pagan) which symbolize the ancient religions of the world. Of the pagan feminine figures the *Libyan Sibyl* is perhaps the most striking (Plate 93). The Prophets, among them *Jeremiah* and *Ezekiel*, are represented by tremendous figures. The character of each is revealed by age, pose, and facial expression, and in some cases by the addition of appropriate symbols. The oblong space extending through the center of the vault is sub-divided into four large and five smaller panels, all filled with titanic figures. At the corners of the panels are decorative nude forms. Childish figures, mounted on square pillars uphold the painted cornices, look over the shoulders of prophets and sibyls or support their manuscripts. These panels, all of which are separated by the simple painted frames, illustrate the creation and fall of man and the great deluge which almost destroyed the race. The general effect of the whole ceiling is that of a dynamic figure-filled, all-over pattern of tremendous twisting, turning, moving, standing, or seated forms.

The first panels are dominated by the enormous energetic figure of God the Father, who with outstretched arms moves through space dividing light from darkness, illuminating the sun, moon, and stars, and assigning space to the seas. Perhaps the greatest of all is the *Creation of Adam* (Plate 93). Protected by a huge cloud-like form, accompanied by a feminine figure—said to be Eve —and surrounded by floating childish forms, God the Father, moving swiftly as if propelled by a rushing wind, extends his hand toward the lifeless form of the recumbent Adam, who rests upon an unadorned triangular space representing the earth. Adam, apparently making an effort to rise, is looking toward the group with a puzzled expression, as if he were reluctant to accept the gift of life which is being—in a sense—thrust upon him. There is a dramatic contrast in the hands, one limp, the other charged with energy, which suggest that when contact is made life will flow from the living form of God to the inert body of Adam. Like the other panels, *The Drunkenness of Noah* (Plate 95) reveals the majestic concept of the artist and his mastery of the painting of the human form. Although other artists, among them Perugino, Raphael, and Botticelli, worked on the decoration of the walls of the Sistine Chapel, Michelangelo's ceiling is the chief glory of the place. As one might naturally expect, this amazing display of nude and draped titanic figures which look like colored statues set against the flat surface of the ceiling is unmistakably the concept of a sculptor.

About twenty years later Michelangelo began his painting of the *Last Judgment* on the altar wall of the chapel, completing it when he was sixty years old. The whole picture suggests restless "cyclonic movement" created by a mighty host of gigantic forms hurtling through space. It seems to have been inspired both by Dante's *Inferno* and Savonarola's graphic descriptions of the day of doom. Surrounded by apostles, prophets, monks, martyrs and church-fathers, Christ is enthroned as Judge with Mary seated at His side. On His right are the blessed and on His left the unfortunate who will soon join the lost souls that are falling through space. This great conception depicting vast energy concentrated in human forms, like that of the Sistine Chapel, displays the artist's amazing skill in anatomical construction and tempestuous movement.

DEL SARTO AND CORREGGIO

Florentine painters are not generally regarded as colorists, for they were chiefly interested in linear movement and producing the illusion of form in space by means of light and shade. Nevertheless Andrea del Sarto (1486-1531), known in his day as the "perfect painter," attained a remarkably deep and radiant color in his *Madonna and Child with Infant John* (Plate 97). In Correggio's *Adoration of the Shepherds,* often called *Holy Night,* a celestial light reflected from the Christ Child illumines the face of the Virgin and shines upon the shepherds who have heard the "glad tidings of great joy." In his *Madonna with St. Jerome,* Correggio (1494-1534) achieves a conception of rare grace and tenderness and reveals a dramatic use of light and dark (Plate 97).

VENETIAN PAINTERS

In the gay city of Venice during the fifteenth century, an art of rich and sumptuous color was being created for the wealthy and worldly-minded merchant princes who, living in a maritime port, enjoyed an extensive trade with the East which enabled them to live in Oriental splendor. Venetian painters tried to recapture the brilliant colors heretofore seen only in the mosaic and stained glass of the Byzantine and Gothic periods. An auspicious beginning for the accomplishment of their aims was the introduction of oil painting, which was brought to Italy by an artist who had spent some time in the Netherlands. The new medium proved to be more satisfactory than tempera; for colors with an oil base were not only richer in hue, they could also be successfully mixed or blended on palette or canvas.

THE BELLINIS AND CARPACCIO

Jacopo Bellini (d. 1470), the head of a family of artists, established a remarkable workshop in Venice. Working with him were his two sons, Gentile and Giovanni, and Mantegna, the Paduan, who married his daughter. Gentile Bellini (1429-1507) developed

an elaborate narrative style and recorded the gay pageants and carnivals which added color to the life of the city. Gentile Bellini's
portrait of *A Turkish Artist* (Plate 96) reflects his contact with
the ceremonial court life of Constantinople, where he was called to
serve the Sultan. This water-color of a princely scribe is the size of
a Persian miniature and is a faithful and delightfully detailed
treatment of contemporary life. In this portrait, Bellini adopted an
Oriental style which contrasts with his other purely Italian paintings. Giovanni Bellini (c. 1430-1516) undertook the painting of
monumental altar-pieces. His Madonnas are serene and gracious
figures often shown in the half-length style which he introduced
and popularized. His power of characterization is shown in the
remarkable portrait of the *Doge Loredano,* with his deep-set, almost
hypnotic eyes, and firm mouth with its "dual expression."

A pupil of Gentile Bellini, Vittore Carpaccio (c.1455-1526),
was a masterly story-teller. His fame rests chiefly on the *St. Ursula
Legend* painted for the walls of a school named for that saint.
Though highly imaginative in content, these paintings are filled
with minutely detailed representations of everyday sights and ordinary objects that make the incredible legend seem plausible. The
theme of the story is the adventures of a betrothed prince and
maiden who, accompanied by eighty virgins, set forth on a quest
of martyrdom. In one panel, the *Vision of St. Ursula,* a young girl
is shown sleeping in a room with furnishings that are accurately
represented in the minutest detail (Plate 98). The light streams
through a window through which a young angel holding the palm
of martyrdom has just appeared. Other paintings describe depar-
tures and arrivals with attendant ceremonies and views of the cities
which were visited. The artist has vividly recorded universal emotions such as anguish, joy, and sorrow which were experienced by
the participants of this strange story.

GIORGIONE AND TITIAN

Giorgione (1478-1510) as a young man also worked in the
studio of Giovanni Bellini, but soon freeing himself from all contemporary fetters, he introduced a new style and new subject

matter. In his idealistic dream world, graceful figures are set in a landscape seen through mist or fog like that which often enveloped his adopted city. The masses of colorful lights and shadows of the landscape contribute almost as much to the poetic quality of his interpretation as do the figures themselves. With color and dark-light he created a beautiful pattern, a wistful mood, pulsating movement, and a golden atmosphere which came to be known as Venetian fire. His *Fête Champêtre* is a landscape of Arcadian peace and contentment in which two musicians are seated on the ground, one playing an instrument, while a nude feminine figure, perhaps a model, holds a pipe and another draws water from a fountain (Plate 101). The spectator's eye wanders easily through the foliage of the trees, past a shepherd and houses set in thick woods to the distant sea beyond. Such pastoral themes, inaugurated by Giorgione, frequently have been employed by later artists who were charmed by the delicate lyricism and idyllic mood of his poetic painting. Giorgione died of the plague when he was only thirty-three years old. Although scarcely a dozen of his works remain, they are perfect expressions of the art of the High Renaissance.

After the death of Giorgione, Titian (1477-1576) assumed the leadership of Venetian art and retained it until his remarkably long productive and prosperous career was ended by the plague when he was ninety-nine years old. He was born in Cadore amid the pine woods, rocks, and waterfalls which he preferred to the canals of Venice as backgrounds for his paintings. Giorgione, a fellow student in Bellini's studio, proved to be a great inspiration to him. Indeed, there are several canvases which have been attributed at various times to one or the other, and some to the combined efforts of the two. Nevertheless, Giorgione's work is suffused with a poetic quality which is not present in the more naturalistic representation of Titian's later work.

Of Titian's earlier life little is known, but after he went to Venice he became an astute businessman. Wisely investing the money derived from the sale of his paintings he accumulated wealth and lived on intimate terms with the notables of his day. Princes, doges, and wealthy merchants sought his favor. His fame soon spread to foreign lands, and he even executed commissions for two enemies of his city; Charles V, who gave him a yearly allowance, and Francis I. When he was called to Rome to paint the portrait of Pope Paul III, he slept in an apartment in the Vatican and was entertained in the Farnese palace. It has been pointed out that Titian was the first "commercial artist."

Although murals were still in demand, the tendency at this time was toward the separation of painting from architecture, thereby increasing the importance of easel paintings (smaller pictures). *Venus and the Lute Player* (Plate 98), with its warm sensuousness, rich background, and glowing color exemplifies an exaltation of physical beauty which is truly Venetian.

Michelangelo's athletic nudes had been clearly outlined, turned, and twisted to represent restless movement. Titian was more prone to observe the surface qualities of his figures, the subtle modeling of lights and shadows, the textures and above all the colors of skin or richly-hued garments. During the latter part of his life his figures were not so clearly defined; parts of them were lost in shadow.

In *Pope Paul III, His Nephew Luigi, and a Cardinal* the characters of the men are ably revealed through the pose and expressions of the figures (Plate 99). Textures of flesh, hair, and rich garments are accurately recorded and fitted into a fine pattern of dark, light, and color. Among his most celebrated religious paintings, the *Assumption of the Virgin,* an altar-piece, is a complex and majestic work designed for the Church of Santa Maria of the Frari in Venice. An open landscape forms a background for two feminine figures, one a nude, the other arrayed in sumptuous garments, shown in *Sacred and Profane Love.* This picture is said to illustrate Plato's dual concept of love; however, the modern spectator, who is impressed by the masterly handling of dark-light pattern and the interplay of rich hues, can imagine that the artist was more intrigued with creating a beautiful picture than with setting forth Plato's ideas.

VERONESE AND TINTORETTO

Paolo Veronese (1528-1588), a contemporary of Giorgione and Titian, was known as Veronese because he came from the city of Verona. Accustomed to painting on a large scale, he portrayed stately spectacles, colorful Venetian pageants, and broad porticoes filled with people. In his detailed and resplendent painting, *The Finding of Moses,* the Holy Family is transported from the true biblical scene to a sumptuous setting in Venice (Plate 100). Our interest centers on the colorful details and brilliant passages, the gay background, aristocratic persons dressed in gleaming silks, and, by way of contrast, the servants and court dwarf.

An important Venetian painter of the second half of the sixteenth century was Jacopo Robusti (1518-1594), called Tintoretto, the son of a dyer. Apprenticed to Titian, he was self-willed and difficult to manage. Dismissed from the studio when only seventeen years of age he was compelled to complete his education as best he could. Nevertheless, Tintoretto, endowed with the vigor and energy of a Michelangelo, soon set up a shop of his own. Here he experimented with lighting effects to enhance the dramatic quality of his painting, and constructed figurines of wax and clay which he suspended from the ceiling and used as models for the study of perspective and foreshortening. Essentially a decorative artist, Tintoretto painted the walls and ceilings of palaces, churches and public buildings with daring renditions characterized by strength, movement, and voluptuous beauty. His *Paradise* in the Ducal Palace is said to be the largest painting in the world. Eighty-four feet wide and thirty-four feet high, it contains over four hundred life-sized figures. *Bacchus and Ariadne* is a poetic interpretation of the classical myth relating that the god of wine comes to console and offer marriage to the Cretan princess whom Theseus had abandoned on the Island of Naxos (Plate 100). The picture shows Bacchus holding out his hand to Ariadne while a goddess, perhaps Venus, lightly floats above them to offer Ariadne a ring and to place a starry crown upon her head. The figures are unified in a wheel-like composition with a hand of each one moving toward the center. Intermittent flashes of light, piercing the transparent shadows, not only serve to mold the forms and produce movement, but they also contribute to the dramatic quality of the painting. The *Origin of the Milky Way,* a highly imaginative work, shows the heavens filled with creatures flying through the clouds, easily turning and swinging in the air. Through his mastery of foreshortening Tintoretto gave the illusion of figures in rapid movement through space. His sweeping rhythms were produced by great swinging strokes of long-handled brushes held at arm's length.

Such composition of swirling lines and rapid movement is termed *baroque,* a word derived from the Spanish "barocco," meaning an irregular pearl with multicurving contours. In a well-controlled baroque composition the movement is unified and rhythmic. In the hands of lesser artists who strove for naturalistic, dramatic effects, the style deteriorated and declined. By the end of the sixteenth century the genius of the Italian school was exhausted. Nevertheless, with her unlimited wealth of past accomplishments, Italy still remained the source of inspiration for European artists though leadership passed to the artists of Flanders, Holland, and Spain.

So many good painters were working in Italy during the fourteenth, fifteenth, and sixteenth centuries that it has not been possible to mention all of them. Included are some of those who made outstanding contributions to the general stream of art or produced unique styles of their own. Many of these painters also contributed to the parallel development of sculpture, for it was the exception to find a Renaissance artist who was skilled in only one medium.

FLORENTINE SCULPTORS

Florence boasted of many fine sculptors, whereas Venice failed to produce any of note. In sculpture, as in painting, the early medieval influence with its linear designs and tendency toward naturalism gave way to the more classical style inspired by the ancient relics and antique sculpture discovered among the Roman ruins. When Nicola Pisano (c.1205-1278) constructed a marble pulpit for the Baptistery of Pisa, he decorated it with panels in high relief illustrating stories from the New Testament. The resemblance to the narrative classical style found on the Roman sarcophagi which Nicola had collected is unmistakable.

At the beginning of the fifteenth century, the Florentines decided to give a new set of bronze doors to the Baptistery of their cathedral as an expression of gratitude for deliverance from the plague. A competition was announced for the purpose of discovering the sculptor who could best design this second set of doors (the first had been planned by Andrea Pisano, c.1270-1348). Seven sculptors submitted models, but the winner was Lorenzo Ghiberti (1378-1455), a youth in his early twenties. Second choice was accorded to Filippo Brunelleschi (1377-1446), who later became one of the most famous architects of the time. Both designs, which comprised a number of panels enclosed in a Gothic frame similar to that used by Pisano, may be seen today at the Bargello in Florence (Plates 102 and 103).

Ghiberti spent twenty-two years on the execution of these doors, which were divided into twenty panels illustrating episodes from the life of Christ. So pleased were the Florentines that they commissioned him to make a third set to be placed on the side of the Baptistery facing the cathedral. They were afterwards known as the "Gates of Paradise" because Michelangelo deemed them worthy to grace Heaven itself. In the "Gates," the ten large panels, enclosed in rectangular frames, depict scenes from the Old Testament, beginning with the *Creation of Adam and Eve* and ending with the *Meeting of Solomon and the Queen of Sheba.* Each panel is treated as a separate entity. Together they show an extraordinary amount of descriptive narration. Variations in the depth of relief planes ranging from high projections in the foreground to barely perceptible elevations in the distance create the illusion of deep space. In the *Prodigal Son* panel the central figure is shown in such high relief that it gives the effect of being in the round. These magnificent doors are enhanced by an outer frame decorated with garlands and fruit clusters which extend upward from vase forms at the base and move along the sides to culminate at the top in an eagle motif. At intervals along the inner frame are niches which contain figures representing the saints. Some present-day critics hold that Pisano's doors, lower in relief and less naturalistic in design, are more appropriate for a flat surface than Ghiberti's, which display greater realism and extraordinary skill.

The effective relief panel of the *Sacrifice of Isaac,* from the great bronze doors, shows Ghiberti's inventive genius and competence in the organization of naturalistic space relations (Plate 103). The biblical actors of the dramatic sacrifice of Isaac to the Lord are placed on a high ledge in a tree-covered rocky landscape. The artist has chosen to illustrate the moment when the uplifted sword of Abraham is stayed by the angel's hand and Isaac is freed. Well-arranged foreground groups show Abraham kneeling before three standing angels on the left; near by is Sarah before the tent door, and on the left, two seated servants await Abraham with his ass. The rich pictorial quality, characterization, foreshortening in the handling of anatomy, and perspective in the landscape indicate Ghiberti's power.

A broad and powerful naturalism characterizes the work of the Sienese sculptor, Jacopo della Quercia (c.1367-1438), who lived contemporaneously with Ghiberti. A satisfying sculptural concept is realized in his *Virgin and Child,* where the vigorous, though generalized, treatment of the garment reveals the massive form beneath, in a manner prophetic of Michelangelo's titanic grandeur (Plate 101). In one of the reliefs designed for the Church of San Petronic at Bologna, the *Expulsion of Adam and Eve,* the background is suppressed to emphasize the figures of the first pair who are being expelled from Eden. This relief, now low, now high, is expressive of the intense emotion gripping the actors in the dramatic scene.

When Filippo Brunelleschi went to Rome to study ancient classical art he was accompanied by his young apprentice, Donatello (1386-1466). Together they dug into the ruins for antique remains and studied the ancient architecture of the Eternal City. Returning to Florence steeped in the classical spirit, Donatello dominated Florentine sculpture for almost half a century. His style, displaying a scientific understanding of anatomy—gained from both close observation of antique sculpture and live models—and an accurate knowledge of the mechanics of the human body, is combined with a classic quietude almost devoid of movement or gesture. His portraits wrought in bronze, marble, or terra-cotta, generalized in the beginning, became completely individualized, implacable, ruthlessly realistic, and startlingly lifelike, as in *Bust of Niccola Da Uzzano* (Plate 102). The colossal equestrian statue of General da

Narni, better known as *Gattamelata*, is reputed to be the first bronze casting of a horse larger than life-size. Like most Florentine artists, Donatello was interested in the portrayal of the lively movements of children. His *Singing Gallery* shows dancing children in a continuous movement, lustily singing. They are set against a flat mosaic background interrupted at intervals by colonnettes.

Donatello's pupil, Luca della Robbia (1399-1482), who also made a choir gallery for the cathedral, divided the oblong space into panels separated by simple classical moldings and treated each space division as a unit, differing in this respect from Donatello's design. Luca developed the phenomenally popular art of glazing terra-cotta. His figures, usually white on blue backgrounds, were encircled by a wreath or border of fruits, flowers, pine branches, and ears of wheat in different colors. Andrea della Robbia (1435-1525) inherited his uncle's workshop and carried on his tradition, as in *Head of a Youth* (Plate 106). Many reproductions have been made of the *bambini* (babies) on the *terra-cotta medallions* which decorate the loggia of the children's hospital in Florence. With an increased range of colors and the addition of more elaborate and detailed decorations terra-cotta, essentially a rough medium, began to decline as a medium of art expression. In the lighter spirit of the della Robbias, Desiderio da Settignano (1428-1464), a pupil of Donatello, created portraits of happy childhood and young women endowed with charm and grace.

The chief representative of scientific realism in the late fifteenth century was Andrea del Verrocchio (1435-1488), the great Florentine teacher at whose shop so many of the painters had studied. He also designed an over-life-size equestrian statue of *Bartolomeo Colleoni* for the city of Venice (Plate 103). In contrast to Donatello's *Gattemelata*, Verrocchio's arrogant rider, completely dominating his spirited steed, stands erect in the stirrups with body slightly turned to the right while he glances to the left. In one intellectual control is suggested; in the other military pomp.

Although the mature work of Michelangelo, sculptor, architect, and painter symbolized "man's hopeless struggle with destiny," a deep spiritual feeling is expressed in an early group of the youthful

Virgin holding the dead Christ in her lap, the tragic *Pièta* of St. Peter's (Plate 106). An early commission for the city of Florence was the statue of *David*. Carved from a thin block of marble eighteen feet high which had been discarded by a former sculptor, it was eventually placed in the Piazza Signoria or public square of Florence. The heroic figure of *Moses,* carved for the proposed tomb of Julius II, remained in the sculptor's studio for forty years (Plate 105). After the death of the Pope it was placed by his tomb, which is too small for it. Every part of the statue bespeaks the determination, inflexible character, and tremendous energy of the great Jewish leader who had seen his people worshipping a strange god. Armed with the stone tablets on which were written the ten commandments, Moses is shown poised for a moment before going into action. Within the simple contour lines of this baroque figure, there are the restless, rhythmic lines of arms, legs, beard, and drapery which unite in a spiral movement that encircles and gives unity to the entire statue.

The mortuary chapel of San Lorenzo at Florence, though planned as a commemorative mausoleum for the Medici family, is in reality a shrine of Michelangelo's art (Plate 104). Here recumbent nudes, a man and woman representing *Night* and *Day* (Plate 104) guard the tomb of Guiliano de Medici, while two similar figures in relaxed and contemplative mood, *Morning* and *Evening,* recline above the sarcophagus of Lorenzo. The architectural scheme employed for both tombs is a wall divided into three high rectangular niches, the central one containing an idealized portrait of the deceased. Guiliano is represented as an alert man of action and Lorenzo as the poet or dreamer.

Benvenuto Cellini (1500-1571) was an expert in metal work such as bronze casting and the molding, chasing and engraving of gold and silver, besides being the author of an outstanding autobiography. One of his famous cups may be seen in the Metropolitan Museum in New York (Plate 107). His celebrated bronze statue of *Perseus with the Head of the Medusa,* showing fine workmanship and delicate detail, still stands in the famous loggia in Florence.

The baroque style with its flowing and tumultuous movement

which seems to belie the ponderous, immobile, and rigid qualities of stone was well suited to bronze and to the purpose of the sixteenth and seventeenth-century artists who sought grandiose and pictorial effects. Some of them placed figures amid rocks or other scenic accessories. All were unified by the movement of line or form. Bernini's *St. Theresa in Ecstasy* (Plate 107) and *Apollo and Daphne* are constructed with technical dexterity especially in the imitation of texture of skin and flesh. Some of the fountains Bernini (1598-1680) and his pupils created exemplify the lastest phase of the baroque style which gradually developed into the lighter rococo, characterized by shorter more animated curves and more ornate detail—not so popular in Italy as in France.

PALACES IN FLORENCE AND VENICE

Although secular architecture became increasingly popular during the Renaissance, churches were still in great demand. A challenge to the architects was the unfinished cathedral of Florence, *Santa Maria del Fiore* (Plate 108). The most pressing problem was that of designing a dome to span the crossing (138 feet wide). Among the contestants in a competition were Donatello and Brunelleschi, who went to Rome to study the dome of the Pantheon. Brunelleschi's design won first choice and to him goes the credit for the first great dome of the Renaissance. By employing a medieval feature, the rib, and elevating the dome on a base or drum pierced by round windows he was able to raise the structure to such daring heights (300 feet) that it not only dominated the cathedral but the city as well, for it is the first thing that catches the eye of an approaching traveler.

Separate and apart from the cathedral, according to Italian custom, stands Giotto's *campanile*, frequently referred to as the world's most beautiful bell-tower. Divided horizontally by string-courses, the sections, low at the base, gain height as they move upward in an ascending rhythm. Likewise windows, divided by column-like mullions in medieval fashion, gradually become taller; thus increasing the appearance of lightness near the top. The tower is constructed of dark and light marble laid in a strikingly patterned effect. Above the base, which is ornamented with bas-reliefs, are statues by Donatello and others, set in niches. With its rhythm, perfect proportions, and sculptural decorations the structure stands a splendid memorial to Giotto, the painter who also proved to be an eminent architect.

The three-storied Florentine palaces served also as fortresses. In the *Medici-Riccardi Palace* the stones of the ground story were rough-hewn with beveled edges, whereas those of the upper stories which were separated from the lower by strongly marked string-courses became successively smoother (Plate 109). This is known as rusticated masonry construction. Overhanging the entire structure was a heavy cornice. Apertures in the ground story were few, a precaution taken for protection from attack. In the upper stories mullioned windows set flush with the wall, medieval-fashion, were surmounted by flat round arches made of smooth stones. Other palaces in Florence and Rome were similarly constructed of different materials; differed also in decorative details which were classical in origin, such as pedimented forms over the windows and classical pilasters at regular intervals. In Venice, where life was safer and gayer, palaces on the banks of the canals were lighter in construction and more elaborate in decoration. The *Ducal Palace* (Plate 108) has arched loggias on the ground story and galleries enclosed by Gothic arcades above. In Venetian palaces, as well as Florentine, it was the façade that held the architect's interest. Often the sides and back were not even made of the same material.

ST. PETER'S IN ROME

The baroque style in architecture was three-dimensional, meant to be viewed from all sides. It is characterized by curvilinear shapes, elaboration of detail, and a dramatic interplay of lights and shadows produced by strongly marked protrusions and deep recessions of architectural masses. A fine example of the baroque, *St. Peter's* in Rome, originally designed to house the tomb of Pope Julius II, is said to be largest church in the world (Plate 109).

Bramante (1444-1514), who had drawn the original plan, died before the church was completed. Among the several architects who succeeded him were Raphael, who died young, and Michel-angelo, who held the position of supervisor of building for seven-teen years. Following Bramante's design, based on the Greek cross with four arms of equal length, Michelangelo eliminated details and planned a magnificent dome (140 feet in diameter) to span the crossing. Reaching the colossal height of 404 feet, it was similar in construction to the one Brunelleschi erected in Florence. But it had a more elaborate base, was larger in scale, and quite different in outward appearance.

Succeeding architects in turn modified Michelangelo's plan. By lengthening the nave and emphasizing the façade they screened the lower part of the dome from view; consequently one gets a better idea of Michelangelo's plan from the rear of the church. Furthermore, the lengthening of the nave made the dome less im-pressive from the interior. Nevertheless, with its carefully con-sidered curves and fine scale, Michelangelo's dome has served as a model for similar structures throughout the Western world. With the solution of the high dome, all the problems of stone construc-tion had now been solved. From this time until the advent of new materials such as steel and reinforced concrete of modern times, no new structural innovations appeared. Renaissance architects, sculp-tors, and painters all reached the heights along the roads they chose to travel.

OUTLINE OF ART OF THE ITALIAN RENAISSANCE

TIME: Thirteenth through 16th centuries A.D.

BACKGROUND: Period of invention, exploration, and discovery. Florence: political turmoil, unrest. Venice: comparatively quiet and peaceful. Scientific attitude toward learning tended to replace earlier superstitious outlook on life. Spread of knowledge with invention of printing press c. 15th century. St. Francis introduced new attitude toward beauties of nature and man's feeling toward his fellow man. The discovery of classical art and literature brought about conflict between Christian and pagan ideas of life. Atheism became prevalent. Church lost unity of control it had exercised in medieval times. Rise of individualism.

ARCHITECTURE: *Palaces:* both medieval and classical motifs used in decora-tion. Emphasis on façade. Materials: marble and stone. Masonry construction. Fort-like in Florence—light and airy in Venice.

    Churches: baroque style in 16th century: protruding and receding volumes unified. Three-dimensional effect—to be seen from all sides. High dome outstanding architectural feature, impressive from exterior. Elaborate sculptural and architectural decorations producing rich play of light and shadow.

SCULPTURE: Intermingling of medieval and classical influences—moving toward naturalism. Later, baroque style: characterized by tempestuous movement. Material: marble, bronze, terra-cotta. Purpose: architectural decoration, portraiture, and free-standing statues.

PAINTING: *Sienese:* mystic religious spirit, closely akin to Byzantine. Linear in style, stiff and formal pose of figures, decorative. *Florentine:* shows close observation of nature. *Giotto* gave volume to his figures, *Masaccio* approached anatomical truth and introduced aerial perspective, *Ucello* and other scientific painters solved the problems of linear perspective and foreshortening, *Leonardo da Vinci* mastered chiaroscuro and *Michelangelo* gained complete control of the most exaggerated movements of the human form. *Raphael* of Urbino excelled in composition. The *Venetians Giorgione, Titian, Tintoretto* and others made great advances in oil technique and the use of color. The Renaissance painters reached the heights in realistic representation. Subject-matter: Christian and pagan themes, Bible stories, legends of the saints, myths, allegories, and portraits. Media: tempera, fresco, and oil painting. The Florentines emphasized line and form; the Venetians, color.

BIBLIOGRAPHY

BERENSON, Bernhard, *The Florentine Painters of the Renaissance* (G. P. Putnam's Sons, N. Y., 1909).

——, *The Italian Pictures of the Renaissance* (London, 1932).

BURCKHARDT, Jacob, *The Civilization of the Renaissance in Italy* (Boni & Gaer, N. Y., 1935).

CELLINI, Benvenuto, *Autobiography,* tr. by Anne McDonald (E. P. Dutton & Co., N. Y., 1919).

EDGELL, G. H., *A Short History of Sienese Painting* (Dial Press, N. Y., 1932).

FINLAYSON, Donald Lord, *Michelangelo the Man* (Tudor Publishing Co., N. Y., 1935).

FRY, Roger, *Transformations* (London, 1927).

HAGEN, O. F., *Art Epochs and Their Leaders* (Charles Scribner's Sons, N. Y., 1927).

MATHER, Frank J., *A History of Italian Painting* (Henry Holt & Co., Inc., N. Y., 1923).

MUNRO, Thomas, *Great Pictures of Europe* (Tudor Publishing Co., N. Y., 1934).

ROEDER, Ralph, *The Man of the Renaissance* (Viking Press, Inc., N. Y., 1935).

SCOTT, Geofrey, *The Architecture of Humanism* (Charles Scribner's Sons, N. Y., 1924).

SYMONDS, John Addington, *The Renaissance in Italy,* 2 vols. (Henry Holt & Co., N. Y., 1935).

TAYLOR, Rachel Ann, *Leonardo the Florentine* (Blue Ribbon Books, Garden City, N. Y., 1927).

VALLENTIN, Antonina, *Leonardo da Vinci,* tr. by E. W. Dickes (Viking Press, Inc., N. Y., 1938).

VASARI, Giorgio, *Lives of the Painters* (Charles Scribner's Sons, N. Y., 1896).

VENTURI, Adolfo, *A Short History of Italian Art* (The Macmillan Co., N. Y., 1926).

WÖLFFLIN, Heinrich, *Art of the Italian Renaissance* (G. P. Putnam's Sons, N. Y., 1913).

CHAPTER XV

Flemish Art

THE awakening of Flanders to the Renaissance of the north
began to manifest itself at the beginning of the fifteenth
century, when that country was governed by the wealthy and
powerful Dukes of Burgundy who presided over an art-loving
court. Bruges and Dijon were among the centers of art where
elaborately illuminated manuscripts and rich tapestries were made.
The *Grimani Breviary* (c. 1500), glorifying Christian life and
portraying Holy Days, and the *Très Riches Heures,* which were
illuminated by Pol de Limbourg and artists of his studio, show
remarkable observation of nature and a realistic rendering of landscape compositions. These books contain a collection of prayers, a
calendar, and appropriate lessons for devotions. The *Turin Book
of Hours,* attributed to Hubert van Eyck, illustrated such common
things of daily life as the labors of each month with its appropriate
seasonal activity, and were enlivened by a wealth of narrative detail. They depict everyday scenes on the farm, animals, birds, and
flowers. Fanciful rendering of bees, butterflies, and squirrels in
bright colors were combined with gold to enhance the borders of
the pages. The artists of the time illuminated these *Books of the
Hours* and the *Gospels* for churches, monasteries, and noble
patrons. Painted for altar-pieces, panels of scriptural subjects based
upon Bible stories and legends of the saints were often made in the
form of *triptychs*—a center panel bordered on either side with a
hinged panel or "wing" which could be folded. If there were more
than three panels the combined group was called a *polyptych*. A
fidelity to detail and impressive perfection of technique are outstanding characteristics of the early art of the north, which owed its
inspiration to the Gothic tradition rather than to the classical move-

ment which exerted such a profound influence upon the art of
Italy.

CONTRIBUTION OF JAN AND HUBERT VAN EYCK

The two van Eyck brothers, Hubert (1366-1426) and Jan
(1385-1441), are credited with first mixing paints with oil, by
means of which a greater brilliancy and intensity of color was
achieved. The extraordinary development of their work reflects
some preliminary school of art in Flanders of which little is known,
but scholars agree that early Flemish artists were inspired by the
illuminators and stained-glass workers. The van Eycks prepared
their panels with a foundation of paint and oils upon which they
skillfully applied layers of transparent glazes. Their aim was to
create paintings that would approximate the chromatic quality
found in stained-glass. The careful preparation of their panels
and the flawless perfection of their painting enabled them to attain
a remarkable luminosity and vibrancy of color and to produce delicate and transparent effects of jewel-like clarity.

Jan van Eyck, as court painter to Philip the Bold, not only
painted religious pictures but also designed costumes for pageants,
tapestries for the ducal palace, and illuminations of devotional
books. *The Adoration of the Mystic Lamb,* a noted altar-piece, was
painted for St. Bavon's Church in Ghent, an ancient city near
Bruges (Plate 110). Comprising twelve separate panels this painting, begun by the van Eyck brothers in 1420 and completed in
1432, is an interpretation of the Christian doctrine of the Redemp-
tion. In the lower zone of the central panel is the sacrificial scene.
Christ, descended upon earth to redeem man from sin, is represented as a bleeding Lamb standing upon an altar. From His heart
a stream of blood flows into a chalice while angels kneel about
Him. In the foreground apostles surround the fountain of life
which purified the world. From above the Dove sheds heavenly
rays of light upon the flower-strewn landscape. From the corners,
groups of people from different walks of life move in toward the
center. Seated upon a throne in the upper zone of the central
panel is God the Father, holding up His right hand with two

fingers raised in benediction. Precious stones adorn the breast and border of his red mantle. On the three panels to one side of Him are the Virgin, singing angels, and Adam; on the opposite three are St. John the Baptist, St. Cecilia, and Eve. St. Cecilia, arrayed in a flowered robe of rich brocade, plays the organ while four angels accompany her on their harps. Adam and Eve, who brought sin into the world, are the two nude figures on the extreme ends of the outer panels. In smaller panels are crowds of crusaders, knights, and others journeying toward Jerusalem.

The central panels were not shown except on Holy Days. At other times the remaining panels were used as shutters to conceal the glorious polyptych from view. On the backs of the shutters are the portraits of the donor and his wife, seen only when those panels are closed. This magnificent altar-piece was among the paintings hidden by the Nazis during World War II and later found by American soldiers in a Salzburg salt mine. It has since been returned to Belgium where it may be seen today in the Cathedral of Ghent. All but one of the panels have been preserved. The deep religious expression of the van Eycks and their introduction of a new medium make a spiritual and material contribution to art. The painters of the fifteenth and sixteenth centuries particularly were greatly indebted to them.

VAN EYCK'S FOLLOWERS DEVELOP NATURALISM

A noted pupil and worthy follower of Jan van Eyck was Rogier van der Weyden (1399-1464), whose *Descent from the Cross* is remarkable for its powerful linear harmonies, strong draftsmanship, and splendid color. It is a dramatic interpretation suffused with pathos and reverent feeling. His landscapes and decorative backgrounds are painted in delicate enamel-like color. The artist's *Madonna and Child* shows a demure Flemish madonna with conventionally oval face, long nose, small lips, and high, round forehead (Plate 110). Rhythmic compositional lines and relations of light and dark are emphasized, instead of minor details of costume, which van der Weyden suppressed.

Hans Memling's (c.1430-1494) *Shrine of St. Ursula,* designed for the Hospital of St. John at Bruges, is a unique reliquary of flawless beauty. On the six panels of the casket are exquisite miniature paintings recounting episodes in the adventures of St. Ursula and her numerous attendant virgins. In the *Arrival at Ghent* may be seen ships in the harbor and the gates of the city with a Gothic cathedral in the background. The typical Flemish realism which stemmed from the austere Gothic style was modified by Memling, who infused an ingratiating note of sweetness and grace in his *Portrait of a Lady* (Plate 111). His fine texture painting of the rich velvet costume, sleeves, veil, and necklace are in the exquisite style of the Flemish primitives.

Another early Flemish master, Quentin Massys (1465/6-1530), who excelled as a colorist, succeeded in giving greater realism to his portraits as in *Man With Pink* (Plate 111).

Hieronymus Bosch (c.1450-1516), a Flemish primitive painter of first quality, possessed an inexhaustibly inventive imagination. His art combines audacious, disorderly, and obscene subjects with the most sacred, as in his *Mocking of Christ* (Plate 112). Bosch's caricatures included chimerical beings which, for satiric reasons, he used to personify human weaknesses. He was a skillful painter of color gradations and a superior draftsman whose understanding of composition influenced his Flemish successor, Pieter Brueghel the Elder.

PIETER BRUEGHEL THE ELDER

At the close of the fifteenth century, Spain under Charles V had attained national unity, France and England had become absolute monarchies ruled by Francis I and Henry VIII respectively, Martin Luther was advocating the Reformation in Germany, and the Low Countries—as Holland and Belgium were called—were experiencing the oppression of the Spanish Inquisition.

These tragic days of political transition when Charles and Francis were warring for the domination of Europe, the religious struggle between Catholic and Protestant, and the constant friction between civilians and mercenary soldiers formed the background against which Pieter Brueghel the Elder (1520?-1569) lived, painted, and reared a family of artist sons. Although not born there, he spent most of his life in Antwerp, a busy seaport to which came people from all parts of the world. He lived among the peasants, sharing such labors as hay-making, plowing, and harvesting;

Proverb, by Pieter Brueghel the Elder. "A leaking roof, a smoking fireplace, a cackling hen, and a quarreling woman are four household plagues." (Bastelaar)

participated in their roistering festivities, carnivals, fairs, dances, and uncouth drinking bouts; attended their celebrations at wedding feasts, baptisms, and even funerals; and joined their hunting expeditions. Although he entered into these activities as one of the people, he was keenly observing the life about him and storing his mind with details of action, pose, and gesture which he was later to record in his virile and characteristically Flemish paintings of peasant life such as *Wedding Dance* and other genre subjects (Plate 113). This realistic rendering of lively action and unrestrained emotional expression of these people who lived so close to nature was in perfect accord with his subject-matter, and through it he was able to capture something of the permanent, the universal in human nature. Another example of his expression of deep human interest is *The Unfaithful Shepherd* (Plate 113) in the Johnson Collection, Philadelphia. In the series of the *Seasons* or the *Months,* he has presented man's activities against the familiar countryside.

Brueghel, like many other artists, journeyed to Rome, but his work on the whole shows little of any Italian influence. But when he crossed the Alps, he was greatly impressed with their grandeur and memories of the Alpine scenes are recorded in the backgrounds of many of his paintings. Throughout his entire life it has been said, he was preoccupied with the entire range of nature and of human life. Toward the end of 1553 he was back in Antwerp where he accomplished most of his work.

RUBENS AND THE GREAT AGE OF FLEMISH PAINTING

Peter Paul Rubens (1577-1640), the outstanding artist of Flanders, brought to northern art an exuberance of expression akin to Venetian painting and expressive of his own hearty zest, joy of life, and appreciation of nature. Born on the Feast Day of Saints Peter and Paul, he was named Peter Paul. As a young boy he served as page in a noble family and there he studied classical and modern languages, which proved to be a great help to him in the artist-diplomat career that he was to follow. Later he was apprenticed to a painter who, recognizing the youth's talent, advised him to study art in Italy. At the age of twenty-three he journeyed south, remaining there eight years, absorbing a knowledge of form in movement from his study of Michelangelo's heroic work and the gorgeous color of the great Venetians, whose monumental decorations he especially admired.

During Rubens' brilliant career he was entrusted with various important diplomatic commissions, and he lived on terms of intimacy with king and princes. While serving as court painter to the Duke of Mantua, he was sent to Spain as ambassador and was cordially received by Philip IV. There he also met the eminent

Spanish artist, Velazquez. The King, impressed with his ability, sent Rubens as Spanish envoy to England to arrange a treaty between that country and Spain. While in England he painted the ceiling of the banqueting hall at Whitehall palace, after which he was knighted by Charles I.

In Italy Rubens had painted portraits of the Pope and several cardinals, but his triumphal career really began when he settled in Antwerp (1609), where he lived in a fine house which contained his rare collection of Italian masterpieces. Because of his popularity both as a man and a painter, the artist, who found himself with more commissions than he could execute alone, employed his pupils to assist him. We are told his studio produced over fifteen hundred paintings of almost every type of subject, including religious themes, portraits, landscapes, animals, historical, and allegorical panoramas.

Descent from the Cross, the center panel of an altar-piece in the Cathedral of Antwerp, has for its dominant motif the long curve of white cloth into which the crucified body of Christ is lowered from the cross by the disciples. Among the latter, Joseph of Arimathea and Peter are strongly characterized. The bearer of Christ's body is St. John and near him is Mary, the mother of Christ. Mary Magdalene kneels in the foreground. The artist's skillful arrangement of figures and the rendering of the crucified Christ are remarkable. Other works of Rubens are *The Crucifixion, Adoration of the Magi,* and numerous portraits, including his wife, with their two children. His brilliant painting of light and color is represented in *The Straw Hat* (Plate 114). When Marie de Medici, who married Henry IV, King of France, went to live in the Luxembourg Palace, she employed Rubens to design a series of murals depicting the importance of her family. With characteristic imaginative power and superb skill he rapidly painted huge canvases in which fantasy, allegory, and mythology are interwoven with historical pageantry. Among the twenty-four murals now in the Louvre are the *Coronation of Marie de Medici* and *Henry IV Receiving the Portrait of Marie de Medici.*

Anton van Dyck (1599-1641) was the master's most gifted pupil. As court artist for James I and Charles I of England he painted a large collection of distinguished and elegant portraits, of which the *Duke of Lennox* is one (Plate 115).

Late fourteenth-century Burgundian sculpture, like painting, showed a realistic interpretation of the human figure. Of the group of remarkable sculptors who worked at Dijon, the most famous was Claus Sluter (d. 1405), whose best-known work is the *Well of Moses* made for the Carthusian Monastery of Champnol. Here are six figures representing prophets of the Old Testament. Carved in a strong realistic manner, the venerable Moses draped in a heavy robe is suggestive of that great leader's forceful character and prophetic vision. Many pretentious tombs in the baroque style, and notable fireplaces, such as the ones in the Hôtel de Ville, Antwerp and the Palace of Justice at Bruges, were carved in the sixteenth century. Most of the early civic architecture was based on the Gothic style.

OUTLINE OF FLEMISH ART

TIME: 14th, 15th, 16th centuries. Rise of cities in the Lowlands. After Peace of Westphalia in 17th century, the northern tradition was greatly strengthened.

BACKGROUND: Weaving of woolen cloth brought prosperity to the cities of Ghent, Louvain, Ypres, Bruges, Antwerp. Each city a civic unit with guilds which controlled each craft. Flemish artists were skillful technicians. Background based on the illuminations and miniatures of medieval time when the country was governed by the Dukes of Burgundy.

ARCHITECTURE: Gothic influences prevailed in Flanders in 14th and 15th centuries. Chief buildings were Town Halls, Belfries, Guild Halls, Cloth Halls. Secular structures with Gothic pointed arches, sharply pitched roofs and dormers. Niches held gilded and painted statues. Many fireplaces account for the large number of chimney stacks on the roofs.

SCULPTURE: Realistic sculpture prevailed in Flanders. Carved, ornate fireplaces were used in hotels, homes, council chambers, and civic centers. Elaborate pulpits were seen in the churches of Brussels. Baroque lavishness was found in carvings and figures made of wood or stone. Since 1850, leading sculptors have exalted the cult of labor in their statues of workers.

PAINTING: 14th century Flemish painting was in the form of miniatures and illuminations. 15th century brought the discovery of oil painting by the van Eyck brothers. Native artists delighted in factual representations of details which were truthfully portrayed. Religious art showed the conventional type Madonna of northern art: oval face, high forehead. Brueghel painted peasants at country dances etc., and extensive landscapes in 16th-century Flanders. Blend of the northern tradition of art with that of the graceful, suave art of Italy was achieved by Rubens, a master of the baroque style.

BIBLIOGRAPHY

Barker, Virgil, *Pieter Breughel the Elder: A Study of His Paintings* (Arts Publishing Corp., N. Y., 1926).

Conway, Sir W. M., *The Van Eycks and Their Followers* (E. P. Dutton & Co., N. Y., 1921).

Fry, Roger, *Flemish Art: A Critical Survey* (Coward-McCann, Inc., N. Y., 1927).

Rooses, Max, *Art in Flanders* (Charles Scribner's Sons, N. Y., 1914).

Valentiner, W. R., *Art of the Low Countries* (Doubleday & Co., Garden City, N. Y., 1914).

CHAPTER XVI

Dutch Art

After Holland's independence was established in 1648, trade increased until the Dutch pushed their commerce to remote parts of the world and monopolized the spice trade of the Indies. Dutch looms produced fine fabrics which were exchanged for the Persian rugs and Chinese porcelains that were brought back by their returning ships. The happiness of the people in their newly acquired freedom found expression in their art. Burgomasters, merchants, corporations, and members of the civic and military guilds were eager to have their portraits painted for their meeting halls. Religious paintings, such as large altar-pieces, were banned by the Dutch Protestants. A democratic, realistic art rendered with perfect craftsmanship took its place. There were portraits of humble housewives, fishermen, pictures of peasants at country dances, and genre scenes interpreting their home life in a warm and sympathetic manner. All classes were represented. Much attention was given to rich textures—fine fabrics, furs, and shining brass utensils. Flower-beds, low-lying fields, farms with animals, and villages were also mirrored in their art.

THE LITTLE DUTCHMEN

A famous group of artists known as The Little Dutchmen painted interiors with gleaming tiles, polished furniture, Oriental rugs, musical instruments, courtyards, and immaculate kitchens. These artists recorded what they saw, whether it was sunlight flooding a garden or parlor, vaporous clouds, wind-mills, the shadows of sails on water, fish nets drying on land, or neat villages with red-brick houses and church spires.

The Big Ships. Hercules Segers.

Jan van der Meer (1632-1675), commonly known as Vermeer of Delft, was interested in the study of color and atmosphere. His paintings are considered "poems of light." *View of Delft* shows a clear light hovering over canal, sky, and water. Here the artist achieved a fine tonal quality. His favorite theme, a young woman standing near a high window draped with rich hangings, is exemplified in *Young Girl with a Flute*, depicting a young girl in a Chinese hat (Plate 119). Dramatically lighted, painted with a delicate attention to matter-of-fact detail, this painting reveals a surprising modernity in its obvious brush strokes and in the decorative, non-realistic handling of background. Yellow and blue seem to have been Vermeer's favorite colors, so frequently has he used them. The artist, who never left Delft, was long forgotten, but since his fine tonal paintings have increasingly come to public attention, Vermeer's fame has steadily increased.

Jan Steen (c.1626-1679), another of the Little Dutchmen, delighted in painting children's games and the festivities of Dutch peasants as in *Fair at Oestgeest* (Plate 116). Gabriel Metsu (1629-1667) rendered Dutch interiors, fruits, and flowers; Pieter de Hooch (1629-c.1683) painted closed court yards with people at work or play. He exhibits fine tonal values and air-filled space, as in *The Mother, In The Pantry* (Plate 116), and the *Interior of a Dutch House*. A representative work of the Dutch genre masters is *A Music Party* (Plate 117), by Gerard Ter Borch (1617-1681). By close acquaintance with these small paintings one eventually begins to distinguish the characteristics of the work of various artists which at first seem so much alike.

DUTCH LANDSCAPE ARTISTS

First among the Dutch landscape painters is Jacob van Ruisdael (c.1628-1682), who usually painted his homeland in a melancholy mood. Sometimes he depicted a mill silhouetted against a calm northern sky, or *The Jewish Cemetery* with tall trees, dark foliage, and a cold gray sky (Plate 117); again he painted the subdued light of setting sun on a vapor-filled marshland, as it breaks through a rift in the clouds, touching trees, fields, and water. He also delighted in painting waterfalls cascading over rocky cliffs. A friend and pupil of Ruisdael was Meindert Hobbema (1638-1709), another landscape painter, whose work was more casual and realistic, wholly lacking in the almost religious feeling of Ruisdael's work. Hobbema's *Avenue at Middleharnais* shows a long road, lined with poplar trees, leading to a village with a church spire rising in the distance. His work is characterized by a peaceful yet majestic grandeur.

DUTCH PORTRAIT PAINTERS

Franz Hals (1580-1666), leader of the Haarlem school, painted his countrymen with realism and a remarkable vitality. His forceful brush-handling was remarkably fluent and flexible; every stroke was sure and accurate. Hals's portraits and guild-hall pictures portray the matter-of-fact character of practical-minded Dutch merchants and soldiers. He painted with ease the textures of lace or velvet, the white ruffs worn by the men or the radiant smile of a soldier. As he often painted sitters who were in a genial mood, as *Yonker Ramp and His Sweetheart* (Plate 118), a certain joviality characterizes many of his portraits, and his expression of spontaneous laughter has earned him the title "The Laureate of Laughter." In his painting, *Officers of the Civic Guard*, like other group pictures of the time, each face is a portrait. The men are in gala dress uniforms bedecked with silken scarves and large hats with waving plumes. In *The Guild of Archers* each of the men is given an equal and proportionate share of attention, yet the whole arrangement is natural and the pose spontaneous. His last painting, *The Lady Regents of the Hospital*, completed when he was eighty-four years of age and his hands were no longer steady, is a remarkable interpretation of the individual character of each of the women.

REMBRANDT, THE UNIVERSAL ARTIST

One of the greatest painters of all time, Rembrandt van Rijn (1606-1669) left over six hundred paintings, three hundred etchings, and fifteen hundred drawings. Rembrandt was born in Leyden, in a house by the Rhine River near his father's windmill, which accounts for the name "van Rijn." He lived in Holland during the seventeenth century, yet his art is universal, transcending all national boundaries and times. His mother was the most important influence of his youth, and he never tired of painting and etching her gentle face. When she read the Bible to her son, his imagination was stirred and he developed an abiding love for Scripture. His father, a well-to-do miller, decided that Rembrandt —the eighth of nine children—should have a university education, and sent him to Leyden University for one year. There he had an opportunity to see great works of art which inspired him to make painting his life work. At Leyden, he painted from nature, portraying his family who willingly served as models and also frequently painting himself, arrayed in varied costumes. It has been said that he has left more paintings of himself than any other artist.

Eventually the artist moved to Amsterdam (1631), then a wealthy commercial city. Because of its numerous canals and bridges, it was often called the Venice of the North. Amsterdam's merchants were prosperous, for ships laden with treasure from all parts of the world sailed into its harbor. Rembrandt, a

successful portrait painter, readily found sitters who paid him
liberally. The *Lesson in Anatomy* (1632), a memorial for the
Surgeon's Guild, was commissioned by the artist's friend, Dr. Tulp.
This work gave the artist a successful start and his fame and fortune grew till he became the most celebrated artist in Holland.
He married (in 1634) Saskia Uylenborch, an auburn-haired beauty,
and they lived happily in a house containing rare Italian paintings,
tapestries, rich fabrics, and old armour; for Rembrandt was an as-
siduous collector. In her portraits Saskia is arrayed in silks, velvets,
and gleaming jewels. These works are expressive of the artist's love
of a gay and luxurious life. His home is still to be seen on a quay
of the Amstel River, silently reminiscent of his happy days there.

A period of misfortune for Rembrandt began in 1642, with the
death of his beloved Saskia. For the care of his child, Rembrandt
hired Henrickje Stoffels, who brought relief to the troubled house
by her devoted service. Although Henrickje could neither read nor
write, her sympathy, understanding, and encouragement were a
great comfort to the artist. By 1656, the artist's unlucky specula-
tions and extravagant habit of collecting had reduced him to bank-
ruptcy. After his home and rare collections were sold to satisfy
creditors he was forced to live in meager lodgings but he continued to paint and became so absorbed in his work that he was
able to rise above his unhappiness. During this period, Rembrandt
painted portraits of Henrickje, and many humble persons, as *Girl
at Open Half Door* (Plate 120). He painted Dutch Jews arrayed
in Oriental robes, representing them as biblical characters. Rembrandt chose to paint faces which were eloquent of struggle and
sorrow, for he sympathized with the poor and burdened and lov-
ingly revealed the dignity and character of the old men and women
who posed for him. No details escaped his penetrating vision, and
he rendered faces and hands with particular care. Becoming more
interested in subjective portraiture of a spiritual kind, he painted
a radiant all-encompassing light which enhanced the human drama
of his works. In many of his paintings and etchings the brilliant
light penetrated the shadow and gave luminosity to even the darkest parts of his pictures.

Rembrandt's method of securing effects by the use of illumination and the massing of brilliant lights against darks is exemplified in the etching *Descent from the Cross by Torchlight* (Plate 121). Here infinite variations of light render the dramatic scene in emphatic chiaroscuro. The use of glowing torchlight gives unity and provides the scene with supernatural power.

The year Saskia died Rembrandt received a commission to paint a company of archers under command of Captain Franz Banning-Cock. This picture, called *The Night Watch*, shows a company of archers leaving their guild hall. It is a light and dark arrangement in which only the Captain and Lieutenant appeared to advantage while the archers were cast in shadow. Of course the picture was unsatisfactory to the archers, who refused to pay the artist when it was completed. This proved to be the turning point in Rembrandt's career; from this time onward he refused to attempt to satisfy the desires of patrons when they conflicted with his ideas of art. The *Syndics of the Cloth Guild*, another portrait group, shows the men assembled in their office. Its five guild members, accompanied by a servant, are gathered for conference and they are shown going over the accounts in a ledger which rests on the table. The artist captured the moment when one man had finished talking and another turns to speak. Each member of the group is rendered as an individual; heads are noble and dignified and facial expressions are varied. Warmth of tone relieves the sobriety of the oak-panelled room, the dark coats, wide white collars, and the broad-brimmed hats.

In the *Supper at Emmaus* (1648) Rembrandt depicted a biblical event which occurred on the first Easter evening when Christ broke bread with two of His disciples (Plate 122). This painting of the risen Christ interprets Him as both human and divine. Clad in a white robe, he is seated at table with two disciples in a bare room enclosed by heavy stone walls. The picture shows the moment when the two disciples suddenly recognize the risen Lord while the servant is still unaware of His presence. One raises his hand in adoration while the other draws back in astonishment as he gazes upon the radiant countenance of Christ which not only illumines the scene, but also penetrates into the deepest shadows of the background.

Although Rembrandt's life was overwhelmed by misfortune and sorrow, his knowledge of man and nature and his complete mastery of his craft brought him peace and contentment. The universality of his interpretations and the originality of his vision gave new meaning to all things. Rembrandt preferred character to beauty; his understanding of human nature was profound. Throughout the course of his life he painted, etched, or drew almost every subject which could claim an artist's attention; his interest ranged from lofty religious themes to such everyday scenes as that depicted in the drawing *Woman Carrying a Child Downstairs* (Plate 120).

OTHER ARTS

Holland's contribution in architecture was not so significant as her painting. There were no great sculptors among the Dutch. Monuments, tombs, choir screens and the pretentious fireplaces designed for public buildings and homes of the wealthy burghers were made by Belgian sculptors who had studied in Italy but later settled in Breda and Utrecht.

OUTLINE OF DUTCH ART

TIME: 17th century.

BACKGROUND: Dutch art reached its height in the 17th century. In 1648, Holland achieved independence from the tyranny of Spanish domination. The Peace of Westphalia ended a long religious and political struggle after which the Dutch Protestants enjoyed freedom. The Protestant Church was not a patron of art, however. The country called Holland consists of northern and eastern provinces known as the Lowlands, or the Netherlands. When these territories were freed from Spain they developed a world trade. The establishment of the East India Company opened world trade routes to the Dutch. With the discovery of the New World, the Dutch became colonizers there. Commerce brought Dutch cities prosperity. Civic pride was evident. Strong guilds which taught effective methods to craftsmen developed thorough skills in all the arts.

PAINTING: Dutch painting is a true picture of the people and their land. Portraits and landscapes are faithful records and, in some cases, exact realistic copies. Dutch genre art reveals the everyday life and the exact appearances of ordinary things, such as exquisite textures, tonal values, and a fine realization of space in courtyard or interior. Consummate craftsmanship was shown. In landscape, the Dutch contributed a grandeur which was characteristic of their interpretation of nature's many moods. Rembrandt painted and etched in both human and realistic terms. His sincere work is universal for it is understood by all men, everywhere. Although the Dutch artists used a predominance of deep brown and green tones, a golden light pervades their canvases.

BIBLIOGRAPHY

CAFFIN, C. H., *The Story of Dutch Painting* (The Century Co., Inc., N. Y., 1911).

FROMENTIN, Eugene, *Masters of Past Time* (E. P. Dutton & Co., N. Y., 1913).

HIND, A. M., *History of Engraving and Etching* (Houghton Mifflin Co., Boston, 1923).

LAURIE, Arthur P., *The Brushwork of Rembrandt and His School* (London, 1932).

VAN LOON, Hendrik Willem, *Rembrandt van Rijn* (Garden City Publishing Co., Garden City, N. Y., 1937).

WILENSKI, R. H., *An Introduction to Dutch Art* (F. A. Stokes Co., N. Y., 1929).

CHAPTER XVII

German Art

G ERMAN art inherited much of the Gothic spirit. The mingling of sentiment, spirituality, and fantasy characteristic of the Gothic was carried over by the Teutonic artists of the Renaissance, particularly in their rendering of fanciful forest scenes. But in line drawings, elaborate wood-cuts and copper engravings, these German artists also gave forthright interpretations of German character and homely scenes. The Reformation in Germany was accompanied by a vital interest in learning and a significant renaissance in art. Local schools of painting flourished in the cities of Nuremberg, Cologne, and Augsburg, where religious works such as illuminations and miniatures were produced. Sacred pictures were also painted on wood panels with gold backgrounds such as the Sienese employed. In Cologne, about 1380, Meister Wilhelm established a school. Here Stefan Lochner (d. 1451) developed a remarkable technical skill and painted the altar-piece *Adoration of the Magi* for the cathedral. Nevertheless, it was not until the sixteenth century that the three great German geniuses, Albrecht Dürer, Hans Holbein the Younger, and Lucas Cranach became world-renowned painters.

DÜRER—THE GREAT GERMAN MASTER

The art of Albrecht Dürer (1471-1528), the most significant master of Germany, typifies the deep spirit of the Reformation. In his childhood the printing press began to reproduce books, and an immediate demand arose for illustrated religious texts. Nuremberg, where he was born, was a prosperous commercial city as well as a center of intellectual life, religious controversy, and art. Craftsmen and artists congregated there from all parts of Europe in order to learn how to cast statues in bronze, set type, carve wood, and design jewelry and watches. Here Dürer's father had found employment with a master silversmith, and following in his father's footsteps, the son entered the same workshop to learn the goldsmith's craft. At the age of fifteen he was apprenticed to Michael Wohlgemuth, a leading artist, whom he assisted in the painting of large altar-pieces. After his apprenticeship the young artist traveled four years, visiting Italy; all the while earning his way by painting. Eventually he returned to Nuremberg, married, and set up a studio. During the following ten years he made several series of wood-cuts and copper engravings which brought him fame and fortune. Among these is *St. Jerome in His Study* (1515), a copper engraving exemplifying excellent draftsmanship which records the scene in minute detail. Following the death of his brother, Dürer engraved *Melancholia,* a composition showing an aged woman brooding over the futility of life. She is surrounded by allegorical symbols, an hour-glass, and ladder in the foreground. An eerie light pervades the scene. The most popular of the series of woodengravings entitled *The Apocalypse* (1498) is *The Four Horsemen of the Apocalypse,* which illustrates the Book of Revelation, VI: 2-8. Completed at the beginning of the Reformation, it was widely reproduced and spread the artist's fame throughout Europe.

Emperor Maximilian visited Dürer's studio and requested the artist to design wood-cuts for his genealogical tree and to depict certain events of his life. Dürer spent three years making ninety-two wood-blocks for this commission, for which he was granted a life pension. While at the height of his powers, he made a second journey to Italy for the purpose of studying art. His genius and gracious personality won hosts of friends among the artists of Italy; he was constantly fêted during his two years' visit. First he went to Venice, where Titian invited him to work in his studio. There the Doge of Venice, as well as Giovanni Bellini, the great painter-teacher, came to see Dürer's paintings and praised them highly. But the artist who influenced him most was Mantegna, the Italian draftsman and engraver, whose representation of form Dürer admired. *Madonna and Child with St. Anne* shows the influence of

Italian color and an increased range of tone (Plate 124). His *Adoration of the Magi* shows the three wise men of different races, one of whom is an Ethiopian. All wear rich colorful robes and carry gifts for the Christ Child.

Although Dürer enjoyed his sojourn in Italy and many inducements were offered him to remain there, he returned to Nuremberg. While traveling homeward over the Alps on horseback, through vast forests, beside swift mountain streams, he was inspired with the idea for his fantastic engraving, *Knight, Death, and the Devil* (Plate 125). This highly imaginative conception shows a helmeted knight in full armour mounted on a dark horse, riding along a rocky pass. At his side stalks grim Death, mounted on a pale horse, and holding an hour-glass to remind the knight of the fleeting of time. Behind is the Devil, who is ready to claim the knight's soul if he should falter. This engraving bears Dürer's unique signature, a monogram made of the letters *D* under *A*, which he placed on the lower margin of his works.

On returning from a visit to the Netherlands, Dürer painted a portrait of *Hieronymus Holzschuher*, a leader in the Reformation and friend of the artist. In this work the strength, decision, and kindliness of the man are seen in the sensitive treatment of his eyes and other features of his face. Dürer's last work, *The Four Apostles*, is a characterization of St. John, St. Peter, St. Paul, and St. Mark. The powerful figures, clothed in flowing garments, are arranged in broad masses and the four faces are deeply expressive of the character of each.

Besides being a versatile artist, Dürer was a poet, philosopher, and the author of numerous books and letters in which he recorded original ideas, discussed his travels and his philosophy of life. Illustrations in the *Treatise on Human Proportion* explained Dürer's scientific text. A friend of Martin Luther, he was deeply interested in the Reformation and thought of his art as having a spiritual function. Still following the native art tradition of the north, he created new ideas and developed a fluid and graceful style which was peculiarly his own.

HOLBEIN—REALIST AND PORTRAIT PAINTER

Although Hans Holbein the Younger (1497-1543) was born only twenty-six years later than Dürer, the work of these artists was quite different both in style and point of view. Dürer was a strikingly imaginative genius; Holbein, the realist, was content to paint what he saw. He found his success through masterly recording of portraits of prominent personages. The work of both artists was alike, however, in accuracy, precision, and technical skill, for both were great draftsmen. Holbein's grandfather, called Old Holbein, and his father, the Elder Holbein, both capable artists, were natives of Augsburg, the leading city of southern Germany. Hans, an infant prodigy, had his first art training in his father's studio where his facility in representing facial expressions was evinced in his earliest work. Later he moved to Basle where he soon found congenial employment as a book illustrator. In 1523 he painted a sympathetic portrait of *Erasmus,* the great leader of the Reformation, showing him at his desk, writing. He also illustrated Erasmus' book *In Praise of Folly* and designed the initial letters and title-page for Luther's translation of the New Testament.

Holbein's large altar-piece, *The Meyer Madonna* (1529), was commissioned by Jacob Meyer, Burgomaster of Basle. The Madonna, holding the Christ Child, is represented as the protectress of the donor's family, who reverently kneel below. After a ban was placed on art by church authorities in Germany, Holbein, leaving his homeland in search of opportunities abroad, went to paint in England. A letter of introduction from Erasmus to Sir Thomas More, Chancellor of Henry VIII, brought him the attention of the king, who made Holbein his court painter. During the two years the artist was a guest of Sir Thomas More, he painted portraits of the chancellor's family and the brilliant circle of friends who gathered there. These striking likenesses brought him many patrons and the doors of England's great houses were opened to him. He was a favorite with "Good King Hal" (Henry VIII) and many anecdotes of his life in the Palace at Whitehall have been recorded. Once when a controversy arose between Holbein and a

Two wood engravings from the series *Dance of Death*, by Hans Holbein.
(Lacroix)

nobleman, the latter complained about the artist to the king, who
replied, "Of seven peasants I can make seven lords, but of seven
lords I cannot make one Holbein, and I shall look upon any injury
to the painter as though it were done to myself." The German artist
painted a veritable gallery of royal portraits, including Henry's
wives and the leaders of court life. His famous drawings now in
the Windsor Castle Collection are rendered in a direct linear style.
A popular subject for artists of the day was the *Dance of Death*.
With his genius for detailed design, Hans Holbein made a series
of forty-one wood-cuts in which Death, in the form of a skeleton,
macabre and grim, ends the lives of all men.

When Henry VIII severed his allegiance to the Pope, Sir Thomas
More, a Catholic, lost favor with the king and was beheaded.
Holbein himself narrowly escaped punishment during these tense
times by escaping to Basle, where he remained two years. Nevertheless, in 1531 he returned to England, and found new patrons
among a large colony of wealthy German merchants who had
settled in London. Among the fine paintings of this period is *Por-*

trait of George Geisze, which depicts the young merchant in a natural and realistic pose.

It was not long, however, before Holbein was again in favor at court, for the king had him design the decorations for Anne Boleyn's coronation. The artist's portraits of Henry's wives, *Catherine Howard* (Plate 125), *Jane Seymour, Anne of Cleves,* together with the portrait of the *Duchess of Milan,* are among his finest works. Holbein's portrait of Henry VIII is a realistic character study of the king. The intricate details of his rich garments and gorgeous jewels are subordinated in the interest of fine design. Holbein was the real founder of portrait art in England, and his many paintings of notables help to make this period of history live again.

LUCAS CRANACH THE ELDER

The third great master of Germany, Lucas Cranach (1472-1553), was born a year later than Dürer. He was also an accomplished painter and an engraver of wood-cuts, an example of which is his *Tournament.* Cranach placed his figure groups in beautiful landscape backgrounds such as that shown in *The Repose in Egypt.* His intimate landscapes, typical of northern art, are characterized by intricate interweaving of lines which produce a rhythmic movement suggestive of the growth and flux of nature. The *Judgment of Paris,* of the St. Louis Art Museum, is one of the versions of this classical subject which the artist painted (Plate 123). His pagan goddesses are gracefully grouped in a pleasingly decorative style though Cranach's naïve treatment of the nude shows his limitations when contrasted with the Italian masters. A romantically conceived landscape background adds interest. After the sixteenth century until recent times, Germany had no outstanding creative artists, for creative impulses were stifled on the one hand by docile imitators of Italian art, called *Mannerists,* and also by wars which devastated the land.

GERMAN ARCHITECTURE

German architecture of town and guild halls and other public buildings followed the traditional Gothic outlines. Steep high-

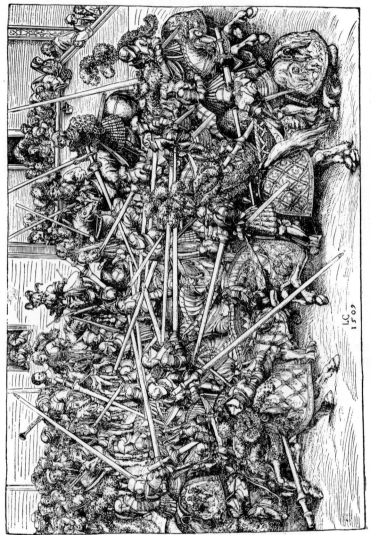

Tournament. By Lucas Cranach the Elder. (Metropolitan Museum of Art)

pitched tile roofs, quaint dormer windows, turrets, and gables were characteristic of domestic and public architecture. The later influence of the Renaissance was manifested chiefly in an enthusiasm for the elaborate baroque style. The *Peller House*, 1605, of Nuremberg, shows the Renaissance style combined with the characteristic German gables.

OUTLINE OF GERMAN ART

TIME: 14th to 17th centuries.

BACKGROUND: Breakdown of Holy Roman Empire in 13th century left Germany in state of collapse. In absence of central government, power was taken over by cities. At end of 14th century art manifested in a style reminiscent of medieval book illustrations. Gold backgrounds retained in paintings. City of Cologne in Lower Rhine, home of Cologne School of Art. The style here showed mystic, gentle piety as seen in altar-pieces of Stephen Lochner. Art of Hamburg, Augsburg, Strasburg, Nuremberg, Ulm, Basle was more realistic in style and characterized by deep love of nature which was rendered with naturalistic accuracy. German artists became great engravers, rendering many details with power and accuracy. Dürer's art is the highest expression of Protestantism; Holbein an accomplished portrait painter, court painter of England under Henry VIII.

ARCHITECTURE: Characterized by high-pitched, steep roofs and dormers which retained irregular Gothic outlines. Renaissance influences came late into Germany and were combined with baroque lines as seen in elaborate Town Halls and mansions built for prosperous merchants.

SCULPTURE: Mostly seen in imposing tombs, reliquaries, statues, monuments. Bronze equestrian statues popular.

PAINTING: Graphic art and painting of Germany show a unique expression of the wonder of nature in an intricate linear art which embodied a minute realism recorded with superb technique. The German painters, original in thought and expression, developed complete intellectual independence.

BIBLIOGRAPHY

DAVIES, G. S., *Hans Holbein, the Younger* (The Macmillan Co., N. Y., 1903).

DICKINSON, Helen A., *German Masters of Art* (F. A. Stokes Co., N. Y., 1924).

HAGEN, Oscar, *Art Epochs and Their Leaders* (Charles Scribner's Sons, N. Y., 1927).

HIND, A. M., *Albrecht Dürer: His Engravings and Woodcuts* (F. A. Stokes Co., N. Y., 1911).

MOORE, T. Sturge, *Albrecht Dürer* (Charles Scribner's Sons, N. Y., 1911).

CHAPTER XVIII

Spanish Art

FROM the time the Moorish galleys crossed over from Africa to Spain and landed on the promontory now called the Rock of Gibraltar, the Spaniards were harassed by the Mohammedans who occupied the peninsula for eight hundred years. It was during the reign of Ferdinand and Isabella that the invaders finally were driven back into the sea, irrevocably losing their terrestrial paradise in Spain. Throughout their long stay, however, the aggressors had intermingled with the natives and out of this mixture came a race in whose veins ran the blood of haughty Spaniard, fiery Arab, and industrious Moor. Due to this rich heritage of peoples from Europe, Asia, and Africa, Spanish architecture reflected the influence of both East and West. In color and pattern the decorations recall both the Byzantine mosaics and Mohammedan arabesques.

New worlds in the west had been conquered in the name of Spain after the Mohammedans were driven out. Spanish power had spread into France, Germany, and the Low Countries when the grandson of Ferdinand and Isabella, Emperor Charles V, began to reign over this vast domain in 1519. A generous patron of the arts, the Emperor collected numerous Italian masterpieces which greatly influenced the Spanish artists, and he also commissioned the Italian Titian to paint his portrait.

Early Spanish art was under strict ecclesiastical control; religious paintings were used to interpret church doctrines and to teach the sacred stories to those who could not read. Such paintings were rendered on wood-panels, miniatures, screens, and altar-pieces for monasteries and churches. Among the most notable of the sixteenth-century artists who painted on wood was Moráles (1509-1586), called The Divine because of the deep religious intensity of his work. The enamel-like quality of his rich reds, greens, and yellows exemplified in his *Christ Crowned with Thorns* are reminiscent of the work of early Flemish masters.

EL GRECO, INTERPRETER OF THE ECSTATIC

Nevertheless, the most important event in the Spanish art world occurred when Domenikos Theotocopoulos (1541-1614), better known as El Greco (the Greek), came to live in Toledo. Although the island of Crete, where the artist was born, was a Venetian colony in the sixteenth century, its culture was primarily Greek. Thus, through the Byzantines El Greco inherited both the ancient and the more modern Greek traditions. With constant communication between Venice and the island, it is not surprising to find the young artist journeying to Italy to complete his training. For fifteen years he remained there. After going to Spain he lived a luxurious though industrious life. Furthermore, it has been said that he became more Spanish than the Spaniards themselves. In a house of twenty-four rooms, which may still be seen, he entertained lavishly, gathering about him a circle of musicians, artists, intellectuals, and Castilian aristocrats, many of whom have been immortalized in his paintings.

Like Leonardo, El Greco, gifted with a versatile mind, was intensely interested in intellectual affairs; but unlike the Florentine, he confined his most serious efforts to painting. A lover of music, he hired musicians to play while he worked. Though extravagant and egotistic, according to some reports, he was equipped with personal charm and high mental attainments, accomplished in the social graces, and endowed with tremendous energy, in addition to being extraordinarily gifted in art. He was active in the social life of Toledo and became the foremost artist of Spain, devoting himself to the expression of characteristic Spanish piety in his paintings.

While in Italy El Greco acquired facility in handling the brush and learned much about color from Titian; he was greatly impressed with the forceful expression and tumultuous movement of Tintoretto's grandiose compositions; but all of these experiences were only a preparation for his peculiar style which had its roots

strongly imbedded in the Byzantine tradition. He abandoned the
Italian *chiaroscuro* (dramatic play of light and shade), in which
forms were partially lost in mysterious shadow for the clearly outlined contours of the Byzantines. In
the former, light seems to come from
some outside source such as the sun,
a candle, or a window. But El Greco's
lighting emanated from no single origin. Darting in sharp zig-zag or flame-
like flashes over the entire canvas, it
served to unify his clearly separated
spots of color and to convey an illusion of pulsating life and movement
to his paintings. For the warm luscious hues of the Venetians, he

Woman from the Espolio.
Drawing by El Greco. (Holme,
Master Drawings in Line,
Studio Publications, Inc.)

substituted cool "honey-yellows,"
wine-reds, and silver-greens which he
combined with dark grass-greens and
blackish-blues to model his forms. To
convey a feeling of heightened emotion and to suggest the supernatural, El Greco exaggerated his drawing by elongating his figures.
El Greco's *Holy Family*, of the Cleveland Museum, is an example
of his effective use of distortion (Plate 126). The Virgin's delicate,
slender face enhances the impression of soulful serenity and her
elongated, pointed fingers emphasize her other-worldliness. For
dramatic purposes he used sharp contrasts of light and dark and
introduced small bright spots of color into large areas of gray. By
applying his paint now thick, now thin, he enhanced the tactile
values of his painting. Many of his pictures are suffused with a
mysticism and emotional intensity approaching ecstasy. Nevertheless, the emotional content of his work was always controlled by
sound architectonic design.

   Surprisingly, El Greco was forgotten for three hundred years.
Since 1912, when he was "rediscovered" by a French essayist, the
art world has marveled at the advanced style, the superb quality,
and the enormous quantity of his works. Both admired and denounced during his lifetime, he nevertheless received so many

commissions from rich nobles and wealthy churchmen that he amassed a fortune. Never one to depreciate the value of his work, he demanded high prices for his paintings. We are told that if his wealthy patrons refused to meet his terms, he would either leave the pictures unfinished or send them to some of his less fortunate friends, explaining that the latter would not have haggled over prices.

A fine example of his earlier work, and one of the Chicago Art Institute's most valued possessions, is the *Assumption of the Virgin,* showing Venetian influence. It was painted as an altar-piece for the Cathedral of Toledo.

In *View of Toledo* the artist's imagination translates the actual scene, which is drab and bleak, into a dramatic landscape (Plate 127). The hills and buildings are shown against a background of heavy clouds, but a blinding bright light bursts through to illumine the scene. The weird grayish green coloring together with contrasting lights and darks produce the effect of an imminent storm. Here is almost an equal balance between realism and design.

VELAZQUEZ, REALIST AND MASTER TECHNICIAN

At the close of the sixteenth century, after El Greco had painted his dramatic compositions, a new master, Diego Velazquez (1599-1660), was born in Seville. His personality and career, like that of Raphael, was unusually happy and triumphant. Well educated and destined to be a lawyer, he showed so much talent for art that his father apprenticed him to the artist Herrera. Later he worked in Pacheco's studio for five years, and while there married the artist's daughter. Then with his bride he journeyed to Madrid where Pacheco had arranged an audience with the king. The artist's success was assured when the portrait which King Philip IV commissioned proved to be so satisfactory that he was invited to become the official court painter. Velazquez was twenty-three years old when he went to live in the palace where he maintained a studio and for thirty-seven years was the trusted confidante and comrade of the king. He painted forty portraits of His Majesty, showing him in court dress, on horseback, and at the hunt, or again representing only his long, thin, melancholy face (Plate 129). Being especially fond of children, the artist has also left charming portraits of *Don Baltazar Carlos*, heir to the throne (Plate 128), *Mariana of Austria*, and the fair-haired *Infanta Margarita*. Indeed, his art depicts court life in its entirety, including the royal jesters, dwarfs, hunchbacks, and dogs which were a familiar part of the scene. The royal personages themselves were treated with a dignity and regal air which they did not always possess.

In *Maids of Honor* Velazquez shows himself at his easel painting the portrait of the Infanta Margarita surrounded by her dwarfs and attendants. Her creamy-silver dress offers a contrast to the soft moss-green of the gown of one of her maids. The faces of king and queen, who are observing the scene, are reflected in a mirror on the wall. Here a complete illusion of reality was attained by the artist's fine treatment of space and masterly arrangement of figures. In *The Surrender of Breda*, a dramatic historical scene, the faces of the men in the immediate foreground are realistic portraits.

Perhaps as a relief and diversion from his usual task of depicting court life, Velazquez executed some remarkably realistic scenes from the life of ordinary people, such as the *Drinkers* and *Tapestry Weavers*. The *Forge of Vulcan* is a realistic rendition of a mythological subject.

Velazquez never allowed his own emotions to influence his expression. His paintings are distinguished by a simple directness and rapid, bold brush-work. Salient accents are focussed on a few important details; everything else is drowned in large masses of grayish tone. He was one of the first artists to record the essentials which the eye sees at a single glance, and in this field he remains supreme. Even in his interpretations of sacred themes he reproduced the outward solidity and substance of forms, for he was entirely concerned with painting the objective world. Silver, rose, and blue are the colors he preferred. A sober realist, this artist is distinguished for his consummate craftsmanship, his sensitivity of vision, and his ability to represent skillfully grouped forms in vast atmospheric space.

Among the contemporaries of Velazquez were Francisco de Zurbarán (1598-1661), a monastic painter who is remembered for such religious pictures as *The Dominican Monk* and the *Flight into Egypt;* Jusepe de Ribera (1588-1652), who was greatly influenced by the Italian Caravaggio, and rendered sombre-hued and vividly realistic paintings of martyrs and saints, such as *St. Jerome;* and Bartolomé Murillo (1617-1682) of Seville, who attained great popularity through his religious subjects and sympathetic interpretations of the life of beggar boys like *The Melon Eaters.* His art, characterized by a suave blending of soft vaporous colors and tonal harmonies, is expressive of the religious teachings of the church and the piety of the people. Murillo's charming *Virgin and St. Anne* exalts the simple joys of family life, for it identifies an unaffected village girl as the appealing Virgin and a local Spanish model as the beatific St. Anne (Plate 131). Sympathy and human kindness pervade this intimate scene which Murillo painted with sincere naturalism. Nevertheless, it is the works of El Greco, Velazquez, and Goya that represent Spain's greatest contribution to painting. After Velazquez the great masters of seventeenth-century art were not to be found in Spain. It would be nearly a hundred years before the third great Spanish painter would arrive upon the scene.

GOYA'S DRAMATIC AND SATIRIC STYLE

Though born a peasant, Francisco Goya (1746-1828) rose to the position of court favorite and became one of the greatest artists of Spain. Egotistic, arrogant, bold and fearless, he brazenly moved through the intrigues, jealousies, and pompous ceremonies of the corrupt court with the same finesse and bravado that he displayed in evading danger in the bull-ring, or eluding death at the hands of a jealous husband or lover. At intervals in disfavor at court, or again just a step ahead of the Inquisition, he not only managed to escape punishment but contrived to recover his favored position as well. Never deeply interested in politics, he easily gave his allegiance to the French invaders and as readily returned it to the Spanish when they revolted and drove the foreigners out. The Spanish king declared that although Goya should be hanged as a traitor, he nevertheless would spare him because he could not afford to lose such a fine artist. In the end, however, Goya was to die in

France a disillusioned old man and an exile from his native country.

Living life to the fullest, Goya delighted in painting games, gay parties, and the vigorous swift action of scenes in the bull-ring which he himself had actually experienced. He gave a realistic interpretation of the life of Spanish beggars, rogues, musicians, and gangsters. In etchings and lithographs he depicted the brutalities of war as in *And There Is No Remedy* (Plate 128), and of the Spanish Inquisition with a power which no sermon could equal. He satirized the weaknesses of a stupid court and ridiculed the vices of his time, sparing neither king nor churchman. He never shrank from depicting with savage realism the misery of the oppressed and the wretchedness of the poor. In addition he was an excellent portrait painter with four hundred examples to his credit varying from charming studies of childhood and a tender, sympathetic rendering of the likeness of his long-suffering wife, to portraits of the Royal Family showing the dull-witted King and the wicked Queen (Plate 129). Perhaps it was his masterly handling of her elegant costume and brilliant jewels that directs attention toward her glittering adornment, and away from the portrayal of her plain features. Another famous example of his portrait work is the *Duchess of Alba* (Plate 130).

Many of Goya's paintings reflect something of his reckless, bold, and dashing personality and his impetuous way of life. In them he sets the stage, presents the actors upon the scene, and directs the attention of the spectator to the center of interest by a brilliant spot of light or a flash of vivid color. To achieve strong patterned effects he depended upon striking contrasts of dark and light. In nature, he said, there are no lines. Although he used color with warmth and perception, Goya regarded it as an accessory rather than as an important structural element. Skillfully unified in groups, his figures move forward and backward as they take their proper places in a bold tonal pattern. His work is intense, spontaneous, and dramatic partly because of the "unfinished" style which leaves something to the imagination.

The three outstanding Spanish painters, strong individuals as well as great artists, differed both in personal character and in their style of painting. El Greco's work is imbued with that ecstatic mysticism which was the very soul of Spain. Rarely penetrating deeply into the character of his subjects, Velazquez, the aloof, objective observer, painted what he saw with remarkable clarity of vision but without emotion or comment. Goya, who not only observed but experienced life, in addition to portraying the passing scene, expressed his personal reaction to it. His lithographs and etchings prove him to be one of the greatest satirists of all time. The works of all three have had a strong influence on modern art.

SPANISH SCULPTURE LARGELY ECCLESIASTICAL

Spanish Renaissance sculpture, which was dominated by Italian influence, is characterized by religious fervor and infused with Jesuit piety. Impressive monuments and tombs were erected in the Royal Chapel of the Cathedrals of Granada and Seville. Usually Italian workers in bronze were imported to execute these large projects. A native sculptor, Alonzo Berruguete (c. 1486-1561), who had studied in Rome expressed a spiritual quality in the elongated, emaciated figures of his *St. Sebastian* and *Sacrifice of Abraham*. Pedro de Mena's *St. Francis* in the Cathedral of Toledo, is deeply expressive of religious feeling. Spanish sculptors made many wood carvings and figures in polychrome which were carried in the Holy Week processions.

SPANISH ARCHITECTURE

Among the cathedrals and monasteries erected when wealth began to flow into Spain from the New World was the magnificent Cathedral of Seville, with its lofty bell tower called *La Giralda,* which is characteristically Spanish (Plate 131). The churches of Gothic construction were enhanced by elaborately carved altar-screens and even the cloisters of the monasteries were embellished with carvings as elaborate as goldsmiths' work in a style known as *plateresque,* a Spanish blend of Italian Renaissance and Moorish architectural features comprising intricate and delicate decorations in the form of garlands, cupids, medallions, scrolls, and niches.

These designs were usually concentrated around doors and windows and in certain other portions of the façade.

An entirely different type of Spanish architecture is shown in the gigantic *Escorial,* a tomb-palace built by Philip II near Madrid. This huge structure, begun in 1563 and completed twenty years later, is solemn and majestic. If the grim plainness of its façade and its immense size make it unique in world architecture, its well-balanced proportions give it dignity and complete unity. The architecture of the Escorial was an extreme reaction from the luxuriousness typical of the plateresque, for it is characterized by an entire absence of such embellishments; instead there was a strict reliance upon the use of classical orders. This austere group of buildings, in which there was a royal mausoleum, church, palace, and a store house for works of art, was constructed of gray granite in a setting of secluded mountain scenery on a rocky Castilian plateau jutting out from a precipitous slope of the Sierras. The façade is a smooth granite wall flanked on either side by a tower with a gateway in between. There are twelve thousand windows, one following the other in endless succession. Juan de Herrera (1530-1597), who built this gigantic structure, had studied architecture with Michelangelo in Rome. Nevertheless, Philip II personally supervised the design and the Escorial reflects his somber temperament and inflexible spirit.

Later Spanish architecture underwent a change from the extreme sobriety and severe style of Herrera's *Escorial* to a new type of design showing baroque freedom which was employed by José Churriguera (1650-1723). It was characterized by fantastic twisted columns, brackets, and ornate projections. After a long popularity in Spain the style spread to South America and Mexico. The museum in Balboa Park, San Diego, California, is a reproduction of this old Spanish-Mexican architecture.

OUTLINE OF SPANISH ART

TIME: 16th and 17th centuries. Goya in latter part of 17th and first part of 18th century.

BACKGROUND: Due to mountainous terrain, Spain more or less isolated. Moorish occupation and Inquisition, strong influences in Spanish art. Rich treasures of silver and gold from New World stimulated building. Inquisition brought bloodshed and fanatical persecution. Moors, the craftsmen, expelled for religious reasons.

ARCHITECTURE: Elaborate and fanciful interpretations of baroque. Churches, Gothic in structure, Spanish in ornamentation. Decoration confined chiefly to doors, windows, and other parts of façade. Ornate panels with intricate carving with emblems and garlands, in style known as plateresque. Escorial designed in severe classical style. José Churriguera combined flamboyant baroque motives with a new style which spread to Mexico and South America. Characterized by fantastic twisted columns, brackets, and ornate projections.

SCULPTURE: Impressive marble monuments, tombs, in 17th century. Renaissance influences seen in work of Berruguete. Sincere piety and deep religious feeling in statues of Pedro de Mena.

PAINTING: Religious frescoes, for the most part, together with miniatures and panels in tempera prior to 16th century. Madonna, a favorite subject. Strong Byzantine and Venetian influence seen in work of *El Greco*. Baroque elements and dramatic use of light and color used by him to express supernatural. *Velazquez'* art based on realism. Achieved visual unity in his paintings through use of proper tones and placement of objects bathed in atmosphere. *Goya*, great satirist, painter, etcher and lithographer. His work is uncompromisingly realistic, bold, dramatic. Emphasis on dark and light. Color added for effect —not used structurally.

BIBLIOGRAPHY

CAFFIN, C. H., *The Story of Spanish Painting* (The Century Co., Inc., N. Y., 1917).

CALVERT, A. F., *Goya* (London, 1908).

MAYER, A. L., *Francisco de Goya* (London, 1924).

———, *El Greco* (Munich, 1916).

POORE, Charles, *Goya* (Charles Scribner's Sons, N. Y., 1938).

POST, C. R., *History of Spanish Painting* (Harvard University Press, Cambridge, Mass., 1930).

RUTTER, Frank, *El Greco* (London, 1930).

STEVENSON, R. A. M., *Velasquez* (The Macmillan Co., N. Y., 1899).

STOKES, Hugh, *Francesco Goya* (G. P. Putnam's Sons, N. Y., 1914).

CHAPTER XIX

English Art

M ANY talented foreign artists enjoyed painting in England, where they were given generous court patronage. Because of the English hospitality accorded imported artists and the high quality of their work, native painters were completely overshadowed in their own land. Numerous Italian artists and craftsmen were employed in the decoration of English mansions, and Henry VIII made Hans Holbein, a German artist, his court painter. When Rubens visited England in 1629, he was royally received and knighted, an honor also conferred upon his favorite pupil van Dyck, the Flemish artist, who became court painter for Charles I. Van Dyck portrayed many court celebrities and is credited with founding the elegant portrait style which set a high standard for English portrait painting. Another foreign-born artist, Sir Peter Lely of Soest (1618-1680) settled in England where he was court painter to Charles II. During a devastating civil war much ecclesiastical and private property was destroyed, and in the Cromwellian regency (1649-1660) art languished into complete stagnation. Finally in the eighteenth century, the leadership of English painting at last passed to native artists.

HOGARTH, PAINTER, ILLUSTRATOR, MORALIST,
AND SATIRIST

During this time, known as the Age of Reason, pictures were used to teach morals and manners. William Hogarth (1697-1764) gave his attention to painting and engraving pictorial comedies and satires designed to uplift morals. Portraying the follies and vices of his time in a spirited if satirical style, he revealed evils which

lay beneath the surface of social life. Among his early works are
the illustrations for Samuel Butler's *Hudibras*, but Hogarth is best
known for his series of popular engravings, *The Harlot's Progress*,

Laughing Audience. Engraving by Hogarth. (Metropolitan Museum of Art)

A Rake's Progress, and *Marriage à la Mode*. The latter presents a
brisk, story-telling pantomime which illustrated the narrative
through the actions and gestures of the figures. This penetrating
descriptive quality, wit, and raillery greatly intrigued the public.
Hogarth's pictures are replete with humorous incidents which contribute to the telling of the story. As one critic has noted, the spectator fails to appreciate fully the beauty of the artist's painting until
he first has had a hearty laugh. Hogarth portrayed varied types:
people of the middle class, the aristocracy, and celebrities of the
stage. His *Shrimp Girl* (Plate 135), executed in only one hour,

is admired for its expression of vitality, delicacy of color, and skillful brushwork.

NOTABLE PORTRAIT ARTISTS

The names of Sir Joshua Reynolds (1723-1792) and Thomas
Gainsborough (1727-1788) are inseparably linked with English
portraiture, for their leadership was supreme in the eighteenth
century. Reynolds' name is also associated with a celebrated London club frequented by the brilliant men of that day. Among these
were Dr. Samuel Johnson, the lexicographer; Garrick, the actor;
Goldsmith, the poet; Gibbon, the historian; and Burke, the states-
man. Under Reynolds' direction, English art was favored by royal
patronage, and the Royal Academy of Art was founded in 1768.
He became its first president; was knighted by George III; and enjoyed prestige and wealth. His discourses on art, read at the Royal
Academy, are famous. Using rich, warm colors and a mellow, ripe
tonality, he painted rapidly, sometimes finishing an entire picture
at one sitting. Among his admired portraits are *Jane, Countess of
Harrington* (Plate 133) and *Lord Heathfield* and many paintings
of children in natural poses. His fine paintings and excellent artistic judgment won him a high place in English art. The poet Oliver
Goldsmith dedicated "The Deserted Village" to "The Prince of
Portrait Painters." Reynolds is buried in St. Paul's Cathedral beside the tomb of Sir Christopher Wren.

Thomas Gainsborough's color is soft and cool compared to
Reynolds' warm, mellow hues. A careful painter of textures, he
achieved beautiful effects in the rendering of lustrous silks, satins,
and jewels. His graceful and dignified portraits of beautiful women
and children include such celebrated works as the *Honorable Mrs.
Graham* and the *Duchess of Devonshire.* In *The Artist's Daughters*
Gainsborough reveals a sincerity often lacking in the portraiture of
his time (Plate 134). Reynolds contended that cool blues and
greens should not be used exclusively in a single painting, but
Gainsborough, who admired these colors especially, set himself the
task of disproving this rule. The result, a remarkable *tour de force,*
was *The Blue Boy,* now in the Huntington Gallery in California
(Plate 132). Besides being a distinguished portrait painter, Gains-

borough was a pioneer interpreter of the English rural scene, which he rendered with convincing charm. Among the native painters who are credited with maintaining the high quality of English portraiture set by Reynolds and Gainsborough are George Romney (1734-1802), a popular artist who painted *The Parson's Daughter* and fine portraits of *Lady Hamilton;* Sir Thomas Lawrence (1769-1830), an excellent painter who became president of the Royal Academy; and Sir Henry Raeburn (1756-1823), who is remembered for his strong, solid style of painting.

Landscapes in water colors and oils, which were especially popular during the eighteenth century, followed the romantic trends manifested in poetry and literature. Paintings of ruins, abbeys, castles, and wild rocky landscapes were favorites. Artists of the time include Richard Wilson (1714-1782), who studied extensively in Italy but returned to live in England. His *Tiber with Rome in the Distance* shows a strong classical influence; nevertheless, a later work, *Thames at Twickenham,* expresses the natural beauty of his native England. John Crome (1768-1821), often called Old Crome, was a self-made artist who delighted in recording the grand and noble moods of nature which he painted in olive-greens and russet-brown tonal effects.

CONSTABLE'S INFLUENCE ON LANDSCAPE PAINTING

The landscapes of Gainsborough and Wilson inspired John Constable (1776-1837) to become the greatest interpreter of nature in English art. Born within fourteen miles of Gainsborough's home, the two artists enjoyed the same countryside with its cornfields, thatched cottages, rivers, mills, and meadows. Constable was concerned with representing nature as a living, changing reality. He studied the land and sky in all their varied aspects as determined by weather and season, and searched diligently for clues to the painting of fleeting effects of light and air. On each of his many studies of clouds he noted the time of day, temperature, and wind direction. Thus, through painstaking research, he was able to record the movement of clouds and flutter of leaves in the breeze with a realism which had never been accomplished before. Instead of using color previously mixed on the palette, he applied varied clear hues, side by side, thereby achieving a stronger chromatic vibration. His grass, for example, contained clear yellow-green, blue-green, blue, and violet, instead of the pre-mixed brownish green used by such artists as Crome. Constable's vibrant painting was acclaimed by contemporary French artists when *The Hay Wain* was shown in the Paris Salon of 1824. Although the team of horses and the wagon are predominant in this composition, the spectator's attention is centered on the beautiful countryside with its trees, bushes, and sky. The influence of Constable's use of color upon the French romantic and impressionist painters of his day is incalculable. Such works as *Stoke-by-Nayland* show the artist's complete realization on canvas of the impressions which first fired his imagination (Plate 134). Although he received two medals at the Paris Salon and was recognized on the Continent, Constable was not invited to membership in the Royal Academy until 1829. Today he is regarded as one of the great landscape artists of all time.

TURNER'S ORIGINALITY; STRIFE AMONG THE CRITICS

The paintings of his contemporary, Joseph Mallord Turner (1775-1851), are broad, generalized impressions in brilliant color harmonies. Turner possessed a romantic imagination and amazing technical skill which enabled him to paint striking effects of color combined with vibrating light. Grandiose expressions of the turbid majesty of the sea are shown in *The Slave Ship, Dawn, After the Wreck,* and *Antwerp: Van Goyen Looking Out for a Subject* (Plate 135). His *Snow Storm* is a remarkable rendering of the color of snow, and *Rain, Steam, Speed* conveys the effect of the rapid motion of a train through fog-laden atmosphere. Here the artist used broken color, that is, hues laid in separate brush strokes without previous mixing on the palette. Turner was championed by John Ruskin, the London critic of art, who wrote "Modern Painters" and "The Art of Painting" in defense of his work, for the public did not appreciate the artist's dripping colors and nebulous forms. Both Constable and Turner made real contributions to impressionist painting of the nineteenth century. The notable collection of paintings which Turner left to the National Gallery are an impressive memorial to this artist, who chose to live as a recluse in conditions bordering on poverty. Although for a time this artist's work gained popular favor, because of its romanticism, Turner's work was later relegated to a less important rôle in the public regard.

WILLIAM BLAKE, THE MYSTIC

William Blake (1757-1827) was a religious mystic whose oil paintings, water-colors, and engravings objectified his visions of the spiritual world, as in *Christ and the Woman Taken in Adultery* (Plate 136). His wood-cuts include illustrations from the Book of Job. He also illustrated his own imaginative poetry: *Songs of Innocence, Songs of Experience,* and *Marriage of Heaven and Hell.* A noteworthy painting by Blake, *God Measuring the Universe,* has been adopted as the motif of a sculptural design on the façade of one of the buildings at Rockefeller Center, New York.

PRE-RAPHAELITE ROMANTICISM

In 1848, the Pre-Raphaelite Brotherhood was formed by Dante Gabriel Rossetti (1828-1882), William Morris (1834-1896), Holman Hunt, John Everett Millais, and others to combat the influence of the factories, which were crushing the creative instinct of the native English craftsmen, that is, the artists of the people. The Brotherhood sought to counteract mechanical trends in England's industrialized society by restoring beautiful hand-crafts, and protested against the Royal Academy's formulating rules for artists because they claimed that this practice had a stultifying influence on art. On the positive side they recommended a return to the simplicity of the methods and ideals of the artist who painted before Raphael's day. Such idealistic paintings as Rossetti's *Beatrice* and *Annunciation* became popular. William Morris promoted creative craftsmanship in the making of beautiful tapestries, stained-glass, wallpaper, furniture, textiles and hand-sewn books. His ideals of honest craftsmanship helped turn popular attention to the arts and crafts.

ARCHITECTS AND CRAFTSMEN IN THE
ENGLISH RENAISSANCE

A great woodcraftsman of England was Grinling Gibbons (1648-1720), who carved the *Choir Stalls* of St. Paul's Cathedral with designs of naturalistic flowers, garlands, swags, birds, festoons, and other forms. He also designed and made many beautiful wood-panels for the fine interiors of England's great mansions. Although sculpture was negligible in England at this time, the large monument of *Lord Nelson,* carved by John Flaxman (1755-1826), is a characteristic work of the period.

The native architects absorbed influences of the Renaissance style and modified these to meet the needs of English life. Magnificent Tudor manor houses reflected the wealth of the time in their oak paneling, ornate over-mantels, elaborate ceilings, and richly decorated walls. During this period brick was used in building *Hampton Court Palace* (Plate 132) and *Windsor Castle.* Elaborate bay windows, called *oriels,* with ornate window tracery were used in the Great Hall of Hampton Court, which is also distinguished for its two-story ceiling. The great achievement of English architects is largely due to the work of two men: Inigo Jones (1573-1652) who received his inspiration from the classical style of Italy and guided architecture toward a beautiful interpretation of classic design; and Sir Christopher Wren (1632-1723), who built St. Paul's Cathedral. The *Banqueting Hall,* Whitehall, which Jones designed for King James I is a handsome classic structure in perfect scale, with restrained ornamentation. Although there was a lull in building during the civil war, a great period of reconstruction followed the fire which almost demolished London in 1666. The task of rebuilding *St. Paul's Cathedral* was entrusted to Sir Christopher Wren, who created this majestic edifice. The famous dome, remarkable for its beauty as well as its construction, reaches a height of two hundred and eighty feet.

Domestic architecture of the first decade of the eighteenth century is generally called Queen Anne, but from 1727 it is known as Georgian in honor of George II and George III. The Adam style represents the influence of Robert Adam (1728-1792), an architect and designer of fine furniture. Other famous wood-carvers and furniture designers were Thomas Chippendale (1718-1779), George Hepplewhite (d. 1786), and Thomas Sheraton (1751-1806). The great English cabinet-makers who created elegant interiors and fine furniture, are largely responsible for making eighteenth-century work a source of inspiration for later periods.

OUTLINE OF ENGLISH ART

TIME: 16th through 19th centuries.

BACKGROUND: 16th century witnesses destruction of monasteries. Restoration in 17th century gave power and wealth to the aristocracy. 18th century Industrial Revolution resulted in the banding together of a group of artist-craftsmen who founded the Pre-Raphaelite Brotherhood, the intention of which was to revive creative impulses which had been stultified by the machine. Protestants were against statues and paintings in churches. This attitude prevailed during the Commonwealth. But with the Restoration, mansions, castles, portraits, and fine furnishings were acquired. The replacing of hand-made articles by machine production required adjustment of art standards.

ARCHITECTURE: Renaissance influences were revealed in the balanced and symmetrical plans of magnificent mansions having superimposed orders, regular openings. Interiors were in the classical style and civic buildings, palaces, churches were built on classic models.

PAINTING: Native painters developed vigorous expression in both portraiture and landscape. Portrait painting developed to meet the demand of the aristocracy. A "grand style" of portraiture presented the English artists with a chance to develop rare brush-work and color. Modern interpretations of rendering of nature developed in the great landscape art seen both in water-color and oil. Advance in use of color made by Constable.

BIBLIOGRAPHY

ARMSTRONG, Sir Walter, *Art in Great Britain and Ireland* (Charles Scribner's Sons, N. Y., 1913).

———, *Gainsborough and His Place in English Art* (Charles Scribner's Sons, N. Y., 1913).

DOBSON, Austin, *William Hogarth* (Dodd, Mead & Co., N. Y., 1902).

FRY, Roger, *Reflections on British Painting* (The Macmillan Co., N. Y., 1934).

HOLMES, Sir C. J., *Constable* (Longmans, Green & Co., N. Y., 1901).

WILENSKI, R. H., *Masters of English Painting* (Hale, Cushman & Flint, Boston, 1934).

CHAPTER XX

Art of the American Indians and of Mexico

I T IS believed that the primitive men who were our predecessors in America came from northeastern Asia by way of the Bering Straits, reaching the Western Hemisphere probably about ten thousand years ago. Pushing their way slowly southward toward the warmer climates beyond the Rocky Mountains, they came to the broad prairies of our Southwest, the valleys of Mexico, and then to Central and South America. In the Americas a remarkable civilization flourished more than a thousand years before the arrival of Columbus.

ART OF THE MAYAN EMPIRE

About three or four thousand years ago, a group of Indians called the Maya lived in Central America, on that narrow neck of land comprising what is now Guatemala, Honduras, and Yucatan. This country, which has beautiful upland valleys between the mountains and tropical forests along the coastlands, looks eastward upon the Atlantic Ocean and westward across the Pacific. The early Mayans planted and harvested maize, or Indian corn. As their agricultural labors were regulated by the seasons and the changing positions of the planets, they studied astronomy and made a calendar which recorded eclipses of the sun and moon and the position of the morning and evening star, Venus. The Mayan calendar recorded eighteen periods of twenty days each with five supplementary days. Square monolithic pillars erected to commemorate the passing of certain epochs of time had special symbolic significance. Between some of these pillars were sun-dials, so placed that when the sun set in direct line with the pillars, it was

April the ninth or September the second, according to whether this occurred at planting or harvest. Our knowledge of Mayan religious festivals and sacrifices is derived from remains such as

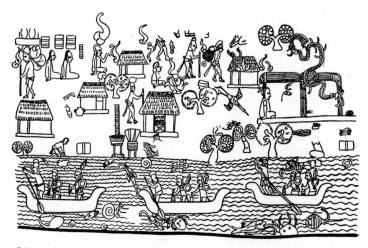

Mayan Village Life at the Seashore. Drawing made from mural fragments found in the Temple of Warriors at Chichen Itza, by Ann Axtell Morris. (Carnegie Institution of Washington)

murals, images, ritual masks, and funeral urns. Their picture writing, like Egyptian hieroglyphics, was a combination of symbols; for example, a bird was indicated by a beak, and war captives signified victory. Brightly colored murals decorated the temple walls, and pictures were painted on fibre papers and on the dry skins of animals. The Mayan system of counting recorded numbers beyond a million.

MAYAN SCULPTURE

Much of Mayan sculpture was in relief and figures were generally shown in profile or three-quarter view. These were set against elaborate backgrounds. A wealth of stone carving adorned the exteriors of their temples, and the interiors contained elaborate sacrificial altars and calendar stones. The designs carved on *stelae*, or grave monuments, and the sculptural renderings of gods have an austere beauty. These sculptors achieved a maximum of beauty from wood or stone, and their carvings have high esthetic quality and plastic feeling. Many representations of the gods who controlled the rain, sun, moon, stars, wind, water, and the maize have been found. Such examples as the *Head of a Maize God* carved in trachyte (c.300 A.D.) are masterpieces (Plate 138).

MAYAN ART FUNDAMENTALLY RELIGIOUS

Because of their elaborate religious rites and pageantry, the Mayans had many priests who served as mediators. It was their duty to offer sacrifices to the gods to insure the success of crops. The chief god and presiding spirit, Itzamma, personified the rising and the setting sun. Another god, Kukulcan, represented as a feathered serpent, was shown on the pyramid temples built in his honor. The finest fruition of Mayan culture, which had developed for thousands of years, was reached in what is now Guatemala and Honduras. In Copan, the chief city of Honduras, were vast shrines with elaborate sanctuaries. Bas-relief stucco carvings on the walls and columns of temples showed grotesque designs of mythical dragon-headed gods and waving serpents. These proclaimed the terrible wrath and endless vengeance which would descend upon the people should they fail to make offering to the gods.

Imposing shrines were placed on terraces with colossal staircases leading to dizzy heights. The magnificent pyramid *El Castillo*, at Chichen Itza, is a temple to the god Kukulcan (Plate 137). Its base, made of limestone blocks, covers an acre of ground. In many of the public buildings of Yucatan, the Mayan builders developed a type of corbeled arch. A huge monument in the form of a single block of stone has been found. This rock, over thirty-five feet long and weighing more than fifty tons, is covered with elaborate incised carvings in geometric designs. The Mayan decorators used brilliant hues on their temple frescoes, and bright designs were incised on ceramic ware and pottery. In recent years there has been a steadily increasing appreciation of the artistic legacy derived from this ancient culture.

After a siege of epidemics, famines, and revolts the remarkable civilization of the Mayans declined. When the Spanish soldiers landed in Yucatan, the natives were not strong enough to resist them. By 1541, they were completely subjugated by massacre, rape, and pillage. The Spanish, unable to read the Mayan calendars or hieroglyphics, destroyed many of these precious relics. Native religious ceremonies were forbidden and the priests and nobles were cruelly persecuted—many of them killed. Their knowledge of astronomy and numbers which had accumulated for over a thousand years was lost to the remaining Indians. If three Mayan codices, which escaped destruction by the Spanish, had not been discovered we would have little proof of this ancient culture.

TOTONAC ART

To the north of the Mayans on the arid plateaus lived many Totonic tribes who developed a comparatively high stage of civilization (c.750-1050 A.D.). The art of these people shows similarity to that of the Mayans and Chinese. Luxuriance of decoration was well adapted to the elaborate Totonac religious rites and ceremonies. The *Human Face with Tattooing* is an example of their art (Plate 137). After the power of the Totonac tribes was broken by civil war, the fierce Aztecs from the central plateaus of Mexico gained control over them.

INCAN ART

In Peru, South America (c.1000 A.D.), another extraordinary people, the Incas, founded their Indian empire—a vast dominion stretching for twenty-seven hundred miles along the fertile uplands where tropical heat is moderated by an altitude of thirteen thousand feet. The capital city was Cuzco, or "City of the Sun," near the present site of Santiago, Chile. Manco Capac, founder of the Incan dynasty, was believed to be a child of the sun god. When he and his followers brought numerous Andean tribes under control, the Incan population numbered ten million Indians. They built stone fortresses and walls with ramparts at strategic points, and maintained a road system from Cuzco to all parts of the empire. Remains of Peruvian temples, palaces and pyramids constructed of great stone blocks have been found near the site of the ancient capital. The immensity of the Inca ruins makes them the most remarkable pre-historic monuments in the Western Hemisphere. One of the temples, decorated with a glittering freize, was called The Place of Gold. Its ornate interior contained burnished plates encrusted with precious stones. The Incas were expert weavers of cloth; they deftly modeled pottery and clay figurines; knew the art of smelting and working metals; and understood the metallurgy of gold, silver, and bronze. The repoussé *Alpaca* (Plate 142), in silver, echoes an interest in geometric form evident in Incan architecture. We learn much about this proud race from other examples of their art such as an *Early Chimu Portrait Vase,* showing a remarkably realistic carving of a tribal warrior's head (Plate 142). A conventional line decoration is painted above the forehead, which is surmounted by stirrup handle and top spout. Primarily an agricultural people, they raised maize, cotton, and potatoes. Their government was a religious despotism, ruled by an emperor. The mass of the people were allowed no freedom. The intellectual culture was confined to the priests and nobles. When the destruction of the rulers and priests occurred in the tenth century, the Inca culture was destroyed. In 1528, Francisco Pizzaro, a Spanish soldier of fortune, accompanied by an army of marauding horsemen with firearms, conquered what remained of the ancient empire. Ruthless Spaniards marched into Cuzco and seized its rich treasures of gold and precious jewels.

TOLTEC AND AZTEC ART

Toltec civilization developed in the highlands of ancient Mexico and reached its highest point during the tenth and eleventh centuries. Prior to the 1930's, when their principal city Tollan was excavated sixty miles from Mexico City, little was known concerning this people; even today our knowledge of their culture is far from complete. Working solely with stone tools, the Toltecs were prolific temple-builders. Some of the finest examples of their decorative sculpture are to be found on the *Pyramid to Quetzalcoatl* (Plate 140), dedicated to their hero-god at San Juan Teotihuacan.

Strange shapes, some half animal and half reptile, appear on the monument; other designs show the feathered serpent associated with the worship of the god. Many of these decorative patterns incorporate coral, shell, precious stones, and gold and silver.

The Aztec culture, contemporary with that of the latter Mayans, flourished several centuries after the decline of the Toltec civilization. The Aztecs, most famous of all the great pre-Columbian tribes, were related to the Indians of the Rocky Mountains and the southern plateaus of the United States. Settling in Mexico because the climate and soil were suited to the cultivation of maize, these migratory hunters and fishers led by Tenoch, their chief, made a settlement (in 1325) at Tenochtitlan on the site of what is now Mexico City, and organized leagues of tribes which spread throughout the Mexican plateaus and valleys. Developing remarkable military strength, in less than two centuries, they dominated the entire territory of Mexico.

Their religion was a barbaric worship of the forces of nature. As the chief Aztec deity was the blood-thirsty god of war, they conquered and absorbed the less militaristic Mayans and annexed their territory. Their cruel religion with its spectacular ceremonies led them to slaughter thousands of war captives and to make sacrifices of children. Twenty stone temples, decorated with carved grotesques of the plumed serpent, eagle, rattlesnake, jaguar, and tiger, stood in the center of their dazzling capital city. They made bronze by alloying copper and tin; developed a calendar; invented a system of counting and symbol writing; and wove and spun cloth. Many domestic utensils, incense burners, and implements have been excavated in Mexico.

Although the Aztecs had a strongly organized empire by the middle of the fifteenth century, they had formidable enemies, the Tlascalans, who lived on the west coast. This tribe, dissatisfied because of the high taxes demanded of them, collaborated with the Spanish in a rebellion. When Hernan Cortez conquered the Aztec Empire (1521) he demanded gold treasure estimated at seven million dollars. After the conquest some Indians sought refuge in the mountains or in the coastal wooded areas where they lived inde-

pendent of Spanish rule, but all the nobles or priests were killed
or reduced to slavery.

NORTH AMERICAN INDIAN ART

In North America there were three major Indian groups: Sioux
Indians of the Plains, who lived between the Rocky Mountains
and the Mississippi River; the Iroquois, of the eastern woodlands;
and the Pueblo of the Rio Grande valley and the Southwest. The
group east of the Mississippi were related to the prehistoric Mayans,
whereas the cliff-dwellers, living in the Southwest, had a culture
based on the Aztec. Although the North American Indians did not
achieve the heights of science and art reached by those of Central
America, Mexico, and Peru, their development of tobacco, cotton,
and peanuts contributed greatly to agriculture. Their handicrafts,
including woven rugs, blankets, baskets, and pottery, were decorated
with conventionalized designs symbolizing reverence for nature.
Leather skins, easily obtainable, were decorated with embroidery,
quill-work, or painting (Plate 142). Conspicuous among fine Indian carvings are colorful totem poles. Elaborate wood carvings on
totem poles and masks represent a form of heraldric and religious
symbolism of the Indians of the Pacific Northwest, British Columbia and Alaska. These symbols, generally derived from nature,
denoted the rank and privilege of certain individuals, families, or
clans. Skillful Indian sculptors carved masks which were used in
ceremonials to invoke magic and to influence the gods (Plate 142).

MEXICAN ARCHITECTURE

The great wealth of Mexico and Central America stimulated the
development of elaborate architecture. The baroque style, introduced by the Spanish, became popular in the seventeenth and
eighteenth centuries. Spanish architecture in Mexico is called *chur-
rigueresque,* a name derived from its Spanish creator, José Churriguera. This style, seen in the *Cathedral of Taxco* (Plate 143)
and the *Church of Ocutlan* of Tlaxcala, is characterized by elaborate carving, gilding, and by graceful belfries decorated with

ornate stucco designs. Although the Indians worked under the direction of Spanish architects, the façade of the Palace in Mexico City shows strong Aztec influence.

Relics of Mexican and Spanish occupation in the southwestern part of what is now the United States, are seen in the monasteries erected by the Franciscan monks (1717-1823). Generally called missions, they are an interesting architectural feature in Texas, New Mexico, and California. Built of stucco and adobe, or sun-dried brick, they have flat roofs and a façade with a portico and vestibule entrance. Many have simple but finely proportioned columns and bell towers. Patios and courtyards of characteristically Spanish design are popular in both domestic and public architecture.

MODERN ART DEVELOPMENTS IN MEXICO

Pre-Columbian art and architecture furnished the basic inspiration for modern Mexican artists, who have influenced twentieth-century international art. Since the revolution of 1910-1920, the Mexican government has fostered a renaissance in native art which reached its height in 1927 when numerous mural paintings of great size were commissioned for the decoration of public buildings. These frescoes treat of social, historical, and political subjects.

Diego Rivera (1886-   ) and José Clemente Orozco (1883-   ) have courageously expressed their ideas on social questions on their large-scale murals which decorate Mexican schools and public buildings, showing rhythmically moving forms painted in rich, earthy colors. Rivera's murals (1933) depicting the *Conquest of Mexico*, on the walls of the National Palace, Mexico City, show the historic struggles of the past in relation to the problems of present-day Mexico. *Zapatá, the Agrarian Leader,* a nineteenth-century Mexican Indian hero, is shown on one of the most striking panels (Plate 139). At the age of twenty-one years, Rivera exhibited his work in Mexico City (1907) with the result that the State of Vera Cruz offered to send him to study art in Spain. The artist spent thirteen years in European art centers where he was associated with three leaders of modern painting, Picasso, Derain, and

Klee. On returning to his native Mexico (1923), he painted his finest work for the *Ministry of Education and Agricultural School* at Chapingo. Rivera's murals for the *Court of Labor*, Ministry of Education, cover three galleries. They show miners, sugar refiners, men weighing grain, weaving, harvesting sugar cane, and working in iron foundries. Following a visit to Moscow, Rivera became radical in his political views, and his representation of communistic doctrines in the murals which he painted for Radio City, New York, resulted in their withdrawal from public view. His Mexican frescoes had included scenes of rich plutocrats and political bosses at banquets while the poor were shown suffering with hunger. In San Francisco he painted murals for the *School of Fine Arts* and the *Stock Exchange*. The vast frescoes in Detroit, entitled *The Machine,* are representations of the machinery which symbolizes that city.

Although excelling in both lithography and murals, Orozco depicts native Indian folklore and religious themes. His art, however, like de Rivera's shows special concern for social and political reform. Orozco studied architecture at Mexico City, but his interest turned to painting in 1909, when he was commissioned to depict scenes of the Revolution. In his murals there is a structural treatment of form which is almost cubistic, and he also uses large intersecting planes. The *Epic of American Civilization, Modern Migration of the Spirit,* painted for Dartmouth College in 1932, is the largest narrative fresco in America. The *Prometheus* at Pomona College, Claremont, California is a modern interpretation of mythology. *Table of Universal Brotherhood* (Plate 141) in the School for Social Research, New York, emphasizes the need for understanding between races and nations and offers appropriate lessons for peace. Perhaps his best work is on the walls of the *Capitol of Guadalajara,* Mexico. The art of Mexican painters, which is expressed in warm, rich colors and compelling rhythms, is a fusion of the ancient Indian culture and modern art tendencies.

OUTLINE OF THE ART OF THE AMERICAN INDIANS AND OF MEXICO

I. PRE-COLUMBIAN CULTURES: MAYA, INCA, AZTEC, NORTH AMERICAN

TIME: Origin of primitive American peoples estimated at 25,000 to 10,000 years ago. A great migration extended southward. Mayan culture developed with capital at Copan, c. 700 A.D. Toltec culture—c.1000 A.D. Aztec capital at Mexico City, 1370. Spanish conquest of Indians.

BACKGROUND: Stone Age culture developed in Central America with Maya in Guatemala, Honduras, Yucatan. Inca in Peru. Aztec in Mexico. Pueblos in southwest of North America. Indians of the central plains and Pacific Northwest. Maya, an agricultural people who cultivated maize. Cities were centers of religious ceremonials. Gods personified processes of nature. Aztecs carried religious fanaticism to hideous extreme of human sacrifice. Government theocratic. Climate varied from hot and humid tropical lands to cooler temperature in high plateaus. Irrigation practiced where necessary. Spanish conquest greatly affected but did not entirely destroy Indian cultures. Dry climate tended to preserve relics.

ARCHITECTURE: Volcanic rock, limestone, forests offered abundant material for building temples for the gods, palaces for the priests and nobles, and thatched huts for the masses of the people. Pyramid temples were built on high bases with broad steps on each side. Bases of temples were of solid concrete faced with stone. Brilliantly colored decoration of stucco and stone carving covered columns, lintels and walls. Skillful engineering of bridges, reservoirs, and canals.

SCULPTURE: Carved stone, clay, diorite, trachyte, rock crystal, onyx, marble, jade, turquoise was used on buildings, grave monuments, and altars. Huge sculpture in the round shows simple masses. Highly decorated freizes and reliefs cover temples. Rich geometric designs show dragons, tigers, reptiles, and convey symbolic meaning. Monumental carvings of the gods in trachyte have impressive sculptural forms.

PAINTING: Found on frescoes, illustrated manuscripts, and figures on pottery. Conventionalized designs show skill in the use of firm lines in both drawings and paintings. Exterior surfaces of columns, lintels and interior walls were decorated. Bowls and jars of baked clay were brilliantly colored. Totem poles of the Northwest Coast were painted in bright colors.

II. MODERN MEXICAN ART

TIME: A vital art renaissance in Mexico beginning after the Revolution is now apparent. (1910-1947). Mexican art reached its height about 1927 and it continues to be a major influence in world art.

BACKGROUND: Indigenous Indian arts lost during the Spanish domination were not forgotten by the natives. Mixture of French and Italian influences with Indian styles manifested by Mexican artists who studied art in Europe. High artistic worth of Mexican folk art has also been a predominant factor.

PAINTING: Large frescoes were designed to fill government commissions for decoration of public buildings such as the Ministries of Education and Agriculture. The artists formed a league with the object of reviving ancient Indian traditions. Subjects relating to local history revealed powerful spatial design. The use of strong, warm colors predominates in the great frescoes in the Palace of Mexico City.

BIBLIOGRAPHY

Boas, Franz, *Primitive Art* (Harvard University Press, Cambridge, Mass., 1928).

Davis, E. C., *Ancient Americans* (Henry Holt & Co., Inc., N. Y., 1931).

Joyce, T. A., *Central American and West Indian Archeology* (G. P. Putnam's Sons, N. Y., 1916).

———, *Mayan and Mexican Art* (Studio Publications, N. Y., 1927).

Markham, Sir C. R., *The Incas of Peru* (E. P. Dutton & Co., N. Y., 1912).

Means, P. A., *Ancient Civilizations of the Andes* (Charles Scribner's Sons, N. Y., 1931).

Rivera, Diego, *Frescoes*, ed. by Ernestine Evans (Harcourt, Brace & Co., Inc., N. Y., 1929).

———, *Frescoes* (Museum of Modern Art, N. Y., 1933).

Spinden, H. J., *A Study of Maya Art* (Peabody Museum, Cambridge, Mass., 1913).

Thompson, J. E., *Mexico Before Cortez* (Charles Scribner's Sons, N. Y., 1933).

CHAPTER XXI

Art of the United States

I N THE New World real obstacles had to be overcome before native artists could respond to the beauty of natural scenery and environment. Only a short time ago our early settlers, occupied with the struggle of carving a new nation out of a wilderness, had little time to spend on anything but the essential needs of pioneers. Both the Puritans of New England and the Quakers of Pennsylvania served an austere God and were governed by religious scruples which inhibited their enjoyment of color and form; they considered sculpture and painting sinful diversions to be severely frowned upon. Nevertheless, as material prosperity increased the colonists began to relax their prejudices and to indulge in some of the refinements of life. They imported beautiful home furnishings from England and the useful crafts became popular. Virginia, Maryland, and Massachusetts drew ideas from London, but a diversity of foreign influences prevailed in neighboring colonies. New England's furniture had its source in old England; New York's brick houses and crafts resembled those of Amsterdam; the Carolinas and Louisiana turned to the French and Spanish for ideas; whereas Delaware introduced Swedish crafts and patterned log cabins after Swedish cottages.

COLONIAL CRAFTSMEN

The early cabinet-makers, adding a personal touch, created new and beautiful variations to the foreign designs which they adapted to meet needs in America. Notable among these are Connecticut chests and Windsor chairs, the latter a distinctly American creation. Duncan Phyfe (1768-1854), the outstanding cabinet-maker of his

day, came to America from Scotland and settled in New York City
about 1790. He introduced original patriotic motifs such as the
American eagle and stars, representing states of the union. Phyfe's
furniture was distinguished by fine proportions and graceful curves.
Since the early cabinet-makers took pride in their custom-made
furniture and set high standards which influenced American taste,
it is small wonder that in later years when the invention of machinery made mass production possible, Americans demanded the
best, for they had been accustomed to good materials, design, and
workmanship. Naturally, the household crafts were the first to
develop. Glass making was introduced by Henry William Stiegel
(1729-1785), who imported Bavarian workers for his factory in
Pennsylvania where bowls, bottles, and window glass were manufactured. The demand for Stiegel's colonial glass was so great that
it was even exported to Europe. This factory is still in operation.
Beautiful household articles, such as pewter and silver tea and
coffee sets, bowls, candlesticks, and clocks, were additions to colonial homes. Housewives wove coverlets, designed bed-quilts of
patchwork, and made hooked rugs and embroidered samplers. A
delightfully spontaneous early American folk art was developed by
untrained painters who created genre pictures such as *By the Fireside* (Plate 145). This art was for the most part anonymous and
expressed the feeling and interest of the painter in a direct and
forceful though naïve manner.

Paul Revere (1735-1818) was a silversmith, and learned his
trade from his father, a French Huguenot. Revere's punch bowls,
tea and coffee sets, designed in the Georgian style, are distinguished
for their simplicity and beauty of proportion and are fine examples
of the silversmith's art. He also worked in pewter, an alloy commonly used in Colonial days, and known as the poor man's silver.
Although Revere engraved the pretentious *Boston Massacre* he was
also glad to use his burin to make collars for the dogs of his Boston
neighbors.

COLONIAL PORTRAITURE

The demand for family portraits came later in New England
than in the royalist colonies of Virginia, Maryland, and the Caro-

linas, where provincial life was more closely modeled after that of the mother country. Cavalier planters who desired to hand down family portraits admired the work of the English painters Reynolds, Gainsborough, and Romney.

The first American portrait artists were anonymous painters who traveled about in the colonies rendering the likenesses of the more prosperous settlers. Although they were called limners and face-painters, it was often necessary for them to supplement their income by painting coaches, carriage wheels, or inn signs. At least four hundred of these "primitives," such as *Baby in Red High Chair*, painted about 1790 are now in the collections of historical societies and museums throughout the country (Plate 144). Among these painters may be mentioned John Simbert, who came to Boston from Edinburgh around 1720 to paint the portraits of those who desired to be "limned." The severity of his style was appropriate for the rendering of the New England divines who sat for some of his best-known portraits. Visiting artists from abroad sometimes instructed the native artists, but there were many, like Robert Feke, who were entirely self-taught.

EARLY PAINTERS—WEST, COPLEY, STUART

Benjamin West (1738-1820), a Quaker, born in Philadelphia, displayed a talent for drawing at an early age. He journeyed to Italy to visit the "cradle of art" and remained for three years. Later he traveled to England where he decided to make his permanent home, in 1765. He maintained a large studio in London where he cordially received young Americans who went abroad to study art, at times offering them financial assistance. West was appointed court painter for George III, who regarded the artist with affection and the highest esteem. The Royal Academy was established in 1767 by the king and at his suggestion West had the honor of being its first president. West's paintings were not all historical or religious subjects, for he also rendered excellent portraits. The *Death of General Wolfe After the Capture of Quebec*, a large historic panorama, shows a group of British soldiers in the uniforms worn at that time—not in the usual classical robes (Plate 146).

The realistic painting of these uniforms was condemned by artists and critics alike when the picture was first shown, but many authorities, including Sir Joshua Reynolds, later retracted their objections. The king also favored West's use of contemporary costume. Historical paintings thereafter were presented with such factual details.

John Singleton Copley (1737-1815) also went to live in England where he became a distinguished and popular portrait painter. Prior to settling in London, the artist spent some time in Italy and while there he painted the portraits of *Mr. and Mrs. Izzard,* a South Carolina planter and his wife. The sincerity and truth and fine characterization of Copley's work compensates for any technical difficulties the artist may have experienced with his drawing. If Copley's style is somewhat formal, his texture painting of silk and lace in the portrait of *Mrs. Seymour Fort* is remarkably realistic (Plate 147).

Another of West's American students who gained fame in London was Gilbert Stuart (1755-1828). After establishing himself as a successful portrait painter, he later returned to America to live. Stuart was an unusually gifted painter; his skill in reproducing the richness of flesh tones, the painting of textures, and the placing of his models in natural poses gives him first rank among early American painters. The best-known of his portraits is the so-called *Athenaeum Portrait* of George Washington in the Museum of Fine Arts, Boston. He was known as the portrayer of George Washington, whom he painted from life only three times. Nevertheless, his admiration and affection for the General was such that he left more than a hundred replicas of the three portraits. The "Athenaeum" portrait was always kept in his studio. It is said that he promised it to Martha Washington when it was completed. This probably accounts for its unfinished condition; he did not want to part with it. Stuart's aim was to reveal the character of his sitters, and to this end he studied his subject long and critically, always centering his interest on the head, to which he subordinated all accessories and details. These characteristics are exemplified in his portrait of *Mrs. Perez Morton* (Plate 148).

PORTRAIT, HISTORY, AND GENRE ARTISTS

Charles Willson Peale (1741-1827), a captain of volunteers, accompanied Washington on his campaigns and fought at the Battle of Trenton. He first painted Washington at Mount Vernon before the Revolution and later portrayed him with Lafayette in a group portrait. Here Washington was attired in impressive military regalia. It is fortunate for posterity that Peale rendered these wartime portraits of Washington, who was then in his forties, for Stuart did not know him until twenty years later. Peale was a prolific artist whose works include such portraits of leaders as *Benjamin Franklin,* now to be seen in Pennsylvania Academy, Philadelphia (Plate 147).

John Trumbull (1756-1843) participated in the war and served on Washington's staff. He fought in the Battle of Bunker Hill which episode he later painted (Plate 146). He is remembered chiefly, however, for two heroic works: *The Signing of the Declaration of Independence* and *Surrender at Yorktown,* both painted in the grand manner reminiscent of West. He also painted four scenes from American history in the Rotunda of the National Capitol.

Caleb Bingham's (1811-1879) *Fur Traders Descending the Missouri* displays an atmospheric painting of the effects of early morning fog and sunlight in a manner far in advance of the artist's time (Plate 150).

HUDSON RIVER LANDSCAPES

In the nineteenth century, Americans began to awaken to an appreciation of the natural beauty and scenic wonders of their country. Native artists, in romantic mood, interpreted such aspects of nature as a thunderstorm, darkness of the forest, or a waterfall. Washington Irving's *Sketch Book,* which includes "The Legend of Sleepy Hollow," shows a similar trend in popular literature. These artists are known as the Hudson River School because many of them painted in the Catskills or on the banks of the Hudson River. This period before the Civil War represents an important development in American landscape painting. Nevertheless, the Hudson

River painters were overshadowed by their nineteenth-century successors, who looked upon them as somewhat old-fashioned. The Chicago Art Institute's exhibition in 1945, showing works of the Hudson River School, did much to restore these artists to their rightful place as founders of American landscape art.

One of the leaders of this group was Washington Allston (1779-1843), who developed a majestic landscape style. *Elijah Fed by the Ravens* was conceived with dramatic intensity and grandeur (Plate 149). His heroic canvases show idyllic though somewhat artificial landscapes. Thomas Cole (1801-1848) carried landscape painting into broader and richer channels. His large paintings of the rugged Catskills, White Mountains, and Connecticut Valley are quite impressive. Somewhat different was the sytle of Asher B. Durand (1796-1886), whose impressive allegorical pictures *Morning of Life* and *Evening of Life* have great distinction. Another noteworthy artist was Frederick Church (1826-1900), a pupil of Thomas Cole who traveled extensively, painting vast panoramas showing the Andes Mountains, icebergs of Labrador, the Rocky Mountains, Pacific Coast scenes, and Mediterranean views. *In the Catskills* combines realism with picturesque beauty. Many other artists expressed their interpretations of nature, believing that man's individuality is best developed by sympathy for his environment. Although most of these men had meager technical training, they traveled abroad, obtaining ideas which they expressed in their own way. Following the Civil War landscape art became sentimental and dull, for the artists painted in sombre, dry color and their compositions lacked unity.

AUDUBON, THE NATURALIST

John J. Audubon (1785-1851), the ornithologist and naturalist, was born in New Orleans. After studying art in Paris, he returned to America, and settled in Pennsylvania in 1813. His magnificent life-size water-colors of hundreds of birds were exhibited in London together with his publication of a text entitled *Birds of America*, which was an authoritative contribution to the knowledge of bird life. Audubon Bird Reservations and Societies, formed to preserve and protect birds, were named in honor of the great naturalist-painter. There has been a recent revival of popular interest in his remarkable bird paintings (Plate 150) and engravings.

GEORGE INNESS; ALBERT RYDER

It was inevitable that new methods of painting should develop when George Inness (1825-1894) returned from France where he studied the landscape art of the French Barbizon school—notably that of Corot. He brought fresh vitality to American art. In *Home of the Heron* he painted the light-effects with a mastery of atmospheric tonality (Plate 149). In *Coming Storm* he conveys the nearness of nature in one of its intimate moods. *Peace and Plenty* shows the serenity and beauty of familiar things as well as the vastness and fertility of his native land. Inness was a painter who did not merely record external nature; instead, he attempted to convey its inward or spiritual realities. The paintings of Albert P. Ryder (1847-1917) are unique expressions of dreams, visions, and phantoms. His method, ultra-modern and intensely individual, uses the minimum of reliance on accurate visual symbols. He often ignores the elements of perspective and uses distortion to heighten the drama of his message. In *Death on a Pale Horse* an air of mystery is enhanced by weird color and the simple outlines of the phantom horse, the bare hillside, and windswept fields (Plate 151). The mood is intensified by the contrasting values in a low key which also give power to the design.

HOMER'S MARINE ART

Winslow Homer (1836-1910), working in both oils and water color, enriched American painting with his independent vision, forceful realism, and untraditional style. Homer's place in American art is assured not only by his paintings but by the journalistic drawings he did for periodicals during the early years of his life. Such drawings, which were largely replaced by photographs after the development of photography, form an important body in the

Union Soldiers Playing Football in Camp. Winslow Homer, in *Harper's Weekly*, July, 1865.

heritage of the graphic arts. In Homer's case, his drawings of the Civil War make an interesting contrast to the magnificent camera documents of the war made by Brady and other early photographers. Homer's paintings never rose far above an illustrative realism, and in this the American artist failed to reach the heights achieved by the great French journalistic draftsman and painter, Daumier. His interpretation of the *Maine Coast* is remarkable for its power and depth. Homer's ability to record the movement of ocean waves against strong, dark rocks, the roar of breakers, the force, magnitude, and mystery of water, and the grandeur of the sea, painted in all kinds of weather, has seldom if ever been equalled. *All's Well* and *Northeaster* and *Herring Net* (Plate 155) portray the life of fisher-folk living by the sea. His realistic painting of the ponderous movement of the ocean combined with his majesty of style brought acclaim at the Paris exhibition of his works in 1900. In comparison with Ryder, who painted dreams and visions, Winslow Homer expressed with reality and force the varied moods of nature.

AMERICAN ARTISTS WORKING ABROAD: WHISTLER, CASSATT, SARGENT

Born in Lowell, Massachusetts, James McNeill Whistler (1834-1903) lived most of his life in Italy, Paris, and London. Nevertheless, the independent spirit with which he fought for his ideals and convictions was typically American. His work incensed John Ruskin, the renowned art critic of London, who said that Whistler's paintings looked as though he had "thrown a pot of paint on the canvas." The controversy caused by this remark resulted in a London court trial in which the artist was awarded a farthing for damages. In his best-known portrait, *My Mother*, the forceful, calm, old lady posed in profile quietly meditates as she sits with hands folded and her feet upon a footstool. His *Portrait of Carlyle*, also treated in broad, simple masses which form a tonal harmony of grays and blacks, is a revealing study of character. In *At the Piano* gradations of tone are subtly related and the color harmonies are exquisite. The interesting line direction of some of the decorative patterns in Whistler's compositions are reminiscent of the Japanese prints he admired. Etching also claimed Whistler's attention. The *Thames Series* and *Scenes of Venice* rank among his best works. *The Pacific* is a notable example of marine art (Plate 154).

Mary Cassatt (1845-1926), was another American painter trained abroad. The delightful portrayal of feminine youth, *In the Loge*, shows her style of visual painting, rare color, vigorous brush-work and strongly planned composition (Plate 157). Although Miss Cassatt's work was influenced by that of Degas and Manet, it was her uniquely personal absorption of nineteenth-century innovations and her creative interpretation of feminine subjects which constitute her contribution to art.

John Singer Sargent (1856-1925), the portrait painter, was born in Italy of American parents, and, like Whistler, lived abroad. His admiration for the realistic technique of Velazquez and Goya led to the development of a similar skill in brush-handling. Sargent's brilliant style is seen in his portrait *Madame X* (Plate 152). Here, energetic brush-strokes, emphatic accents and simple but effective pose combine to produce the verve typical of Sargent. Sargent's dashing style of painting won many patrons who paid high prices for his skill. It was his skillful texture painting, light effects, and the elegant ease in the poses of aristocratic patrons which made him a popular painter. His art, based on the factual, accurately records the outward appearance, whereas Whistler's is characterized by a decorative style and psychological penetration.

THE REALISM OF THOMAS EAKINS

Although he studied extensively abroad, Thomas Eakins (1844-1916) returned to live in America. He painted with vigorous realism, combining keen, intellectual perception with amazing accuracy of observation. He specialized in the study of anatomy, which, together with a command of three-dimensional form, resulted in a remarkable portrayal of objective reality. A characteristic example is *The Agnew Clinic*. Such portraits as *The Thinker* are penetrating character studies. Another work, *Lady with a Setter Dog*, shows Eakins' skill as a portrait painter (Plate 153). His uncompromising accuracy of observation links him to Homer, while in his individualism and independence he is akin to Ryder. Although somewhat neglected during his life, Eakins is now regarded as a great artist. His influence was greatly felt by a group of younger artists, including Robert Henri (1865-1929), John Sloan (1871-), and George Luks (1867-1933), who admired the objectivity of his work. These men painted their version of the American scene with vitality, courage, and humor, in such characteristic works as *Old Clown Making Up* (Plate 155), *Fifth Avenue, Dance Hall*, or *City Slums*. George Bellows (1882-1925) dramatically painted prize fighters, *Men of the Docks, Polo Crowd*, and *The Circus* (Plate 154).

CONTEMPORARY ARTISTS

Following the decline of impressionism and the rise of post-impressionism, American art developed a search for the solidity of form as exemplified by the French master, Cézanne. Among many capable artists who are painting their environment and time with sincerity are John Marin (1875-   ), and Charles Burchfield (1893-   ). Marin's *On Morse Mountain* and Burchfield's *Ice Glare* are typical works (Plates 158 and 156). Thomas Benton (1889-1947) has produced strong mural compositions having spatial depth and spirited subject-matter. His easel painting, *The Meal*, is a representative work (Plate 157). Grant Wood (1892-1942), who has been associated with the mid-west, shows true insight in his *American Gothic* (Plate 156). His landscapes show three-dimensional forms arranged in a rhythmical decorative style. Benton's murals are brilliant in color, and dramatic in the arrangement of forms. Rockwell Kent (1882-   ), who says, "I cannot trust myself to paint what I see . . . I paint only what I remember," depicts desolate, frozen wastes or lonely shacks at nightfall, all rendered in a clean-cut technique reminiscent of his wood-block prints.

PIONEER SCULPTURE

The earliest American sculptors carved figure-heads for the sailing ships; later patriotic impulses brought a demand for statues and monuments to commemorate American heroes and patriots. Some of the early statues of Washington were those made by Houdon of France, among them a bust at Mount Vernon and a statue in the Rotunda of the Capitol at Richmond, Virginia; both are realistic likenesses. In the nineteenth century there was a revival of sculpture.

SAINT GAUDENS—THE IDEAL SCULPTOR

Augustus Saint Gaudens (1848-1907), born in Dublin, was brought to America as an infant. At the age of twenty he went to Paris to study. His early work, *Memorial to Admiral Farragut*, represents the hero in alert posture, with feet somewhat spread apart as though he were on the swaying deck of his ship. The base on which the figure stands was designed by the architect Stanford White. Showing the strength and character of the great man, Saint Gaudens' masterly portrait statue of *Lincoln*, in Lincoln Park, Chicago, is an impressive memorial. Here the dignified, pensive Lincoln stands before the chair of state. It has been described as "The glorification of the common man, the apotheosis of democracy." A replica of the statue was presented to Great Britain by this country in 1920 to commemorate one hundred years of friendship between the two nations.

ARCHITECTURAL SCULPTURE

Modern American sculptors have simplified their expression and restored to sculpture a certain monumental character, a trend which is exemplified in Daniel Chester French's (1850-1931) portrait statue of *Lincoln* in the Lincoln Memorial, Washington. This large seated statue, more than twenty feet high, is perfectly suited to its architectural background. The brooding figure symbolizes the strong and sympathetic character of the great leader.

Lorado Taft's (1860-1936) *Fountain of the Great Lakes* in Grant Park, Chicago, shows a group of five bronze figures in classical style, each holding a water-filled shell representing one of the five Great Lakes. His concrete statue of *Blackhawk,* a blanketed Indian chief, stands forty-eight feet high on a bluff near Oregon, Illinois, with head thrown back, gazing across the vast landscape which had been his hunting ground. Gutzon Borglum (1871-1941) carved from marble a heroic head of *Lincoln* for the Rotunda of the Capitol, Washington. The work of Paul Manship (1885-   ) shows the influence of Archaic Greek and Oriental sculpture as exemplified in his decorative works such as *Antelope, Indian Hunter, Playfulness.*

COLONIAL ARCHITECTURE

The first American settlers built churches and public buildings of timber, which was more plentiful than stone or brick. Southern plantation homes were constructed of wood. George Washington, a "gentleman builder," designed his spacious mansion, *Mount Vernon,* with a low veranda of eight slender pillars surmounted by a cornice which gives the structure a strong horizontal emphasis (Plate 159). Thomas Jefferson designed *Monticello,* with its Doric portico. Architecture was a major interest of Jefferson. The popularity of his designs for the *University of Virginia* (Plate 160) and the *State House, Richmond,* encouraged the use of the classical style later seen in countless structures.

The Georgian architectural style, originated by Sir Christopher Wren, derived its name from the Georges during whose reign it was popular. Imported in the eighteenth century, this style combines the dignity of the classic with the charm and elegance of the Renaissance. It is characterized by stately regularity of spacing, carved cornices, decorative pilasters, and interiors of spacious elegance. The southern version is exemplified in the mansion *Westover* and the *Governor's Palace* at Williamsburg in Virginia, whereas *Independence Hall,* Philadelphia represents the northern adaptation (Plate 159).

ADAPTATIONS OF CLASSICAL STYLES

Following the Revolution there was a renewed interest in building. The classical style was dominant in civic and domestic structures. The first professional architect in America, Charles Bulfinch (1763-1844), designed the *Massachusetts State House,* Boston. The French architect Benjamin Latrobe (1764-1820) came at Washington's request to take charge of building additions to the Capitol. Among Latrobe's work there is the semicircular *Statuary Hall,* famous for its echo. Latrobe's classical design for the *United States Bank, Philadelphia,* became the model for similar structures. Classical porticoed buildings soon appeared in various parts of the country such as the *Taft House* in Cincinnati, the *Cotton House* built over a hundred years ago in Green Bay, Wisconsin, and the *Lanier House* of Indiana, both of which are now state museums.

Classic architecture held sway until its spell was broken by Henry H. Richardson (1838-1886), who had studied abroad. He pioneered in adapting the Romanesque style in his design for *Trinity Church, Boston.* He also adapted the sturdy, round arches, robust mouldings, and heavy roofs to other types of structures.

AMERICAN-RENAISSANCE ARCHITECTURE

McKim, Mead, and White employed the American-Renaissance style in many structures, including the *Boston Public Library.* Cram, Goodhue, and Ferguson adapted the old Gothic principles to the more modern construction of the *Cathedral of Saint John the Divine,* New York. The *Nebraska State Capitol,* Lincoln, the last building designed by Goodhue, is a departure from the domed style of state capitol which has been traditional in America (Plate 160). It has a plain tower rising from a low, wide base. Here is a complete adaptation of architectural design to the civic needs and functions of present-day life.

OUTLINE OF ART IN THE UNITED STATES

TIME: Colonial period to the 20th century.

BACKGROUND: Puritans and Quakers had religious scruples, inhibiting to the development of art. Gradually, home furnishings and paintings imported from England and the Continent inspired native artists to create beautiful works of their own. Anonymous traveling artists painted portraits of prosperous citizens. After the vast territorial expansion and growth of wealth, native artists studied in Paris, returning later to paint the American scene.

ARCHITECTURE: Classic ideals expressed by Thomas Jefferson in Virginia were continued in American architecture until 1850 when certain architects developed original variants of the Renaissance style, especially in the state capitols with Renaissance domes. Later, the French Renaissance styles were used in 5th Avenue, N. Y., mansions. Romanesque and Gothic were used in popular adaptations for churches, colleges and mansions.

SCULPTURE: In colonial days this art was negligible although wood-carvers made figureheads for ships. Occasionally prosperous citizens or civic leaders commissioned statues, memorials, or tombs which were elaborated with sculpture. In the 19th century native sculptors created superior portrait sculpture, reliefs and monumental works. Modern sculptors have achieved a complete unity with architectural forms.

PAINTING: Portrait painting, genre art, and mural painting has flourished since colonial days in America. A strong native landscape school developed 1815-1913. The technique of impressionism, learned in Paris, became popular. Varied styles were followed and many artists were realists, others became mystics and abstractionists. No one style predominated. The "American Scene" is a popular subject. An important influence in American art came from the French painter, Cézanne. The growth of museums and the encouragement given artists by civic groups and the government are responsible.

BIBLIOGRAPHY

BOSWELL, Peyton, *American Painting* (Dodd, Mead & Co., N. Y., 1939).

CAFFIN, C. H., *American Masters of Sculpture* (Doubleday & Co., Garden City, N. Y., 1913).

——, *Story of American Painting* (F. A. Stokes Co., N. Y., 1909).

CAHILL, Holger, and BARR, Alfred H. Jr., *Art in America in Modern Times* (Reynal & Hitchcock, Inc., N. Y., 1934).

EBERLEIN, H. D., *The Architecture of Colonial America* (Little Brown & Co., Boston, 1915).

——, and McCLURE, Abbot, *The Practical Book of Early American Arts and Crafts* (J. P. Lippincott Co., Philadelphia, 1916).

EDGELL, G. H., *American Architecture of Today* (Charles Scribner's Sons, N. Y., 1928).

GOODRICH, Lloyd, *Thomas Eakins* (Whitney Museum, N. Y., 1934).

HAMLIN, T. F., *The American Spirit in Architecture* (Yale University Press, New Haven, 1926).

ISHAM, Samuel, *History of American Painting* (The Macmillan Co., N. Y., 1927).

JACKMAN, Rilla Evelyn, *American Arts* (Rand, McNally Co., Chicago, 1928).

KIMBALL, Fiske, *American Architecture* (Bobbs-Merrill Co., Indianapolis, 1928).

LA FOLLETTE, Suzanne, *Art in America* (Harper & Bros., N. Y., 1930).

NEUHAUS, Eugen, *The History and Ideals of American Art* (Stanford University Press, Palo Alto, 1931).

PRICE, Frederic Newlin, *Ryder: A Study in Appreciation.*

SHERMAN, Frederick Fairchild, *Early American Painting* (The Century Co., Inc., N. Y., 1932).

SULLIVAN, Louis, *The Autobiography of an Idea* (W. W. Norton & Co., Inc., N. Y., 1927).

TAFT, Lorado, *History of American Sculpture* (The Macmillan Co., N. Y., 1930).

TALMADGE, Thomas, *Story of Architecture in America* (W. W. Norton & Co., Inc., N. Y., 1927).

CHAPTER XXII

French Art

THE Gothic influence persisted in France through the fifteenth century. By mid-century, however, so many churches had been erected that there was little need for ecclesiastical architecture. The now powerful kings gave their attention to the construction of châteaux and palaces. The wing of the *Château Blois,* built by Francis I (1494-1547), combines Italian and French-Renaissance architectural forms (Plate 161). Most notable is the projecting, polygonal staircase with oblique railings which rise in gradual ascent. Friezes are elaborately carved and the railings contain medallions of heraldric motives. Large niches have statues and gargoyles jutting from the roof. The stairway is a distinctly French feature as are the many mullioned windows and the steep roof. The classical façade is reminiscent of the Italian manner showing pilasters, pediments, columns, galleries, and loggia. When Francis I moved his capital to Paris, he built his palace at *Fontainebleu* and commenced the *Palace of the Louvre*—which Napoleon later converted into an art gallery. Francis also collected Italian paintings and employed Italian painters and sculptors to adorn his palaces. Leonardo and Raphael were among the artists who came to France at his request.

THE "ERA OF GREAT KINGS"

When Louis, the "Sun King" (1638-1715), ascended the throne at the age of twenty-three, France was already strong and unified. Authority once centered in the church was now vested in the state, and the power of Louis XIV who declared, "I am the State," was absolute. He allowed the Huguenots to be persecuted and the peasants to be exploited to support the indigent nobility who spent their time in frivolity and court ceremonial. France, become the most powerful country in Europe, gradually weakened under the reigns of the dissolute Louis XV (1710-1774) and the incompetent Louis XVI (1754-1793), whose reign terminated in the terror of the French Revolution. During the "Era of Great Kings," however, Paris had become a handsome city with wide boulevards and vast palaces.

Louis XIV employed both native and Italian artists and architects to collaborate with the French painter, Lebrun, in the designing and construction of the *Palace of Versailles* (Plate 161). This Renaissance structure, set amid terraced gardens ornamented with statues and sculptured fountains, was a fitting monument to Louis' glory and a fine setting for the pomp and ceremony of his court. To accomplish the king's plans to make Paris the art center of the world, his able minister, Colbert, together with Lebrun, founded the *Académie des Beaux Arts*.

The furnishings of châteaux and palaces were embellished with gilded reliefs, carvings and inlays of tortoise shell, metal, and precious woods. Much admired were the Sèvres porcelains. The famous Gobelin works manufactured tapestries with realistic designs showing flowers, animals, figures, and castles set against landscape backgrounds. These remarkable textiles gave a feeling of warmth and color to walls of plaster or stone. Enormous fireplaces reaching almost to the ceiling were the focal points of interest in the great halls. The straight or slightly curved lines of the strong massive furniture of the Louis XIV period gradually gave way to a lighter more intimate rococo style with less restrained curves, a type of ornamentation that appealed to the frivolous feminine-dominated court of Louis XV. Nevertheless, despite Italian refinements and an outward show of elegance there were no such comforts as the effective heating systems or adequate sanitary facilities which the inhabitants of early Crete or ancient Rome enjoyed.

The style known as Empire reflected Napoleon's enthusiasm for Roman architecture and classical decorations, such as are exemplified in the *Pantheon of Paris*, the *Church of the Madeleine*, and the *Arc de Triomphe*—triumphal arch—erected in 1806-1836

(Plate 162). The exterior of the *Madeleine* is reminiscent of a Corinthian temple.

FRENCH SCULPTORS

One of the most important French sculptors of the Renaissance was Jean Goujon (1510?-1568). The *Fountain of the Innocents* is perhaps his most famous work (Plate 163). Designed to stand near Saint Denis cemetery in Paris, the fountain was moved in the eighteenth century to the new market place of Paris. The elongated nymphs carved in low relief on the fountain are in the naturalistic Italian manner.

During the eighteenth and nineteenth centuries sculpture was not confined to the ornamentation of palaces. A new demand had arisen for a civic art which would express the national spirit. François Rude (1784-1855), working in the emotional romantic style, carved his well-known group entitled *Departure of the Volunteers* for the *Arc de l'Étoile* in Paris.

Antoine Louis Barye (1796-1875) devoted most of his efforts to animal sculpture, which hitherto had not been practiced as a separate art. In *Theseus and the Minotaur* (Plate 162) the sculptor departs from his usual naturalistic style. Here Barye uses simple rhythmic forms in a way we associate with work of later artists such as Manship.

The last of the great romantic sculptors was Auguste Rodin (1840-1917) who worked in two different styles: the first naturalistic, pictorial and dramatic; the second, known as his unfinished style. To the former belongs the *Thinker,* a realistic minutely detailed work, anatomically correct and emotionally expressive. In his more poetic and impressionistic style he avoids strong contour lines and emphasizes the play of light over the undulating surfaces. In Rodin's sculpture *By the Sea* there is definite contrast between the roughly chiseled stone background and the polished surface of the girl's form (Plate 163).

EARLY FRENCH PAINTING

Painting in the form of murals was employed as architectural ornamentation. Portraits and smaller easel paintings both religious and secular, also appeared. A formal and delicately refined religious painting of the fifteenth century is a *Pièta* by an unknown artist called the Master of Avignon, who worked in a style reminiscent of the Sienese (Plate 164). Here the grief-stricken Madonna, seated between John and Mary Magdalene, holds the limp body of the dead Christ, while the donor who is included at the left, kneels humbly in a prayerful attitude. All are set against a gold background ornamented with tooled and raised inscriptions or designs such as borders and a faint suggestion of the towers of Jerusalem. Deep but restrained emotion is shown by a contrast of light-dark and in the controlled movement of the figures which participate in the dramatic scene.

Among the early French portrait painters who recorded the likenesses of their sitters with remarkable skill and their garments with meticulous attention to multitudinous detail, were the Fouquets and the Clouets. Jehan Fouquet (c.1420-c.1477) painted the *Virgin and Child* which hangs in the Antwerp Museum. Jean Clouet, (fl. c.1516-1546), known as the Elder Clouet because his son François was also an artist, painted the gracious portrait of *Charlotte of France* which may be seen in the Art Institute at Chicago (Plate 164). Here the hard clear-cut lines characteristic of the *Pièta* have given way to softer broad areas of dark and light. *Diane of Poitiers,* attributed to François (1500?-1572), is now in the Worcester Museum.

PAINTING IN THE SEVENTEENTH CENTURY

Two traditions developed in French painting of the seventeenth century: a democratic expression of the life of the people as exemplified in *Peasant Family* by Louis le Nain (1593-1648), and an aristocratic style derived from the classical art of Italy. In a sense, the two schools, depicting common people on the one hand and court life on the other, were prophetic of the collision of opposing political forces which precipitated the French Revolution.

The landscape painting of Nicolas Poussin (1594-1665) and Claude Lorraine (1600-1682) formed the background of French art of the seventeenth century. Both were native Frenchmen who spent most of their time in Rome. The intellectual, meditative Poussin came of a poor but noble family who lived in Normandy, while the impulsive and almost illiterate Claude was born of humble parents in the Duchy of Lorraine.

Using classic ruins as an exotic setting for numerous figures illustrating historical or mythological incidents borrowed from the legendary lore of Greece and Rome, Poussin developed a panoramic style. Painted in the grand manner is *Shepherds of Arcadia* (Plate 165). *Diogenes Throwing Away his Bowl*, somewhat formal and coldly classical in style, may be seen at the Art Institute in Chicago. In contrast, Claude's landscapes are infused with a poetic beauty and romantic feeling for nature as in *Figures on the Bank of a Stream* (Plate 165). Goddesses and shepherds are posed amid classical ruins, among hills, groves, rocks or beside flowing streams, irrespective of meaning of even appropriateness. The warm glow of a mellow light, which is his special charm, may be seen in *Landscape with a Piping Shepherd, Cleopatra Landing at Tarsus,* and *Seaport at Sunset.* There was an immediate popular response to Claude's works and commissions came in from various parts of the world.

WATTEAU; BOUCHER; FRAGONARD

A lowly-born genius of the eighteenth century was Antoine Watteau (1684-1721). Destined by his father to be a carpenter, the youth, with high hopes of becoming an artist, tramped all the way from Valenciennes to Paris, where he lived in poverty and semi-starvation until a Paris dealer employed him to paint religious pictures. Later as a theatrical scene painter, he became assistant to the manager of the Luxembourg Palace. Looking out upon the gardens he saw graceful lords in colorful array and ladies dressed in elegant costumes with bouffant skirts and powdered hair, masquerading as shepherds and shepherdesses, gesticulating, bowing, or waving their fans. The lonely artist caught the spirit of their laughter and make-believe and with the magic of his art he wound a fanciful garland of beauty and gaiety about the lives of the pampered court favorites as shown in *Danse dans un pavillon de jardin* (Plate 166). Watteau's *Fêtes,* as these gay pictures were called, proved to be a fortunate turning point in his career. When the exquisite quality of his art was at last appreciated he had only a short time to enjoy the acclaim now freely accorded, for he was a victim of tuberculosis and constantly aware of impending death.

Watteau's *Embarkation for the Island of Cythera* depicts a fanciful voyage of lovers to an imaginary isle dedicated to Venus. His *Gilles* is a sympathetic study of a comedian. Like Daumier, Watteau took a lively interest in depicting the strolling comedians who were an important part of the theatrical life of Watteau's day.

Inspired by Watteau, François Boucher (1703-1770) and Jean Honoré Fragonard (1732-1806) also painted pastoral and allegorical scenes enlivened with gay lords and ladies amid Arcadian settings. A spirit of revelry and frolic is seen in Boucher's *Cupid a Captive* and Fragonard's *The Swing.* A delicately lyric gaiety pervades Fragonard's "The Artist," a detail from his painting *The Lover Crowned* (Plate 166). Foliage, roses, silks and satins form the setting against which Fragonard, with rare draftsmanship and color, painted this enchanting and fanciful interpretation for Madame du Barry.

GREUZE; CHARDIN

During the reign of Louis XVI the promised "deluge" broke over France. When infuriated masses revolted from the long-endured oppression, beheaded the nobles, and put an end to the frivolities of Versailles, a new art expression was required for a new era dominated by revolutionary impulses. Diderot, the art critic and literary authority of the day, denounced the art of Boucher and Fragonard as being licentious and frivolous and decreed that pictures should preach morals and encourage such virtues as benevolence, kindness, and charity. By an order of Napoleon, Fragonard was ousted from his luxurious quarters in the Louvre. Democratic subjects and genre scenes illustrating the moral philosophy of Jean Jacques Rousseau become popular. Jean Baptiste Greuze (1725-1805) acquired fame and popularity by exhibiting works like the *Paternal Curse,* a sermon in paint, and *A Father Explains the Bible to His Family.* He also painted pictures of sentimental young girls such as the *Broken Pitcher* now in the Louvre.

With sound craftsmanship and a feeling for fine design, Jean Baptiste Chardin (1699-1779) rendered interiors and genre scenes which set a high standard for realistic painting. Employing unpretentious subject-matter, such as that of the *House of Cards,* entirely divorced from the fashionable world that was painted by Watteau and Fragonard, he entered a field in which he has rarely if ever been surpassed (Plate 167). *Grace Before Meat* shows a skillful rendition of the beautiful textures of common things.

DAVID; INGRES; GROS

Napoleon made Jacques Louis David (1748-1825) the official artist of France. Declaring that the only proper subjects of art were those derived from the history or mythology of Greece and Rome, David, who became a real dictator of art in all its forms, inaugurated the reign of classicism; "patriotic" subject-matter was presented through the depiction of dramatic incidents in the lives of the old Romans. *Youth with a Horse* is an excellent example of David's use of a dramatic pose and his careful drawing of sculpturesque anatomical forms by employing forced lighting to create strong cast shadows (Plate 168). He added cool coloring merely to complete the obviously posed picture. David had no comprehension of the integrating or functional use of color.

A greater technician than his teacher was Jean Auguste Dominique Ingres (1780-1867), David's most famous pupil, and one of the most subtle draftsmen in the history of art. In portraits and such paintings as *Madame Rivière,* and *Portrait of a Gentleman* (Plate 167), distinguished by linear grace, Ingres emphasized beauty of form. Modeling with true classical restraint, he gave little attention to the structural quality of color.

Baron Antoine Jean Gros (1771-1835), another pupil of David, painted many battle scenes for Napoleon and recorded subjects of contemporary life and such unusual aspects of nature as the smoke of conflagrations, snow, and blizzards. The stern reality of the *Pest of Jaffa* is characteristic of his exotic subject-matter and romantic appeal. When David went into exile he selected Gros to be his successor, but being in sympathy with the romantic movement and the revolt of the young French artists against the doctrine of authority, Gros found it impossible to continue in David's tradition. Upset by conflicting emotions, he ended his life by casting himself in the Seine River.

GÉRICAULT

Art as well as literature was now coming under a new influence conducive to heightened emotions. Everyone was reading the romantic authors, Wordsworth, Goethe, Schiller, Dante, Shakespeare, Scott, and Byron. The public had grown weary of pictures about Greece and Rome, and the artists themselves were seeking more vital subject-matter. The first definite assertion of revolt from formal classical painting came when the young artist Théodore Géricault (1791-1824) claimed the right to choose his own means of expression and to paint the world as he saw it. His *Raft of Medusa*, founded upon the true account of a shipwreck described in the Paris newspapers, created a sensation in the exhibition of 1819. Géricault's spirited studies of animals as *Riderless Races at Rome* shows his early interest in the study of photographic movement in painting (Plate 168). His concern with the effects of movement have been demonstrated also in his many paintings of the races in England. By study of anatomy and momentary poses he achieved naturalistic effects. Géricault placed his animal forms in a convincing natural setting well adapted to the element of movement involved in the picture.

DELACROIX

Eugène Delacroix (1789-1863), the leader of the French Romantic movement of painting, achieved a highly personal use of pigment which permitted him to convey emotional effects of great intensity with colors keyed higher than the dull tones commonly used. Delacroix gained a new concept of the use of color from the canvases of Constable, and this he utilized to depict the richly exotic life he observed during an artistic sojourn in Morocco and North Africa. Like Ingres, Chassériau, and others of the day, he delighted in portraying sinuous ladies of the harem and fiery Arabs on their horses. His religious paintings of scenes from the life of Christ are full of dramatic feeling and vigorous movement. Among his paintings were the *Massacre of Scio, Arab Phantasy* and *Liberty Leading the People* (Plate 170). Delacroix gave vitality and movement to dramatic themes suggestive of stirring times or life in distant places.

Though modern regard is somewhat tempered by Delacroix's preoccupation with overdramatic effects and illustrative art, his often superb color, stemming from the Venetians and Rubens, and his mastery of draftsmanship assure continuing interest in his work. In addition to his production in the visual arts, Delacroix also left an imposing literary legacy. His *Journals* record not only the activity of a fruitful, turbulent life, but share with such documents as the *Notebooks* of Leonardo da Vinci the rare distinction of being articulate about the purposes and mechanics of the practicing artist.

THE BARBIZON PAINTERS

In contrast to the classical panoramic scenes of Poussin and Claude, the romanticists developed an intimate style of landscape which was inspired by the poetry of Wordsworth. A group known as the "Men of 1830" went to live in Barbizon, at the edge of the lovely forest of Fountainbleau about thirty-five miles from Paris. This forest had been the hunting grounds of the kings of France. Among the group who went there to devote their lives to landscape painting were Rousseau, Corot, Millet, Daubigny, Diaz, and Tryon.

Theodore Rousseau (1812-1867), known as the Poet of the Foliage, painted ancient oaks with twisted trunks and knotted branches such as those which appear in *The Path, The Sunlit Oak,* and the *Outlet from the Forest.* Jean Baptiste Camille Corot (1796-1875) developed a poetic type of landscape with silvery harmonies, mist-laden willow trees, and skies seen at dawn, or dancing nymphs. These pictures brought him enormous popularity, a large income from their sale, and often inconvenient flattery of innumerable imitators who flooded the markets with sentimental landscapes. As the wave of popular favor gradually receded from these low-keyed pastoral rhapsodies, Corot's truer stature as an artist emerged. Sometimes called the painter with a divided artistic personality, his now prized pre-Barbizon period landscapes and excellent figure paintings show distinctive superiority over Corot's work of the mist-laden romantic phase. Such solidly constructed pieces as *The Inn* at Wellesley College and *View of Subiaco,* and in general the paintings stemming from his early artistic pilgrimage to Italy, reveal the artist's often brilliant design and intelligent observation. The nudes and figure studies once regarded as almost negligible constitute Corot's outstanding production. Though painted in a mood akin to the lyrical quality of the Barbizon period, such paintings as *Mother and Child* at the Metropolitan and *Agostina* are vibrant in tone and brushed in with arresting dexterity. *Portrait of a Girl, 1859* is a distinguishing example of his figure work (Plate 174). The painting reveals the artist's feeling for plastic expression and a use of color which marks him as a forerunner of the impressionists.

The humble peasants of Jean François Millet (1814-1875), wearing coarse garments and heavy shoes, are portrayed as austere laborers. Their bent figures and knotty hands are symbolic of the dignity of honest toil and the drama of man's struggle with the soil. The *Sower* shows a figure striding along with rhythmic motion as he flings the grain into the furrows (Plate 169). In *The Angelus,* the peasant stands with head uncovered while his wife lifts her hands in prayer.

DAUMIER; COURBET; CHAVANNES

Honoré Daumier (1808-1879), lithographer, cartoonist, and painter, remained in Paris and gave his sympathy and attention to the suppressed masses of the city. In his lithograph *Rue Transnonain,* Daumier portrays with great emotion one of the bloody incidents in the social upheaval of his day (Plate 169). As in his paintings, form is subordinated to simple, dramatic presentation. Daumier was the leader of a group of exceptionally competent Parisian newspaper cartoonists who utilized the then newly evolved

Three ink sketches. Daumier.

medium of lithography to dramatize the people's struggle against the tyranny of the monarchy, their poverty and misery, and in general to satirize the foibles of Parisians of all classes. While often hastily drawn since they were intended for publication in newspapers, Daumier's incisive lithographs and sketches are unsurpassed as powerful, often satirical comment on the social scene.

Superb draftsmanship and the infusion of human warmth distinguish the impressive body of oil painting which Daumier left behind. His interest in the use of color was secondary to his concern with structure and tonal effect. Like an architect, Daumier built up his compositions to form a massive unity. For subject-matter he chose mainly the poor, the working people, bedraggled carnival performers, and those who struggle against injustice, as in his *Prison Choir* in Baltimore and *Washerwoman* in the Museum of Modern Art. One of his masterpieces, *The Uprising*, depicts an almost formless mob groping, surging ahead, while a single figure emerges into the light to lead the group forward (Plate 171).

As an artist concerned with the life of his times and capable of giving it visual form, Daumier has had unique impact on artistic thinking and vision.

Maintaining that an artist should paint what he sees, exactly as he sees it, Gustave Courbet (1819-1877) set out to prove the falsity of the doctrine that the artist should necessarily seek "noble" classical subjects or paint romantic themes, and thereby succeeded in reaching the heights in realistic representation. His bold vigorous style is exemplified in *Mère Gregoire* (Plate 172) and in *Courbet's Studio*. *The Funeral at Ornans,* a melancholy scene, shows a sympathetic understanding of the common people. Here the mourning peasants wearing the provincial costume topped with a large white linen head-dress, are painted in sombre tones against a bleak landscape stretching out toward a fog-laden sea.

A dynamic personality as well as an important figure in art, Courbet, a communist, refused a decoration proffered by the French government in recognition of his contribution to art. Having served on the Council of the Commune in Paris in 1871, he was sentenced to death after its fall. Finally he won a reprieve, but was forced to leave France and, like David, he died in exile.

Puvis de Chavannes (1824-1898) created a two-dimensional dignified type of mural painting which is associated with nineteenth-century decoration. In simplified designs suggesting quiet repose, his delicate tones of color take their place without destroying the flatness of wall or ceiling. *Sainte Genevieve Watching Over Paris,* the last of his series of frescoes illustrating episodes of her life, shows the patron saint at twilight, standing in quiet meditation as she gazes wistfully over her city.

MANET

The reaction toward realistic subject-matter which Courbet had launched was continued by Edouard Manet (1832-1883). If not of the real aristocracy, Manet was nevertheless a man of wealth and position who enjoyed the smart society of the Parisian well-to-do. After leaving art school he traveled over Europe studying and copying the works of Rembrandt, Titian, Tintoretto, and also the paintings of the Spaniards, Velazquez and Goya. The influence of the latter is apparent in his earlier work. Thus he broadened his vision and developed a high degree of technical ability.

By insisting upon extreme simplification he eventually modified the traditional method of imitating nature. Indeed, some of his canvases are almost posterlike in their forceful expression. Clearly defined figures and objects are represented almost in silhouette, just "as one might see them with eyes half closed," that is, the objects are neither lost in atmosphere nor are the lines of contour broken by the play of light on their surfaces—which is often the case in nature. Manet laid on his colors with broad, sweeping brush strokes and set dark masses against light areas without benefit of unifying intermediate tones. He subordinated both form and color to this contrapuntal (interweaving of contrasting elements) use of dark and light areas. During his later years he painted out-of-doors for the most part, using a modified form of the impressionist technique which was practiced by his friends Monet and Pissarro.

After the camera was invented about the middle of the nineteenth century, the famous daguerrotypes offered strong competition to portrait painting. The church was no longer a great patron of the arts, royalty was on the decline, and the artist found himself drifting farther away from the people. Nevertheless, there are always men who feel impelled to paint just as there are always musicians who must compose. Consequently various schools of painting attempted to attract attention, each in its own peculiar manner: the romanticists, by painting exotic subject matter rendered in bright colors and swirling lines; the realists, by depicting ordinary people going about their daily tasks, and by making caustic comments on life in general and the landscapists who went out-of-doors and painted directly from nature, substituting brighter hues for the brown tones of earlier painters.

Turner and Constable had pioneered in the field of color, Delacroix had made additional contributions of a pseudo-scientific nature, and now Manet was raising his color key. Painting with great economy of means, he also chose unusual subject-matter, and became a leader of what was later to be known as the impressionist group—a name which had been applied in derision to one of Manet's own paintings of a sunset which he called *An Impression*. Although he made few innovations and did not advance very far in the actual recording of light effects—the problems with which the impressionists were concerned—he was chosen as their logical leader because he was well known and had already exhibited in the Paris Salon from which they had been excluded. He succeeded in bringing their cause to the attention of Napoleon III, who set aside space in the same building as the original Salon which later came to be known as the Salon des Refusés, a place where rejected pictures might be shown. Because people have a tendency to dislike what they do not understand, they were vociferous in criticism of the reactionary art of the impressionists which today seems quite conservative.

Although Manet's sympathies were with the younger men, his work had not yet been sufficiently revolutionary to provoke adverse criticism. To give more active encouragement to them, he deliberately produced two paintings in which he used provocative subject-matter. *Olympia* and *Luncheon on the Grass* both showed nudes which were neither idealized nor did they illustrate an allegorical or mythological theme in the traditional manner. The former was shocking because the figure, a realistic representation of a demi-mondaine, was not considered a proper subject to be displayed in respectable society; the latter, probably suggested by Giorgione's poetic *Pastoral Symphony*, showed two nude studio models together with clothed figures in an out-of-door setting, without comment of any kind. Thus Manet alienated the critics and lost the high place in public esteem which he had hitherto enjoyed. His pictures were thrown out of the Academy and he himself became a target for such insults as those heaped upon the impressionists who dared to defy tradition. In *Luncheon on the Grass,* showing figures sharply silhouetted against the landscape background, Manet succeeded in recording the impression which the eye catches at a single glance (Plate 173). Nevertheless, he did not employ the impressionist method of using color to create the effect of brilliant illumination. Instead he emphasized the tonal quality of the dark-light pattern. Technical skill is shown in the poster-like *Boy with the Sword* and *Portrait of Madame Michel-Levy* of the Chester Dale Collection (Plate 175). If, as in some of his later work, the flat masses of color laid on with broad strokes seem to be merely a confusion of blobs and spots when seen too close, the objects represented are clarified when seen from a distance.

The impressionists were also realists who merely centered their interest upon a different aspect of nature, the fugitive effect of light on an object and its enveloping atmosphere. Observing that a ray of light passing through a glass prism is refracted into pure prismatic colors, they concluded that an approximate effect of sunlight could be obtained by placing its component colors side by side on the canvas without previous mixing on the palette. By thus laying on paint with short quick brush strokes, they were able to convey a brilliancy which had not otherwise been achieved. Simply stated, yellow and blue juxtaposed on the canvas in the impressionist manner, produced a brighter green than if the two colors had been mixed on the palette. With some modification of hues necessary to secure the proper tonal values, and also some contrasts in intensity, all of the impressionists used the above method—with variations in their manner of application. Since the blending of hues occurs in the eye of the spectator the new technique took advantage of optical illusion. Included in the group led by Manet, who, however, never became an impressionist in the strictest sense of the word, were Pissarro, Monet, Sisley, and Renoir.

MONET; PISSARRO; DEGAS; TOULOUSE-LAUTREC

Well known for his paintings of sunshine on the façades of cathedrals, haystacks, flowers, or other objects as they appeared at different hours of the day, Claude Monet (1840-1926) is considered the true originator of impressionistic painting. His *Westminster* is unintelligible when seen close to, but when viewed from the proper distance the structure emerges from the light-bathed atmosphere. Whether the scene was laid in Normandy, Venice, or London, Monet's theme was really the painting of sunlight, as in his *Gladiolas* (Plate 172). In *La Gare Saint Lazare* the artist caught an instantaneous effect of billowing clouds of smoke which veiled the panting engines and enveloped the roof of the station. Here the predominating color is blue. Since nature derives her harmonies from light, Monet, like the other impressionists, deleted black from his palette.

Camille Pissarro (1830-1903) strove to contribute to the scientific aspect of the impressionistic theory, but being an artist as well as a scientist, he succeeded in imparting art quality to his painting. Edgar Degas (1834-1917) combined the new knowledge of color with an unusual treatment of linear rhythms. His angular line schemes, together with a peculiar perspective based on strong diagonals, an asymmetrical composition, and strange arrangements of moving figures, show a direct influence from the Japanese prints that were attracting the attention of artists at the time. Degas, an impersonal observer whose interest was focussed on vigorous movement, painted ballet dancers in casual and natural poses, as in *The Rehearsal* (Plate 178), race-horses, scenes from the circus, cafe or opera, and a few portraits. More concerned with creating effective patterns than in portraying figures as individuals, he also painted working women—milliners and laundresses at their daily tasks. Both his oils and pastels are characterized by movement, effective line-schemes, and decorative arrangements of unusual subject-matter.

A great admirer of the work of Degas was Henri de Toulouse-Lautrec (1864-1901), who was descended from a noble French family. Many of his works are bitterly satirical. They are strikingly designed and full of color and movement as *At the Circus* and *The Ringmaster*. His many versions of *Au Moulin Rouge* exhibit his supreme interest in sketching and painting the habitués, dancers, drinkers, and smokers of this cafe on which he lavished his great skill as an illustrator (Plate 178). When painting the Parisian life of Montmartre he followed unusual patterns of line and dark and light in his search for characteristic poses of certain individuals, sometimes viewing the scene from high perspective or with tables and figures in oblique position on the canvas. In his pattern plans he shows a strong influence from Japanese prints.

RENOIR

Going a step farther than Monet and other members of the impressionist group, Pierre Auguste Renoir (1841-1919) added form to color. Born at Limoges, France, famous for its enamelers and decorators of fine china, he was apprenticed to a porcelain painter when he was only thirteen years old. There he learned to love the bright colors which he later applied in short whipping strokes, thus making his canvases throb with the vibrating energy of light. He said that he spent his entire life "in the conquest of the sun," and that his models were chosen from women whose skin had the power to reflect light, rather than for their physical beauty. Renoir is so famous for his exceptional use of color that his very name immediately calls to mind warm, luscious, scintillating hues. Under his hand even grays became opalescent. Black and white prints fail to convey the real charm and esthetic value of his work.

Realizing that intense light, like intense dark, tends to destroy form, Renoir used different tones of color to create form. If some portion of a cheek, shoulder, or brow seemed too flat, he unhesitatingly placed a spot of light where it needed to be raised, regardless of whether he saw it there or not. Hence his tones and colors are structural as well as warm, brilliant, and pulsating or life-giving. Besides creating a joyous art full of grace and beauty, he also may be said to be a documentary painter, for he recorded the entire life of the Parisian bourgeoisie, at the opera, boating on the river, dining at the boulevard cafes, in the ballrooms, the studio, or strolling along the streets. His exuberance of expression and the fullness of his forms are reminiscent of Rubens, and like that Flemish master, he seems to have accomplished his work with effortless ease.

The gaiety of the lively scene depicted in *La Bal à Bougival* is heightened by a vibrating light and scintillating jewel-like color (Plate 179). This painting, now in the Boston Museum, shows Renoir's skill in painting textures, such as the shimmering quality of silk or the reflection of light on hair and soft flesh. The *Three Bathers*, a subject which he painted in his earlier period and again during his last years, exemplifies the development of a more flexible technique. His treatment of form later became more sculpturesque, but without loss of his usual fullness of color.

CÉZANNE

At the close of the century, Paul Cézanne (1839-1906) abandoned the impressionist technique, left Paris, and returned to his home in southern France. In the quiet country about Aix he worked alone searching for an enduring order that lies deeper than momentary light or naturalistic appearance. Each day he took his canvases out into the country, but never satisfied with his work, he often returned without them. The art world might have been deprived of some of its greatest treasures if his wife had not searched for his paintings among the bushes where he had left them. It has been said that the artist cared so little for his finished pictures that his young son was allowed to amuse himself by cutting out the doors and windows of the houses, while other canvases were used for lighting fires and scrubbing the kitchen floor. Cézanne's mind was focussed on the problem that he was attempting to solve. To him each painting was only a step along the road of progress.

Besides landscapes, flowers, or figures he repeatedly painted apples or other fruits arranged among the folds of a table cloth. His *Still Life with Apples* is illustrative of Cézanne's purpose, namely, perception of forms, their relation in space, and their color and solidity (Plate 177). Probably because he was a slow worker, it was difficult to find models—with the exception of his patient wife who could "sit still as an apple." Carefully calculating the effect of each brush stroke, we are told that he sometimes spaced them half an hour apart.

Turning his attention to the eternal aspect of nature, Cézanne stated that everything in nature could be reduced to geometric forms: the cube, cone, or cylinder. To create three-dimensional forms, which the impressionist technique had destroyed, and also to suggest spatial depth, he employed advancing and receding hues in varying values and intensities. Thus he strove to give permanence to form and poise to flickering light. In this hitherto unex-

ampled use of color, he moved away from the traditional imitation
of nature; nevertheless, he retained recognizable, if abstract subject-
matter. "I am the primitive of my way," he said. While Renoir's
work was spontaneous and intuitive, Cézanne's was intellectual,
verging on the scientific, for he was a true product of his age.

The bare rocks and mountains, the reddish soil and dark-foliaged
trees of Provence, clearly defined against an azure sky together
with the roofs and walls of the houses, are "re-presented" in a
simplified geometric manner. There is a fine sweep of space and
monumental grandeur in the mountain form of *Mont Saint Vic-
toire* and *Village of Gardanne* (Plate 176). His fruit compositions
are carefully arranged even to the folds of the table cloth. The
men seated about a table in *Card Players* are a part of a fine structural organization to which everything in the picture contributes,
including the pipes on the wall, the curtain and the cards on the
table (Plate 177).

SEURAT AND SIGNAC

Other French artists who abandoned the impressionist style in
favor of their own individual methods were Georges Seurat (1859-
1891) and his co-worker Paul Signac (1863-1935), the leaders of
a small group of painters known as the neo-impressionists or post-
impressionists, who strove to reduce their forms and figures to the
simplest geometrical designs. These artists, sometimes called Poin-
tillists or Divisionists, followed a scientific system of divided color
which they applied to their canvases in small dots, wedges,
"stitches," or patches. Seurat believed that anyone could paint if
the method were made scientifically simple, but he lived too short
a time to satisfactorily prove his theory or to experience the inevitable disappointment which would have followed. Being a real
artist himself, he was able to create a masterpiece of great distinction despite his cumbersome system.

The Parisians of Seurat's day often went to enjoy a peaceful
Sunday outing on an island in the Seine River. Such a scene is
represented in his *Sunday on the Island of La Grande Jatte*, at the
Chicago Art Institute (Plate 173). Here the artist saw people

lying on the grass or strolling idly among the trees of the park; the men wearing tight trousers, and the women dressed in basques and full skirts with bustles in the style of the 1880's. In this painting the ladies carry small parasols, while their children, pet dogs, and monkeys furnish added interest. Before beginning to paint the large picture—some seventy square feet in area—the artist made forty or more sketches; some were tone drawings made with conte crayons; others were freely rendered in oils somewhat in the impressionist technique. First the landscape was recorded without the figures. Then groups of figures were sketched. After the ground work had been laid, the artist returned to his studio and built up his organization just as an architect constructs a building. A definitive sketch combining the landscape and figures was made in oils before work on the final canvas was started. An analysis of the painting reveals that a carefully planned straight-line scheme, composed of trees and figures reduced to geometric forms, was superposed on the landscape. Darker areas stretching horizontally across the canvas unify the figures and balance the vertical lines of trees and people. These, together with the lighter areas and strategically grouped figures, give an impression of deep space. Opposing the straight-line scheme is a curved-line pattern built on the bustle motif and repeated in the curved unbrellas, the backs of some of the figures, and the tail of the monkey.*

Seurat's method was to juxtapose small dots of pure spectrum colors laid on with machine-like precision. These colors, when seen from a distance, mix optically. The small dots are placed so close together that the contour line of the forms is preserved and a clear-cut tonal effect is achieved. Throughout the entire composition there are correctly adjusted proportions of warm and cool or complementary colors. Standing close to the picture, one can not help but marvel at the detailed method which the artist employed to produce this presentation of figures strolling about in a sun-drenched park.

* Daniel Catton Rich, *Seurat and the Evolution of "La Grande Jatte,"* University of Chicago Press, Chicago.

GAUGUIN

Paul Gauguin (1848-1903) is famous for his tropical landscapes and paintings of Tahitian natives of the South Seas. Of French and Peruvian ancestry, he lived in South America until his parents

Women at the River. Color wood-cut by Gauguin. (Museum of Modern Art)

took him to France when he was seven years old. Joining the French navy at the age of seventeen, he had an opportunity to visit the tropics. Later he became a successful stockbroker in Paris, using his leisure time and Sundays to paint for pleasure. After exhibiting two of his landscapes in the now famous Salon des Refusés, he was so encouraged by the favorable reception of his work that he decided to abandon business and devote all of his time to art. Breaking away from the current styles of painting, he began to work in a free and personal manner, simplifying his forms and applying wide patches of strongly outlined colors to a rough canvas which suggested the texture of tapestry.

About 1883 Gauguin joined the Dutch artist Van Gogh at Arles, in southern France. During this time Gauguin's work shows some of the Dutchman's influence—particularly in the vital use of color. After an unpleasant experience with his maladjusted friend, Gauguin's romantic temperament again asserted itself, and in 1891, he was off to Tahiti in search of a land where both man and nature were untamed. Moving inland with the natives far from what he considered the "annoyances of civilization," he painted exotic landscapes in brilliant hues such as yellows, greens, cerise, and rose—regardless of the natural colors which he actually saw. To his friends in Paris, he wrote, "I have escaped everything that is artificial, conventional, customary. I am entering into truth, into nature." Gauguin's simplified drawing, broad masses of warm color, quiet lines, and patterned textures are imbued with something of the calm dignity and restrained force that characterizes the simple people he depicts. Gauguin, "the savage" among the painters of his day, is now regarded as a great decorative artist. He was buried in the Marquesas Islands among the natives he immortalized in his colorful canvases. In *The Moon and the Earth* (Plate 180) the artist uses form and color to create a decorative pattern and carry out the symbolism of the title. A mystic atmosphere is induced through diffused and unnatural lighting, without sacrificing a feeling that this is an allegory expressed in simple terms befitting a simple people.

VAN GOGH

His friend, Vincent Van Gogh (1853-1890), was the son of a Dutch protestant pastor who lived in Brabant. The influence of his pious parents and the constant reading of the Bible from early childhood probably account for his continuous, if unsuccessful, efforts to be of service to suffering humanity. After trying various kinds of work, he became an assistant pastor and was stationed among the poor miners of Borinage in Belgium. Later encouraged by his brother Theo, who fortunately was employed and could provide him with a small sum to defray living expenses, Van Gogh began to study painting when he was thirty years old.

In Paris he met Pissarro and Seurat, who inspired him to paint with bright color in the out-of-door sunlight. While he did not wholly accept their methods, he did retain the principle of color dissection. Working with feverish energy and varying his brush strokes, Van Gogh sometimes applied his paint with a palette knife;

again he squeezed it directly from the tube on to the canvas; but his most characteristic strokes were the thin, ribbon-like, wiry ones with which he endowed all nature with vital motion. Indeed, the observer can almost feel the wind blowing through the trees and surging fields of grain in his paintings. His flowers fairly glow with life; he even made ordinary inanimate objects such as a pair of shoes or an old chair seem important by imparting to his painting something of his own intensity and vitality. He constantly sought to reveal the mysteries of growth and the life-giving force of all creation.

Van Gogh was happy while painting in Arles in southern France where he worked with frenzied enthusiasm, often producing a picture at a single sitting; but due partly to long hours of exposure in the blazing sun and dry wind, he suffered a nervous collapse, and during one of his many disagreements with Gauguin, who had gone there to live with him, he attacked his friend with a knife. Before this unfortunate occurrence there had been similar distressing experiences when he reacted violently to anyone who opposed him. Finally he lapsed into recurrent cycles of insanity and, realizing that he had lost his reason, he consented to enter an asylum. Theo placed him under the care of Dr. Gachet, a nerve specialist who was also an art enthusiast. When the artist recovered normalcy, he suffered remorse for his irresponsible actions and at the age of thirty-seven he finally ended his stormy life by shooting himself. Dr. Gachet, who had been an understanding friend and whose portrait Van Gogh had painted, buried the artist near his own home. Beside the grave he planted the sunflowers which the artist had loved to paint. His paintings, which had offered some release from the hardships and tragedy that filled his life, reflect Van Gogh's own emotional intensity. Van Gogh's portrait of The Postman (Plate 182) is alive with vital color which gives the painting a freshness and expressiveness. Moving brush strokes model the face and form in a direct statement characteristic of the intense quality of Van Gogh's portraits. His Stairway at Auvers (Plate 182) shows a typical French village scene, brought to movement and life through the artist's use of bold outline and the strong light which diffuses the picture. Van Gogh's paintings have enjoyed exceptional popularity among a most diverse audience following an exhibition at the Museum of Modern Art in New York in 1935. Through reproduction, prints of the paintings are distributed widely and may be seen on the walls of homes and offices in every section of the country.

REDON

As a frail, sensitive child, Odilon Redon (1840-1916), wandered alone among the rocks and hills of the country surrounding Bordeaux. His mystical paintings are suffused with a subtle transient quality suggestive of the ever changing imagery of floating clouds and the restless sea which he knew so well. Thus combining realism with fantasy, his poetic works are expressive of his inner vision. A competent lithographer, he also worked in pastel as well as painting in oils. Pastel was a medium particularly suitable for suggesting the evanescent mystery in which he enveloped his favorite subjects: flowers, women, and children. His colors were always personal and imaginative, never purely imitative. Now radiant and animated, or again delicate in hue, they were strongly contrasted with rich blacks. Without undue confusion he often surrounded his figures with arabesques of trailing vines and fragile flowers. While his work may not be so strong in formal qualities as that of some of his contemporaries, it nevertheless has its own special charm. He has been classified as a symbolist—one who uses objects from the visual world to express his own personal emotions. His work entitled *Mystery* is closely akin to that of the expressionists (Plate 181).

ROUSSEAU

Among the primitives—artists who had little or no formal training, or at least who painted in a naïve manner—was Henri Rousseau (1844-1910), who was born at Laval. This former clerk in the custom house of Paris was only a "Sunday painter" until he reached middle age, when he was able to retire and devote his entire time to art. When he was about eighteen he began his service in the army and was sent to Mexico during the reign of the

ill-fated Maximilian. There he was impressed with the tropical
foliage which occurs frequently in his work. He also haunted the
botanical gardens of Paris, where he made literal and detailed
sketches of plants which aided him both in recording Mexican
scenes from memory and in creating his imaginative jungle compositions showing monkeys disporting themselves among orange-
laden trees or ferocious wild beasts lurking amid forests of palms,
lotus, and long grasses. He also recorded peasant festivals, landscapes, and family portraits with a primitive intensity and a meticulous attention to detail. To aid him in achieving a likeness of a
sitter, we are told, he took careful measurements of the face in
order to copy it exactly. This detailed literalness, quite unexpected
at the time, coming as it did in the midst of the determined movement away from photographic representation, provided a great deal
of amusement for the sophisticated, who brought their friends to
view Rousseau's paintings. Undiscouraged, the artist continued to
trundle his pictures in a cart to the Salon des Refusés, but it was
not until he was sixty-three years old that he began to sell some of
the works which now adorn the walls of the world's most famous
art galleries. Those who ridiculed the paintings he had worked so
hard to perfect had failed to observe that this self-taught peasant
intuitively possessed that feeling for formal design which gives life
to painting. His naïve technique contributed to the imaginative
quality and nostalgic mood which pervades his painting *The Sleeping Gypsy* (Plate 181). Among the artist friends who encouraged
him during his last years were the younger painters Picasso, Braque,
and Marie Laurencin.

The emotional freedom achieved in the works of Gauguin, Van
Gogh, and other post-impressionists inspired a group of young
artists who welcomed a reaction from the complexities and hyper-
scientific methods of Seurat and his followers. Through a careful
study of the gradual development of art from Giotto to Cézanne
they began to seek new idioms of expression. French artists no
longer went to Italy as did Poussin and Claude, for after the seventeenth century the art capital of the Western world was definitely
established in Paris, where many artists who came to study remained to paint.

OUTLINE OF FRENCH ART

TIME: 15th through 19th centuries.

BACKGROUND: The "Great Kings" were important patrons of the arts. Masterpieces were imported from Italy, and Italian artists were invited to live in Paris. When the power of the king became absolute, nobles abused their privileges, lived in luxury at expense of the masses, who finally rebelled. French Revolution followed, out of which a new social order emerged. The Industrial Revolution heralded the modern mode of life.

ARCHITECTURE: Chiefly secular: chateaux palaces, and civic buildings. *Chateaux:* a combination of Renaissance and Gothic styles. Features: dormer windows, numerous chimneys, elaborate fireplaces and stair cases, niches, statuettes, grotesques, gargoyles. Lower part of structure classical; pilasters, colonnades and pedimented ornamentation. Interiors of *palaces:* plaster-reliefs, gilding, intricate metal-work, pale blue and pink walls. Tapestries made in Gobelin factories, *Civic Buildings:* the *Louvre* in Renaissance style with Baroque decorations. *Hotel des Invalides,* chapel covered with Renaissance dome. Magnificent landscaped gardens, such as those of Versailles, with statues, fountains, lagoons, clipped hedges, flowers and trees in formal arrangement.

SCULPTURE: 17th century baroque and rococo influences characterized by naturalism, restless movement, momentary pose and skillful use of drapery—tending toward a fanciful and ornate style. Return to the classical during Napoleonic era. Later realistic rendering of figures in contemporary garb—naturalistic animal sculpture. *Rodin:* emphasis upon pictorial and dramatic effects. Contrasts between rough unfinished backgrounds and completed parts of modeled forms.

PAINTING: Remarkable realism and strong linear style in portraits of 16th century—late Gothic. Idealistic landscapes of Poussin and Claude, classical—17th century. Art of Watteau, Fragonard, Boucher, light subject-matter, airy elegant style. Napoleonic era: David dictator of art and arbiter of fashion. Martial subject-matter, cold *classical* style, emphasis on line and form rather than on color. *Romanticism* with exotic subject-matter, followed the classical style. Delacroix became interested in scientific aspect of color. *Naturalism* stressed by Courbet, Millet and others. In *impressionism*—(later part of 19th century) interest was focused upon the portrayal of light on objects. Later *post-impressionism* reveals a search for permanent form instead of the representation of fleeting light. Independent artists like Van Gogh and Gauguin worked in individual manner.

BIBLIOGRAPHY

BELL, Clive, *Landmarks in Nineteenth Century Painting* (Harcourt, Brace & Co., Inc., N. Y., 1927).
CAFFIN, C. H., *Story of French Painting* (The Century Co., Inc., N. Y., 1915).
CLUTTON-BROCK, Alan, *An Introduction to French Painting* (Henry Holt & Co., Inc., N. Y., 1932).
HOEBER, Arthur, *The Barbizon Painters* (F. A. Stokes Co., N. Y., 1915).
HOURTICQ, Louis, *Art in France* (Charles Scribner's Sons, N. Y., 1917).

MOORE, C. H., *The Character of Renaissance Architecture* (The Macmillan Co., N. Y., 1905).

MOUREY, Gabriel, *French Art in the Nineteenth Century* (London, 1928).

MUNRO, Thomas, *Great Pictures of Europe* (Coward-McCann, Inc., N. Y., 1930).

RODIN, Auguste, *Art* (Small Maynard & Co., Boston, 1912).

WARD, W. H., *Architecture of the Renaissance in France,* 2 vols. (Charles Scribner's Sons, N. Y., 1926).

CHAPTER XXIII

Art of the Twentieth Century

THE first half of the twentieth century has witnessed the rapid development of the Machine Age. Today man is able to escape static restrictions and to travel great distances with speed. We are now experiencing the growing pains of an epoch in which all nations of the earth are learning to be neighbors. Our efforts to understand the ideologies, cultural patterns, and art of all peoples are a present responsibility. The chance for peace and survival depends upon the degree to which we can harmonize the opposing tensions of our time.

The machine has so broadened man's vision that he can now observe the world from a vast new perspective. The modern artist, looking from a fast-moving airplane, sees the earth below as a pattern of geometric forms of varying hues and textures. Contemporary paintings may show objects from more than one point of view. The artist may disregard objectivity when recording from memory the significant aspects of remembered things.

The esthetic expression of the world's artists, working as they are against a background of flux and change, has aroused wide public interest and controversy. It is generally agreed that the modernist movement in America began with the Armory Show in New York in 1913. The works of modern artists showing varied visual trends have aroused both interest and controversy. Museums offer the modern artist a chance to display his work and the public the opportunity of seeing it. The Museum of Modern Art and the Solomon R. Guggenheim Foundation for Non-Objective Painting in New York, as well as the Institute of Contemporary Art in Boston, are largely devoted to the display of "living" art. Since World War I many artists have come from all parts of the world to live in America; since 1933 the influx of European artists has been especially great.

PAINTING

PAINTERS OF THE TWENTIETH CENTURY

Henri Matisse (1869-) became the leader of a group of young artists in Paris who were known as the Fauves (wild men) because of their radical ideas about painting. In this group, between 1905 and 1910, were Derain, Rouault, de Vlaminck, and Dufy. These men, experimenting in modernism, are largely responsible for the development of new vistas in twentieth-century art. Matisse had received a thorough academic training at the Beaux-Arts after which he was commissioned by the French government to copy masterpieces in the Louvre. While seeking ways to paint with greater vitality than impressionism permitted, he experimented with various methods and adopted a naïve style, "a rapidity of statement, a sort of shorthand of what is taking place in the mind," which had the advantage of adding fresh new life to his expression. Finally, his style crystallized into a highly decorative manner and he became preëminently a designer of surface patterns. A striking portrait, *Woman in White Dress,* was exhibited at the Paris Salon, 1946 (Plate 188). A decorative background and chair cover are significant elements of the whole design pattern. Vivid but subtle color adds emphasis and unity to the painting. Simplifications have reduced the portrait to a mere impression of the model, for all but essentials are eliminated. Distortions enhance the effect of the organization which is all-important to the artist, for he is not interested in recording a representational impression of the sitter. Neither is Matisse interested in or concerned with three-dimensional painting. About 1910, when the Fauves realized that their leader would not follow the trend toward abstraction of form, the group dispersed. Various factions then developed, some following a decorative emphasis while others became neo-realists, abstractionists, cubists, or expressionists.

Matisse has continued consistently in his decorative style. He combines colors in daring harmonies, and his distorted figures, reminiscent of exotic Persian miniatures, are posed against screens gaily decorated in bold, rhythmic patterns and arabesques. Matisse

Odalisque. Matisse. 1928. (Museum of Modern Art)

was inspired by the rhythms found in African Negro sculpture. Another influence was his stay in north Africa where he reveled in the brilliant color and sunshine of Morocco. Matisse frequently employs a decorative harmony of rich red-rose tones in his oriental interiors.

Georges Rouault (1871-   ), one of the Fauves, lived apart from the controversies which surrounded other members of the group. His paintings reveal some of the gorgeous color and firm linear tracery found in Gothic stained glass windows. Rouault is fond of painting portraits of unfortunate characters of the Paris scene and melancholy old clowns (Plate 194). He has often rendered religious themes, for his moods are profoundly serious. Although his contemporaries have turned to abstractions, Rouault has consistently retained a distinct subject interest as in *Christ Forever Flagellated* (Plate 195). Rouault's work includes many line drawings, which, like his paintings, are distinguished by their simple and strong conception.

Maurice de Vlaminck (1876-   ) delights in clear bright color applied with a heavy impasto. Raoul Dufy (1877-   ) paints the familiar Parisian scene at the beach, races, or the boulevard with simplicity of treatment using a characteristically light, dextrous brush-stroke. Clarity of form has been the entire aim of André Derain (1880-   ), another of the Fauves. He follows the Cézanne tradition in the solution of space problems and the painting of solid form. Derain uses dull colors and broad brush-strokes in *Window on the Park,* which is painted with special consideration for still life and the growth patterns of nature (Plate 183).

The Spanish painter, Pablo Picasso (1881-   ), an established artist in Barcelona, went to Paris at the age of twenty-two, where he soon received recognition as an outstandingly able and versatile artist. The most inventive of contemporary painters, Picasso has ever been at the heart of twentieth-century art experimentation. His work has ranged from realism to abstractionism, to develop in its later phases toward a type of semi-abstract painting, with free use of distortion to create a powerful emotional impact.

Unlike many artists, Picasso has an equal facility for handling color and structural form. His excellent draftsmanship is also evident in all of his work. The first decade of the century saw Picasso's "blue" period, when he rendered elongated, melancholy figures, and his "rose" period, during which he frequently painted acrobats, musicians, clowns and other circus folk.

Around 1907 Picasso developed a strong interest both in African Negro sculpture and in Cézanne's treatment of form. From there he continued to carry the study of spatial relations in painting much further, and out of these studies became the dynamic leader of the cubist movement. Simply stated, cubism may be called a system for simplifying and arranging forms in space, based on an intellectual, almost mathematical approach to the problems of composition in painting. Cubism has greatly influenced twentieth-century painting, architectural and furniture design, and advertising art. *Three Musicians* (Plate 185) though painted in 1921, long

Four Ballet Dancers. Picasso. 1925. (Museum of Modern Art)

after Picasso had passed through his cubist phase, demonstrates the influence of cubist thinking on his art.

Neo-classicism next occupied Picasso, from about 1915 to 1923, and during part of this period he painted colossal, massive women reminiscent of some of the Greek and Egyptian sculptures. *Woman in White* (Plate 189) displays the combination of classical dignity with simplification of form characteristic of this period.

Picasso was greatly affected by the Spanish civil conflict during the 1930's. His panorama-mural *Guernica* (Plate 186) depicts the suffering and despair which were an aftermath of the bombing of Spain's holy city. In its dramatic distortion, this powerful indictment of modern warfare, on canvas, is by way of becoming a classic; it was viewed by thousands of people when it was displayed at New York's Museum of Modern Art.

While the *Guernica* is in some ways typical of Picasso's later paintings, its subdued, grayed tones are completely different from the strong, often raw color which characterizes his work in the late 1930's and the 1940's.

In order to achieve variety and interest, the cubists painted segments of familiar objects such as guitars, pipes, playing-cards, or other paraphernalia on their canvases. The texture of cubist pictures was varied by the addition of fragments of such materials as corrugated paper, news-print, or wall-paper, which were pasted on the painting. These fragments were combined with the composition and the resulting pattern was called collage. Cubist paintings which include recognizable objects generally use an extreme perspective; colors are reduced to low intensities, so that the importance of color, as hue, is subordinated. Contrasting lights and darks are a major interest while straight lines and angles replace the curves and arabesques so well loved by the Fauves.

Associated with Picasso in Paris was Georges Braque (1882-   ), who adopted the cubist style in 1908. He was successful in unifying geometric elements in the organization of his paintings, which show a fine balance. By 1911 the cubists were exhibiting their paintings, often named "Abstraction." Braque is a master of a style which is semi-abstract, as seen in *Plums, Pears, Nuts, and Knife* (Plate 185). Here the artist's interest is concentrated upon the organization of line directions—horizontals, obliques, and the rhythms of circles and ellipses which are combined with masses and colors. This still-life study achieves a unified simplification of appearances of natural objects.

Another of the cubists, Ferdinand Léger (1881-   ) produced clean-cut geometrical works expressive of the Machine Age with its power, force, movement. Léger delights in strong contrasts and his present style of painting is in the non-objective manner. In *Treillage Noir*, the artist renders his emotional reaction instead of making a representational interpretation of reality (Plate 196). He is concerned primarily with abstract form and his experiments created stimulating patterns which are the result of contemplation rather than observation of reality. When considering his ideas about things he is often impelled to distort the actual in the interest of his pattern. Many of Léger's paintings may be hung in either a vertical or horizontal position according to the decision of the spectator, for the artist does not designate that the painting be viewed from a certain position.

A group of Italian artists called futurists settled in Paris in 1909. These artists believed that art should express the multiple movements of the Machine Age. The futurists stressed movement in their paintings by means of emphatic and forceful lines. They restored color to an important rôle following its neglect by the cubists. The best known of the Futurists is Gino Severini (1883-). His *Pan-pan in Monaco* describes a dance in which fragments of abstracted planes convey the effect of motion (Plate 191). Concentrating on the dynamics of movement, the futurists painted objects as they would appear to the stroboscopic camera. *Nude Descending a Staircase*, 1912, by Marcel Duchamp (1887-   ) demonstrates a cubist method of abstracting "sheaths of planes" and a futurist treatment of the positions assumed while walking down a staircase (Plate 184). The artist aimed to portray a space-time idea of motion and a kaleidoscopic view of the dynamics of movement.

A group of Russian artists led by Wassily Kandinsky (1866-1944), who had been working in the field of non-objective art, developed a style called expressionism shortly before World War I. These painters used strong, primary colors and their aim was to show the rhythms of industry through simplifications of forms. Kandinsky's writings have analyzed the theory of expressionism and abstractionism in an instructive defense of his art. Unfortunately, by the time the expressionist mode of painting was well launched as a definite style, the Russian government denounced it. As a result many of these artists suffered hardships and turned from fine arts to industrial design. Kandinsky and Marc Chagall (1889-   ) moved to Germany where they enriched the development of expressionism in that country. Chagall's paintings contain various symbols. His imaginary environment is indicated by the use of fragments of objects unrelated to the laws of logic and gravity. In his paintings, for example, forms may float with ease above the earth. In *I and My Village* symbolic and fragmentary forms are combined in a fanciful manner (Plate 198). It should be noted that Chagall's forms are representational, not abstract. Kandinsky, who was trained in Russia to be a lawyer, began to paint as a pastime. He decided to study art in Munich and he became a brilliant painter. From expressionism he later turned to an abstract and then to a non-objective style. Kandinsky depicts his subconscious emotional response in *Calm* (Plate 192). This painting has a quiet and soothing color pattern of greyed values in decided contrast to the bright effects of his work called *Joy*. Lines and masses in *Calm* contain arcs and circles which give serenity while explosive action is portrayed in *Joy*. Kandinsky believed that art should be as abstract as music, which he often used to assist in evoking his interpretations. His last works are clear-cut, two-dimensional paintings which are completely non-objective.

Other leading artists who have developed non-objectivism exhibit with the cubists and purists at the Solomon R. Guggenheim Foundation for Non-Objective Painting in New York. Among them is Rudolph Bauer, a German artist, whose *Red Square* expresses the artist's entire freedom from objectivity (Plate 193). Interest centers on the clean-cut pattern of this strong abstract organization. Hilla Rebay's painting, *Animation* expresses the artist's conception of "serene and eternal rhythms" (Plate 193).

The modern art movement in Germany resulted in the establishment of the famous Bauhaus, an architectural-industrial school, first at Weimar, later at Dessau. Kandinsky, who was a leading teacher became associated with Paul Klee, at that time an artist and writer for the magazine called the *Blue Rider*. This publication was the journal of a fellowship of painters who called themselves the Blue Rider Group. These artists developed expressionist paintings in Germany between 1911 and 1916. The well-known Blue Rider Franz Marc (1880-1916) met an untimely death in World War I. His vital paintings of animals have become popular because of their strong linear rhythms, motion and brilliant color.

Käthe Kollwitz (1867-1945), a German expressionist artist, has devoted her talent to recording the suffering and tribulations of the war-driven poor of Germany. She depicts hunger and unemployment and privation in her drawings, engravings and wood-cuts. Her

Volunteers. Wood-cut by Käthe Kollwitz. (Brooklyn Museum)

style is reminiscent of Daumier, the French master, in both theme and treatment. In *Volunteers,* a wood-cut, she emphasizes a dramatic and forceful theme. The artist conveys an emotional mood by the skillful use of her knife and graver. As wood presents a difficult surface to cut, technical skill is needed to indicate delicate details of the individuals shown in the grouped figures.

Although expressionist paintings had gained appreciation for a number of years in Germany, they were denounced by Nazi officials, who banned them. Many of the German artists fled to London, Paris, and America. Among them was Oscar Kokoschka (1886-   ) an Austrian painter, educated in Vienna, though he later worked with the expressionists in Germany. His strongly outlined work has a rugged style as seen in *Self-Portrait,* one of his best-known works.

Lyonel Feininger (1887-   ), an American who has spent most of his life in Germany, painted for a time in the cubist manner, but later developed a distinctly personal style characterized by the use of cubist line and shape in the depiction of ships, the sea, and dynamic mechanical forms. His *Side-Wheeler* (Plate 190), a dramatic fusion of visualized sensation and memory impressions, conveys the idea of the motion of a ship in a storm.

Another art "ism," called dadaism, developed out of the efforts of a group of painters and poets who lived in Zurich. Disillusioned by their difficulties following World War I, these painters denounced all recognized values and systems and set up their own art standards. Enthusiastic converts from various countries joined the group and dadaism became international in scope. Several well-known painters who had been identified with the Blue Rider group joined the dadaists. Prominent among the dadaists were Hans Arp, Paul Klee, Francis Picabia, Marcel Duchamp, and Man Ray. Although dadaism was short lived, some of the theories on which it was based were absorbed in the newer style called surrealism.

Paul Klee (1879-1940), a Swiss who experimented in many techniques and was at one time a dadaist, became interested in children's drawings and the art of the insane. In an effort to achieve a spontaneous technique, Klee developed a personal style of art expression which he called "a child of five" manner of drawing. He used zig-zag lines and scribblings which are naïvely direct. *Tight-Rope Walker* is executed in Klee's characteristic outline style (Plate 191).

Although the style of painting known as surrealism started about 1919, it was not until 1924 that the manifesto of this group was issued. Simplifications are stressed by the surrealists and this style requires a neat, tidy, clean technique. Surrealists believe that dreams reveal an accurate reality denied the conscious mind. Accordingly, surrealism fosters the interpretation of images from the subconscious as a revelation of the deeply hidden mysteries of the heart. The best known of the group is Salvador Dali (1904-   ), who uses realistic treatments of objects, though his subject-matter is illogical, in much the manner of dreams. His excellent draftsmanship is expended upon subjects which are unrelated, unreal, dreamy, or even weird. Titles of his paintings are often mystifying, as *Paranoic-Astral Image* (Plate 197). The highly creative Spanish artist, Joan Miro (1893-   ) has painted numerous improvisations and fantasies in a spontaneous surrealistic style. In his *Person Throwing a Stone at a Bird* (Plate 199), the shapes vaguely suggest natural forms and the painting is "free" in its expression. All of Miro's subject-matter refers to images, dreams, or is of subconscious inspiration.

The Italian painter, Amedeo Modigliani (1884-1920) died tragically in Paris, a victim of starvation and tuberculosis. His work is almost exclusively that of portraiture. Instead of attempting to imitate the outward appearance of nature or of his subject, Modigliani strove to convey his personal feeling for, or his reaction to, the object or individual. Many of his portraits recall the simple Italian primitives which Modigliani loved and which inspired him. The intense facial expression of his portraits show the influence of Negro sculpture. Modigliani was ever searching for the realization of satisfying rhythmic harmonies, such as in *Chanteuse de Café* (Plate 195). Here, as in many others of his canvases, a single, dark and severe figure dominates the composition. The artist often uses a figure motif with elongations and distortions—accentuation of the oval of the face or length of neck or arms. His color is satisfying, though somber, and his backgrounds are simple.

Stuart Davis (1894-   ), the American painter, has developed skill in abstract art. His method of painting *House and Street* (Plate 197) included the following activities: First, he observed the actual New York street scene in all its details, after which he made numerous sketches. On returning to his studio, Davis translated his impression into a strong pattern of dark and light and color. This was followed by improvisation or free-painting, after which he reduced his creation to an abstraction. Piet Mondrian (1872-1944), a Hollander, studied in Paris before coming to America in 1934. *Composition in White, Black, and Red* (Plate 192) demonstrates his austere and purely non-objective art. This painting is executed with mathematical precision and simplification. Mondrian divides his canvas into rectangles, using heavy black lines with which he combines sharp color accents.

Giorgio de Chirico (1888-   ) an Italian, though born in Greece, painted in Germany and France where he was influenced by the cubists. His subject-matter is remote or dream-like. *Delights of the Poet* contains an architectural arrangement indicating a dream memory, though the whole is organized with strong pattern interest (Plate 190). Line direction and dramatic use of light and dark add force to the poetic theme.

Max Weber (1881-   ), who was born in Russia, came to this country as a youth. He is a leader of modernism in America today. *Music* is an example of his powerful, emotional, and individual style (Plate 199).

Marie Laurencin (1885-   ) was strongly influenced by the simple style of the French painter, Rousseau, although her work is not characterized by that artist's naïvete. She has become famous because of the development of an essentially feminine style and specialization in the painting of graceful, young girls which possess an elfin charm. Laurencin combines cool colors with subtle greys in delicate harmonies.

Georgia O'Keeffe (1887-   ) is a strongly individualistic American painter. She developed many changes of style between 1926 and 1936, ranging from vital expressionism to abstraction, and non-objectivity. At intervals, however, she has rendered studies in a representational manner. Notable among her works are semi-abstract treatments of flowers and still-life, landscapes in simplified renderings of the Southwest and other sections of the country. Her *Long Island Sunset* is a creative interpretation revealing the artist's concern for plastic, rhythmic effects in painting (Plate 198).

Ben Shahn (1898-   ), though Russian born, works distinctively in the American tradition. A versatile and gifted craftsman, he has made outstanding contributions in the fields of easel and fresco paintings, photography, and poster art. Shahn's interest has always centered around social statement, and his carefully designed and painted posters for various government agencies and labor organizations, are classed as examples of fine art (Plate 200). His dramatic, powerfully composed paintings combine realism with a poetic use of form and color.

Paralleling the many movements which form a part of the general development of modern art is the creative achievement of contemporary Mexicans and many regional American painters. These sincere artists, too numerous to mention, are carrying on the modern tradition begun by Cézanne, Van Gogh, and Gauguin.

SUMMARY OF CONTEMPORARY PAINTING

In an age of speed, experiment, and conflict it is small wonder that the artist should seek a new idiom in which to express his reaction to the world about him. Impressed by scientific discoveries, the development of the camera, and the multiple motion of the machine, he has at the same time experienced the quietude and inner rhythm of Oriental art, which suggests rather than transcribes, and the simplified, impersonal, and emotionally moving sculptural forms created by the primitive African Negro sculptor. Stimulated by the impact of his own environment, the contemporary artist has, nevertheless, endeavored to bring to his work something of the simplicity, poise, and unity felt in the older arts.

Great art of all periods has been based upon a fine underlying composition or structure, and distortion for the sake of better design has been practiced in almost every epoch. To mention only a few examples, the Greeks distorted natural proportions to achieve isocephaly * in their sculptured borders; Michelangelo twisted his forms to emphasize strength and power; El Greco elongated his fingers to suggest spirituality, and by an arbitrary use of dark-light and color achieved a pulsating movement which gave life to his paintings. So the modern artist, reorganizing material gathered from nature, has employed abstract forms which in the end have become wholly non-objective. This art, according to the artist Abraham Walkowitz, is "wholly independent of picturization in any form or of any object. It has a universal language and dwells in the realm of music with an equivalent emotion. Its melody is attuned to the receptive eye as music is to the ear." †

With art moving away from naturalism, the old linear perspec-

* A principle of representing the heads of figures, whether seated or standing, at about the same level.

† Sidney Janis, *Abstract and Surrealistic Art in America.* (New York, Reynal and Hitchcock, Inc.)

tive with a fixed focus has been abandoned. An extended vision makes it unnecessary for the artist to limit himself to only one point of view. He can move around an object and represent top, bottom, and side views simultaneously. The various planes are flattened and rearranged in new non-naturalistic yet recognizable forms like those in some of Braque's still-life paintings or in Picasso's abstract organizations. The cubists originated this "circulating viewpoint," which was further developed by the futurists, who attempted to make the artist not merely an observer but a participator by suggesting that he is in the midst of the movement revolving about him. The spectator is likewise invited to enter this new world, the picture, which has a life of its own. The confident young futurists arriving in Paris from fascist Italy attacked with audacity and varying degrees of success such technical problems as capturing on canvas man's reaction to a world in constant motion.

The so-called elements or tools with which the artist works, such as line, light-dark, color, form, and so forth, have become increasingly functional in new designs which have been constructed or built up rather than copied from nature. Seurat employed horizontal lines or planes contrasted with vertical figures or objects to give the effect of spatial depth. A close study of *Sunday on the Isand of Grande Jatte* (Plate 173) reveals both straight and curved line schemes, with each line contributing to the unity of the whole. Rouault's heavy lines, reminiscent of the supports of stained glass windows, give power and strength to his painting. Kandinsky's emphatic black lines, seen in some of his earlier impressionistic work, provide a strong contrast to his explosive color organizations. The Fauves simplified and distorted lines for the sake of better design. The cubists discarded the curves and arabesques of the Fauves for straight lines and angles. The futurists paralleled lines to indicate the force and direction of movement.

Color had been employed by the impressionists to achieve a naturalistic effect of light. Seurat and the neo-impressionists extended the unbroken-color technique to construct form rather than to envelop objects in an atmospheric veil of light. Cézanne utilized the advancing and recessive properties of color to indicate volume and to reveal spatial depth. The Fauves decorated their canvases with exotic hues, but the cubists, more closely related to Cézanne in their concentration upon the organization of forms and planes, either omitted color or reduced it to such low intensities and somber tones that its importance as hue was practically nullified. The futurists, however, attempted to restore its former brilliance.

Texture has come to mean more than a naturalistic representation of different materials such as silks, satins, skin, or hair. The modern painters regard it as surface enrichment to be achieved by flat pattern or the manipulation of the actual materials of the painter's craft. Van Gogh squeezed paint directly from the tube on to the canvas or applied it with knife or thumb in raised ribbon-like strokes. Monet and Seurat reduced color areas to small spots which they laid side by side, thus producing a rough surface. The Fauves employed exotic textured patterns as contrast for plain surfaces. The cubists, who first reduced recognizable objects to essential parts, finally resorted to pasting up pieces of newspaper, matches, cigarettes or other bits of studio paraphernalia in an effort to emphasize texture. The futurists' restless patterns of dark-light and color produced an all-over kaleidoscopic textural effect of forms in motion.

Forms or objects distorted by the Fauves were decomposed by the cubists and set in motion by the futurists. All have sought to arbitrarily arrange plastic elements for more effective expression. If by this method representational and associational values are lost, the composition as a whole gains in unity, and a rhythmic order which is both pleasing to the eye and stimulating to the mind has been achieved. In short, abstract art is more closely related to music.

In addition to abstract art there was a contrasting movement, surrealism, in which an attempt was made to restore naturalism to a limited extent. A group of artists, impressed by the psychologists' explorations into both the normal and irrational mind, sought to externalize the unseen intangibles of the realm of fantasy and dream. Like the dadaists, they discarded limitations and endowed objects and figures with unrestricted movement in boundless space. The work of these introspective artists who have

attempted to fuse dream and reality tends to be extremely symbolical and personal. Likewise, the titles of their pictures are more
mystifying than enlightening. Both Klee and Chagall were picturing an unreal, imagined, or remembered world before the surrealists declared their intentions. With convincing naturalism, Dali
has displayed an extraordinary amount of skill in representing unrelated objects in unusual combinations, such as the limp watch
hanging upon the limb of a tree.

Few artists of the century have achieved their best work by
adhering strictly to one of the various "isms," not all of which
have been mentioned here. Like Picasso they have worked in first
one then another retaining what they needed for the development
of their own peculiar style. In the most advanced of the paintings
emphasis has been placed upon structural organization.

SCULPTURE

EXPERIMENTS IN PROCESSES, METHODS, MATERIALS

Contemporary sculpture is the result of successful experiment
and fertility of invention by which the moderns have achieved
a new concept of beauty. About 1910, a keenly searching attitude
developed among progressive sculptors who were dissatisfied with
existing styles and a purely representational approach to art. They
felt that sculpture of true value could not be achieved by merely
copying the model. These men experimented with new methods,
processes, and materials and brought greater vitality to the art of
modeling by adding texture and color interest. The period of ques-
tioning and growth which followed World War I encouraged the
use of a variety of materials. Marble, bronze, lead, stone, cement,
wood, alabaster, aluminum, white onyx, ceramics, and various
alloys are now successfully utilized by the sculptor. The natural
restrictions of material form a major consideration in the organization of the sculptor's concept. The material under the sculptor's
chisel is never allowed to lose its peculiar quality and identity.
The modern sculptor's problem is to emphasize such essentials of
form as his material may embody. The numerous styles which have

developed in twentieth-century sculpture range from classical simplicity to extreme distortion and abstraction. Form may be representational, symbolic, abstract, geometric, non-objective, or expressionistic. Decorative sculpture is enriching modern architecture and bringing about a more satisfying relation between sculpture and architecture.

INFLUENCE OF AFRICAN NEGRO SCULPTURE

A group of painters and sculptors in Paris were strongly influenced by the simplifications found in African Negro sculpture, which presents an abstract and harmonious treatment of form. The primitive Negro was not interested in the representation of realistic forms. Negro sculpture was intended for religious purposes and the primitive artists avoided representational treatment by organizing their concept in imaginative terms or symbols. Negro sculpture presents an abstract form of beauty both lofty and formal (Plate 183). The study of Negro idols and masks has aided the modern sculptor's experiments in geometric and abstract form. Cubist and futurist paintings, expressive of the machine age, have profoundly influenced modern sculpture. The futurist manifesto, 1912, defined sculpture as a medium for the expression of the inner life of man. The modern sculptor aims to render his subject in a formal abstract style, independent of actual appearances. The modern approach is direct and simplified, but not representational.

ABSTRACT AND NON-OBJECTIVE SCULPTURE: BRANCUSI: ARCHIPENKO: ZORACH: MOHOLY-NAGY

Constantin Brancusi (1876-   ), a Roumanian who studied in Paris, was influenced by Negro sculpture. His work emphasizes simple curves and beautifully molded surfaces. *Bird in Space* (Plate 204) shows the play of light and dark upon exquisitely molded bronze. A flowing outline is expressive of elemental and momentary movement. Likewise, in his abstract treatment of life-size portraits, Brancusi expresses beauty envisioned by his fertile imagination and feeling. Alexander Archipenko (1887-   ), who was born in Kiev, Russia, and studied in Paris, has founded an art school in New York. Archipenko's interesting experiments with various media—silver, diorite, colored ceramic, marble, stone, and bronze—have attracted world-wide attention. His *Reclining Torso* (Plate 202) has austere charm because of its rare purity of line and exquisite surface treatment. William Zorach (1887-   ), an American, is working with varied materials including red granite which incorporates a new texture and color interest. *Affection* (Plate 203) is a delightful work which gives a feeling of leading the eye through the forms, planes, and masses the sculptor uses to indicate movement and gesture. Zorach's sculpture is expressive of his statement, "The meaning of art is found in the play of organized form and color . . . color is beautiful only if related to the organization of form."

Ladislaus Moholy-Nagy (1895-1946), who had been identified with the Bauhaus abroad, became a leader in the development of the German school of non-objective art in America. He experimented with compositions on more than one plane, using various manufactured materials. His *Space Modulator*, 1940 (Plate 204), utilizing chromium and plexiglas, is suspended from a wire to permit a free play of light on its polished and transparent surfaces. As the light changes, so the pattern of the design varies. Moholy-Nagy established a school of industrial design in Chicago.

EXPRESSIONISM: MILLES: LACHAISE: MAILLOL

Carl Milles (1875-   ), born in Sweden, was a gifted woodcarver when a young lad. His success in life was assured when he won a scholarship for the study of sculpture in Stockholm and later worked with Rodin in Paris. Milles has created some of the world's most beautiful fountains, all of which he has adapted to the setting in a most satisfying manner. *Fountain of the Tritons*, in the McKinlock Court of the Art Institute, Chicago (Plate 201), and also in the sculptor's garden at Lidingo, near Stockholm, is a work of massive bronze. Charming mermen and mermaids are rendered with an imaginative treatment of delicate flowing lines. The whole effect is enhanced by the display of falling water emerging from numerous jets. Milles' figures suggest beauty of line and mass in conformity with the finest ideals of plastic sculptured form. He is a skilled sculptor of animal life who uses varied treatments to assist in the interpretation of his feeling.

One of the masters of modern sculpture, the late Gaston Lachaise (1882-1935), who worked in America from 1906, developed unique experiments in the use of metal. The strong rhythms of his lightly-poised volumes are seen in *Floating Figure*—a work of great individualism (Plate 202). A well-known French master, Aristide Maillol (1861-1944), has produced powerful abstract organizations in stone, bronze, and terra-cotta. Others of his works, such as *Seated Woman* (Plate 200), are less in the non-objective style and show an approach to subject-matter which is direct and simplified, yet not in the least representational. His figures realize a complete repose in the harmonious arrangement of planes, lines, masses. A monumental quality of Maillol's forms recalls the serene timelessness of the art of antiquity.

DECORATIVE EMPHASIS: MANSHIP: HERZOG: LAWRIE

Paul Manship (1885-   ), born in Minnesota and educated at the American School of Sculpture in Rome, has developed a strongly decorative style. His *Dancer and Gazelles* shows an intensely individual expression. Manship's treatment of hair and drapery in this work is reminiscent of Archaic Greek sculpture. His fountains, fanciful centaurs, dryads, animal studies, portraits, and decorative reliefs have originality and thorough craftsmanship.

Decorative sculptural reliefs have achieved an appropriate unity with architecture. Oswald Herzog, a German sculptor, designed the series of metal grilles and sculptural reliefs for the entrance of the Chanin Building, New York, 1929. Here abstract designs interpret such concepts as "Energy" and "Endurance." Likewise, the sculptural designs of Lee Lawrie (1887-   ) for Rockefeller Center, New York, show the successful decorative use of sculpture as an integral part of architecture.

STYLIZED SCULPTURE: MESTROVIC: FAGGI

Civic sculpture has been enhanced by the contribution of Ivan Mestrovic (1883-   ), a Yugoslav, whose monumental bronze *Bow and Arrow* in Grant Park, Chicago, is a modern treatment of two Indians on horseback. Strong angularity of pose gives force to this dynamic interpretation. Alfeo Faggi (1885-   ), an Italian sculptor, now an American citizen, has created impressive ecclesiastical sculpture in a modern simplified style. His designs include a series of remarkable bas-reliefs, *Stations of the Cross*, for the Church of St. Thomas the Apostle, Chicago. These have strong linear emphasis in the treatment of the low relief. Faggi's work represents a unique contribution in it departure from the strictly naturalistic religious sculpture. His interpretation enforces a religious mood by the moving quality of its abstract beauty.

EXPRESSIONISM IN GERMANY AND ENGLAND

The late Wilhelm von Lehmbruck (1881-1919) of Germany, used extreme distortion and elongation of proportions to achieve highly expressionistic effects as in his famous *Kneeling Figure* (Plate 203). George Kolbe (1887-   ) has been accorded high acclaim among contemporary German workers for his fountains, war memorials, and single statues which indicate a quiet modern type of naturalism and simplified form.

Jacob Epstein (1880-   ) an American now working in England, has created unusual portrait busts, for he retains essentials of the outward appearance of subjects without permitting his sculpture to be realistic in the representational sense. His *Bust of Mademoiselle Gabrielle Soene* has interesting texture treatment (Plate 201). Frank Dobson (1887-   ) of England, has achieved noteworthy results in wood-carving by utilizing the beauty found in the natural grain. Dobson's strong, personal style is seen also in clay, stone, and marble. *Marble Woman* exemplifies the simplifications and dignity of his volumes. Eric Gill's (1882-   ) work includes skillful stone carvings for reliefs, steles, memorials, and decorative sculpture. His work is somewhat reminiscent of the style of Italian primitives because of a dynamic line quality which suggests movement. Henry Moore (1898-   ), an English sculptor whose work was exhibited in 1946-47 in many American cities, has accomplished remarkable plastic integrations in the extremely rhythmic style which he has developed. The simplifications of Negro sculpture are evident in his work. *Reclining Figure* is distinguished by its fluid lines and expressive use of distortion (Plate 187). Henry Moore is contributing much to the creative development of modern sculpture today.

ARCHITECTURE

CLARITY OF FORM AND FUNCTION

Modern "living" architecture is fulfilling the needs of twentieth-century life by the construction of efficient and beautiful buildings. Architecture today is concerned with housing the world's people during their working and leisure hours in well-planned offices, factories, schools, libraries, railroad stations, airports, broadcasting stations, hospitals, theatres, churches, and homes. Recognition by modern architects of their responsibility to all the people has resulted in significant structural advances international in scope. Architects in every part of the world are attaining a type of construction which has clarity of form and which offers convenience and comfort. Leaders of the modern movement in architecture have erected simple and efficient buildings systematically planned to meet every requirement of function. Varied designs for steel construction are objects of utility, strength, and beauty. Reinforced concrete creates a construction form which is the dominant motif of beautiful modern design.

Vast achievements, directed by American architects and engineers, such as the Boulder and Bonneville dams, and the Tennessee Valley power plants evidence coöperative planning by modern builders and engineers. Tall structures, known as skyscrapers, America's contribution to the development of modern architecture, have been made possible in our time because of mass production by the machine. These upward soaring towers give distinction to the skylines of American cities and are monuments to the combined skill of modern architects, engineers, and builders.

THE SKYSCRAPER: ZONING LAWS

Contemporary architects have met the demand for more office space in the congested urban areas such as downtown Manhattan and the Chicago Loop. The skyscraper makes possible larger rental capacity on a minimum ground area while offering a construction well suited to such centers. Only since the invention of the steel skeleton have builders been able to create structures which rise to great heights though based on small ground area. Steel-cage construction offers adequate support for the building's weight and provides the needed strength to sustain the soaring vertical height. The skyscraper's steel skeleton has slender upright supports to which light materials are attached, as to a frame. For example, the walls of shops occupying lower floors of a building may be made entirely of glass, which allows more light and is practical for window display.

When skyscrapers became more numerous and more closely grouped in small areas, the streets below were darkened like deep canyons and the lower stories of the structures had constant need of artificial light. The New York City Council passed zoning laws requiring that buildings in certain locations and of specified height have set-backs, or recessed construction, on their higher levels. This resulted in a twofold architectural advance, for conformity to zoning laws allowed more light and air to reach the streets and lower floors, while the recessed upper floors presented a new and unique design which has become the dominant characteristic of skyscraper construction.

PIONEER OF MODERNISM: LOUIS SULLIVAN

Credit for the creation of the modern skyscraper is generally given to Louis Sullivan (1856-1924), who realized in his design for the Guaranty Building, Buffalo, in 1895, an office structure of steel which offered the first successful solution of the problem of the skyscraper. Here Sullivan expressed principles which were epoch-making in their influence upon modern architecture. He developed the idea that new forms must be evolved to fit new materials. The dictum "form follows function" is the controlling thought of his book, *The Autobiography of an Idea*, in which he envisioned the improvements of the twenty-five years since his death. In his pioneering work on the skyscraper he emphasized the construction of vertical shafts which convey the appearance of great height while also suggesting stability and strength. Sullivan advocated the use of larger windows, fireproof bricks, and the combined use of metal and glass for shop windows. He anticipated the mass production of strong, resilient steel, the fastening of steel beams with rivets applied by the machine, and the use of powerful machines to erect the steel skeleton. Sullivan insisted that a building should frankly express its material and construction and that decoration should be integrated with basic form.

Following the extensive use of modern steel and reinforced concrete, many new mechanical processes and materials have been found useful by architects. The creative use of materials offers a challenge to the modern architect. Ceramics, glass, onyx, marble, copper and other metals, and plastics have been given new adaptations. The architect today may use glass for entire walls.

FRANK LLOYD WRIGHT'S CREATIVE ARCHITECTURE

Associated with Sullivan for a time as his chief draftsman was Frank Lloyd Wright (1869-   ), who established himself in the nineties as a creative designer of homes, though his work today includes a variety of construction. His original designs have consistently emphasized the relation of the building to its out-of-door setting. Wright has advocated the use of larger windows to bring man closer to nature. His designs show spacious expanse of open areas, and a simple horizontal and vertical arrangement combined to give a satisfying unity with the environment. Like Sullivan, Wright creates architecture which has organic unity of form and function. In the *Kaufman House, "Falling Water,"* Bear Run, Pennsylvania, he unites the building with its setting of natural beauty by arranging cantilever construction to project horizontal sun decks and porches over a flowing stream (Plate 206). Wright's designs for houses on the West Coast meet the needs of a climate which offers all year round out-of-door living. The *Millard House*, Pasadena, is built of precast concrete blocks. A beautiful textured appearance results from the incorporation of a design in each block.

Wright is not bound by any definite style, for this leader among modern architects is always seeking ways of building better structures for better living. His design for the *Administration Building* of S.C. Johnson and Son, Racine, Wisconsin, employs hollow, reinforced concrete columns which spread, flowerlike, at the top (Plate 206). The creative use of glass is noteworthy in this structure, the beautiful simplicity of which offers maximum light, space, air. Wright's desert development in southern Arizona, *Taliesin West*, begun in 1937, is his winter home and workplace. It houses a colony of apprentices who have sought to learn his theory of logical planning. Built of simple, rough materials, it has large stone walls with broad masonry beams. These walls are molded concrete, in vibrant tones of yellow, rose, gray, and orange. Redwood boards and huge canvases are arranged as sun shelters. Some walls are inclined obliquely to adapt the structure to its setting, the topography of which shows distant mountain slopes.

SKYSCRAPER DESIGN: ELIEL SAARINEN

The *Tribune Tower*, Chicago, was built according to a design submitted by Raymond Hood which won first place in a worldwide contest. This beautiful structure reveals the soaring vertical line typical of the modern skyscraper combined with certain Gothic features such as ornament, buttresses, and tracery. The second prize was awarded to Eliel Saarinen, a Finnish architect, whose design was a stark geometric form having an upward line of entirely modern style. Mass, with its height increasing after the first set-back, or recession, was symmetrically balanced. The modern emphasis of this plan was acclaimed by architects, who urged that it be displayed in leading American cities. Saarinen's design has had great influence on the development of the modern skyscraper.

FUNCTIONAL STRUCTURES

Rockefeller Center, New York, an outstanding triumph of modern architecture, comprises several related buildings designed to house many activities—offices, shops, restaurants, theatres, radio broadcasting stations (Plate 208). This steel and reinforced concrete structure meets the needs of urban life today. The entire unit is dominated by the R.C.A. Building which towers to a height of almost a thousand feet. The construction of modern factories and grain elevators has received much emphasis in America. An example of the practical adaptation of new materials is seen in the clean-cut and beautiful efficiency of the *New York City Municipal Asphalt Plant* with its simple, unadorned surfaces, large openings, frank use of brick, concrete, steel, glass, tile, and metals (Plate 207).

LOW-COST HOUSING PROJECTS FOR WORKERS

Twentieth-century architects have concerned themselves with the problem of better housing for industrial workers of lower income groups (Plate 207). In many cities slum districts have been leveled to the ground to make way for low-cost civic housing which aims to improve the living condition of thousands by offering improved comfort, more sunshine and ventilation. At Amsterdam and Rotterdam in Holland, fine examples of large-scale developments for workers' housing were designed by J. J. P. Oud. His plans for a group of houses on the Hook of Holland illustrate simplified modern construction which allows plenty of light, air, and sunshine (Plate 205). Plain walls enhanced by the use of beautiful color, large windows, balconies, flat roofs used for decks, unusual use of brickwork and glazed tiles are notable features. Oud's designs show the influence of pure colors and of cubism's austere angles. About 1927, several low-cost housing projects were developed in Germany at Weissenhof, near Stuttgart, in Frankfurt, and in Berlin.

THE BAUHAUS

At the famous Bauhaus (Plate 205), a modern school of architecture and industrial design established first at Weimar and later moved to Dessau, a group of architects, artists, designers and industrial craftsmen worked under the leadership of Walter Gropius. The Bauhaus was founded to create designs appropriate for modern living by applying machine-age principles to the planning of factories, shops, apartments, and domestic housing, as well as the interiors and furniture for these structures. The idea behind the Bauhaus was to facilitate coöperation of architects and artisans, industry, and craftworkers. The buildings which housed the shops, classrooms, and studios were designed by Gropius. Each workshop was a separate unit, differentiated according to its function and utility, although all were connected by covered passageways. Glass walls separated sections of the shops and the studios had balconies, decks, and ramps. The development of modern functionalism at the Bauhaus brought a new, unfettered emphasis into architecture.

THE INTERNATIONAL STYLE

As modern architects abandoned all added ornamentation and developed a clear-cut simplicity of outline expressive of the dynamics of the machine age, a new beauty emerged which fulfilled the demand of Louis Sullivan that "form follow function." The modern style has a geometric purity of outline which combines with simple textured surfaces such as plain stuccoed walls. The style is now called International because it is adapted to the needs of all the people of the world, whether they live in western Europe, the Americas, or in the Orient. The structural needs of different people and climate are of first consideration. Across the Pacific, the Japanese have long been accustomed to ordered simplicity. Flexibility of space arrangement was achieved there by the use of removable screens for walls, which make it possible for a single rooms to serve many uses.

In western Europe architects have been influenced by the cubist painters, who have done much to bring a new daring into architectural design. Designs without ornament, emphasizing curving walls, were introduced by the Art Nouveau group. Henry van de Velde, a member of this group, was very successful in the handling of simple, unadorned curving walls. Mies van der Rohe's (1886-   ) plan for the Tugendhat House, 1930, at Brnö, Czechoslovakia, contains an interior whose large areas may be divided into rooms by walls of glass to be raised or lowered at will. The furniture which he designed for this house is notable for comfort, lightness, and beauty of line. Entirely functional in character, the house and its interior meet the needs and taste of contemporary living.

This International style of modern architecture has sought to break with the eclecticism of the past. Modern architects all over the world have united in their desire to improve architecture through the best use of machine-age devices and the more creative uses of new materials. These men sought to build better structures for the social good of all men. One of the leaders of this movement is Charles Edouard Jeanneret, a French architect, known by his pseudonym "Le Corbusier." He wrote a treatise entitled *Towards a New Architecture,* in which he explains how the great machines that are the foundation of modern mass production must be made to serve mankind in newer and more creative ways. By frank acknowledgement of the exact needs of twentieth-century life architects can erect structures which are wholly practical. Organic construction must satisfy function and beauty. The spirit of today's architectural developments is not fixed by set styles or formulas but is flexible and mobile.

OUTLINE OF THE ART OF TWENTIETH CENTURY

TIME: The latter part of the 19th through first half of the 20th century.

BACKGROUND: Modern life, complex. Development of airplane increased speed and made all nations neighbors. Clash of cultural patterns. Disordered economic, political, and social conditions. Within half a century two wars of global significance, leaving in their wake maladjustment and bewilderment. Aggressive materialism. Experimental attitude toward life resulting in scientific advances. New influences on art: diversified materials including products of machine, also extended vision largely due to machine, and the clean-cut hard lines and sharp edges of the machine itself. Structural use of color due to scientific experimentation marked a great development in painting. Art became international.

ARCHITECTURE: New materials: textured concrete, glass and metals. New forms and fluid space made possible by advent of steel construction. Tendency toward elimination of decoration other than that inherent in structural materials, such as color and texture, or the arrangement of windows to emphasize lofty lines or to create textured patterns. Attention given to low-cost housing—notably in Holland. Unique American contribution, the skyscraper. Experimentation in pre-fabricated houses.

SCULPTURE: Usually allied with architecture, if monumental. More often reduced to a size suited to display in museums. Materials: marble, stone, bronze or other metals, alabaster, cement, wood, wire and plastics. Either stationary or mobile. Progressed from neo-classical forms to purely abstract. Sculptor concerned with balanced movement and the relationship of mass or volume.

PAINTING: Moved away from naturalism of the 19th century to non-objective art devoid of subject-matter or associational qualities. Emphasis placed upon carefully controlled organization of line, color, space, and texture. Painters also experimented. The *Fauves* under Matisse used simplified drawing, disregarded light and shadow, employed pure colors in daring harmonies, and distorted lines to produce figures non-naturalistic yet recognizable and decorative. Picasso and the *Cubists* influenced by the hard lines and sharp edges of modern architecture, broke down objects into planes which they put together in new compositions. The *Futurists* were primarily concerned with movement. The *Surrealists* explored the unseen world of fantasy and dreams, which they attempted to externalize through hte use of recognizable objects. The *Dadaists* broke all art traditions. *Non-Objective* painters strive to express emotional reactions through abstract art elements such as space, color, etc. Their work is characterized by balanced tensions and ordered movement.

BIBLIOGRAPHY

BARNES, Albert C., and DE MAZIA, Violette, *The Art of Cézanne* (Harcourt, Brace & Co., Inc., N. Y., 1939).

——, *The Art of Henri Matisse* (Charles Scribner's Sons, N. Y., 1933).

——, *The Art of Renoir* (G. P. Putnam's Sons, N. Y., 1935).

BARR, Alfred H. Jr., *Cubism and Abstract Art* (Museum of Modern Art, N. Y., 1936).

——, *Modern Architects* (Museum of Modern Art, N. Y., 1932).

——, *Picasso, Fifty Years of His Art*

BELL, Clive, *Since Cezanne* (Harcourt, Brace & Co., Inc., N. Y., 1929).

CHENEY, Sheldon, *The Story of Modern Art* (Viking Press, Inc., N. Y., 1945).

——, *The New World Architecture* (Longmans, Green & Co., N. Y., 1930).

DAVIDSON, Morris, *Understanding Modern Art* (Coward-McCann, Inc., N. Y., 1931).

EPSTEIN, Jacob, *The Sculptor Speaks* (Doubleday & Co., Garden City, N. Y., 1932).

FAULKNER, Ray, and HILL, Gerald, *Art Today* (Henry Holt & Co., Inc., N. Y., 1941).

GEIDEON, S., *Space Time and Architecture* (Harvard University Press, Cambridge, Mass., 1942).

GORDON, Jan, *Modern French Painters* (London, 1929).

Janis, Sidney, *Abstract and Surrealist Art in America* (Reynal & Hitchcock, Inc., N. Y., 1944).

Le Corbusier (Charles Edouard Jeanneret), *The City of Tomorrow and Its Planning* (Harcourt, Brace & Co., Inc., N. Y., 1929).

——, *Toward a New Architecture* (Harcourt, Brace & Co., Inc., N. Y., 1931).

Morrison, Hugh, *Louis Sullivan* (W. W. Norton & Co., N. Y., 1935).

Ozenfant, Amedee, *Foundations of Modern Art* (Harcourt, Brace & Co., Inc., N. Y., 1931).

Read, Herbert, *Art Now* (Harcourt, Brace & Co., Inc., N. Y., 1934).

Raynal, Maurice, *Modern French Painters* (Brentano's, N. Y., 1928).

Starrett, W. A., *Skyscrapers and the Men Who Build Them* (Museum of Modern Art, N. Y.).

Sweeney, J. J., *Plastic Redirections in Twentieth-Century Painting* (University of Chicago Press, Chicago, 1934).

Van Gogh, Vincent, *Dear Theo,* letters to his brother (Houghton Mifflin Co., Boston, 1937) and *Autobiography of Vincent Van Gogh* (Houghton Mifflin, Co., 1937).

Wilenski, R. H., *French Painting* (Hale, Cushman & Flint, Inc., Boston, 1931).

——, *The Modern Movement in Art* (F. A. Stokes Co., N. Y., 1927).

Wright, Frank Lloyd, *Modern Architecture,* Kahn Lectures, Princeton University, 1930.

——, *An Autobiography* (London, 1932).

Wright, W. H., *Modern Painting: Its Tendency and Meaning* (Dodd, Mead & Co., N. Y., 1927).

Booklets from Museum of Modern Art such as: *What Is Modern Architecture? Art in Our Time, Fantastic Art, Dada, Surrealism* (edited by A. H. Barr), etc.

Fifth catalogue of the Solomon R. Guggenheim Collection of Non-Objective Paintings, 1939.

General Bibliography

BARNES, Albert C., *The Art in Painting* (Harcourt, Brace & Co., Inc., N. Y., 1937).

BLUM, André, and TATLOCK, R. R., *A Short History of Art* (Charles Scribner's Sons, N. Y., 1926).

CHASE, G. H., and POST, C. R., *A History of Sculpture* (Harper & Bros., N. Y., 1925).

CHENEY, Sheldon, *A World History of Art* (Viking Press, Inc., N. Y., 1937).

CRAVEN, Thomas, *Men of Art* (Simon & Schuster, Inc., N. Y., 1931).

FAURE, Elie, *History of Art,* 5 vols., tr. by Walter Pach (Harper & Bros., N. Y., 1921-33).

FLETCHER, Sir Banister, *A History of Architecture on the Comparative Method* (Charles Scribner's Sons, N. Y., 1931).

GARDNER, Helen, *Art Through the Ages,* third ed. (Harcourt, Brace & Co., Inc., N. Y., 1948).

HAMLIN, A. D. F., *A Text Book of the History of Architecture* (Longmans, Green & Co., N. Y., 1923).

HAMLIN, Talbot, *Architecture Through the Ages* (G. P. Putnam's Sons, N. Y., 1940).

HILDEBRAND, Adolf, *The Problem of Form in Painting and Sculpture,* tr. by Max Meyer and Robert M. Ogden (G. E. Stechert & Co., N. Y., 1932).

LAMPREY, L., *All the Ways of Building* (The Macmillan Co., N. Y., 1937).

McMAHON, A. Philip, *The Art of Enjoying Art* (Whittlesey House, McGraw-Hill Book Co., N. Y., 1937).

MUNRO, Thomas, *Great Pictures of Europe* (Tudor Publishing Co., N. Y., 1934).

PIJOAN, Joseph, *History of Art,* 3 vols., tr. by R. L. Roys (Harper & Bros., N. Y., 1927).

POST, C. B., *A History of European and American Sculpture from Early Christian Period to the Present Day* (Harvard University Press, Cambridge, Mass., 1921).

READ, Herbert, *Art and Society* (London, 1937).

RINDGE, A. M., *Sculpture* (Brewer & Warren, Inc., N. Y., 1929).

ROBB, David M., and GARRISON, J. J., *Art in the Western World* (Harper & Bros., N. Y., 1935).

ROOS, Frank J., *An Illustrated Handbook of Art History* (The Macmillan Co., N. Y., 1937).

ROTHSCHILD, Lincoln, *Sculpture Through the Ages* (Whittlesey House, McGraw-Hill Book Co., N. Y., 1942).

SCHOOLMAN, Regina, and SLATKIN, Charles, *The Enjoyment of Art in America* (J. B. Lippincott Co., Philadelphia, 1942).

STITES, Raymond S., *The Arts and Man* (McGraw-Hill Book Co., N. Y., 1940).

VENTURI, Lionello, *Painting and Painters from Giotto to Chagall* (Charles Scribner's Sons, N. Y., 1945).

WHITAKER, Charles Harris, *Rameses to Rockefeller: The Story of Architecture,* (Random House, Inc., N. Y., 1934).

Index

Italic numbers refer to Plate illustrations

āle, câre, ăm, ärm; ēve, ĕnd, makēr; īce, ĭll; ōld, ôrb, ŏdd; ūse, ûrn, ŭp, ü as in Fr. *menu;* fōōd, fŏŏt; κ as in Ger. *ich;* ɴ as in Fr. *bon*

(1)